THE WIRELESS COOKBOOK

THE WIRELESS COOKBOOK

Build Real Projects and Master Wi-Fi, Bluetooth, and LoRa

by Bill Zimmerman

no starch press®

San Francisco

Printed in the United States of America

First printing

29 28 27 26 25   1 2 3 4 5

ISBN-13: 978-1-7185-0436-3 (print)
ISBN-13: 978-1-7185-0437-0 (ebook)

Published by No Starch Press®, Inc.
245 8th Street, San Francisco, CA 94103
phone: +1.415.863.9900
www.nostarch.com; info@nostarch.com

Publisher: William Pollock
Managing Editor: Jill Franklin
Production Manager: Sabrina Plomitallo-González
Production Editor: Jennifer Kepler
Developmental Editor: Jill Franklin
Cover Illustrator: Garry Booth
Interior Design: Octopod Studios
Technical Reviewer: Lawrence Yau
Copyeditor: Rachel Head
Proofreader: Sharon Wilkey
Indexer: BIM Creatives, LLC

Figure 3-4 is licensed under the Creative Commons Attribution-ShareAlike 4.0 International license (*https://creativecommons.org/licenses/by-sa/4.0/*). Figures 6-12 and 10-9 are licensed under the Creative Commons Attribution-ShareAlike 2.0 Generic license (*https://creativecommons.org/licenses/by-sa/2.0/*).

Library of Congress Control Number: 2025027006

For customer service inquiries, please contact info@nostarch.com. For information on distribution, bulk sales, corporate sales, or translations: sales@nostarch.com. For permission to translate this work: rights@nostarch.com. To report counterfeit copies or piracy: counterfeit@nostarch.com. The authorized representative in the EU for product safety and compliance is EU Compliance Partner, Pärnu mnt. 139b-14, 11317 Tallinn, Estonia, hello@eucompliancepartner.com, +3375690241.

What I cannot create, I do not understand.
—Richard Feynman

About the Author

Bill Zimmerman is a passionate software engineer (formerly at Microsoft), a successful startup founder, an educator, and a Linux evangelist of more than 30 years. He has created teaching labs and curriculums, delivered workshops, and mentored learners of all ages in technology and entrepreneurship at locations across Europe, the Middle East, and Africa. When not working on open source projects, he's often found trail running or wrenching on his old Land Rover.

About the Technical Reviewer

Lawrence Yau got his first computer at age six and has been immersed in technology ever since. He has worked in IT since 2007, with experience in coding, systems and network administration, and most recently, project management. A Raspberry Pi enthusiast since its debut in 2012, Yau developed a number of utilities for the platform and planted the seed for what would grow into the popular RaspAP project. In his spare time, he enjoys playing badminton and spending time with his family over dim sum and other Cantonese and Taiwanese dishes.

BRIEF CONTENTS

CONTENTS IN DETAIL

PART I
THE BIG PICTURE

1
WIRELESS FUNDAMENTALS   3

4
BASIC AND ADVANCED CAPTIVE PORTALS   **91**

5
BLUETOOTH AUDIO IN TWO WAYS

6
EXPLORING LONG RANGE WITH LORA   157

7
INTRUSION DETECTION WITH KISMET   201

8
WIRELESS AIR QUALITY MONITORING 227

9
PWNING WI-FI WITH PWNAGOTCHI   261

11
WIRELESS DISPLAYS IN TWO WAYS

343

APPENDIX: THE ENGINEER'S MINDSET 375

FOREWORD

In 1999, I watched Steve Jobs unveil the first iBook with AirPort wireless networking during the MacWorld keynote. Since that first exposure to Wi-Fi, I've watched and participated in the Wi-Fi revolution—mostly as a casual user. Wi-Fi went from a slow networking standard that cost hundreds of dollars to add on to a computer to the primary method of connecting computers, phones, tablets, cars, and even modern appliances today.

You might be forgiven for believing the radio frequency (RF) and code behind modern wireless protocols is indiscernible magic. But it's not, and no book I've seen cuts to the heart of it as quickly as *The Wireless Cookbook*, written by an expert I discovered through his involvement with the Raspberry Pi.

I've used Bill Zimmerman's RaspAP software to set up my own Wi-Fi networks. His software removes the difficulty of a confusing process. It turns a Raspberry Pi into an easy and approachable Wi-Fi access point or router.

Similarly, this book takes wireless concepts that can be hard to grasp and distills them into digestible recipes. It builds on a base-level understanding of RF principles (see Chapter 1) and walks you through practical and relevant examples of Wi-Fi and Bluetooth debugging.

Wireless protocols will continue to evolve, and this book sets you on a path to understanding that evolution. Unlike many technical books, it has timeless information and examples.

I first heard about this book during its development in 2022, and I was happy to talk to (and learn from) Bill about some of the Wi-Fi portions, especially as it pertains to modern Raspberry Pis.

Whether you're building wireless products; integrating Wi-Fi, Bluetooth, or LoRa into a project; or simply interested in wireless communication, this book has a lot to offer.

Jeff Geerling
Saint Louis, Missouri
June 2, 2025

PREFACE

My first foray into computer programming began with following a recipe
when I was 12 years old. My guide for those early coding adventures was a
print magazine called *COMPUTE!*, which offered readers access to cutting-
edge games (by early 1980s standards, anyway) with impressive graphics,
for the low price of a monthly subscription. *COMPUTE!* made you work for
those programs, though: Pages of source code had to be painstakingly typed
in by hand. It was a tedious process. I would diligently enter code, line by
line, into my Atari 8-bit computer, only to have cryptic errors returned when
I finally entered RUN at the command prompt . . . errors that, more often
than not, referenced line numbers buried deep in some eye-wateringly dense
block of machine bytecode.

    I persevered through it all, motivated by the fantastical artistic render-
ings of these games on the magazine covers. The games themselves were
simple and lacked replayability, but that was beside the point. Without being
aware of it, or even thinking of it as educational, I was acquiring the fundamental principles of computer programming. In the process of designing
and coding my own animated game character "sprites," I learned about the
base-2 numeral system. By repurposing snippets of code and concepts introduced in different issues, in time I was creating my own programs from
scratch.

    Another popular magazine from this era, *Scientific American*, was influ-
ential for A.K. Dewdney's "Computer Recreations" column. His writing explored topics like hypercubes, genetic algorithms, fractals, simulated robots,
and more, often with pseudocode that could be translated into working
programs. I'll never forget the wonder I felt when my Atari rendered a

quarter-screenful of the Mandelbrot set, in glorious monochrome, after countless hours of CPU time.

Compared with modern programming, those early experiences seem almost medieval. While I appreciate the vast availability of information today, part of me misses the early days of having to imagine solutions with next to nothing to go on. It's hard to accurately describe just how much we had to figure out for ourselves. Without access to online resources, it often felt like we were coding on a desert island. And yet, since we had no alternative, it was never a burden.

This process of following code recipes as a teenager cemented my future career as a software engineer. The Atari and Commodore home computers of my youth were eventually retired for an x86 Intel machine. Later, in college, I had my first exposure to shared computing resources from a VAX terminal. Shortly thereafter, in 1991, Linus Torvalds announced the first official release of Linux. I delved headlong into the Linux kernel and haven't looked back since.

Today, this algorithmic learning approach remains a viable and highly effective way to develop skills in many diverse areas of computing. I'm grateful to the authors who guided me along this path of growth and development.

In the same spirit, I hope you'll enjoy taking this journey with me.

Bill Zimmerman

ACKNOWLEDGMENTS

Writing a technical book is seldom a solitary endeavor, despite the many hours spent largely in isolation coding, testing, parsing logs, and doing research. This book exists thanks to the contributions and support of many individuals.

First, I'd like to express my gratitude to the team at No Starch Press. Jill Franklin saw potential in this project from our first conversation and provided valuable guidance throughout. I thoroughly enjoyed collaborating with Bill Pollock on how best to position the book, and I greatly appreciate his sage advice. Thanks also to the entire production team at No Starch who refined and polished these pages.

Technical accuracy in this work owes much to Lawrence Yau, whose expert eyes caught potential pitfalls and who suggested improvements that significantly enhanced the material. Special thanks to beta reader Rob White for his meticulous review of Chapter 4, which vastly improved its content. Jeff Geerling graciously agreed to read Chapter 1 long before much of the book was written and kindly granted permission to use his photography. His encouragement early on in the writing process was truly invaluable.

I'm indebted to Olga Vishnyakova and Nikolay Lipko for their creative and technical input, respectively, from the outset of this project, not to mention their unconditional support and our enduring close friendship. Likewise, Roderick Knowles acted as a superb sounding board; his discerning eye and enthusiasm for the project boosted my resolve on many occasions.

My deepest appreciation goes to members of my family, Jamie and Vincent Delaney, for their willingness to read draft chapters and provide equal doses of genuine praise and critical feedback, as necessary. I spent many an hour at their kitchen island writing large portions of the material in this book.

Finally, to readers like you who are passionate about wireless technologies and Linux: Your curiosity and dedication to continuous learning inspire works like this. I hope this book serves you well in your personal and professional journeys.

INTRODUCTION

The Wireless Cookbook is designed so that you can read it linearly, from start to finish, or skip around and choose recipes at random. Each project is designed to stand on its own; no given recipe is dependent on any other or requires that you develop skills in a different area before proceeding to that one. At the same time, if concepts presented in one recipe can be used to enhance others, this will be pointed out along the way.

In choosing which recipes to include in this book, priority was given to selecting a variety of practical applications that touch on various aspects of 802.11 Wi-Fi, Bluetooth, and LoRa (short for *long range*) wireless technologies in a Linux context. The book's emphasis is on building complete projects that are practical and useful day-to-day, with easy-to-follow, step-by-step instructions. Along the way, we'll take a closer look at some of the fundamental concepts relating to each project, to help you develop a deeper understanding of what you're building. Of course, you may skip ahead to the practical implementation steps of any recipe and return to the theory sections at any time.

Who Is This Book For?

If you are a hobbyist, do-it-yourself enthusiast, or educator new to Linux and are seeking to build your knowledge of practical wireless applications for single-board computers (SBCs), including the Raspberry Pi family of devices, this book was written for you. Equally, seasoned developers looking to expand their skills will find an entry point into more advanced Linux wireless projects. Think of this book as providing a clear path to building practical, real-world applications with a variety of wireless technologies that you can start using straight away.

Each recipe walks you through building a functional and feature-rich project that may be customized, extended, or repurposed for other applications. I've made every effort throughout to explain things in plain English for the benefit of new Linux programmers, but with enough technical detail to satisfy more advanced users.

You'll need a minimum level of technical ability to make the most of this book. For example, I assume you know how to prepare an SD card with a compatible operating system (OS), access your Raspberry Pi (or similar device) remotely, and enter commands and code in a Linux environment. Where relevant, tips and tricks are provided that will help you develop fluency in Linux while also building your knowledge of wireless services and applications.

With the recipes presented here, you will develop the necessary skills and gain the confidence to create entirely original wireless projects of your own.

Why This Book?

There were three main motivations behind the writing of this book. First, there's no denying that wireless technologies today have become vital commodities in and of themselves, not unlike electricity. Our work and leisure time often depend on them. In our hyper-connected world, it's increasingly rare to find a consumer electronic device or appliance that doesn't rely on wireless connectivity in one form or another. This is more true now than ever, with the rise of Internet of Things (IoT)–enabled devices.

Most of the time, the presence of wireless connectivity is taken for granted; it's only in its absence that our dependence is truly felt. As a result, you can choose to be a passive consumer of these devices or seek to develop an understanding of the wireless technologies that underpin them. Along the way, you can even engineer some of your own solutions to meet your specific goals.

Second, as the principal developer of the popular free and open source RaspAP wireless router project, shown in Figure 1, I'm naturally drawn to this subject. Of the recent innovations in consumer SBCs, arguably none have done more to democratize access to Linux programming than the Raspberry Pi (abbreviated *RPi* or simply *Pi*), created by the UK-based Raspberry Pi Foundation.

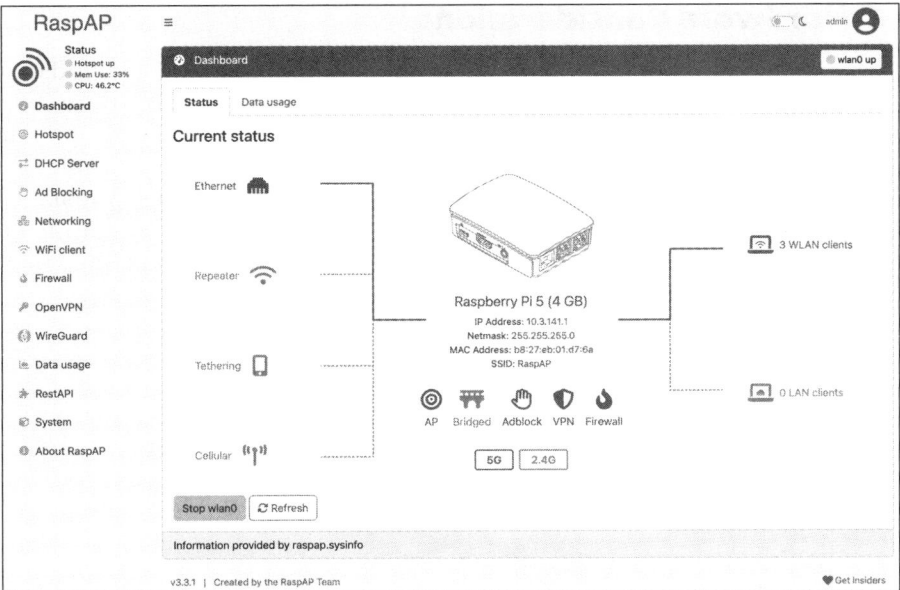

Figure 1: The RaspAP open source wireless router project

With capabilities making them suitable as server appliances, there has been a proliferation of uses for the RPi, ranging from smart homes to environmental monitoring, medicine, adaptive therapies, smart energy meters, computer vision, amateur astronomy, robotics, 3D printing, and much more. All of these applications rely on connectivity in one form or another for remote control, data access, and so on, and wireless is an attractive solution for several reasons. RaspAP evolved as an extensible access point (AP) and software network router that can be used as a component in these and many other kinds of projects.

While you may find projects similar to the ones in this book in the form of GitHub README files, blog posts, or other online walk-throughs, it's often challenging to find resources that are complete and up to date and that accurately guide the reader through the steps of creating them. Moreover, general concepts may not be explained at a deep enough level of detail to satisfy the curiosity of a developer or hobbyist exploring some new facet of wireless networking in Linux. Likewise, other guides may assume too much foreknowledge or experience and gloss over important details. *The Wireless Cookbook* seeks to strike a balance here and provide clear instructions with enough detail to satisfy all readers.

That brings us to the third motivation for this book. Until now, print resources with a specific focus on wireless projects for Linux have been lacking. The broad interest and questions I've received about applying RaspAP and similar wireless projects in various ways have highlighted the demand for a cookbook-type approach to implementing popular (and some lesser-known) wireless projects. This is where *The Wireless Cookbook* delivers.

Hardware Considerations

A diverse array of SBCs can be found on the market today, including not only the Raspberry Pi, shown in Figure 2, but also devices such as the Rock Pi, ASUS Tinker Board, Pine64, NanoPi, Orange Pi, and Banana Pi. A variety of supported operating systems are also available for these devices, although the majority are Linux based. The most popular choices include Raspberry Pi OS (based on Debian and optimized for the Pi's hardware), Armbian, Debian, and Ubuntu. You can also find SBCs that run Android and Windows.

Figure 2: The RPi Zero W is a small but capable Linux computer.

The opportunities for developing applications for these devices are virtually endless. In fact, the primary limiting factor isn't what an SBC can do, but rather what a specific device can accomplish. For this reason, I'll narrow down the vast range of possibilities to the Raspberry Pi family of devices and the Raspberry Pi OS Lite (32- or 64-bit) distribution. Each recipe in this book has been rigorously tested and validated to work on these systems. Other devices and OSes, such as the Orange Pi with Armbian, will usually work with some modifications. However, for the sake of simplicity, I'll focus on using the Pi running Raspberry Pi OS Lite as the reference environment.

This may sound obvious, but be sure that you have an official 5.1-volt (V) power supply for your specific Pi model. Each model has unique power requirements, and undervoltage due to a mismatched power supply or having several external USB devices connected to the system can lead to intermittent errors down the road. I'll discuss ways to identify these and other common problems later in the book.

A final note on wireless adapters: Each recipe makes use of the family of built-in wireless chipsets on recent Pi models, supported by the Broadcom kernel driver. The capabilities of these chipsets vary between, for example, the Pi Zero W and the Pi 5; however, they all fulfill the basic requirements of each project. Some recipes will recommend an external USB wireless adapter for specific purposes. In these cases, I've selected inexpensive yet capable and widely available adapters that you should have little trouble procuring.

How to Use This Book

The recipes in this book were selected by identifying popular use cases for various technologies and developing project frameworks around them. The flow of recipes generally progresses from simple to more complex; however, you are not required to work through them in order from start to finish. You should be able to skip to any project that catches your eye.

Each chapter opens with an overview of the topic covered in the recipe and suggested use cases. The hardware and software requirements are listed up front, followed by relevant background information and topics of special interest (with pointers to additional resources where helpful).

None of these recipes requires expensive, difficult-to-source, or otherwise exotic hardware. In fact, several require only a compatible Raspberry Pi model. However, a big part of the appeal of these affordable Linux computers is their extensibility—that is, the ability to expand their basic capabilities in various ways with add-on hardware components. Details on additional required or recommended hardware components, such as external wireless adapters, sensors, displays, and so on, will be provided in the recipe's list of materials, along with estimated costs. All of the components mentioned in the "Hardware Required" section of each chapter should be readily available from several online vendors, and you'll find that several of the add-on components are common to multiple recipes in this book and can be reused for different purposes.

Online Materials

This book includes many detailed code examples and Linux shell manipulations. While I encourage you to develop the practice of using a Linux text editor, it isn't strictly necessary to do so for every project (I won't force you to repeat my experience of entering thousands of lines of code into the Atari!). These days, modern distributed source code management systems like Git and hosted code repository sites like GitHub and Bitbucket make the process of sharing code much simpler. You will find all the source code for this book, organized by chapter, hosted at *https://github.com/wirelesscookbook*. Instructions for pulling source code from GitHub to be used on your system are provided in subsequent chapters.

The aim of this book is to help you build practical wireless projects quickly and efficiently. You are free to use the code examples provided in the book and the resources available in the companion GitHub repository in your own programs and documentation. You don't need to contact the author or publisher for permission unless you are selling or distributing materials with examples taken from this book, in whole or in part.

The recipes in this book rely on many third-party open source software components. The maintainers of these code repositories will indicate the licensing models used for their projects. Most often, this will be defined in a README file or a separate LICENSE file associated with the project. If you're considering using one of these projects for commercial purposes, be sure to review the licensing agreement before doing so.

Finally, the libraries and tools used in this book have their own comprehensive online documentation. Links to relevant documentation will be provided in case you would like to learn more.

Conventions Used

This book contains many source code examples that you will use in the course of building the projects. These typically take the following form:

```
def signal_to_bars(signal):
    bars = ['\u2581', '\u2583', '\u2585', '\u2587']
    ranges = [
        (-100, -80), # 1 bar
        (-79, -67),  # 2 bars
        (-66, -56),  # 3 bars
        (-55, -30)   # 4 bars
    ]
    signal = int(signal) # cast to integer
--snip--
```

The # indicates a comment or a line of code that should not be executed; uncommenting a line involves removing the # at the start of that line. The *--snip--* in this example indicates that code not vital to understanding the relevant part of the content has been omitted to save space.

The same convention may be used for command output. Commands entered in the Linux terminal and the output returned are often displayed in a single listing. In these instances, the user input will appear in **bold**. For example:

```
$ ping nostarch.com

PING nostarch.com (104.20.17.121): 56 data bytes
64 bytes from 104.20.17.121: icmp_seq=0 ttl=57 time=32.997 ms
64 bytes from 104.20.17.121: icmp_seq=1 ttl=57 time=41.216 ms
--snip--
```

The $ prompt is a Linux convention that indicates a user is executing a command in the bash shell. The shell powers the text interface of many Linux operating systems, including Raspberry Pi OS. It isn't necessary to enter the $ symbol when executing a command.

Code examples, variable names, parameters, commands, and terminal output appear in a monospaced font, as shown here. *Monospaced italics* are used for placeholders in code listings.

You'll also see the following additional styles used throughout this book:

- New terms being introduced for the first time and important words or concepts appear in *italics*.

- Individual keystrokes appear in all caps: ENTER, F3, ALT, and so on. Keystroke combinations like CTRL-C indicate that the first key should be held while pressing the second key.

- Menu and dialog box selections and other user input appear in **bold**.

- Supplementary or tangential material that may be of interest to the reader will appear in a boxed callout.

How This Book Is Organized

I've organized the book's chapters into two parts.

Part I: The Big Picture aims to equip you with the tools and understanding you will need to work through the projects in the second part of the book.

Chapter 1: Wireless Fundamentals   Provides a broad overview of the wireless technologies covered in this book and how they work.

Chapter 2: Getting Started   Guides you through the steps of setting up the Linux development environment that you'll be using for the recipe chapters that follow and introduces the basics of programming in a Linux environment, with some recommended approaches.

Part II: The Recipes is the real "meat and potatoes" portion of the book. The chapters present a selection of unique projects in a recipe format, complete with detailed background information on the underlying technologies and descriptions of use cases, software and hardware used, implementation, troubleshooting, and next steps.

Chapter 3: Monitoring Wi-Fi with a Mini TFT Display   Uses an attached display device to visualize two different yet related characteristics of Wi-Fi networks. Python, the general-purpose I/O (GPIO) header, and add-on hardware are introduced here.

Chapter 4: Basic and Advanced Captive Portals   Examines the technology behind Wi-Fi hotspots and demonstrates the use of open source software most often applied in OpenWrt-based wireless routers to create two kinds of captive portals.

Chapter 5: Bluetooth Audio in Two Ways   Details two unique and practical applications that use Bluetooth for audio output, plus a third bonus one. This chapter is recommended for audiophiles but will be equally interesting to anyone wanting to know how Bluetooth works.

Chapter 6: Exploring Long Range with LoRa   Introduces very long range and low-power wireless applications using LoRa and discusses methods for evaluating range and connecting to LoRaWAN networks.

Chapter 7: Intrusion Detection with Kismet Focuses on the threats posed by poorly secured wireless networks. You'll build a powerful Kismet Wi-Fi monitoring node as part of a wireless LAN security test bench.

Chapter 8: Wireless Air Quality Monitoring Presents a wireless IoT project that delves into air quality sampling technologies. You may also participate in citizen science by pushing your sensor readings to the cloud via Wi-Fi.

Chapter 9: Pwning Wi-Fi with Pwnagotchi Provides a comprehensive guide to building a Pwnagotchi unit. This AI-based open source project has made big waves in the Wi-Fi security and hacking communities.

Chapter 10: Exploring Mesh Networking Dives into the topic of building resilient, extensible mesh networks. You'll use an ad hoc wireless routing protocol and off-the-shelf components to create mesh-capable nodes, with optional add-on network traffic indicators.

Chapter 11: Wireless Displays in Two Ways Explores how you can use two popular wireless display technologies to stream high-definition video to an external device, such as a TV or monitor. In the process, you'll free yourself from digital surveillance with these open source alternatives.

The **appendix** opens with a discussion about developing an engineer's mindset. From this foundation, a problem-solving methodology is presented that you can apply not only in a Linux context but also in any technical endeavor. Tips and strategies are also provided to assist you with debugging and otherwise tracking down issues you might encounter in the course of implementing these projects.

Wrapping Up

Now that you have an idea of what you'll find in this book and how to use it, let's get started! If you're already intimately familiar with wireless technologies, have a working Linux development environment set up, and are impatient to get building, you can skip straight to the recipes in Part II. If you're new to these concepts or would like a refresher or additional details on the technologies and the recommended setup for this book's projects, the following chapters will provide the foundation you need.

PART I

THE BIG PICTURE

1

WIRELESS FUNDAMENTALS

Wireless networks have become so ubiquitous in our daily lives that it's easy to take them for granted. Whether at home or in public spaces, there's a high probability that at any given moment we're bathed in wireless traffic of all descriptions. Most of the time, our devices automatically establish links to known 802.11 and Bluetooth networks without any intervention on our part, and usually without our knowledge. If we have a decent wireless signal that enables us to perform our desired tasks, we're generally content to go about our routines, blissfully unaware of the complexities behind the scenes of these transformative technologies.

As consumers of wireless technology, we can hardly be blamed for assuming a passive role. With each technological advancement, friction in the various domains of our lives is incrementally reduced. This conditions us to expect each new generation of tools to be faster, easier to use, and more intuitive than before.

In this chapter, I'll break us out of this passive mode, pull back the curtain, and help you develop an understanding of what makes wireless work. The end goal here is to provide non-network engineers with a conceptual model of the technologies underpinning Wi-Fi and related Bluetooth and LoRa (short for *long range*) networks while offering sufficient detail to satisfy more advanced readers. With this foundation, you'll be well equipped to tackle the material in the subsequent chapters of this book.

Electromagnetic Radiation

In physics, electromagnetic radiation travels in waves that are described in terms of their spatial period, or *wavelength* (the distance over which a wave repeats), often denoted by the Greek letter *lambda* (λ). The number of oscillations that pass a particular point in a given period of time is called the *frequency* and is measured in cycles per second, or hertz (Hz), commonly denoted by the Greek letter *nu* (ν). This is illustrated in Figure 1-1.

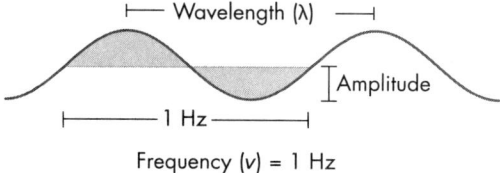

Figure 1-1: The elements of a typical waveform

The *amplitude*, or *vertical height*, of a wave is defined as one-half of the peak-to-trough height. As the amplitude of a wave with a given frequency increases, so does its energy. All forms of electromagnetic radiation, whether microwaves, visible light, or gamma rays, travel at the speed of light (c). They differ only in their wavelengths and frequencies. Wavelength is typically expressed as a unit of distance. Common wavelength units range from meters (10^0) in the case of radio waves, to centimeters (10^{-2}) for microwaves, to nanometers (10^{-9}) for X-rays, and so on.

A given range of wavelengths or frequencies is called a *spectrum*. This term was originally used to describe the visual light spectrum but is now applied to the entire *electromagnetic spectrum (EMS)*, ranging from short-wavelength (high-frequency) gamma rays to long-wavelength (low-frequency) radio waves, as shown in Figure 1-2.

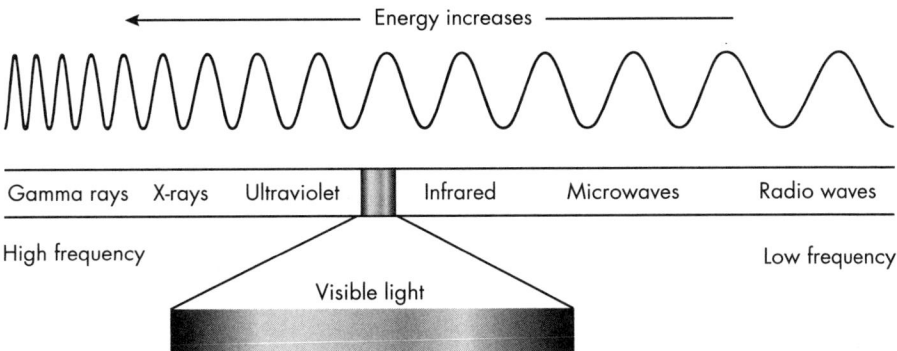

Figure 1-2: An overview of the electromagnetic spectrum

Our focus is on the radio end of this spectrum. Radio frequencies, often abbreviated *RF*, range from 3 kilohertz (kHz) to 300 gigahertz (GHz). Microwaves utilize the RF spectrum from 300 megahertz (MHz), or 300,000 kHz, up to 300 GHz. So where do Wi-Fi signals fit in?

Wi-Fi devices transmit and receive signals on the 2.4 GHz, 5 GHz, or recently approved 6 GHz bands, all of which fall within the microwave and radio wave frequency range. As a point of reference, microwave ovens operate at frequencies of about 2.45 GHz, or λ = 12.23 cm. While this is slightly lower than a Wi-Fi signal, your microwave oven operates at a significantly higher power output, in the range of 800 to 1,800 watts (W).

By contrast, a typical home Wi-Fi router uses 5 to 30 W, with 10 to 15 W being average. The power consumption of the Raspberry Pi 4's wireless chipset tops out at a minuscule 400 milliamps (mA), or 0.4 W, while transmitting at 20 decibel milliwatts (dBm) on the 2.4 GHz band. If these figures are unclear, don't worry; we'll break this down when we discuss signal strength later in this chapter.

What's in a Name?

Let's begin with a brief examination of one of the most often used terms in the wireless domain. Although it's commonly believed to be an abbreviation of *wireless fidelity,* the shorthand *Wi-Fi* is actually a brand name that was introduced by the Wi-Fi Alliance to make wireless technology more accessible to consumers. The technical standard, *IEEE 802.11*, was considered too complex for general audiences, so the Alliance was formed to promote adoption and ensure interoperability among devices. The Wi-Fi name is trademarked and can be used only by devices that have passed certification testing in a laboratory setting.

Today, the Wi-Fi CERTIFIED seal of approval has been granted to more than 50,000 consumer wireless products. The certification process includes standardized testing for security, interoperability, and backward compatibility with previous generations of Wi-Fi products.

Wi-Fi Technology Working Principle

In this and the following sections, I'll break down 802.11 wireless into its individual components. It's important to bear in mind from the outset, however, that Wi-Fi is just one part of the wireless story. Later in this chapter, I'll touch on the related short-range (Bluetooth) and long-range (LoRa) wireless networking technologies. Let's begin with the fundamentals behind 802.11 Wi-Fi before looking at the technology more closely.

Wi-Fi, like broadcast radio and cellular telephone signals, is based on scientific discoveries dating back to the late 19th century. Traditional AM/FM radio and TV stations broadcast using analog signals. Wi-Fi signals are transmitted digitally as discrete values—the 0s and 1s of binary data—between a wireless *access point (AP)* and one or more connected client devices equipped with a *wireless adapter*. This data is converted by a router or an adapter so it can be transmitted (abbreviated *Tx*) or received (*Rx*) via Wi-Fi radio waves. When a connected device receives this encoded radio signal, that device decodes the signal back into the original data. We'll examine this process in more detail in "Making a Connection" on page 33.

In communications, Wi-Fi is classified as a *half-duplex* system, meaning that only one device may transmit data at any given time. If two wireless devices were to try to transmit at the same time, they would interrupt each other. In the half-duplex mode, data packets are sent back and forth in sequence over a shared channel. This is analogous to how a walkie-talkie or push-to-talk system works. Normally, this happens so quickly on a wireless local area network (WLAN) that it mimics seamless two-way (*full-duplex*) data transmission.

The more wireless devices are added to a given channel, however, the fewer opportunities each device has to talk. This is known as *co-channel interference*. The devices take turns to communicate, with the slower ones taking longer to transmit the same amount of data. For this reason, one way to mitigate co-channel interference is to keep data rates fast by disabling the slower wireless devices. In larger WLAN implementations, multiple APs may be deployed to create smaller coverage cells, thereby limiting the number of devices sharing a channel.

The two-way communication process requires wireless adapters and the router to work in tandem on a WLAN. For communication to proceed, each device must adhere to a set of agreed-upon wireless protocols and encryption standards. The IEEE 802.11 standard defines the protocols that enable communications with current Wi-Fi−enabled devices, including routers and access points. Wireless access points may support a range of IEEE standards, discussed in the next section.

IEEE 802.11 Standards

Wi-Fi standards are established by the Institute of Electrical and Electronics Engineers (IEEE), the organization responsible for the various types of

Wi-Fi that are familiar to anyone who has shopped for a home router or looked at the technical specifications of a Raspberry Pi or similar device. Known as the IEEE 802.11 Wireless LAN standards, they are identified by the number 802.11 with a letter suffix. There's nothing magic about the number 802.11; it simply refers to the body of networking standards developed by the IEEE 802.11 working group. For comparison, working group standards for other types of networks are summarized in Table 1-1.

Table 1-1: IEEE 802.11 Working Group Standards

Name	Description	Notes
802.3	Ethernet	Describes the physical and networking characteristics of an Ethernet network, including how physical connections between nodes (such as routers, switches, and hubs) are made through various wired media like copper coaxial or fiber cable.
802.15	Wireless specialty networks (WSNs)	Focuses on wireless personal area networks (PANs). This category covers technologies such as Bluetooth, the Internet of Things (IoT), wearables, mesh networks, body area networks, and visible light communication.
802.16	Broadband wireless metropolitan area networks (MANs)	Concerned with point-to-multipoint wireless access, often referred to as "last mile" broadband. One wireless mechanism defined by this standard is WiMAX (Worldwide Interoperability for Microwave Access), which can cover several miles with a single base station.
802.22	Wireless regional area networks (WRANs)	Defines fixed wireless broadband access for rural and remote areas. WRAN systems based on this standard take advantage of broadcast TV *white spaces* (unused channels in the frequency band) that exist in sparsely populated areas.

Each 802.11 standard is a ratified amendment to the original specification. The standards operate on varying frequencies, deliver different bandwidth, and support different numbers of channels. Given the order in which the 802.11 WLAN standards were ratified, higher letters generally correspond to faster network speeds (with the notable exception of 802.11a and b). At first glance, they can look a bit like alphabet soup. For simplicity, I'll broadly classify each network by two distinct attributes (I'll discuss a third one, broadcast range, in the next section):

Speed   The amount of data the network can transmit. This is expressed in megabits per second (Mbps), where 1 megabit is 1 million bits.

Frequency   The radio frequency the network is carried on. The available frequencies are 2.4, 5, or 6 GHz.

Table 1-2 summarizes the most common IEEE 802.11 WLAN standards based on their designations.

Table 1-2: IEEE 802.11 WLAN Standards

Name	Speed	Frequency	Notes
802.11a	54Mbps; 6–24Mbps is typical	5 GHz	One of the oldest standards but still used by many devices today. Incompatible with 802.11b or g standards and newer 5 GHz Wi-Fi technologies.
802.11b	11Mbps	2.4 GHz	Designed to be backward compatible with previous 802.11 standards that provided for speeds of 1, 2, and 5.5Mbps. Compatible with 802.11g.
802.11g	54Mbps	2.4 GHz	Combines the best qualities of 802.11a and b. Popular for its combination of speed and backward compatibility.
802.11n	Up to 600Mbps; 100Mbps is typical	2.4 and 5 GHz	The first standard to use multiple-input multiple-output (MIMO) technology. Significantly increased speed and range by operating on both 2.4 GHz and 5 GHz bands.
802.11ac	450Mbps or 3.5Gbps	2.4 and 5 GHz	The fifth generation of Wi-Fi, established in 2013. Developed to operate primarily on the 5 GHz band, to reduce interference in the 2.4 GHz band.
802.11ax	450Mbps up to 9.6Gbps	2.4 and 5 GHz; 6 GHz for Wi-Fi 6E	Wi-Fi 6 offers practical performance gains of 2–2.5 times over 802.11ac (Wi-Fi 5). Backward compatible with 802.11g and n standards, and introduces support for the 6 GHz frequency band.

Each of the standards listed here can operate in either an infrastructure mode or an ad hoc network design mode. The vast majority of wireless networks use *infrastructure mode*, where all devices on the network communicate through a single access point. *Ad hoc mode*, also known as *peer-to-peer* mode, doesn't require a centralized access point. These are typically short-lived networks with weak or no security, often used to connect devices for the purpose of data sharing (used with wireless printers, for example). Mesh networks, which are examined in detail in Chapter 10, are a notable exception.

Broadcast Range

The 802.11 standards were all developed with not only speed but also effective range in mind. A general rule of thumb is that the broadcast range of most 2.4 GHz wireless routers is about 45 meters (or 150 feet) indoors and roughly 90 meters (300 feet) outdoors. Newer 802.11n and 802.11ac routers that operate on both 2.4 GHz and 5 GHz bands are able to reach greater distances. However, there's a trade-off between speed and range on the 5 GHz band. This is a limitation imposed by physics; because of its narrower wavelengths, a 5 GHz Wi-Fi connection is more susceptible to obstructions than a 2.4 GHz connection. As a result, somewhat shorter effective ranges are typical. Two maxims influencing Wi-Fi broadcast range are worth bearing in mind here:

- The higher the data rate, the shorter the effective range.
- The wider the channel bandwidth (20, 40, 80 MHz, and so on), the shorter the effective range.

As anyone who has experienced a Wi-Fi "dead spot" knows, indoor range may also be significantly affected by the physical layout of a structure and the type of building materials used. If you have multiple neighboring Wi-Fi networks nearby, *channel interference* is another factor that can reduce the delivery of your network. This is particularly true of 802.11b/g/n networks on the 2.4 GHz band. While 14 available channels are designated for use in this band, a great deal of overlap occurs between them, as shown in Figure 1-3. This issue is discussed in greater detail in "Channel Surfing" on page 13.

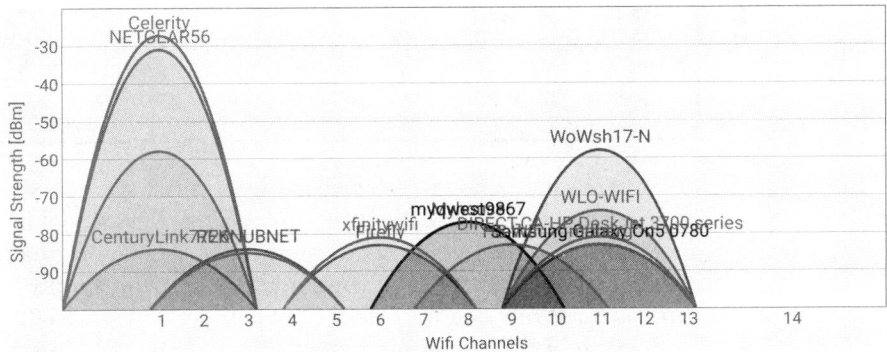

Figure 1-3: A crowded 2.4 GHz band with overlapping wireless networks on the same or adjacent channels

In addition to the problem of overlapping wireless networks, a wide variety of devices can create interference and thus limit the effective range and speed of your network. The lower frequency of the 2.4 GHz band allows signals to travel farther, which may seem like a good thing. However, the longer reach means that there's a greater likelihood of neighboring access points interfering with one another. As the number of devices connected to the 2.4 GHz band increases, so too do the levels of interference and congestion. A valid comparison is trying to hold a conversation in a room that is slowly becoming more and more crowded, with competing loud voices eventually making effective communication effectively impossible.

Radio sources such as cordless phones, wireless video cameras, Bluetooth devices, microwave ovens, and wireless peripherals all compete for the 2.4 GHz spectrum. This congestion is less of a problem on the 5 GHz band, which has a lot more usable spectrum (up to 500 MHz, compared to about 80 MHz on the 2.4 GHz band). Still, despite being less crowded, the 5 GHz band remains susceptible to interference from sources such as radar, some variable frequency drive (VFD) electronic motors, and motion detectors.

The effective distance at which a device can connect to an access point also depends on the orientation of the antenna. Directional antennas can enable longer reach to specific areas, at the expense of a shorter reach to other areas.

SIGNAL BOOSTING

A common misconception is that powered Wi-Fi "booster" antennas are an expedient way of solving the range issues of wireless networks. There are a few problems with this idea. For starters, amplifying your router's wireless signal runs the risk of being illegal in many places. Most countries treat 802.11 wireless LANs as license free, but to qualify, radio devices' power levels must be limited to relatively low values. For example, in the United States, the Federal Communications Commission (FCC) has set the maximum transmit power for unlicensed wireless equipment at 30 dBm (1 watt, or 1,000 milliwatts). Second, while boosting your signal may sound like a good thing, it creates a big source of RF noise for your neighbors. Finally, communication requires devices on both sides of a wireless link to be able to reach each other. While you may succeed in making your router transmit a stronger signal, there's no guarantee that the signals returned by your wireless clients (phones, computers, and so on) will be capable of reaching the router.

A technique known as *beamforming* uses the science of electromagnetic interference to increase the precision of a wireless signal by focusing it in a specific direction. In effect, this method uses an array of antennas to "steer" a radio signal in a particular direction, rather than simply broadcasting in all directions. While beamforming has been around since 802.11n, with the introduction of MIMO, improvements have been made in subsequent WLAN standards. The latest standard, 802.11ax, doubles the number of MIMO antennas from four to eight, which has the effect of improving data transfer rates as well as extending the signal range.

Bandwidth, Throughput, and Latency

The performance of any network (wired or wireless) can be measured in a number of ways. The following terms are sometimes used interchangeably, but it's important to understand the differences between them:

Speed   The rate at which data is transferred from a source system to a destination.

Bandwidth   The maximum capacity of a wired or wireless link to transmit data over a network in a given period of time, typically expressed in Mbps. Bandwidth can be compared to the volume of water that is able to flow through a pipe of a specific diameter. A common misconception is that bandwidth is a measure of network speed, but it defines only *potential* capacity. It's also important to note that bandwidth is a finite resource in any given deployment.

Throughput The actual amount of data transmitted over a network in a given period of time. While bandwidth concerns theoretical data transfer rates across the network, throughput reflects the real-world data transfer achieved.

Generally speaking, higher-bandwidth networks tend to be faster. However, network performance can be influenced by another factor: *latency*, or the amount of time required for data to get to its destination across a network. Sometimes called *round-trip time (RTT)* or *lag*, network latency is commonly measured as a round-trip delay value, taking into account the time it takes for a request to travel from sender to receiver and back. It's usually expressed in milliseconds (ms). Low latency (a short delay) is desirable, while high latency (a longer delay) is not.

One of the primary causes of network latency is distance, or how far the device making a request is from the device responding to it. A data packet sent over a Transmission Control Protocol/Internet Protocol (TCP/IP) network must pass through a number of routers, switches, bridges, and gateways. Each of these transitions, known as a *hop*, incurs a small but measurable time delay. Other factors, such as packet size, *jitter* (variability in the network delay), and network congestion, also come into play. The protocols used are a consideration as well: TCP, for example, requires an acknowledgment before sending more data, whereas the User Datagram Protocol (UDP) doesn't keep track of what it has sent.

LATENCY EFFECTS IN FIBER OPTICS

Despite operating on optical waveguides, fiber-optic networks are not immune to latency effects created by distance. Based on the speed of light in a vacuum (299,792,458 meters per second), there is a latency of 3.33 microseconds (μs), or 0.00000333 s, for every kilometer spanned by a fiber-optic cable. However, light travels more slowly through the glass core of a cable because of differences in its refractive index. This means the latency of light traveling in a fiber-optic cable is slightly higher, at around 4.9 μs per kilometer (km) of distance traveled.

You can perform your own latency test on the Raspberry Pi with a network tool called `mtr`. This combines the functions of `ping` and `traceroute`, two common utilities found in most Linux distributions. (A *ping* is a basic network test that sends a small data packet to another device and measures how long it takes to get a response; during speed tests, latency is sometimes referred to as *ping rate*.) Results are reported as round-trip response times in milliseconds and the percentage of packet loss. Install and test it like so, replacing the remote address with one of your choosing:

```
$ sudo apt update
$ sudo apt install mtr-tiny -y
$ mtr --report github.com
Start: 2025-04-18T03:58:47-0700
HOST: rpitest                     Loss%   Snt   Last    Avg   Best   Wrst StDev
  1.|-- 192.168.8.1                0.0%    10    1.3    1.4    1.1    2.0   0.3
  2.|-- 192.168.235.172            0.0%    10    3.2    3.4    2.8    6.5   1.1
  3.|-- 172.29.177.129             0.0%    10   28.1   26.0   18.7   38.8   6.5
  4.|-- 10.49.60.173              10.0%    10   30.5   36.6   29.4   50.9   7.7
  5.|-- ae7-100-xcr1.mal.cw.net    0.0%    10   35.1   36.9   28.9   50.8   6.5
  6.|-- ae1-xcr1.max.cw.net        0.0%    10   39.8   35.3   30.3   41.8   3.5
  7.|-- mad-b3-link.ip.twelve99.n 20.0%    10   34.4   36.4   30.9   43.9   4.5
--snip--
 18.|-- lb-140-82-121-4-fra.githu  0.0%    10   60.6   59.8   56.4   66.0   3.2
```

As shown here, mtr provides latency and packet loss statistics for each hop that packets take to reach their destination. The first few hops typically correspond to your router's gateway and your internet service provider (ISP). A high packet loss percentage can indicate a problem with that particular hop. You can perform similar latency tests with ping or traceroute and compare the results.

Signal Strength

As discussed in "Broadcast Range" on page 8, you can expect the usable range of Wi-Fi signals to degrade with distance and other factors. Signal strength is measured from the perspective of the receiving wireless device. The most accurate way to measure it is in milliwatts (mW), but because of Wi-Fi's ultra-low transmit power, we end up with lots of decimals, making these numbers difficult to read. For this reason, most Wi-Fi networks use decibels *relative* to 1 mW, or simply *decibel milliwatts (dBm)*, as a way of defining signal strength. Using dBm is a logarithmic, rather than linear, way to express power level or signal strength.

Given that Wi-Fi signal strength is typically less than 1 mW, dBm values are expressed as negative numbers. For most applications, an ideal Wi-Fi signal strength is in the range of −50 to −67 dBm (where −50 dBm is 0.00001 mW) and will largely be a function of the distance from the wireless access point. Below this range, connectivity issues become noticeable. Table 1-3 provides a summary of different signal strengths and their perceived quality.

Table 1-3: Wireless Signal Strengths and Their Perceived Quality

Signal strength	Expected quality
–30 dBm	A perfect signal, probably measured within a meter or two of the router
–50 dBm	An excellent signal
–60 dBm	A very good, reliable signal
–67 dBm	An acceptable signal, considered the minimum for services such as non-high-definition streaming video
–70 dBm	A degraded but still usable signal, able to support services such as email and light web use
–80 dBm	An unreliable signal, insufficient for most services
–90 dBm	A poor signal with a very low likelihood of establishing a connection

You can use the Linux utility iw to perform a scan of nearby networks with a Raspberry Pi's onboard wireless adapter. Fetching dBm values for the detected service set identifiers (SSIDs) is simply a matter of filtering the command output with awk, like so (replace the wlan0 interface with your own, if different):

```
$ sudo iw dev wlan0 scan | awk '/signal:/{sta=$2$3} /SSID:/{print $0" "sta}'
    SSID: Home-Router -30.00dBm
    SSID: RaspAP -52.00dBm
    SSID: SFR WiFi Mobile -66.00dBm
    SSID: SFR WiFi FON -68.00dBm
    SSID: NETGEAR N300 -79.00dBm
--snip--
```

As you might expect, changing the location (and even orientation) of your Pi can influence the output of this basic WLAN survey. Repeat this command with your Pi in different locations and compare the results.

For the most part, network engineers use dBm as a standard measurement. Many manufacturers have adopted *received signal strength indicator (RSSI)* to gauge signal strength, although this is a somewhat arbitrary measure: Some wireless adapter vendors use a scale of 0 to 60, others 0 to 100 or even 0 to 255. RSSI is often used to represent signal strength graphically, in the form of indicator bars, for example. For our purposes, we'll standardize on dBm throughout this book.

Channel Surfing

The Wi-Fi frequency bands can be subdivided into smaller frequency ranges known as *channels*. These are roughly analogous to lanes of traffic or television channels, although with somewhat fuzzier boundaries. Channel numbers indicate the specific frequency range a device's center frequency operates on. The operating channel of a home or business WLAN is defined by the AP or wireless router, not the wireless client devices. The bands and channels used for a network can greatly impact performance and reliability.

These days, most Wi-Fi routers will scan your wireless neighborhood and automatically select the best channel for your locality. However, some routers ship from the factory with a preset channel and do not have this auto-select facility.

Given that you'll be taking manual control of WLANs in this book, it pays to know how to determine these settings yourself. Before delving into the channels on these bands, let's first briefly discuss channel widths.

Channel Widths

Broadly speaking, *channel width* refers to the amount of bandwidth used within the radio spectrum during a transmission. The 802.11 standards specify an allotment of 22 MHz for a single channel, with a 5 MHz incremental step between each one. It's common to see a nominal value of 20 MHz used to describe Wi-Fi channels, so I'll use that value here. A 20 MHz segment with a channel separation of 5 MHz means that adjacent channels overlap and signals on adjacent channels will interfere with each other. We'll see what this means for each of the wireless bands later in this section.

The 802.11b and 802.11g wireless standards rely on a single channel to send and receive information. A technique known as *channel bonding* gives one the ability to use two adjacent channels simultaneously, creating a wider 40 MHz segment. 802.11n was the first standard to allow channel bonding, which effectively doubles the potential data transmission rate. Bonding can boost throughput from the 54Mbps offered by the 802.11g standard to a theoretical maximum of 600Mbps, although lower rates are more typical.

ARE TWO CHANNELS BETTER THAN ONE?

A 40 MHz channel can deliver higher throughput than a 20 MHz channel, but bonding also has its downsides. Wider channels reduce the number of nonoverlapping options and therefore increase the likelihood of interference. As a result, using bonded channels can actually lead to poorer wireless performance.

It's quite common, particularly in crowded wireless environments, to observe the effective throughput of an 802.11n wireless AP being reduced by half. This occurs when a 40 MHz channel "falls back" to 20 MHz because of interference on the 2.4 GHz band. The most common reason for this is when the AP or router detects another wireless network, or *basic service set (BSS)*, within 40 MHz (that is, two channels) of its own. For example, if an AP is set to channel 6, another network operating anywhere from channel 4 to 8 will trigger a fallback. When this happens, hostapd, the Linux service providing the AP, will report an error like the following:

```
20/40 MHz operation not permitted on channel pri=3 sec=7 based on overlapping
BSSes
```

Indeed, this caution is included in the notes for hostapd's configuration file:

```
# Please note that 40 MHz channels may switch their primary and secondary
# channels if needed or creation of 40 MHz channel maybe rejected based
# on overlapping BSSes. These changes are done automatically when hostapd
# is setting up the 40 MHz channel.
```

To understand why this happens, let's take a closer look at the channels on the 802.11 2.4 GHz band.

Channels on the 2.4 GHz Band

A total of 14 channels are defined for use by Wi-Fi devices on the 2.4 GHz band. Of these, the ones available in your area will depend on your wireless regulatory domain. For example, 11 are allowed for use in what is known as the North American domain. In the United States, channels 12, 13, and 14 are restricted by the FCC and are not supported on equipment sold in the country. In Europe, regulators allow the use of 13 channels. We'll look at this important concept more closely in "Wireless Regulatory Domains" on page 19.

Figure 1-4 displays the 2.4 GHz channels, with their 22 MHz segments and center frequencies (in GHz).

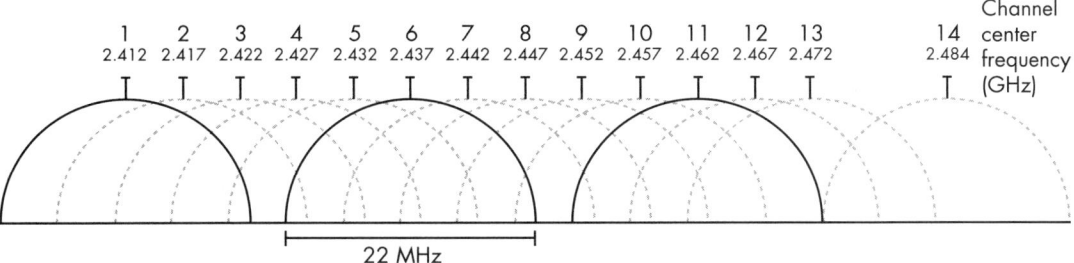

Figure 1-4: A visual representation of the channels on the 2.4 GHz band

Unlike with television channels, you'll notice some overlap between adjacent 802.11 wireless channels. In fact, only 3 of the 11 channels can operate simultaneously without overlapping or interfering with one another: channels 1, 6, and 11, as shown in Figure 1-5.

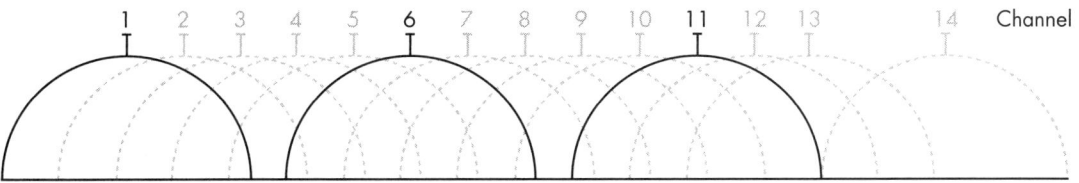

Figure 1-5: The three nonoverlapping channels on the 2.4 GHz band

One might reasonably ask, why contend with overlapping channels in the first place? The first part of the answer is that the RF spectrum, of which Wi-Fi is a part, is a finite natural resource with limitations imposed by physics. As a result, wireless is known as a *shared medium*, which means that the clients in a given area must all share the available bandwidth. The second part of the answer is that the IEEE, mindful of these physical limitations, designed the 802.11 standards with overlap in mind.

Wi-Fi uses some sophisticated techniques to minimize channel noise, including direct-sequence spread spectrum (DSSS), which employs a type of modulation to reduce signal interference. DSSS was defined in the original 802.11 specification and first implemented with 802.11b. More efficient transmission methods, such as orthogonal frequency division multiplexing (OFDM), were added with 802.11g. The technology surrounding Wi-Fi is constantly evolving, so you can expect to see these techniques further refined and newer ones rolled out by the 802.11 working group.

Wouldn't it be simpler to just have a wider frequency band with no overlapping channels? The short answer is yes, and the solution already exists in the form of the wider and less crowded 5 GHz band.

Channels on the 5 GHz Band

As the 2.4 GHz band becomes more crowded and newer consumer hardware enters the market, many users are opting to use the 5 GHz band for their wireless LANs. Not only are there significantly more nonoverlapping 20 MHz channels available on the 5 GHz band, but this band also supports wider Wi-Fi channels: 40, 80, and even 160 MHz. It's a fundamental rule of wireless networking that more spectrum enables higher throughput, and that is borne out here.

With about 10 times the usable bandwidth of the 2.4 GHz band and far fewer competing devices, the 5 GHz band is comparatively interference-free (at least for now). There are 25 predefined nonoverlapping 5 GHz Wi-Fi channels available for use in the United States. The availability of these channels varies in other countries based on wireless regulatory domain restrictions, discussed later in this chapter.

The channels are grouped into six blocks or sub-bands, as shown in Figure 1-6. The available channels for Wi-Fi appear in a lighter shade.

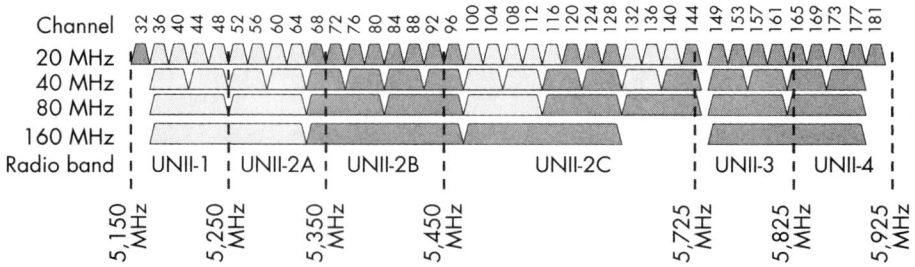

Figure 1-6: A visual representation of the channels on the 5 GHz band

The first block, comprising channels 36, 40, 44, and 48, is known as *UNII-1* and is allocated for domestic use, such as indoor wireless APs. The next blocks, *UNII-2A*, *UNII-2B*, and *UNII-2C* (aka *UNII-2 Extended*), support both indoor and outdoor operation, although UNII-2B is not currently available for unlicensed Wi-Fi use in the United States because of radar protections. The *UNII-3* band, sometimes called *UNII-3/ISM* because its upper channels border or fall within portions of the radio spectrum reserved for industrial, scientific, and medical purposes, is intended primarily for outdoor WLAN bridges and indoor APs. It's not widely available outside the United States. The *UNII-4* band was originally reserved for dedicated short-range communications (DSRC) for vehicle safety applications but is now being partially opened for unlicensed Wi-Fi use.

As you can see in Figure 1-6, in addition to 20 MHz channels, 40, 80, and 160 MHz channels are also supported. For example, the UNII-2C band is capable of accommodating three 80 MHz channels or one continuous 160 MHz channel.

You can use the Linux utility `iwlist` to retrieve the 5 GHz channels available for use with your Raspberry Pi's onboard wireless adapter. Here, I've used an 802.11ac-capable Raspberry Pi 4 with the wireless regulatory domain set to US. Compare the output with the visual map of the 5 GHz band shown in Figure 1-6 (your results may differ):

```
$ sudo iwlist wlan0 freq
wlan0     32 channels in total; available frequencies :
--snip--
          Channel 36 : 5.18 GHz
          Channel 38 : 5.19 GHz
          Channel 40 : 5.2 GHz
          Channel 42 : 5.21 GHz
          Channel 44 : 5.22 GHz
          Channel 46 : 5.23 GHz
          Channel 48 : 5.24 GHz
          Channel 52 : 5.26 GHz
          Channel 56 : 5.28 GHz
          Channel 60 : 5.3 GHz
          Channel 64 : 5.32 GHz
          Channel 100 : 5.5 GHz
--snip--
```

You may also notice that, unlike in the 2.4 GHz band, 5 GHz channel numbers are not sequential: They increment by four. This is because while each channel is 5 MHz wide, the usable channels are spaced 20 MHz apart to avoid overlapping ($4 \times 5 = 20$ MHz).

In time, of course, we can expect the 5 GHz band to fill up as well. However, hopefully by then we'll have access to the high-frequency 60 GHz WiGig band with 7 GHz of free spectrum to meet our wireless networking demands.

A Word on MIMO

The 802.11ac standard realized most of its gains by extending techniques developed for 802.11n. As mentioned previously, one of the breakthrough technologies of 802.11n was multiple-input multiple-output (MIMO), pronounced *my-moh*. MIMO uses multiple antennas to transmit and receive data over multiple data streams, significantly increasing network performance and range. Wi-Fi equipment manufacturers commonly use terminology like "2×2" (two by two) to indicate which MIMO technology is used in a product.

MIMO exploits a radio-wave phenomenon known as *multipath*, in which transmitted signals bounce off walls, doors, and other objects and reach the receiving antenna multiple times via different routes, at slightly different times. Uncontrolled, multipath can distort the original signal, making it more difficult to decode and degrading Wi-Fi performance. MIMO harnesses this effect by using a technique known as *spatial multiplexing*, or *space-division multiplexing (SDM)*. The transmitting WLAN device splits a data stream into multiple parts, called *spatial streams*, and transmits each one through a separate antenna to corresponding antennas on the receiving end. Doubling the number of spatial streams effectively doubles the raw data rate: A 2×2 MIMO device can transmit two 150Mbps streams, resulting in a total data rate of 300Mbps, while a 3×3 MIMO device supports up to 450Mbps.

The 802.11n specification provides for up to four spatial streams (4×4 MIMO) and a channel width of 40 MHz. By contrast, 802.11ac can utilize eight spatial streams (8×8 MIMO) and channels up to 80 MHz wide, which can then be bonded to make 160 MHz channels. The 802.11ac standard also further refined this technology into *multiuser MIMO (MU-MIMO)*. Sometimes advertised as "Next-Gen AC" or "AC Wave 2" wireless, MU-MIMO allows a Wi-Fi router to communicate with multiple devices simultaneously, thereby reducing wait time. If you have more than a handful of devices connected to your 802.11ac access point, MU-MIMO can noticeably improve network performance. In addition, the AP scrambles data before transmitting it, so only the intended receiving device can unscramble it. This has the effect of boosting Wi-Fi security by masking the data from eavesdroppers.

There are trade-offs to MIMO, such as increased power consumption and, to a lesser extent, equipment cost. With regard to the Raspberry Pi, the 3B+, 4, 5, and Compute Module 4 (CM4) models use the Cypress (formerly Broadcom) CYW43455 wireless chipset with a single radio that supports 1×1 802.11ac, which is not MIMO capable. While you won't see 2×2 or greater MIMO capabilities from the Pi's onboard Wi-Fi adapter, it pays to have some familiarity with the technology if you're in the market for an external adapter.

Wireless Regulatory Domains

The 802.11 wireless modes available for use are not simply a function of your device's hardware capabilities. Wireless spectrum regulations must also be taken into account. There are lots of international issues with Wi-Fi that restrict channel use, transmission power, and other factors on a regional and per-country basis. This becomes important when, for example, you configure an 802.11ac wireless access point using your Pi's onboard adapter.

The regulatory database for `brcmfmac`, the Linux kernel driver that supports the Broadcom wireless chipset, is embedded in the firmware of all current Wi-Fi–capable Raspberry Pi models. To get details on your currently configured wireless regulatory domain, execute the following command:

```
$ sudo iw reg get
global
country US: DFS-FCC
    (2400 - 2483 @ 40), (N/A, 30), (N/A)
    (5150 - 5250 @ 80), (N/A, 23), (N/A), AUTO-BW
    (5250 - 5350 @ 80), (N/A, 23), (0 ms), DFS, AUTO-BW
    (5470 - 5730 @ 160), (N/A, 23), (0 ms), DFS
    (5730 - 5850 @ 80), (N/A, 30), (N/A)
--snip--
```

In this case, the currently configured regulatory domain is US (an ISO 3166 Alpha-2 country code), and the relevant regulatory body is the FCC. The lines that follow contain four pieces of information:

- The frequency range and maximum channel width for this particular rule; for example, (2400 - 2483 @ 40)

- The maximum antenna gain and effective isotropic radiated power (EIRP); for example, (N/A, 30)

- The dynamic frequency selection (DFS) channel availability check time; for example, (N/A) or (0 ms)

- Any applicable flags, such as dynamic frequency selection (DFS) or automatic bandwidth selection (AUTO-BW)

If the wireless domain configured on your Pi does not allow use of a particular channel on the 5 GHz band, an 802.11ac-configured AP will fail to start. Errors like these are common:

```
nl80211: Failed to set channel (freq=5180): -22 (Invalid argument)
hostapd: Could not set channel for kernel driver
```

You can set your wireless domain through `raspi-config` or by setting the country value in *wpa_supplicant.conf* to an appropriate ISO 3166 Alpha-2 country code. If this isn't clear now, don't worry; we'll look at this in more detail later. For now, the important thing is to be aware of how this regulatory framework is applied at the firmware level.

Evaluating Performance

One of the most common sources of confusion about Wi-Fi networks concerns performance. In the wired networking world, interface speeds are generally thought of as constant: A 1Gbps wired Ethernet connection is expected to consistently produce 1Gbps transfer speeds. With wireless networking, there are many more complexities to consider. The bottom line is that, unlike a wired connection, wireless transfer speeds cannot be guaranteed.

While many factors may impact wireless performance, some of the most common are:

- Devices transmitting simultaneously on the same channel
- Interference from external sources, including non-Wi-Fi devices
- Poor signal due to devices being too far away from each other (aka *path loss*)
- Signal reflection, absorption, and diffraction caused by the physical environment

To mitigate these issues, wireless devices transmit data in small chunks, each followed by a *checksum* or *cyclic redundancy check (CRC)* as a means to verify the integrity of the received data. If the check passes, the receiving device sends an acknowledgment (known as an *ACK* response) to the sending device, letting it know that it can transmit the next data chunk. Additionally, to prevent co-channel interference, only one wireless device is allowed to "talk" on a channel at any given time, which introduces further overhead to ensure devices are communicating in turn.

As you might imagine, the methods that enable wireless communications incur a cost. The rated performance of a given wireless standard, such as 54Mbps with 802.11g, assumes a near perfect link quality. A weaker signal or increased interference can significantly affect the actual transfer speed. Considering their relatively low power output, Wi-Fi technologies are capable of transmitting over surprisingly long distances. To achieve this, devices in the network must negotiate slower transmission rates. The resulting signal strength and negotiated speed are usually represented to the user in an approximate visual form, like signal bars. In this section, we'll devise a more detailed and precise measure using a tried-and-true technique.

Given what you know about 802.11 standards, latency, channels, and so on, let's consider some objective measures of network performance. Specifically, here you will perform a WLAN bandwidth test using a Raspberry Pi's onboard wireless adapter. The method you'll use differs in several important ways from that used by popular "speed test" websites, such as the one shown in Figure 1-7, and mobile applications. The reason for this is partly revealed by the latency test you performed earlier: You're seeking to isolate a WLAN by minimizing the influence of external network factors (for example, hops between routers).

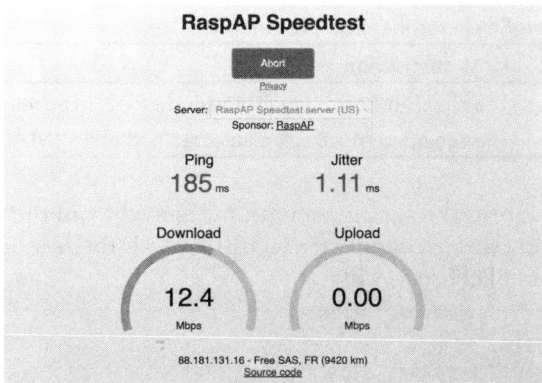

Figure 1-7: An example of a network speed test website
(https://speedtest.raspap.com)

To do this, you'll make use of *iPerf*, a tool that measures the maximum achievable bandwidth on IP networks. The `iperf3` executable you'll be using contains both client and server functionality. To perform the test, you'll need two hosts running iPerf: one acting as the client and the other as a server. Unlike online speed tests and Linux tools like `ping` and `mtr`, which generate minimal network load by default, iPerf attempts to consume all the available bandwidth a network can deliver. For this reason, it's advisable to use it only for brief assessments and only on networks under your direct control.

iPerf has broad cross-platform support and may be installed on any system running Linux, macOS, or Windows, as well as iOS and Android devices. Installing it on a Raspberry Pi is straightforward:

```
$ sudo apt update
$ sudo apt install iperf3
```

Next, choose another computer on your network and install iPerf there. In my case, I installed `iperf3` on a MacBook using Homebrew. Here, I'll walk you through evaluating an IEEE 802.11ac 5 GHz WLAN using a Raspberry Pi 4 Model B Rev 1.1, which features an onboard Broadcom BCM4345/6 wireless chipset.

To perform the test, configure the Raspberry Pi as an 802.11ac 5 GHz wireless access point with 80 MHz channel support. The Pi will act as a client during the iPerf test, and the test machine (the MacBook, in my case), disconnected from Ethernet and associated with the Pi's WLAN, will act as the server. Be sure to place the test machine within line of sight of the Pi to minimize signal loss.

Table 1-4 shows the IP addresses assigned to each device for the purposes of this test.

Table 1-4: Device Setup for the iPerf Performance Test

IPv4 address	Host description
10.3.141.1	The client: a Raspberry Pi 4 with an 802.11ac wireless access point
10.3.141.197	The server: a MacBook connected to the Pi's WLAN via the AP

Prior to the test, the signal strength measured from the MacBook (acting as the server) was excellent, at −55 dBm. With the test bench prepared, you can start the iPerf server like so:

```
$ iperf3 --server
-----------------------------------------------------------
Server listening on 5201 (test #1)
-----------------------------------------------------------
--snip--
```

After the server has started, it will listen for connections from iPerf clients (that is, the iperf3 program running in client mode) over the network on the default 5201 port. You can now start iPerf on the Raspberry Pi in client mode, specifying the remote server as the host it should connect to:

```
$ iperf3 --client 10.3.141.197
Connecting to host 10.3.141.197, port 5201
[  5] local 10.3.141.1 port 56588 connected to 10.3.141.197 port 5201
[ ID] Interval           Transfer     Bitrate         Retr  Cwnd
[  5]   0.00-1.00   sec  10.7 MBytes  89.8 Mbits/sec    0    454 KBytes
[  5]   1.00-2.00   sec  11.3 MBytes  94.9 Mbits/sec    0    510 KBytes
[  5]   2.00-3.00   sec  10.8 MBytes  90.7 Mbits/sec    0    537 KBytes
[  5]   3.00-4.00   sec  10.8 MBytes  90.2 Mbits/sec    0    563 KBytes
[  5]   4.00-5.00   sec  11.5 MBytes  96.4 Mbits/sec    0    563 KBytes
[  5]   5.00-6.00   sec  10.9 MBytes  91.2 Mbits/sec    0    600 KBytes
--snip--
- - - - - - - - - - - - - - - - - - - - - - - - - -
[ ID] Interval           Transfer     Bitrate         Retr
[  5]   0.00-10.00  sec   108 MBytes  90.9 Mbits/sec    0         sender
[  5]   0.00-10.04  sec   107 MBytes  89.4 Mbits/sec              receiver
```

The benchmark will run for several seconds and output a report like the one shown here. To stop the iPerf server process, use CTRL-C. The bitrate, expressed in Mbps, is reported for each second of the test. The summary at the bottom shows that the sender (the Raspberry Pi, acting as the iPerf client) achieved an average upload speed of 90.9Mbps to the server, while the receiver (the MacBook, running the iPerf server) averaged 89.4Mbps in download throughput from the client. The Retr (retransmissions) column shows the number of TCP segments that had to be resent. Nonzero values here typically indicate a problem with the network, such as congestion or a weak Wi-Fi signal.

Testing with iPerf is an excellent way to objectively evaluate the performance of your WLAN. It's also a common approach for comparing the relative performance of wireless adapters. We'll take a closer look at these hardware components in the next section.

Wireless Adapter Hardware

Network adapters enable communication with other computers, servers, or devices over a local area network connection. Adapters may be used for wired or wireless LANs and take a variety of physical forms, such as network interface cards (NICs), integrated chipsets, or USB adapters (commonly referred to as *dongles*). A special class of virtual adapters are software-only implementations designed to mimic a physical hardware NIC. These types of adapters are often used for virtual private networks (VPNs) to handle the flow of data between a VPN tunnel and the local physical network adapter. You'll get firsthand experience with many of these adapter types throughout this book.

All Wi-Fi–capable Raspberry Pi models use an integrated single-chip solution for wireless LAN connectivity. As you might expect, the manufacturers and WLAN capabilities of these chipsets have changed over the years. Table 1-5 shows the chipsets used in several of the more popular Pi models.

Table 1-5: WLAN Chipsets Used in Popular Pi Models

Raspberry Pi	Release year	Wireless LAN chipset
3 Model B	2016	Broadcom BCM43438, 2.4 GHz WLAN IEEE 802.11 b/g/n
Zero W	2017	Broadcom BCM43438, as above
3 Model B+	2018	Cypress CYW43455, 2.4 GHz and 5 GHz IEEE 802.11 b/g/n/ac
4 Model B	2019	Cypress CYW43455, as above
Compute Module 4	2020	Cypress CYW43455, as above
400	2020	Synaptics SYN43436, similar to the BCM43438 used in the Pi 3 Model B and Zero W
Zero 2 W	2021	Synaptics SYN43436, as above
5	2023	Infineon CYW43455

You'll notice that several generations of WLAN chipsets have been used across various Pi models, with some models sharing the same chipset.

Let's take a closer look at two of the more recent chipsets listed in Table 1-5, the Cypress CYW43455 and Synaptics SYN43436.

The CYW43455 Chipset

The Cypress CYW43455 chipset, used in several popular Raspberry Pi models, is a WLAN adapter module that supports dual-band Wi-Fi (2.4 GHz and 5 GHz) as well as Bluetooth 5.0 and Bluetooth Low Energy (BLE). The chipset and its associated components are housed under an RF-shielded metal cover located in the upper-left corner of the Pi's top side, just below the general-purpose I/O (GPIO) header. This design is known as a *system on a chip (SoC)*, as it integrates multiple related functions—in this case, Wi-Fi and Bluetooth—into a single electronic system along with an ARM-based CPU, RAM and ROM, radio transceivers, power management, host interfaces, and more.

The RF shield obscures one's view of the chipset itself. It's possible to gradually heat the printed circuit board (PCB) with a hot air gun and remove the shield by using a vacuum pen, although doing so is generally not recommended, at the risk of ruining your Pi. Even with care, I managed to partially melt the plastic bases of the first few pairs of GPIO pins. The CYW43455 chipset appears just above the Raspberry Pi logo in Figure 1-8.

Figure 1-8: The Cypress CYW43455 chipset on a Raspberry Pi 4, revealed by removing the metal RF shield (upper left)

The chipset is connected to the Pi's primary SoC via a secure digital input/output (SDIO) v3.0 host interface. This means wireless traffic doesn't compete with other USB devices for bandwidth.

CHIPSET SPEED LIMITATIONS

Linux tools like `iwconfig` will often report a bitrate of 325Mbps or more for the CYW43455, while `iperf3` tests show significantly less (in the neighborhood of 100Mbps) even with 80 MHz channels. What's going on here? The CYW43455 chipset is connected via a 4-bit SDIO link that typically runs at 41.7 MHz, giving an upper limit on throughput of about 160Mbps. In practice, iPerf tests won't get close to this figure because it's a *simplex* link (that is, half-duplex, or only one direction at a time) and there is overhead in each of the protocol and transport layers. Given this restriction, a "real-world" speed of 100Mbps is actually quite good for this hardware. It's also worth noting that the ability to properly use 80 MHz channels means that the channel (a shared medium) is occupied for a shorter period, leaving more time for other devices.

An ARM Cortex-R4 (ARMCR4) 32-bit processor with tightly coupled, on-chip memory (800KB SRAM and 704KB ROM) forms the controller backbone of the integrated WLAN subsystem. A compact dual-band radio transceiver module, labeled "TINY Radio" in block diagrams, is responsible for low-power communication on the 2.4 GHz and 5 GHz bands, with support for 20, 40 and 80 MHz channels. The chipset includes a power management unit so it can function as a mobile platform with extended battery life. These and several other components of the CYW43455 are highlighted in the block diagram shown in Figure 1-9. The WLAN submodule is pictured on the right side of the diagram, while the Bluetooth submodule appears on the left.

One item of particular interest in the WLAN submodule is the 1×1 IEEE 802.11ac PHY component. This represents the *Physical (PHY) layer*, which is the first and lowest layer in the seven-layer Open Systems Interconnection (OSI) model of computer networking (discussed in greater detail in Chapter 10). In this context, its role is interacting with the actual hardware to send and receive RF signals. A PHY chip implements the physical layer of electronic circuits to handle the functions of the wireless technology being used. The PHY layer's primary job is converting data it receives from the Data Link layer into electrical pulses, which represent the binary data. This process involves RF transceivers and a digital baseband chip that uses a digital signal processor (DSP) to handle the work of digital-to-analog translation.

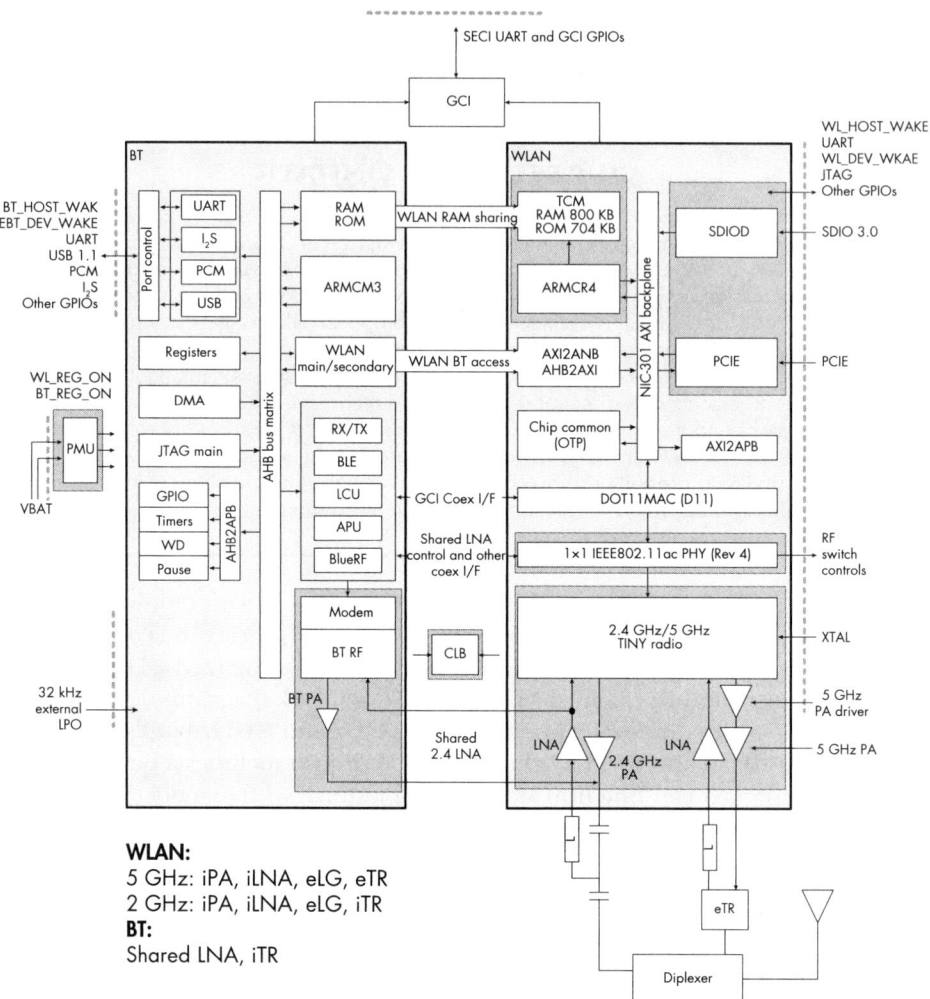

Figure 1-9: A block diagram of the CYW/BCM43455 chipset

Recalling the discussion of MIMO earlier in this chapter, you can probably guess what the "1×1" designation refers to. This PHY layer supports a single transmit and receive radio chain, also referred to as *single-input single-output (SISO)*. Some practitioners in the wireless industry use the notation *T x R : S*, where *T* is the number of transmit radio chains, *R* is the number of receive radio chains, and *S* is the number of supported spatial streams. Applied here, this means that the CYW43455's radio may be designated as *1 x 1 : 1*. As a SISO adapter, the maximum data rate will therefore be capped at 150Mbps.

It's important to differentiate between the Wi-Fi hardware (the PHY layer) and the interface, or Media Access Control (MAC) layer. Usually, we set parameter values for the PHY layer, such as a frequency or channel, and then associate the Wi-Fi interface with an AP at the MAC layer. The Linux command iw makes this distinction between the hardware (phy) and the interface (also called dev, or *device*, following Ethernet's naming convention).

To see how this works in practice, let's view a summary of the available Wi-Fi hardware and interfaces on a device. Here, I'm using a Raspberry Pi 4 with an external USB wireless adapter (your output may differ):

```
$ iw dev
phy#0
    Interface wlan0
        ifindex 4
        wdev 0x1
        addr 74:da:38:ed:5e:94
        ssid Home-Router
        type managed
        channel 6 (2437 MHz), width: 20 MHz, center1: 2437 MHz
        txpower 20.00 dBm
phy#1
    Interface wlan1
        ifindex 3
        wdev 0x100000001
        addr dc:a6:32:3d:ff:9d
        ssid RaspAP
        type AP
        channel 52 (5260 MHz), width: 80 MHz, center1: 5290 MHz
        txpower 31.00 dBm
```

In this example, notice that two wireless adapters are present on the system, identified by their PHY indexes, phy#0 and phy#1, with their associated interfaces (wlan0 and wlan1, respectively). The first interface, wlan0, is operating in managed mode and is connected to Home-Router on the 2.4 GHz band. The second interface, wlan1, is operating in AP mode on the 5 GHz band. I'll return to these concepts many times throughout this book, so it's good to have some familiarity with them from this stage.

The SYN43436 Chipset and Antenna

In the previous section, we looked at the CYW43455 chipset's internals in some detail. Here, we'll explore the SYN43436 chipset and antenna.

While block diagrams are mainly conceptual, they afford us a view of a wireless chipset's design architecture. Removing the RF shield to reveal the chipset might be useful as part of a hardware teardown, but if not done carefully, that removal can easily render a device nonfunctional. A less destructive method uses radiography, or X-ray imaging, to let us peek inside the Pi's hardware. Raspberry Pi experimenter Jeff Geerling has done exactly this. His radiograph of the Pi Zero 2 W is shown in Figure 1-10.

Figure 1-10: An X-ray image revealing the inner workings of a Pi Zero 2 W. Courtesy of Jeff Geerling (https://www.jeffgeerling.com).

The BCM/SYN43436 chipset, indicated with an arrow, is visible beneath its intact metal RF shield. This WLAN adapter supports IEEE 802.11 b/g/n and is limited to the 2.4 GHz band. While it's very similar architecturally to the BCM43438 used in the Pi 3 Model B and previous Zero W, it does require dedicated firmware.

One particular item that stands out in this X-ray view is the SYN43436's antenna circuit. The Pi Zero's antenna is an ingenious design; it's highly efficient for such a small component and deserves a closer look. We'll examine it in the next section, after a general introduction to wireless antennas.

Wi-Fi Antennas

While they may appear simple at first glance, a surprising level of engineering has been invested into wireless antenna development and testing. This section is by no means exhaustive; rather, it's intended to provide an overview of the fundamentals so you can better understand the *how* and *why* of the antennas in your Wi-Fi devices. Of particular interest here is the embedded PCB antenna design of the Raspberry Pi.

Wireless signals are electromagnetic (EM) waves containing packets of information. In simple terms, an antenna is a device that converts these EM waves into electrical signals, and vice versa. Devices communicating on a wireless LAN, such as mobile handsets, laptops, and access points, require both receiving and transmitting antennas. *Receiving antennas* capture EM waves and convert them into electrical signals for further processing. *Transmitting antennas* convert electrical signals from a circuit into EM waves and radiate them into the atmosphere.

The size of an antenna depends on the frequency of the signal it's intended to transmit or receive. The wavelength (λ) of a signal can be calculated by dividing its velocity (v) by its frequency (f), like so:

$$\lambda = \frac{v}{f}$$

A wave's velocity is almost always expressed in metric units, typically as meters per second (m/s). As you learned earlier in this chapter, frequency is generally expressed in Hertz (Hz), which is shorthand for *cycles per second* (cycles/s). Knowing these values, we can plug them into the equation and solve for wavelength.

Wireless signals travel at the speed of light, which is equal to 299,792,458 m/s. To keep things simple, we'll round this up to 300,000,000 m/s, or 300 $\times 10^6$ m/s. For the frequency, let's use the popular 2.4 GHz from the wireless spectrum. 1 GHz is equal to 1 billion cycles/s, so 2.4 GHz is 2.4 billion cycles/s. Using the formula for wavelength with engineering notation, this works out to:

$$\frac{300 \times 10^6}{2.4 \times 10^9} = 0.125$$

Since I'm using meters as the unit of measure, this is equal to 0.125 meters, or 12.5 cm.

Antennas are typically constructed with dimensions that correspond to a fraction of the desired wavelength. One of the simplest designs is the *half-wave dipole*, so named because it measures one-half of the wavelength. This type of antenna is made of two halves, each measuring one-quarter of the wavelength. Some familiar RF services and their corresponding antenna dipole sizes are shown in Table 1-6.

Table 1-6: Common RF Services and Their Antenna Dipole Sizes

Service	Frequency	Wavelength	Antenna dipole length
Radio	95 MHz	3.15 m	≈ 78 cm
Wi-Fi 4	2.4 GHz	0.125 m	≈ 6.25 cm
Wi-Fi 5	5 GHz	0.06 m	≈ 3.0 cm

To optimize performance, antennas are often sized to match a multiple of the quarter-wavelength (sometimes called a "$\lambda/4$" radiator) of the radio signal. As it happens, 5 GHz is roughly double 2.4 GHz, which means its wavelength is about half as long (and therefore a multiple of the 2.4 GHz quarter-wavelength). For this reason, a single antenna works reasonably well for both Wi-Fi bands. It is also conveniently less expensive for manufacturers to supply just one antenna.

Gain is a measure of an antenna's efficiency and directivity. This is a key performance figure in determining how well input power is amplified. Antenna gain is typically expressed in decibels relative to an *isotropic radiator* (a theoretical antenna that radiates equally in all directions), or *dBi*. The internal antennas in wireless access points usually have gains in the range of 1 to 1.5 dBi, compared to 2 to 5 dBi for external antennas. A 3 dBi gain increase represents double the transmit power, so the performance increase with an external antenna can be quite significant. Some wireless products with so-called high-gain antennas are available that offer even higher dBi values.

Many antennas are external and easy to spot, like the familiar black rubber antennas on wireless routers, while others are etched directly into the PCB of the device itself. The latter is common in mobile handsets, tablets, and so on, with the most rudimentary antennas often visible as a simple line of copper.

Returning to the X-ray image of the Pi Zero 2 W, Figure 1-11 shows a close-up view of its antenna design.

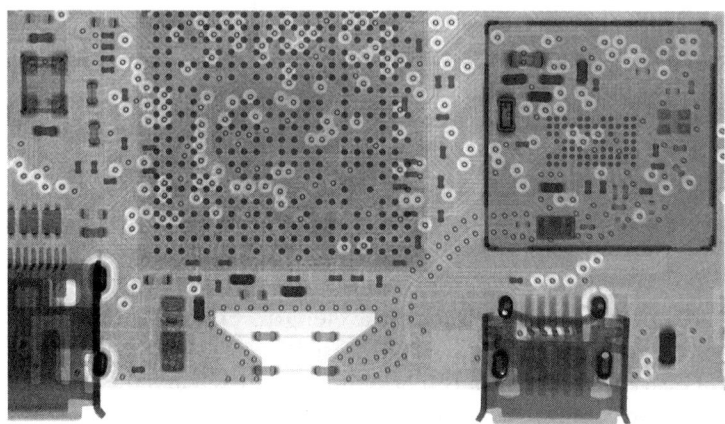

Figure 1-11: The Pi Zero 2 W's PCB antenna. Courtesy of Jeff Geerling (https://www.jeffgeerling.com).

Positioned along the Pi Zero's lower edge, between the mini HDMI display and micro USB data port, is the PCB antenna. This is visible as a translucent trapezoid when viewed with a light source behind the Pi's board. The antenna's circuit can be seen below the RF shield in the X-ray view, leading to a series of capacitors. This antenna technology, licensed from Proant AB, is the same as that used on the previous Pi Zero W and later Wi-Fi–capable Pi models. The antenna is formed by etching away copper on each layer of the PCB to create a resonant cavity. Within this space, radio waves interact and resonate at specific frequencies. The resulting signal is directed toward the narrow end of the cavity, where the capacitors are situated.

This PCB antenna is many times smaller than a typical 2.4 GHz dipole antenna (the kind you'd find attached to a Wi-Fi router, for example), yet surprisingly sacrifices only a fraction of the gain. Independent test results in environments like the one shown in Figure 1-12 indicate that its radiated signal performs well, demonstrating both strong gain and high efficiency within the target 2.4 GHz band.

Figure 1-12: A Raspberry Pi Zero W in a wireless antenna test chamber

This underscores the idea that there's always something to be learned from clever designs and smart engineers.

Kernel Drivers

I briefly mentioned brcmfmac, the Linux kernel driver that supports the Pi's wireless chipset, in the previous discussion of wireless regulatory domains. What exactly is a kernel driver, and what role does it play in the wireless hierarchy?

In Linux, a *driver* is a piece of code that runs in the kernel and manages the specifics of a piece of hardware, such as a disk, network adapter, or display. Drivers abstract, or hide, the details of how the hardware device works, instead exposing a well-defined programming interface for communicating with it. User activities are performed by mapping standardized calls to device-specific operations that act on the hardware level. Each device driver is, effectively, a "black box" that can be plugged in or loaded at runtime as needed.

Device drivers were traditionally built directly into the kernel, as they require the low-level access that the kernel provides. Today, however, most drivers exist as kernel modules. This approach is more flexible, because kernel modules can be loaded and unloaded on demand. This allows you to add or remove functionality while the system is up and running. It's also slightly riskier, because improper access by a less privileged piece of software (operating in so-called userland) could potentially crash the host machine or cause it to behave unpredictably.

You can use the `lsmod` command to display the currently loaded modules in the Linux kernel. This command produces output like the following:

```
$ lsmod
--snip--
Module              Size  Used by
fuse               99603  3
cmac                3239  1
rfcomm             37723  6
bnep               12051  2
hci_uart           20020  1
btbcm               7916  1 hci_uart
bluetooth         365780  29 hci_uart,bnep,btbcm,rfcomm
brcmfmac          292632  0
brcmutil            9863  1 brcmfmac
cfg80211          544545  1 brcmfmac
rfkill             20851  6 bluetooth,cfg80211
--snip--
```

Near the end of this snippet, you'll notice that `brcmfmac` appears several times: once as a loaded module and again as a dependency of two other ones required for wireless networking.

Broadcom is a worldwide provider of solutions for wireless LAN infrastructure. The company initially provided limited GNU/Linux driver support for its Wi-Fi devices, requiring users to tinker with the firmware to use them. This changed in September 2010, when Broadcom released a fully open source driver, `brcm80211`. This was later subdivided into two other open source drivers, `brcmfmac` and `brcmsmac`. I'm primarily concerned with `brcmfmac` here, because it supports newer wireless chipsets, AP mode, monitor mode, and hardware encryption. On Linux systems, the `bcrmfmac` driver gives you an interface to your wireless adapter that you can use to interact with Wi-Fi networks in the real world.

You can fetch some details about the specific `brcmfmac` driver on your system by searching the journal:

```
$ journalctl -b | grep brcmfmac
brcmfmac: F1 signature read @0x18000000=0x15264345
brcmfmac: brcmf_fw_alloc_request: using brcm/brcmfmac43455-sdio for chip BCM4345/6
usbcore: registered new interface driver brcmfmac
brcmfmac: brcmf_fw_alloc_request: using brcm/brcmfmac43455-sdio for chip BCM4345/6
brcmfmac: brcmf_c_preinit_dcmds: Firmware: BCM4345/6 wl0:
   Nov  1 2021 00:37:25 version 7.45.241 (1a2f2fa CY) FWID 01-703fd60
--snip--
```

Firmware: BCM4345/6 indicates the current `brcmfmac` firmware version. You can further probe the source of this driver by searching the apt repository:

```
$ apt search bcm4345
Sorting... Done
```

```
Full Text Search... Done
firmware-brcm80211/stable 1:20230210-5~bpo11+1+rpt1 all [installed]
  Binary firmware for Broadcom/Cypress 802.11 wireless cards
```

Here, you can see that the parent device driver is brcm80211 and that it's currently installed on the system.

You'll be interacting with wireless adapters by using the Linux brcmfmac driver throughout this book. Now that we've looked at wireless hardware and drivers in some detail, let's move up a level in the hierarchy and examine what happens when you connect a client to an access point.

Making a Connection

Imagine a typical scenario in which a client device (often referred to as a *station* or simply *STA*) wishes to connect to an access point. How do these two devices agree to a connection? Let's take a brief look at the steps involved in this process. The terminology introduced here will appear throughout this book.

The station initiates the process by performing an active or passive scan to discover available access points. During an active scan, the station transmits a *probe request* and listens for a *probe response* from any AP within range, as illustrated in Figure 1-13. In a passive scan, the STA listens for *beacon* frames broadcast by APs. These beacons contain information about the access point, such as the SSID, supported data rates, network capabilities, and a timestamp to help with synchronization. If a STA wishes to join a detected wireless network, it will send a probe request management frame. The AP will answer with a probe response frame. A passive scan generally takes more time, since the STA must listen and wait for APs to broadcast beacons rather than actively probing to find one.

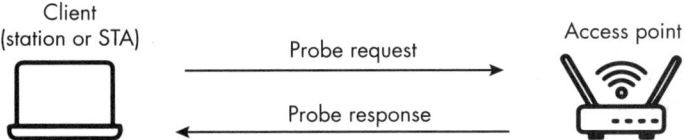

Figure 1-13: A wireless client (STA) probe request and AP probe response

This first probing or scanning phase occurs while the STA is unauthenticated and unassociated. In the wireless world, authentication is analogous to plugging a computer into an Ethernet port on a switch. While it may sound backward, the STA must be authenticated before it can be associated. So, the next step is for the STA and access point to exchange *authentication request* and *authentication response* frames.

Once a STA is authenticated to the access point, it will then proceed with *association*. Similar to the previous phases, the STA and access point will exchange association frames. If the AP accepts the association, its response frame will contain a success status code along with details about its supported wireless capabilities.

Here, you can see the authentication and association phases captured in a hostapd service log:

```
wlan0: STA 24:62:ab:fd:24:34 IEEE 802.11: authenticated
wlan0: STA 24:62:ab:fd:24:34 IEEE 802.11: associated
wlan0: AP-STA-CONNECTED 24:62:ab:fd:24:34
--snip--
```

When these phases are complete, the STA and AP are successfully connected. However, they have not yet started communicating over the wireless medium. One of the primary challenges in wireless networking is providing sufficiently strong protection for the data packages exchanged over the airwaves. Attackers equipped with radio receivers can eavesdrop on WLANs with minimal effort, so wireless transmissions between the STA and AP need to be secured with an encrypted connection. This is done with some additional frame exchanges collectively known as a handshake.

A *handshake* in this context, commonly referred to as a *four-way handshake*, consists of the first four messages that are exchanged during the establishment of an encrypted connection between a client and an access point. In this arrangement, the AP is usually referred to as the *authenticator*, while the client device is known as the *supplicant*. The process is initiated by the access point and serves to accomplish the following:

1. Confirm that the client holds a valid *pairwise master key (PMK)*.
2. Confirm that the PMK is current.
3. Derive a new *pairwise transient key (PTK)* from the PMK and install the pairwise encryption and integrity keys.
4. Transport the *group temporal key (GTK)* to the client.
5. Install the PTK and GTK on the client and the PTK on the AP.

The "messages" in the four-way handshake are specific data packets that contain information needed to establish a secure communication channel. These messages are passed back and forth, each carrying specific instructions or keys:

- Message 1 is the AP saying, "Let's start the secure connection process." This message contains a random number called an *authenticator nonce*, or *ANonce*, used by the API in the derivation of encryption keys. The AP is essentially saying, "Here's my random number; now you create yours, and together we'll compute our shared secret keys."

- Message 2 is the client responding with, "Received; here's my part." This message includes the client's random number (the *supplicant nonce*, or *SNonce*) and, importantly, a signature, or authentication code, called a *message integrity check (MIC)*. This proves the client knows the shared secret (PMK) and can correctly generate the encryption keys. You can think of the MIC as the client saying, "Here's my random number, and proof that I know our shared password."

- Message 3 is the AP's confirmation message. It says, "I see that you know the shared secret. Here's the group key (GTK) you'll need for broadcast traffic." The AP includes its own authentication signature to prove it also knows the PMK, and securely delivers the GTK that's used for multicast and broadcast communications on the network.

- Finally, message 4 is the client saying, "Received and understood, good to go!" It's an acknowledgment that the client has received the GTK and is ready to start using the secure connection.

Each message is carefully choreographed such that both sides prove they know the shared secret without actually transmitting it. The handshake with its four messages is illustrated in Figure 1-14.

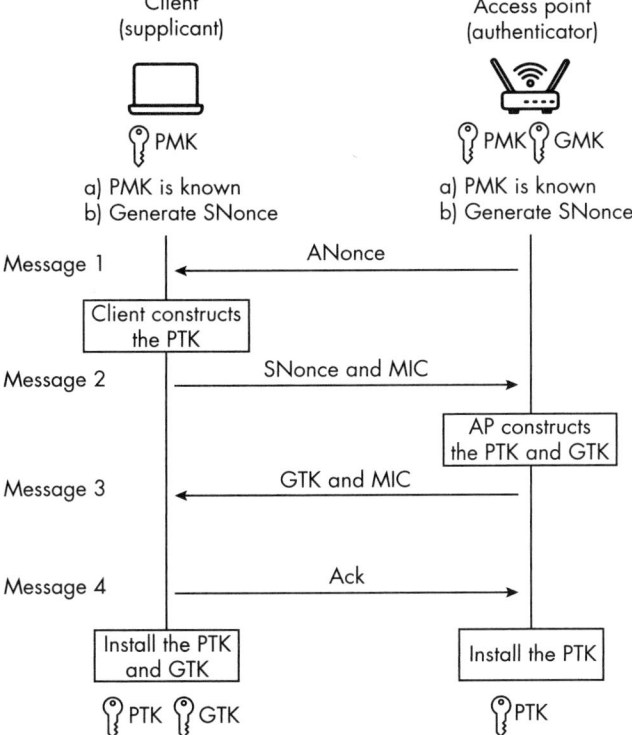

Figure 1-14: The steps involved in the four-way handshake process

When a wireless client first associates with an access point, two logical *ports* are created:

- The *uncontrolled port* remains open and allows only specific types of authentication traffic to pass through: primarily 802.1X authentication frames and Extensible Authentication Protocol over LAN (EAPOL) frames. This is the pathway used for the initial authentication process and the four-way handshake itself.

- The *controlled port* is initially blocked and remains that way until the four-way handshake successfully completes. This port controls access to the actual network resources and user data traffic. All *unicast* (one-to-one) traffic is encrypted with the PTK, while all *multicast* (one-to-many) traffic is encrypted with the GTK.

The hostapd service will capture the key exchange in its log output:

```
wlan0: AP-STA-CONNECTED 24:62:ab:fd:24:34
wlan0: STA 24:62:ab:fd:24:34 RADIUS: starting accounting session ...
wlan0: STA 24:62:ab:fd:24:34 WPA: pairwise key handshake completed (RSN)
--snip--
```

The RSN here refers to the *Robust Security Network* protocol, used to establish secure communications between APs and wireless clients. At this stage, the STA and AP are connected and securely communicating over an encrypted wireless channel. This channel will remain open until the STA is disconnected by the AP. Again, you can observe this in the hostapd log:

```
wlan0: AP-STA-DISCONNECTED 24:62:ab:fd:24:34
wlan0: STA 24:62:ab:fd:24:34 IEEE 802.11: disassociated
--snip--
```

There are many reasons why a client might be disassociated by an AP, either intentionally or unintentionally, and perhaps even as the result of a third party (I'll revisit the deauthentication/disassociation process in some of the later chapters in this book). Users may observe this occurring without knowing why; an ability to parse an AP's logs and identify these events is key to understanding the problem.

Bluetooth Wireless

Most people are familiar with Bluetooth but often associate it with the devices they're accustomed to pairing rather than the technology itself. Bluetooth uses radio waves in the 2.4 to 2.485 GHz unlicensed ISM band to transmit data over short distances. Depending on the Bluetooth version and device class, ranges of anywhere from 10 meters (33 feet) up to 100 meters (328 feet) are typical. Similar to Wi-Fi, which also operates in the 2.4 GHz band, effective Bluetooth ranges are highly dependent on factors like the physical environment and interference from other radio sources. Likewise, both technologies have evolved significantly over the years, with improvements in range, data rates, power efficiency, and more. Beyond these superficialities, however, Wi-Fi and Bluetooth are fundamentally very different.

The radio technology used by Bluetooth, known as *frequency-hopping spread spectrum (FHSS)*, relies on rapid switching of radio signals between different frequency channels. This frequency hopping improves the reliability of a signal by mitigating the effects of interference. (If you'd like to learn more about this technology, another form of spread spectrum radio modulation is discussed in "LoRa Modulation in Detail" on page 174.)

A Bluetooth signal's frequency hops are visible on the right side of the radio spectrum graph in Figure 1-15. For this to work, the pseudorandom sequence must be known to both the transmitter and the receiver.

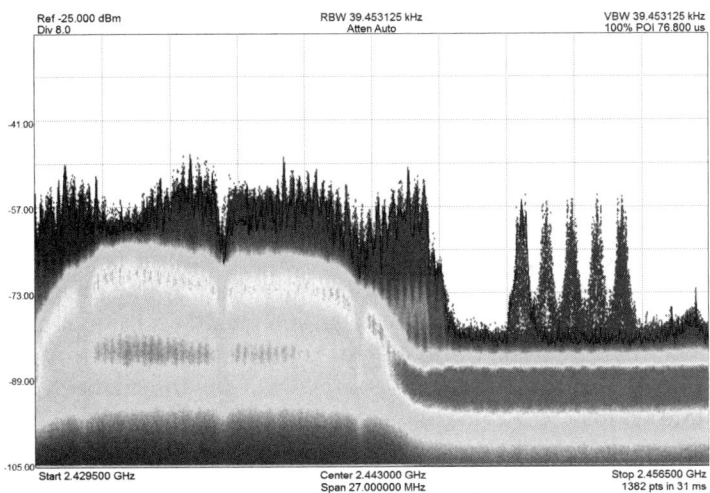

Figure 1-15: A radio spectrum graph of Wi-Fi and Bluetooth coexisting on the 2.4 GHz ISM band

In Bluetooth Classic (aka *Bluetooth Basic Rate/Enhanced Data Rate*, or *BR/EDR*), data packets are transmitted on one of 79 designated channels, each spaced 1 MHz apart. With *adaptive frequency hopping (AFH)* enabled, Bluetooth will perform up to 1,600 hops per second to avoid channels with interference. BLE uses half the number of channels, with 2 MHz spacing.

Whereas Bluetooth Classic is designed for continuous data streaming, BLE remains in sleep mode until a connection is initiated. The net effect is significantly reduced power consumption, making it better suited for battery-constrained devices. In BLE, packet transmissions last for only a few milliseconds and the effective data rates are reduced, with version-dependent speeds of up to 1–2Mbps. As you might guess, the periodic transmission pattern and reduced data rates make this less well suited for applications that require continuous streaming, such as listening to music or holding a phone conversation. For this reason, you'll find that BLE is most often used in scenarios involving IoT devices, sensors, fitness trackers, smartwatches, and the like.

The Infineon/Cypress CYW43455 chipset described earlier in this chapter has support for Bluetooth 5.0, BLE, and adaptive frequency hopping.

Long Range Wireless

LoRa is an RF modulation technology designed for low-power wide area networks (LPWANs). According to its creator, Semtech, the name is a reference to the extremely long-range data links the technology enables: In rural areas a LoRa-based gateway can receive and transmit signals over a distance of 10 miles (16 km) or more, and even in dense urban environments signals can travel up to 3 miles (5 km). This is much further than technologies like Wi-Fi or Bluetooth can reach. Another key characteristic of LoRa-based solutions is their ultra-low power requirement, which allows battery-powered devices to last for many years.

Given these properties, LoRa is ideal for applications that transmit small chunks of data with low bitrates, such as IoT applications that operate in low power mode. Since the packets are small and sent only a few times each day, little energy is required to transmit them, and when the end devices are asleep, the power consumption is measured in milliwatts.

LoRa operates on unlicensed sub-gigahertz frequencies such as 915 MHz, 868 MHz, and 433 MHz. Like those used by 802.11 Wi-Fi and Bluetooth, these frequencies are part of the internationally designated ISM bands.

The LoRa Physical Layer

Although some vendors add Data Link layer functionality on top, LoRa itself is purely a Physical layer implementation (the so-called bits layer), as defined by the OSI seven-layer network model and illustrated in Figure 1-16. Instead of using cables, LoRa uses the air as a medium for transporting radio waves between an RF transmitter, perhaps located in an IoT device, and an RF receiver in another LoRa node, relay, or gateway. By contrast, *LoRaWAN* (discussed in the following section) is a protocol built on top of the LoRa modulation technique. This protocol operates at the Network layer of the OSI model.

The LoRa physical layer is optimized for low throughput, low data rates, and long-range applications. LoRa signals are robust and very resistant to both in-band and out-of-band interference. The modulation scheme also provides immunity to multipath (where a transmitted signal takes multiple paths to reach a receiver) and fading, making it well suited for use in urban and suburban environments where these effects are common.

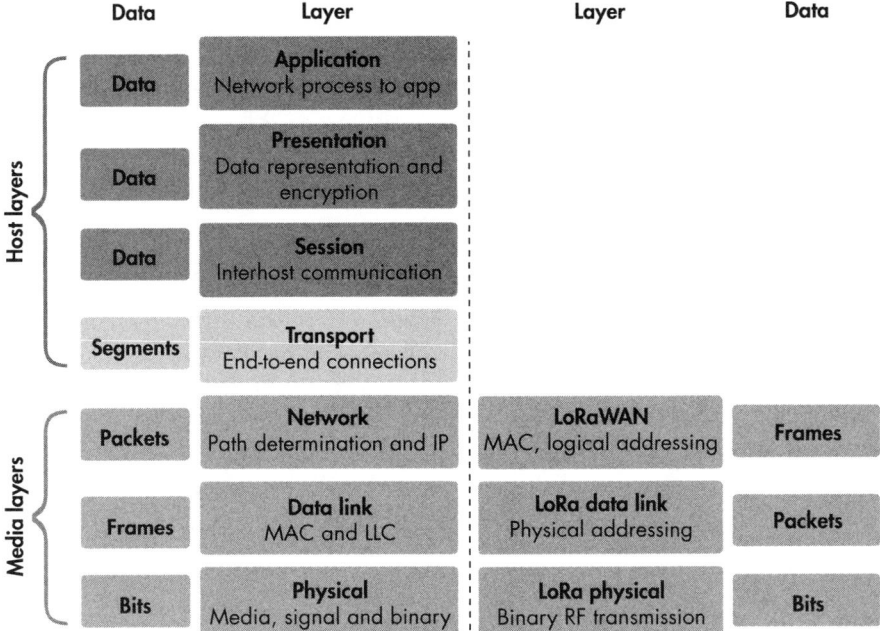

Data	Layer			Layer	Data
Data	**Application** Network process to app				
Data	**Presentation** Data representation and encryption				
Data	**Session** Interhost communication				
Segments	**Transport** End-to-end connections				
Packets	**Network** Path determination and IP		**LoRaWAN** MAC, logical addressing		**Frames**
Frames	**Data link** MAC and LLC		**LoRa data link** Physical addressing		**Packets**
Bits	**Physical** Media, signal and binary		**LoRa physical** Binary RF transmission		**Bits**

Figure 1-16: The roles of LoRa and LoRaWAN in the OSI reference model

The way LoRa's radio modulation works is fascinating and deserves a much closer look. This topic is examined in greater detail in Chapter 6.

LoRaWAN

In simple terms, LoRaWAN is a software layer that defines how devices use the LoRa hardware. For example, LoRaWAN specifies when they transmit and the format of the messages. LoRaWAN is designed to manage communication between LoRa-enabled devices and a centralized network infrastructure, typically through gateways. Typically deployed in a star topology, a network based on the LoRaWAN protocol is well suited to applications that require long-range communication among many devices that collect small amounts of data and have low power requirements.

In terms of capacity, a LoRaWAN network can support millions of messages. However, the number of messages supported in any given deployment depends upon the number of gateways that are installed. For example, a single eight-channel gateway can support a few hundred thousand messages over the course of a 24-hour period. If each end device sends 10 messages a day, such a gateway can support about 10,000 devices. If the network includes 10 such gateways, it can support roughly 100,000 devices and one million messages. If more capacity is required, all that is needed is to add additional gateways to the network.

Wrapping Up

This chapter covered many aspects of how Wi-Fi works in practice, from the low-level adapter hardware to the antenna, the firmware, and out into the atmosphere where a connection is made with a client device. We examined the channels on the 2.4 and 5 GHz bands, explored concepts such as bandwidth and signal strength, and looked at a robust method of measuring wireless network performance. In addition, I touched on the roles filled by short-range Bluetooth and long-range LoRa networks in the wireless landscape.

The information provided here should give you a solid foundation for building real, hands-on projects using these wireless technologies. In the next chapter, I'll discuss preparing your development environment and cover some prerequisites and common software components.

2

GETTING STARTED

The chapter focuses on preparing your programming environment for the projects that follow. You'll use the setup you create here throughout the rest of the book, so it's worth investing some time up front and getting comfortable with it. Though simple, it will offer enough functionality to enable you to become productive immediately and start coding the recipes in the next part of the book.

We'll look at several approaches to coding, consider editor choices, and discuss prerequisites and common software components. To wrap up, I'll introduce a few shortcuts that will help you manipulate the Linux terminal like a seasoned pro, and we'll take a brief tour of the Linux filesystem.

While you'll be using the tools and techniques introduced in this chapter in the context of Linux and single-board computers, a bonus is that the skills you develop here will be transferable to other programming languages and environments you are likely to encounter in the future.

Choosing Your Environment

A *development environment* is a workspace consisting of tools and processes that allow you to build the components of a software project or product. Depending on a developer's specific needs, this environment may contain tools for writing and compiling code, testing, debugging, benchmarking, source control, system log monitoring, and more.

In the not-so-distant past, developers were limited to what was available in the terminal: usually text editors with varying degrees of sophistication. Today, modern graphical operating systems with *integrated development environments (IDEs)* offer standard features such as smart code completion, syntax validation, and, more recently, AI pair programming.

With all the tools available to choose from, there are nearly as many ways to build software projects for single-board computers like the Raspberry Pi as there are developers doing it. Opinions vary as to which toolset is best, but ultimately, what matters is finding the approach that works best for *you*. In the following sections, I'll introduce three approaches to setting up your development environment.

Direct Access via the Terminal

The first option is to do everything in the terminal, or a *terminal emulator*, which is a program that lets you interact with a system via a text-based interface. Because the program relies entirely on text, this approach is well suited to lower-spec computers like the RPi Zero, as it requires fewer system resources. You can access a terminal either locally, with a keyboard and monitor connected to the device, or remotely, typically via *Secure Shell (SSH)*, a cryptographic protocol that enables secure remote login between systems. Both Windows and macOS have built-in SSH clients that work perfectly well. Other popular third-party options are available as well, including PuTTY, iTerm2, and Terminus, so you needn't feel constrained by the limitations of a default SSH client.

In simple terms, the *shell* is a program that accepts commands from the keyboard and passes them to the operating system to execute. This mode of interaction is often referred to as a *command line interface (CLI)*. In the old days, CLIs were the only interface available on Unix-like systems. Today, they remain an integral part of many modern software tools, often working in tandem with *application programming interfaces (APIs)* to provide services to other pieces of software.

On most Linux systems, a program called *bash* (an acronym for the GNU Bourne Again SHell, an enhanced version of the original Unix shell program sh, written by Steve Bourne) serves as the shell program. It's enabled by default on Raspberry Pi OS. To confirm this, try the following:

```
$ printf "my shell is %s\n" $(readlink /proc/$$/exe)
my shell is /bin/bash
```

While it can feel intimidating at the outset, especially if you're more familiar with IDEs, developing in the Linux shell with bash can be a liberating experience. Working with files in the terminal requires using a text editor, with GNU Nano, Vim, and Emacs being popular choices. While these tend to have steeper learning curves than their IDE counterparts, the upside is their extreme portability and universality. Human-readable plain-text configuration files (often called *dotfiles*) for terminal programs are generally much more portable than the equivalent settings for IDEs.

By saving these dotfiles (for example, your Vim configuration, contained in *.vimrc*) to an online source code repository like GitHub, you can effectively "bring your configuration with you" by cloning them onto whichever system you happen to be working on. In this way, creating a familiar editor configuration on a new device can be done in just a few steps:

```
$ sudo apt install git vim -y
$ git clone https://github.com/billz/.vim.git
$ cp .vim/.vimrc ~/
$ vim ~/.vimrc

" Basic Settings
filetype plugin indent on
syntax on
set guifont=Menlo:h14
set nocompatible
set modelines=0
set tabstop=4
set shiftwidth=4
set softtabstop=4
set expandtab
--snip--
```

Text editors like Vim and Emacs are generally much more widely available than OS-specific IDEs, so in a minute or two you can have your familiar development environment up and running on a new machine. This is extremely handy if you happen to be working with several Raspberry Pis, for example.

With the addition of a terminal multiplexer like Tmux, you can split a single terminal window into multiple panes, as shown in Figure 2-1.

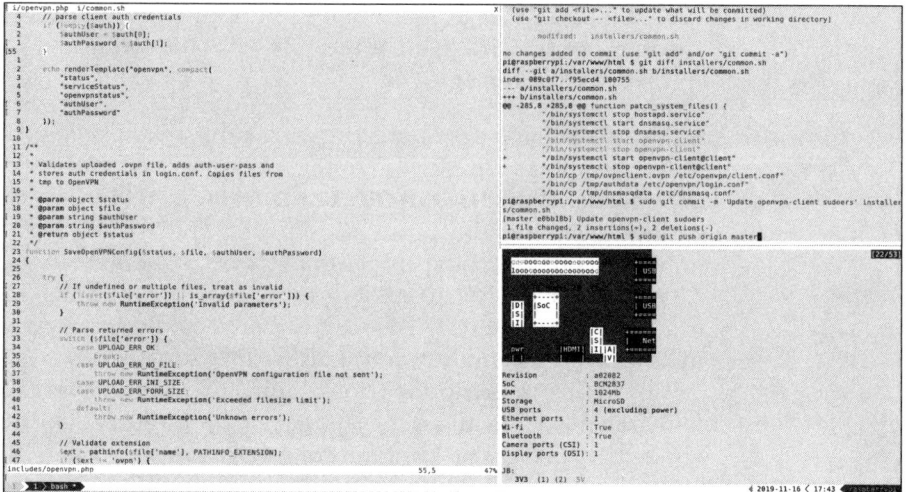

Figure 2-1: My development environment, with Tmux used to provide multiple panes in a single terminal window

Though by no means a requirement, using a terminal multiplexer may be very helpful when working through the recipes in this book. For example, you might devote one pane to a text editor, another to navigating the Linux filesystem, and a third to monitoring system log output. Tmux also has a dotfile, *tmux.conf*, which is portable and can be version controlled like other dotfiles.

Key-Based Authentication

A useful pro tip when working via the terminal is to copy your public SSH key to the Raspberry Pi. Known as SSH *public key authentication*, this method allows you to log in securely without entering a password each time. It works by pairing a local private key with a public key that's associated with your user account on the remote system.

First, check to see if you already have a key pair on the computer you're using to connect to your remote device. This will usually be located in the */.ssh/* directory on macOS and Linux, or in the *.ssh* directory in your user profile folder on Windows (for example, *C:\Users\your-user\.ssh*). On a Linux or macOS computer, execute **ls ~/.ssh**. If you see files called *id_rsa* and *id_rsa.pub*, you can skip to the next step. Otherwise, generating them is easily done:

```
$ ssh-keygen -t rsa -b 4096
Generating public/private rsa key pair.
Enter file in which to save the key (/home/username/.ssh/id_rsa):
--snip--
```

Accept the defaults and, optionally, add a passphrase to encrypt your private SSH key. You can then use a related SSH utility available on macOS and Linux to securely copy your public key to the remote device:

```
$ ssh-copy-id -i ~/.ssh/id_rsa.pub pi@raspberrypi.local
```

Substitute your device's IP address or hostname for `raspberrypi.local`, if necessary. You will be prompted to provide a password for the *pi* user, whereupon the public key from your computer will be stored in */.ssh/ authorized_keys* on the remote system. You can then simply connect with `ssh pi@raspberrypi.local` and use your SSH key for authentication.

Editor Choices

In the Linux shell, editing configuration files and code is typically done using a command line text editor. This is a big change from the GUI-based editors you might be familiar with. While there are many editors to choose from, I'll focus on three of the most popular: Nano, Vim, and Emacs. For a humorous comparison of these editors, see Figure 2-2.

Figure 2-2: A satirical take on command line text editors (in truth, Nano isn't so bad!). Courtesy of Curtis Lassam (https://cube-drone.com).

When it comes to simplicity, Nano wins hands down. It sits on the easy-to-use end of the spectrum and is preinstalled on most Linux systems. Shortcuts are displayed at the bottom of the user interface, making it beginner-friendly. It's minimal and perfectly suitable for editing configuration files of the type you'll be using throughout this book. Using Nano is straightforward: Execute `nano *filename*` to edit a file, navigate with the arrow keys, and use the keyboard shortcuts CTRL-O to save and CTRL-X to exit.

If you don't need more advanced features from a command line text editor, Nano is the perfect choice. As for the other two—Vim and Emacs—the question of which one is superior has been the subject of debate bordering on religious zealotry for decades.

Vim, short for *Vi IMproved*, is an enhanced version of the classic vi text editor available on most Unix-like systems. It is highly configurable and known for its efficiency once mastered. Fluency with Vim is virtually a requirement for gray-bearded Linux system administrators. Despite it having a reputation for using an arcane set of keystroke inputs, developing basic Vim literacy is fairly straightforward with the help of its integrated tutorial paired with a quick reference, or "cheat sheet," and a healthy dose of patience.

Only vi is installed on Raspberry Pi OS by default. To get the full features of Vim, you'll need to install it:

```
$ sudo apt install vim
```

To learn more about editing in Vim, execute `vimtutor` in the shell and follow the tutorial. To exit the tutorial, enter the command `:q!`.

Emacs (originally standing for *Editor MACroS*) is the oldest and arguably the most versatile text editor of the bunch. The original version was created in 1976 by GNU Project founder Richard Stallman, but the Emacs family of text editors has continued to evolve up to the present day. A likely explanation for its remarkable longevity is its package support, which lets you transform Emacs into just about anything you can conceive of. More than a mere text editor, Emacs can be customized into a full desktop productivity environment.

As with Vim, you can install it via apt:

```
$ sudo apt install emacs
```

In the examples in this book, I'll assume you're using Nano. However, your choice of editor, like your environment setup as a whole, is a matter of personal preference. If you find you're more comfortable with a different text editor, simply substitute it in the code examples in place of nano.

SSH key access, some basic familiarity with a text editor, and optionally a multipane terminal environment are all you need to get up and running with the recipes in this book. That said, in the next section I'll introduce an alternative environment setup that allows you to use a full-featured, browser-based IDE on your Raspberry Pi.

Self-Hosted code-server

Unlike the terminal and text editors, which are steeped in Linux tradition, this next environment upends things and brings development into the modern era. Created by Microsoft, *Visual Studio Code*, commonly referred to as *VS Code*, is a free and open source editor for Windows, Linux, and macOS. VS Code has all the features you'd expect from a modern IDE: *IntelliSense* (word-based code completions), syntax highlighting, debugging, themes, parameter hints, and Git integration are all standard. VS Code has built-in support for a wide array of programming languages, from Java to C++, Python, PHP, Go, and more. What's more, VS Code's plug-in system allows you to add on and even create new extensions to suit your needs.

These days, it seems everything is migrating to the cloud, and VS Code is no exception. The team at Coder.com has brought VS Code to the cloud and open sourced it under the MIT License. The result is *code-server*, a VS Code instance that runs on a remote server and is accessible through any web browser, as shown in Figure 2-3.

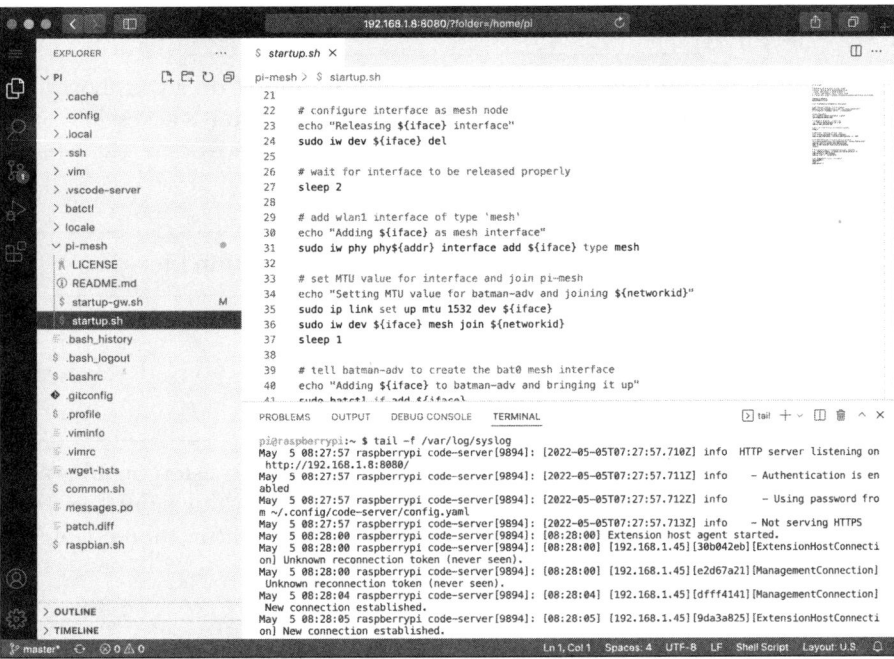

Figure 2-3: A self-hosted code-server instance in a browser

This approach is functionally equivalent to using the VS Code IDE on a local machine, but it offers several advantages. First, it shifts processor-intensive tasks, such as compiling code, to a more powerful hosted server. Using code-server also allows you to code from virtually anywhere and on any device. For example, if you code at home on a Mac, use a Windows machine at the office, and travel with an iPad or Android tablet, a code-server instance acts as a portable development environment accessible from all these devices. The interface is modern, responsive, and provides access to a full suite of desktop-like tools.

According to the code-server documentation, a self-hosted instance requires a Linux machine with WebSockets enabled, 1GB of available RAM, and two CPU cores. If you're using a Raspberry Pi 3B+ or 4 with at least 1GB SDRAM (more is better), code-server will work without any problems. Given that the Pi Zero models are limited to 512MB of SDRAM (and the original Zero has a single-core 1 GHz ARMv6 CPU), they won't support hosting code-server. Don't worry, though; in the next section I'll demonstrate a different method for using VS Code that works fine on these devices.

The easiest way to install code-server on Raspberry Pi OS is to use the install script provided for Linux. The script will automatically detect the distribution type and attempt to use the system package manager, if possible. You can preview what will occur during the install process with:

```
$ curl -fsSL https://code-server.dev/install.sh | sh -s -- --dry-run
```

To install code-server, run:

```
$ curl -fsSL https://code-server.dev/install.sh | sh
```

The install may take several minutes on a Raspberry Pi. When it's done, create a code-server configuration file so it's accessible on your network:

```
$ mkdir -p ~/.config/code-server/
$ nano ~/.config/code-server/config.yaml
```

Add the following to this configuration file:

```
bind-addr: 0.0.0.0:8080
auth: password
password: my-password
cert: false
```

The first line instructs code-server to listen on all available IP addresses on port 8080. Replace the placeholder value `my-password` with your user password. Save your changes and exit the editor, then enable and start the code-server service for the *pi* user:

```
$ sudo systemctl enable --now code-server@pi
```

You can confirm that code-server started correctly by checking its status with:

```
$ sudo systemctl status code-server@pi}
```

If the service state indicates `active (running)`, you can now access the code-server UI in your browser. Depending on your environment, the address might be *http://raspberrypi.local:8080* or *http://<local-ip-address>:8080*. To determine your Pi's IPv4 address, execute `hostname -I` in the shell. Replace *<local-ip-address>* with this value in your browser's address bar and press ENTER.

Since you're not using SSL certificates on your local server, code-server will warn you that it's being accessed in an insecure context. This is fine for now, so you can safely dismiss this warning. At the welcome prompt, enter your password to proceed, as shown in Figure 2-4.

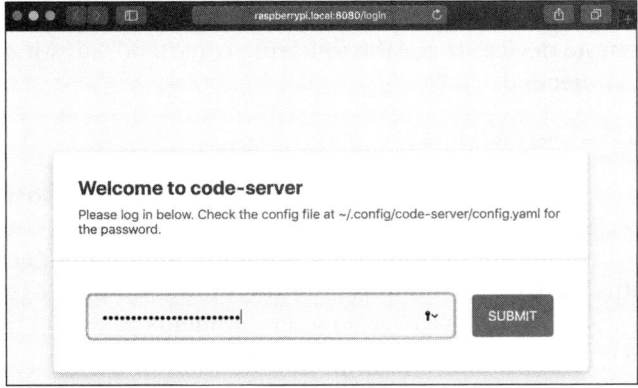

Figure 2-4: The code-server login dialog, self-hosted on a Raspberry Pi 4

When you access code-server for the first time, it will present you with a "Get Started with VS Code in the Web" walk-through. This allows you to create an initial configuration, tune your preferences, and so on. For our purposes, the Terminal and Explorer panels will be useful as you proceed through this book. You can enable these from the View menu and further tweak the layout to your liking.

Next, we'll look at one more possibility for setting up your development environment, which provides a solution for those who would like to use the approach described here but are using a resource-constrained device.

Remote Development

This approach is recommended if you're using a Pi model or other device that doesn't meet code-server's minimum requirements. The VS Code *Remote - SSH* extension lets you open a remote folder on any machine running an SSH server, so you can take full advantage of VS Code's feature set. Once connected via SSH, you can interact with files and folders anywhere on the remote filesystem. To enable remote development with SSH, you'll need to take these steps:

1. Configure your Pi or other device for SSH access.

2. Optionally, configure key-based authentication for your remote SSH host.

3. Install VS Code on your local development machine running Windows, Linux, or macOS.

4. Install the Remote Development extension pack.

Before connecting with VS Code, verify that SSH access is enabled on your remote device. Enter the following command, substituting your Pi's address if needed:

```
$ ssh pi@raspberrypi.local
```

Next, in VS Code, select **Remote-SSH: Connect to Host** from the Command Palette (**F1**), and use the same pi@raspberrypi.local user login as in the previous step. At this stage, VS Code should indicate "Opening Remote" in the status bar while it downloads the necessary software to enable remote SSH access to your device. After a few moments, it should indicate "SSH: raspberrypi.local" in the status bar, as shown in Figure 2-5.

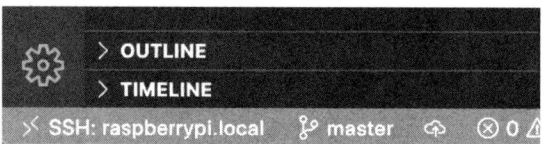

Figure 2-5: The VS Code remote SSH option enabled on a Raspberry Pi

While it's being configured for remote SSH, you may notice that VS Code Server is being downloaded to your remote device. This is different from code-server, the self-hosted server package described in the previous section. There's no harm running both on the same device, but practically speaking, you will generally use one or the other.

To confirm remote SSH access is working correctly, open an Explorer pane (available from the View menu) and try viewing a file in the *pi* user's home directory. You may do the same with a Terminal pane and try executing a bash command. The interesting thing about remote SSH mode is that no source code "lives" on your local machine; the extension runs commands and other extensions directly on the remote machine. This is illustrated in Figure 2-6.

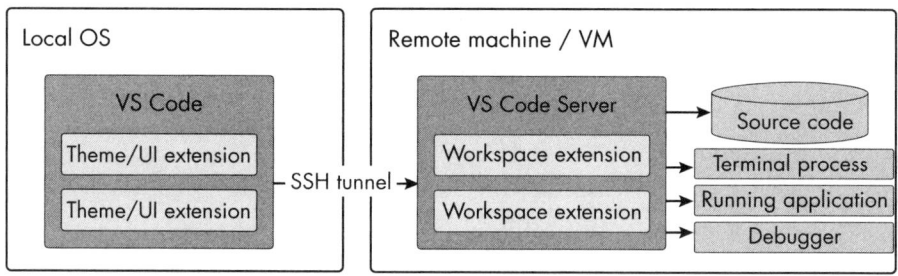

Figure 2-6: The remote SSH extension gives you access to an editor, terminal, and debugger on the remote host.

For the developer, remote SSH with VS Code provides a local-quality experience, meaning that all the features of the desktop IDE are available while working remotely on the Pi. This includes Git source control and extensions for popular languages such as Python (both of which are used extensively in this book).

The main limitation of this approach is that your local machine needs to be able to run VS Code, which, at least for the time being, excludes mobile devices such as tablets and phones. However, with the release of Apple's iPadOS and Samsung's DeX, the boundary between tablets and traditional computers is already starting to blur. We may very well be able to run VS Code on these devices in the near future.

Prerequisites

With your development environment set up, you can now prepare your device to begin implementing the projects in this book. This typically involves using a clean install with the latest updates as your starting point. Flashing an SD card with the latest release of Raspberry Pi OS Lite (32- or 64-bit) is the first step in this process.

It might be tempting to create a Swiss Army knife–type setup that combines many different software projects on a single device. The idea that you can carry a "do-it-all" Linux system in your pocket certainly has appeal. However, while it is technically possible to combine several of these recipes in a single installation, I highly recommend that you start each project with a fresh OS install. Stacking the Linux services you'll be using on top of one another can sometimes lead to unpredictable results. For example, network ports may already in use by another service, software packages may conflict with one another, or configuration errors may arise.

Minimizing the time you spend troubleshooting will leave you with less frustration and more time to spend building. Besides, SD cards are cheap, so you can easily pick up a few extra ones, label them, and swap them as needed as you proceed through the book.

Kernel and Package Updates

Kernel and firmware updates may become available after a general release, including fixes to mitigate security holes, so it's important to install the latest versions of these packages as well. Update your system's package list, upgrade the installed packages to the latest versions, and reboot:

```
$ sudo apt update && sudo apt full-upgrade
$ sudo reboot
```

Note that full-upgrade is used rather than a simple upgrade, as this also picks up any dependency changes that may have been made. With your packages and possibly kernel updated, you can fetch some details about your setup by using a system information tool written in bash. Install and run it with the following commands:

```
$ sudo apt install neofetch
$ neofetch
```

If you like, you can then compare your installed kernel version against the latest available general release from the OS provider.

Wireless LAN Countries

I touched on the topic of wireless LAN countries in the previous chapter; it's a common stumbling block that tends to confound many users, so let's put it to rest here. On first boot of a fresh install of Raspberry Pi OS, you might be confronted by the following message:

```
Wi-Fi is currently blocked by rfkill.
Use raspi-config to set the country before use.
```

Telecommunications radio bands are subject to regulatory restrictions to ensure interference-free operation. The Linux OS complies with these rules by requiring users to configure a two-letter Wi-Fi country code. In Raspberry Pi OS, 5 GHz wireless networking is disabled until this country code has been set, usually as part of the initial installation process.

Recent versions of the official Raspberry Pi Imager software include an option to set the WLAN country when writing the SD card. However, if you run into this issue, you can fix it easily using the sudo raspi-config command. Select **Localisation Options** from the parent menu, then **WLAN Country** in the next menu. Choose your two-letter country code from the list, then select **OK** and **Finish**. After running this utility, you can execute a script to check the status of your WLAN adapters:

```
$ sudo apt install rfkill
$ rfkill list wifi
0: phy0: Wireless LAN
      Soft blocked: no
      Hard blocked: no
```

You can use the following command to confirm the details of your wireless regulatory domain:

```
$ sudo iw reg get
global
country US: DFS-FCC
    (902 - 904 @ 2), (N/A, 30), (N/A)
    (904 - 920 @ 16), (N/A, 30), (N/A)
    (920 - 928 @ 8), (N/A, 30), (N/A)
    (2400 - 2472 @ 40), (N/A, 30), (N/A)
    (5150 - 5250 @ 80), (N/A, 23), (N/A), AUTO-BW
    (5250 - 5350 @ 80), (N/A, 24), (0 ms), DFS, AUTO-BW
--snip--
```

In this example output, you can see that the country code is set to US. The list of supported frequencies should be familiar from your explorations in Chapter 1.

Headless Access

Throughout this book, I'll assume that you are accessing your device without connecting it to a monitor or keyboard (often referred to as *headless mode*). This is a common arrangement when a Raspberry Pi is embedded in another device or is in a remote location. You can certainly use a monitor and keyboard if you prefer, but connecting headlessly is a good exercise, and you may find it useful to develop a habit of using the tools discussed in this chapter.

You'll perform all the operations in this book's recipes over SSH. The Secure Shell protocol uses encryption to secure the connection between a client (your computer) and a server (a Raspberry Pi, in this case). There are a few simple steps you can take when preparing an SD card to enable remote access from the start.

On Raspberry Pi OS, the SSH server is disabled by default. There are several ways to enable it, but I'll describe the simplest method for enabling a headless setup here. After flashing the OS image onto the SD card, insert it into a card reader connected to a Windows, macOS, or Linux machine so that the boot partition can be accessed. To enable headless access with SSH, place an empty file named *ssh* (no extension) in the boot partition of the SD card. When the device boots, the system will check for this file. If it's found, SSH is enabled and the file is deleted.

To access your device remotely, you'll need to connect to it via either Ethernet or Wi-Fi. Some SBCs, such as the Raspberry Pi Zero W, lack an Ethernet port and are designed to be accessed wirelessly (another method, often called *USB On-The-Go* or simply *gadget mode*, is possible but won't be discussed here). In this case, you'll make use of wpa_supplicant, a software implementation of an IEEE 802.11 supplicant for Linux, to configure wireless networking. Just as you did with the *ssh* file, create a file called *wpa_supplicant* in the boot partition of your SD card. Add the following contents to this file:

```
ctrl_interface=DIR=/var/run/wpa_supplicant GROUP=netdev
update_config=1
country=your_ISO-3166-1_two-letter_country_code

network={
    ssid="your_SSID"
    psk="your_wi-fi_password"
}
```

When the Pi first boots, this file will be copied to the Linux root filesystem, and the settings defined here—including your network's name and pre-shared key (PSK)—will be used to enable wireless networking. We will revisit this configuration for several of the recipes later in this book.

Software Components

You'll be installing many Linux software packages as you work through the recipes that follow, but one component you'll use often is a routed wireless access point. Setting up a wireless AP requires several software services working together. In this section, we'll look at two methods for creating a wireless AP: using NetworkManager, the standard suite of Linux networking tools, and RaspAP, an independent project that turns a Pi into a lightweight wireless router.

Using NetworkManager

NetworkManager is a software utility that aims to simplify the creation and management of both wired and wireless network connections. In recent releases of Raspberry Pi OS, this tool has taken on a more prominent role.

You can use NetworkManager's command line interface, nmcli, to create a hosted wireless access point from the shell. Begin by checking the status of the wireless interface by running nmcli without any arguments. If your device's wireless interface status appears as sw disabled, execute the following command to enable the wireless adapter:

```
$ sudo nmcli radio wifi on
```

Then run this command, optionally replacing the WirelessCookbook SSID and ChangeMe password with your own values, to create a Wi-Fi hotspot using your device's Wi-Fi interface:

```
$ sudo nmcli device wifi hotspot ssid WirelessCookbook password ChangeMe
```

After a moment, nmcli should respond with output similar to the following:

```
Device 'wlan0' successfully activated with '9925f219-d1f7-4b25-8b62-504a71d197cb'.
Hint: "nmcli dev wifi show-password" shows the Wi-Fi name and password.
```

Use another wireless device, such as a laptop or smartphone, to connect to the network. Look for a network with an SSID matching WirelessCookbook, and enter your network password to connect to it. If your Raspberry Pi is connected to the internet via Ethernet or a second wireless adapter, your connected device should now also have internet access. Confirm this with a ping test:

```
$ ping nostarch.com
PING nostarch.com (104.20.17.121) 56(84) bytes of data.
64 bytes from 104.20.17.121 (104.20.17.121): icmp_seq=1 ttl=51 time=57.1 ms
--snip--
```

Monitoring Connections

To obtain some basic insights into what's happening behind the scenes, you can use the NetworkManager CLI's `monitor` command. First, disable the hotspot by executing the following command:

```
$ nmcli device disconnect wlan0
Device 'wlan0' successfully disconnected.
```

Then run the `monitor` command:

```
$ nmcli monitor
NetworkManager is running
```

Next, in a separate bash shell, restart the hotspot by using the command you used in the previous section. The output of `nmcli monitor` should display output similar to the following:

```
Hotspot: connection profile changed
wlan0: using connection 'Hotspot'
wlan0: connecting (prepare)
wlan0: connecting (configuring)
--snip--
wlan0: connected
```

You can also perform a simple network connectivity check by executing this command:

```
$ nmcli networking connectivity
full
```

This indicates that the host is connected to a network and has full access to the internet. Other possible return values are `limited`, `portal` (if the host is behind a captive portal and cannot reach the full internet), and `none`.

Modifying Settings

Throughout this book, you'll be changing network configurations to achieve various goals. For example, you might want to modify the Dynamic Host Control Protocol (DHCP) settings for a given connection to enable dynamic IP address assignment. Let's explore how to do this with NetworkManager.

First, display the available network connections:

```
$ nmcli connection show
```

This will show a list of connections set up in NetworkManager:

```
NAME       UUID                                  TYPE   DEVICE
MyNetwork  02335dcf-62e0-4266-a45c-459dd2135c62  wifi   wlan0
```

Let's assume the connection you want to modify is `MyNetwork`. To change DHCP settings such as Domain Name System (DNS) servers, you can use the connection modify command. For instance, you could execute the following command to specify Quad9's public DNS server:

```
$ nmcli connection modify MyNetwork ipv4.dns "9.9.9.9"
```

You can also modify other settings, like the DHCP hostname:

```
$ nmcli connection modify MyNetwork ipv4.dhcp-hostname "myhostname"
```

After making changes, bring the connection down and then up again so they take effect:

```
$ nmcli connection down MyNetwork
$ nmcli connection up MyNetwork
```

Finally, verify your changes by executing the following command:

```
$ nmcli connection show MyNetwork
```

As you've seen here, NetworkManager simplifies the process of creating a wireless access point by abstracting various Linux networking services, such as DHCP, wpa_supplicant for Wi-Fi authentication, and systemd-resolved for DNS resolution. Of course, there's much more you can do with NetworkManager's CLI. It's worth taking some time to familiarize yourself with its capabilities by consulting the man pages with man nmcli.

In the next section, we'll look at an alternative method to create a wireless access point. This tool offers an intuitive web-based interface for advanced control over wireless networking services.

Using RaspAP

Developers have a long history of using prebuilt software components for their work. You can, of course, download a piece of source code, add any required dependencies, and compile and install a package manually. Indeed, for some software this might be the only option. Alternatively, you may be able to employ a package manager like apt to do the heavy lifting for you and deliver a ready-to-go executable or library with a single command.

The RaspAP open source software project and its associated Docker container are conceptually similar to the latter approach. That is, they let us bypass the usual steps of building an application and give us a feature-rich wireless router with a graphical user interface, all bundled in a single package. While it's by no means required, you can use RaspAP in any recipe in this book that requires a wireless access point to simplify and speed up the build process.

Introducing Containers

In this context, a *container* is an isolated environment in which your code runs. This means that a container has no knowledge of your operating system, dependencies, or even your files. It operates entirely within the environment provided by a tool such as Docker Desktop or Docker Engine.

Containers include everything needed to run your code, down to a base operating system.

Here, I'll focus on using Docker Engine to deploy and manage a containerized RaspAP application stack. Docker containers have several advantages over other methods of developing and deploying code. As sandboxed processes, containers are isolated from all other processes running on the host machine. This isolation is made possible by features like kernel namespaces and control groups (cgroups) that have been part of Linux for a long time.

A RaspAP Docker container is a runnable instance of a container image. This container can be started, stopped, moved, or deleted using the Docker CLI. The container can be run on a local device or a virtual machine, or deployed to the cloud. Isolation from other containers also means that it has its own software, binaries, and so on.

Installing Docker Engine

Since RaspAP is built for Debian-based systems, the instructions here will focus on this OS family. To get started with Docker Engine on Debian, you will need the 64-bit version of one of the following:

- Debian Bookworm 12 (stable)
- Debian Bullseye 11 (oldstable)

Docker Engine for Debian is compatible with x86_64 (or amd64), armhf, arm64, and ppc64le architectures.

Some Linux distributions include unofficial Docker packages in their repositories, which can conflict with the official Docker Engine. So, prior to installing it, it's important to first uninstall any conflicting packages. You can do this by running the following command:

```
$ for pkg in docker.io \
    docker-doc \
    docker-compose \
    podman-docker \
    containerd \
    runc; do \
    sudo apt-get remove $pkg;
done
```

Note that apt-get might report that you have none of these packages installed.

A convenience script to install Docker noninteractively is available at *https://get.docker.com*. Prior to executing it, be sure to familiarize yourself with the potential risks and limitations. You may want to run the script with the --dry-run option first, to learn what steps it will perform when invoked:

```
$ curl -fsSL https://get.docker.com -o get-docker.sh
$ sudo sh ./get-docker.sh --dry-run
```

Change into your home directory, then download and execute the convenience script to install the latest stable release of Docker:

```
$ cd ~/
$ curl -fsSL https://get.docker.com -o get-docker.sh
$ sudo sh get-docker.sh
```

Verify that the installation was successful by running the `hello-world` image:

```
$ sudo docker run hello-world
```

This command downloads a test image and runs it in a container. When the container runs, it prints a confirmation message and exits. The output should appear similar to the following:

```
Unable to find image 'hello-world:latest' locally
latest: Pulling from library/hello-world
478afc919002: Pull complete
Digest: sha256:4bd78111b6914a99dbc560e6a20eab57ff6655aea4a80c50b0c5491968cbc2e
Status: Downloaded newer image for hello-world:latest

Hello from Docker!
This message shows that your installation appears to be working correctly.
```

You have now successfully installed and tested Docker Engine. The Docker service starts automatically on Debian-based distributions.

At this stage, you may perform some post-installation steps to simplify using Docker. The Docker daemon binds to a Unix socket, not a TCP port. By default, the *root* user owns the Unix socket, and other users can only access it using sudo. The Docker daemon always runs as the *root* user. If you don't want to always have to preface the `docker` command with `sudo`, you can create a Unix group called *docker* and add users to it. Then, when the Docker daemon starts, it will create a Unix socket accessible by members of the *docker* group.

To create the *docker* group and add the current user, execute these commands:

```
$ sudo groupadd docker
$ sudo usermod -aG docker \$USER}
```

Log out and log back in so that your group membership is reevaluated. With these steps completed, you're now ready to deploy RaspAP.

Deploying with Docker, Two Ways

In this section, I'll show you two different ways of deploying RaspAP in a Docker container: using Docker Compose and using the container registry.

The first method allows you to deploy the entire RaspAP application stack with a single command, `docker compose up`, as well as to configure things like environment variables and network settings in a centralized manner.

Advanced users may also use this option to define a multicontainer environment of which RaspAP is one component, using the *docker-compose.yml* file.

Begin by cloning the `raspap-docker` GitHub repository into your home directory, then change into it:

```
$ cd ~/
$ git clone https://github.com/RaspAP/raspap-docker.git
$ cd raspap-docker
```

For ARM devices such as the Raspberry Pi, you must uncomment the cgroup: host line in the *docker-compose.yaml* file:

```
version: "3.8"
services:
  raspap:
    container_name: raspap
    image: ghcr.io/raspap/raspap-docker:latest
    #build: .
    privileged: true
    network_mode: host
    cgroup: host # uncomment when using an ARM device
    cap_add:
      - SYS_ADMIN
    volumes:
      - /sys/fs/cgroup:/sys/fs/cgroup:rw
    restart: unless-stopped
```

Edit this file with **nano docker-compose.yaml** (or a similar command if you're using a different text editor), remove the # at the start of the cgroup line so it looks like it does here, then save the file and exit the editor.

With this configuration done, run **docker compose up -d**. It's important to use docker compose (with a space) rather than using the older docker-compose syntax. If docker compose isn't available on your system, refer to Docker's installation instructions. You should see output similar to the following, indicating the progress of RaspAP's Docker image being built:

```
$ docker compose up -d
[+] Running 2/8
  raspap 7 layers        [] 12.83MB/337.8MB Pulling
    5665c1f9a9e1 Downloading [===>                        ]   3.547MB/49.59MB
    4311202aff18 Downloading [=========>                  ]   4.98MB/24.95MB
    ac4d205394f0 Download complete
    baf57b850085 Download complete
    18a1ed9b4ba8 Downloading [=>                          ]   4.307MB/263.3MB
--snip--
```

During this process, Docker will build an image containing RaspAP's application stack on your system. This build always pulls the latest RaspAP release from its main GitHub repository.

Behind the scenes, Docker has used the image it just built to start a containerized instance of the RaspAP application stack. You can confirm this by executing the following command:

```
$ docker container ls
CONTAINER ID   IMAGE           COMMAND                CREATED       STATUS       NAMES
8d7b32b8373a   raspap:latest   "/bin/bash -c '/home..."  2 hours ago   Up 2 hours   raspap
```

At this stage, the RaspAP application is running, and you can access the web interface as you normally would. Depending on how you connect to your device, this will typically be one of the following URLs:

- *http://raspberrypi.local*
- *http://10.3.141.1*

Note that RaspAP and all its dependencies are wholly contained within the running Docker container. The host system does not have any of the apt packages or application files used by RaspAP, unless you've explicitly installed them.

As an alternative to Docker Compose, you can deploy RaspAP by using its prebuilt Docker container image, available as the `raspap-docker` package on the GitHub Container Registry. This method defines a single container from the base image, sets up the environment, and configures the application within the container.

Given that everything needed to deploy RaspAP is stored within this package, it isn't necessary to clone the `raspap-docker` repository. Instead, you can simply execute one of the following `docker run` commands.

For ARM devices, the `cgroups` must be made writable:

```
$ docker run --name raspap -it -d --privileged --network=host \
    -p 8081:8081 --cgroupns=host \
    -v /sys/fs/cgroup:/sys/fs/cgroup:rw \
    --cap-add SYS_ADMIN \
    ghcr.io/raspap/raspap-docker:latest
```

For non-ARM devices, execute this command:

```
$ docker run --name raspap -it -d --privileged --network=host \
    -v /sys/fs/cgroup:/sys/fs/cgroup:ro \
    --cap-add SYS_ADMIN \
    ghcr.io/raspap/raspap-docker:latest
```

Both commands should produce the output shown next, followed by a progress indicator of the state of the various package components as they are downloaded to your system:

```
Unable to find image 'ghcr.io/raspap/raspap-docker:latest' locally
latest: Pulling from raspap/raspap-docker
```

When the container image download is completed, you can verify its operational state like so:

```
$ docker container ls
CONTAINER ID  IMAGE        COMMAND                CREATED       STATUS         NAMES
4257b8aa3c7e  ghcr.io/...  "/bin/bash -c '/home..."  5 minutes ago  Up 5 minutes  raspap
```

The RaspAP application should now be up and running, and you can access the web interface as you would normally.

Using the RaspAP Quick Installer

When deploying RaspAP in a Docker container, the associated *Dockerfile* executes the *Quick installer* to download the application files and dependencies. You may, of course, dispense with Docker and run the Quick installer directly. This will not run the application in an isolated container, but it gives you greater control in terms of optional components.

RaspAP's Quick installer has been designed to assist users with creating an instance of RaspAP both quickly and with a great deal of flexibility. The installer accepts several command line options, or *switches*, that allow you to customize your installation. To activate an option, append -s -- *option* to the installer command. You can chain several options together to tailor the installation to your specific needs.

To run the installer, use curl to fetch the script and pipe the output to bash. In this example, I'm passing the --help flag. This option outputs usage notes and exits:

```
$ curl -sL https://install.raspap.com | bash -s -- --help
```

Each option has an abbreviated and a descriptive form, separated by commas. For example, -v, --version indicates that you can pass either -v or --version (but not both) to the installer. You will find this pattern to be extremely common among Linux applications.

The Quick installer will automatically detect your device's OS, install compatible packages, and apply a *known good* default configuration. As an added bonus, you will be able to subsequently manage your wireless access point with a responsive web interface. By using RaspAP's installer, you can get this piece of your setup up and running quickly so you can focus your attention on other tasks. It also eliminates a great deal of redundancy across recipes by installing most of the basic software packages you'll need.

Install RaspAP from your shell prompt with the following command:

```
$ curl -sL https://install.raspap.com | bash
```

After a moment, the installer's welcome screen will appear. The current release version will be indicated along with your device's detected OS:

```
888888ba                                      .d888888  888888ba
88     8b                              d8    88  88      8b
a88aaaa8P' .d8888b. .d8888b. 88d888b. 88aaaaa88a a88aaaa8P
88     8b. 88     88 Y8ooooo. 88    88 88      88  88
88     88 88.  .88       88 88.  .88 88      88  88
dP     dP 88888P8 88888P 88Y888P 88      88  dP
                                 88
                                 dP       version 3.3.2
```

```
The Quick Installer will guide you through a few easy steps
RaspAP Install: Configure installation
Detected OS: Debian GNU/Linux 12 (bookworm) 64-bit
--snip--
```

You will be prompted at each step of the install process to confirm destination directories, add any custom components, and so on. Alternatively, you can perform an unattended installation by appending the -s -- --yes option, like so:

```
$ curl -sL https://install.raspap.com | bash -s -- --yes
```

This option assumes a "yes" response to all prompts, similarly to how the apt package manager works. You can pass additional options to specify which add-on components, such as OpenVPN or WireGuard, you want (or don't want) during a noninteractive installation. Refer to the Quick installer documentation at *https://docs.raspap.com/quick/* for more details.

Accessing the Web UI

When RaspAP's installer completes, you will be prompted to reboot your device. Following a reboot, your new wireless network will be configured as follows:

IP address   10.3.141.1

Admin username   admin

Admin password   secret

DHCP range   10.3.141.50 to 10.3.141.254

SSID   RaspAP

Password   ChangeMe

At this stage, you have two options for accessing RaspAP's web UI. If you choose to connect to the RaspAP SSID, you can access the administrative web interface by entering **http://10.3.141.1/** into your browser's address bar. Alternatively, if your device is connected via Ethernet to your local network, you can access it on your LAN with its hostname (for example, *http://raspberrypi.local*). Note that if you've changed your hostname or aren't running Raspberry Pi OS (which has the avahi mDNS/DNS daemon enabled by default), you may need to replace this with the IPv4 address assigned to your device. In this event, check your router's list of attached peripherals.

You will initially be prompted to authenticate with the previous admin credentials. Once this is done, RaspAP's administrative interface should appear in your browser.

If SSH is enabled on your device, you may also access it using that method. Begin by authenticating with the RaspAP access point by using the credentials shown. Next, assuming your device is running Raspberry Pi OS and the default *pi* account is present, use a terminal client to connect to it with:

```
$ ssh pi@10.3.141.1
```

A Brief Tour of Linux

Throughout this book, you'll be working almost exclusively in the GNU/Linux terminal and exploring various parts of the Linux filesystem hierarchy. Don't fret if you're coming from the desktop world; navigating Linux effectively will become easier and, dare I say, even intuitive with a bit of practice.

Common Keystrokes

The terminal is a powerful tool for interacting with a Linux system, but making the most of it requires some familiarity with various keyboard shortcuts and commands. Using the shell is a keyboard-only affair; there's no mouse input. Fortunately, you can use some terminal tricks to streamline your work. Even if you've chosen VS Code as your preferred environment, you will need to spend some time interacting with the terminal, so it's a good idea to get comfortable with it.

Table 2-1 shows a list of common Linux CTRL key shortcuts that will have you using the terminal like a seasoned pro.

Table 2-1: Common Linux CTRL Key Shortcuts

Keystroke	Action
CTRL-N	Navigates down through the command history.
CTRL-P	Navigates up through the command history.
CTRL-R	Begins a backward search through the command history. Each keystroke moves backward one step in the history.
CTRL-S	Halts output to the terminal.
CTRL-Q	Resumes output to the terminal after CTRL-S.
CTRL-A	Moves the cursor to the beginning of the current line.

(continued)

Table 2-1: Common Linux CTRL Key Shortcuts *(continued)*

Keystroke	Action
CTRL-E	Moves the cursor to the end of the current line.
CTRL-D	Deletes the character under the cursor or exits the current shell, depending on context.
CTRL-K	Deletes the text from the cursor to the end of the line.
CTRL-X-BACKSPACE	Deletes the text from the beginning of the line to the cursor.
CTRL-T	Transposes the character before the cursor with the one under the cursor.
CTRL-W	Cuts the word before the cursor; use CTRL-Y to paste it.
CTRL-U	Cuts the line before the cursor; use CTRL-Y to paste it.
CTRL-_	Performs an undo of the last character typed.
CTRL-L	Clears the terminal screen.
CTRL-C	Forcefully terminates a running process in the terminal.
CTRL-Z	Suspends a running process in the terminal.

The final two keystrokes in this list, CTRL-C and CTRL-Z, are among the most common shortcuts you'll encounter in the terminal, yet they are often misunderstood. When CTRL-Z is used to *suspend* a process, this means its execution is temporarily paused and moved to the background, allowing you to continue using the terminal. This is useful when you want to halt a process without terminating it.

For example, let's say you're monitoring the hostapd process with the system journal, like so:

```
$ sudo journalctl -u hostapd -f
```

Using CTRL-Z pauses the journal output and returns you to the terminal prompt. You may then use the jobs command to display tasks currently running in the background:

```
$ jobs
[1]+  Stopped     sudo journalctl -u hostapd -f
```

You can resume this process later using the foreground command, fg. Running fg with no arguments resumes the most recently backgrounded job in the queue. If you have multiple jobs running in the background, you can bring a specific one to the foreground by executing fg %*number*, where *number* corresponds to the job's numeric ID in the queue.

By contrast, using the CTRL-C keystroke instructs the terminal to send an interrupt signal (SIGINT) to the process, causing it to stop immediately. This is an expedient way to exit a running process or command. For example:

```
$ ./my_program.sh
^C
```

Here, the ^C represents the interrupt signal. This effectively terminates the execution of *my_program.sh*.

Overview of the Filesystem

This might be your first experience navigating the Linux operating system. If you're coming from Windows, the Linux filesystem structure can seem particularly alien. The familiar *C:* drive and other lettered drives are gone, replaced by forward slashes (/) and directories with cryptic, often three-letter names. Throughout this book, you'll encounter references to many common Linux directories. If a code example or bash command mentions an unfamiliar path, refer to Table 2-2 for a quick reference.

Table 2-2: Common Linux Directories

Directory	Description
/	Known as the root directory. Everything in a Linux system is located under / (note that this is distinct from /root).
/bin	Contains binaries needed for the boot process and to run the system in single-user mode, including essential commands such as cd and ls.
/boot	Holds files used during the boot process, along with the Linux kernel itself.
/dev	Contains files that represent devices attached to the local system.
/etc	Stores system configuration files and directories.
/etc/init.d	Contains various service startup scripts, such as /etc/init.d/raspi-config.
/home	User home directories.
/lib	Holds common library directories, files, and links. For example, /lib/modules stores Linux kernel modules.
/mnt	The typical mount point for user-mountable devices and temporary filesystems.
/opt	Contains optional software packages. Typically used by proprietary software that doesn't follow the standard filesystem hierarchy.
/proc	A virtual filesystem that provides system statistics. Doesn't contain real files, but provides an interface to runtime system information.
/root	Home directory for the root user.
/sbin	Holds commands used by the superuser for system administration.
/tmp	A standard repository for temporary files created by applications and users.
/usr	Contains most user-level libraries, source code, programs, and so on. A mini Linux-like directory structure.
/usr/bin	Contains commands available to normal users.
/usr/include	Holds include files used in C programs.
/usr/share	Contains shared directories for architecture-independent textual help files, resources, and more.
/usr/lib	Holds library files searched by the linker when compiling programs.
/usr/local/bin	Stores executable application files local to this system.
/var	Contains administrative files such as logfiles, locks, spool files, and temporary files used by various utilities.

While we're discussing the Linux filesystem, it's worth mentioning some key differences in how files are treated compared to an operating system like Windows. As the popular saying goes, "Everything in Linux is a file." This includes physical devices like screens, keyboards, and printers, as well as conceptual items such as processes and network sockets. Directories themselves are actually files that contain links to other files.

Physical devices are virtualized as files in */dev*, while processes and system resources are virtualized as files in */proc*. For example, try the following:

```
$ cat /proc/cpuinfo
--snip--
Revision : a02082
Serial   : 000000005254823f
Model    : Raspberry Pi 3 Model B Rev 1.2
```

Notice that the file */proc/cpuinfo* contains details about what type of processor your system is running, including the revision, model name, and more. I'll explore these and many related concepts in the subsequent chapters.

Wrapping Up

In this chapter, we explored a few of the most popular approaches to working with code in Linux. As I mentioned at the start, there are nearly as many coding environments, tools, shortcuts, and processes as there are developers using them. The best path is to test out these approaches for yourself and decide which one is most appropriate for you.

Whichever development environment you land on, I'm confident that it will set you up well for the recipes that follow. This chapter marks the end of the introductory material in this book. Now, prepare to roll up your sleeves and start building.

PART II

THE RECIPES

3

MONITORING WI-FI WITH A MINI TFT DISPLAY

In this chapter, I'll introduce an external hardware display that connects to your Pi and show you how to use Python to visualize two key Wi-Fi metrics: a signal strength meter and statistics for a wireless access point (AP). The components used here are widely available and affordable. If you've never used add-on hardware with a Raspberry Pi or are looking to get your feet wet with Python, this is a great starting point.

The majority of the recipes in this book use software to render a web interface or display information to a user via a secondary device, such as a mobile phone or laptop. This project is unique in that it uses a specialized piece of hardware, a tiny color thin-film transistor (TFT) liquid crystal display, to output information to the user in real time.

This chapter also introduces general-purpose input/output (GPIO), which extends the hardware capabilities of the Raspberry Pi. You've likely noticed the 40-pin GPIO header on all current Pi boards (the pins are unpopulated on the Pi Zero models) and perhaps wondered what they are used for. In the world of integrated circuit design, these pins can be thought of as a convenient "accessory" to some other primary function. Most of the time, they have no predefined purpose and are not used by default. Here, we'll use the Pi's GPIO header to send instructions to the attached TFT display.

Use Cases

A connected mini display can be extremely useful when you want to know the state of a running service or another process at a glance, without remote access. In this recipe, I'll show you how to produce two kinds of output with the same display module:

- A signal strength meter that you can use to evaluate your wireless environment
- Statistics related to an access point, including its current status, IP address, and data transfer rate, plus general system information

For each use case, you'll use Python code to update the display in real time.

The display you'll use, the Mini PiTFT, also includes two integrated tactile hardware buttons. I'll show you how, with some additional coding, you can program these buttons to make them function as a tiny interactive user interface. Finally, I'll present ways to modify the code to display values for another service or measurement of your choosing.

Hardware Required

This project relies on basic hardware components that are both affordable and readily obtained. These items are described in this section.

Compatible Raspberry Pi Models

Any WLAN-capable Raspberry Pi model will suffice for this project, including the original Pi Zero W and the Pi Zero 2 W. However, if you're using one of these models, you will need to attach a 40-pin GPIO header by soldering it yourself. Alternatively, several online retailers offer Zero W and Zero 2 W units with a presoldered header, usually for little extra cost.

For the access point portion of this chapter, your device will need an available wireless interface to host the AP. For this purpose, the Pi 3B, 3B+, 4, and 5 models with integrated Wi-Fi and Ethernet will work well. Alternatively, you can use a Pi Zero W model with a micro USB Ethernet adapter, or an older Pi model with a USB wireless adapter.

Mini PiTFT Add-on

I recommend the excellent Adafruit Mini PiTFT, shown in Figure 3-1, for this project. Designed specifically for the Raspberry Pi, its low cost, compact form factor, and bright 240×135-pixel color display make it well suited as an add-on. No soldering, special connectors, or other hardware is required.

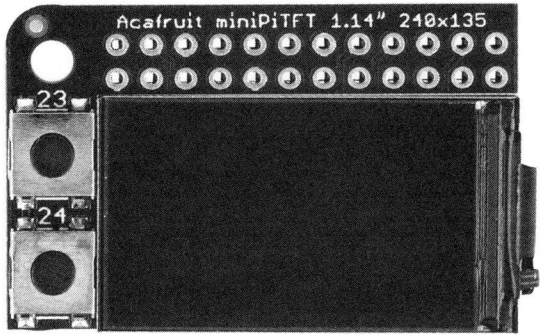

Figure 3-1: The Adafruit Mini PiTFT is a compact
and affordable color TFT display.

The Mini PiTFT is available for purchase directly from Adafruit Industries and other online resellers for approximately $10.

Lithium-Ion Polymer Battery

While not a strict hardware requirement, a lithium-ion polymer (LiPo) battery can be helpful when taking Wi-Fi signal strength measurements. A portable power source will make it easier to move around the area covered by the wireless router. Of the many LiPo battery HATs (short for *Hardware Attached on Top*) available, two models made by Waveshare are both affordable and well suited for this project.

The Waveshare Uninterruptible Power Supply (UPS) HAT shown in Figure 3-2, available from Waveshare for about $24, is designed for the Pi Zero W models. It attaches to these devices via a clever six-pin "pogo" connector. No soldering is required.

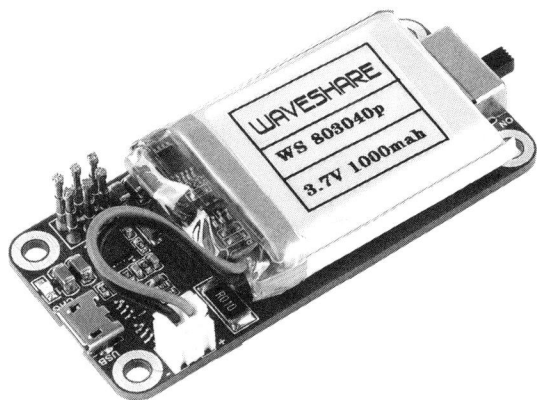

Figure 3-2: The Waveshare UPS HAT for Raspberry Pi Zero

The Waveshare Li-polymer Battery HAT, shown in Figure 3-3 and available from Waveshare for approximately $19, has a capacity and form factor designed for Raspberry Pi models 3B, 3B+, 4B, and 5.

Figure 3-3: The Waveshare Li-Polymer Battery HAT

ESTIMATING COVERAGE AREA

If you're considering whether to add a LiPo battery to your project, let's indulge in a brief thought experiment. The coverage area of a typical Raspberry Pi WLAN module depends on many factors, such as the wireless band used, transmit power, and environmental considerations. In real-world "open-air" tests (that is, with a clear line of sight and minimal interference), the effective range can extend to around 50 to 100 meters (165 to 330 feet). Using a radius of 50 m as a conservative figure, we can estimate the potential coverage area, A, as being equivalent to $\pi \times (50)^2$. In other words:

$$A = 3.14159 \times 2{,}500 = 7{,}854 \text{ m}^2$$

For comparison, this is roughly equal to 30 tennis courts or 6 Olympic-sized swimming pools. In a survey area of this size, a power extension cord will get you only so far. Naturally, an interior space in a crowded Wi-Fi neighborhood will have a considerably smaller coverage area, but still, being untethered with a LiPo battery HAT will make your wireless survey considerably easier and more fun. A LiPo battery is a handy component that will be useful in several other recipes in this book.

Software Used

This recipe introduces the Python programming language and a library called *CircuitPython*, an extension that lets us program microcontroller boards. We'll be using a fork of Adafruit's example CircuitPython program (a copy of the original Git code repository that we can customize for our needs).

You're encouraged to fork this repository (or *repo*, for short) and experiment further with it yourself. Perhaps you'd like to monitor a different service, adjust the wireless signal levels, or change the display colors. You can make whatever changes you like, then commit them to your own repo. Such is the nature of open source software.

In addition to doing some Python coding, you will also need to configure a routed wireless access point. You can achieve this in a few ways, which I'll discuss shortly.

A Closer Look at GPIO

Since we're discussing hardware, this is a good opportunity to briefly look at the Pi's hardware interfaces. Each Pi model has three types of serial interfaces on its GPIO header (the row of 2×20 pins across the right edge of the of the board, as illustrated in Figure 3-4). If you've ever opened a login session from a serial terminal application, such as PuTTY on Windows or screen on Linux, you've already used the *universal asynchronous receiver-transmitter (UART)* interface. UART is a convenient way to control the Pi over GPIO or access its serial console. The other two serial interfaces are the *serial peripheral interface (SPI)* and *inter-integrated circuit (I^2C)* bus. SPI on the Pi allows for up to two attached devices, while I^2C can support many devices, as long as their addresses don't conflict.

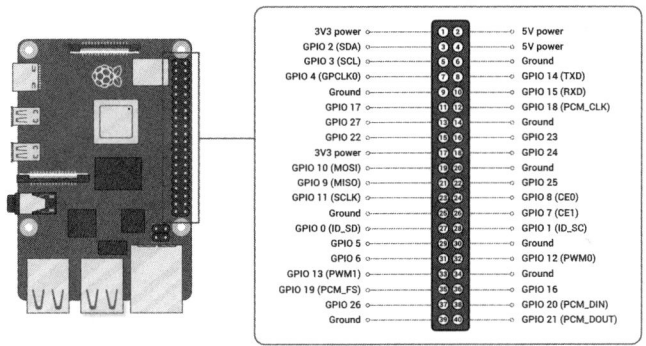

Figure 3-4: A GPIO pinout diagram for the Raspberry Pi (Raspberry Pi, CC BY-SA 4.0)

The Mini PiTFT uses only the SPI port, so it's very fast. This has the added benefit of leaving plenty of GPIO pins available for buttons, LEDs, sensors, and so on. Its compact form factor also allows it to fit into just about any Pi case. The display itself is quite small, about 1.14 inches (29 mm) diagonally. Since it uses in-plane switching (IPS) display technology, it's very readable, with high contrast and wide viewing angles.

Pinout Guide

In electronics, a *pinout* refers to the arrangement of contacts, or pins, on a component and their associated functions. The GPIO Zero Python library provides a command line utility called `pinout` that you can use to display the Raspberry Pi's GPIO pinout information. This tool is installed by default in all current Raspberry Pi OS distributions. On other operating systems, you can install it from the apt repository as follows:

```
$ sudo apt update
$ sudo apt install python3-gpiozero
```

Executing **pinout** on its own will output a board schematic and GPIO header diagram for the current Raspberry Pi. It's also possible to manually specify a revision of Pi or, by configuring remote GPIO access, to output information about a remote system. Example output on a Pi Zero W looks like this:

```
$ pinout
Description         : Raspberry Pi Zero W rev 1.1
Revision            : 9000c1
SoC                 : BCM2835
RAM                 : 512MB
Storage             : MicroSD
USB ports           : 1 (of which 0 USB3)
Ethernet ports      : 0 (0Mbps max. speed)
Wi-fi               : True
Bluetooth           : True
Camera ports (CSI) : 1
Display ports (DSI): 0

,--oooooooooooooooooooo---.
|   1oooooooooooooooooooo J8|
---+ PiZero W    RUN o1    c|
 sd| V1.1 +---+   TV 1o    s|
---+      |SoC|            i|
| hdmi    +---+   usb pwr  |
`-|  |-----------| |-| |-'
--snip--
```

A useful companion utility is the Raspberry Pi GPIO pinout guide hosted at *https://pinout.xyz*. This website contains detailed pinout information not only for the Raspberry Pi boards themselves but also for dozens of HATs, partial HATs (pHATs), sensors, and more.

Figure 3-5 shows a simplified Raspberry Pi GPIO pinout schematic.

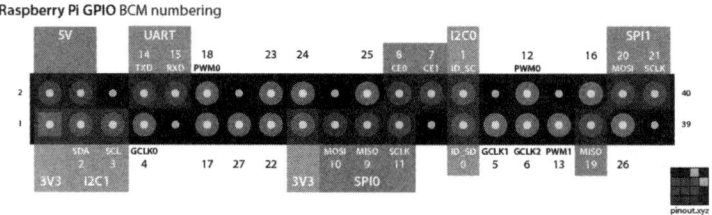

Figure 3-5: A Raspberry Pi GPIO pinout diagram (source: https://pinout.xyz*)*

This visual corresponds to the first two rows of the diagram output by pinout, with pin 1 in the bottom-left corner. Notice that pin 1 is the only pin with a square solder pad (this may be visible only from the underside of your Pi).

If you rotate your Pi such that the GPIO header is at the top and the HDMI port(s) are at the bottom, the orientation will match these diagrams.

Mini PiTFT Pinout

Now that you have some basic familiarity with the Pi's GPIO header, let's examine the Adafruit Mini PiTFT's pins. The pinout schematic is shown in Figure 3-6.

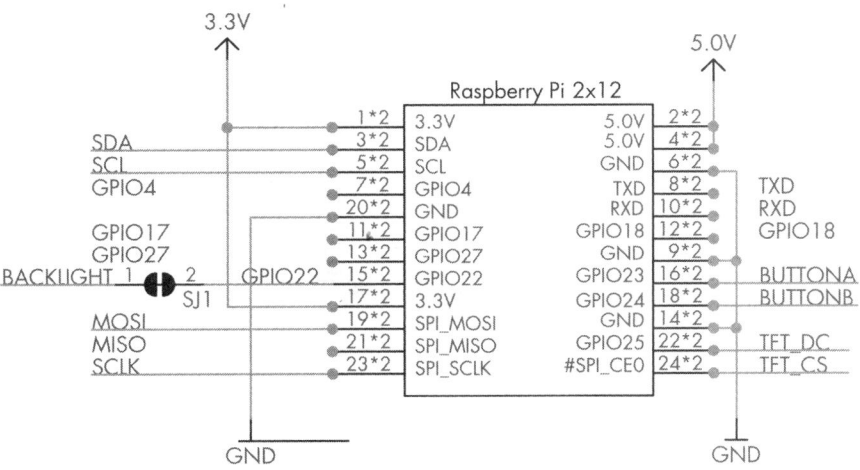

Figure 3-6: The pinout diagram for the Adafruit Mini PiTFT

Note that the orientation of this schematic is rotated 90 degrees to the right relative to the GPIO diagram in Figure 3-5. It's often helpful to start with pin 1 as a reference when consulting diagrams such as this.

Orient the PiTFT with the screen facing you and the tactile buttons on the left side. You should now be able to map the PiTFT's pins to one of the pinout diagrams displayed in the pinout output and Figure 3-5:

5.0V   Connected to the display backlight

3.3V   Connected to the display power and the STEMMA QT/Qwiic connector

GND   Ground for everything

SDA and SCL I^2C data for the STEMMA QT/Qwiic connector

GPIO22   Used to turn the backlight on and off

GPIO23 and GPIO24   Connected to the two front buttons

SCLK, MOSI, CE0, and GPIO25   The display control pins

Note that the Mini PiTFT is *stackable*, meaning that you can attach additional hardware to the Pi by using a stacking header.

Assembling the Components

Some basic component assembly is required for the Pi Zero. If you've elected to solder a 40-pin GPIO header to the Pi Zero yourself, be sure to complete this step before proceeding. The remaining steps do not require special tools and can be done with relative ease if care is taken.

Attaching the PiTFT Display

Before attaching the PiTFT, execute `sudo shutdown -h now` to shut down your Pi safely, then disconnect the power. The PiTFT connects to the top 2×12 section of the Pi's 2×20 GPIO header (the leftmost GPIO pins), as shown in Figure 3-7. It comes preassembled and tested, so it can be attached directly with no soldering or special connectors required.

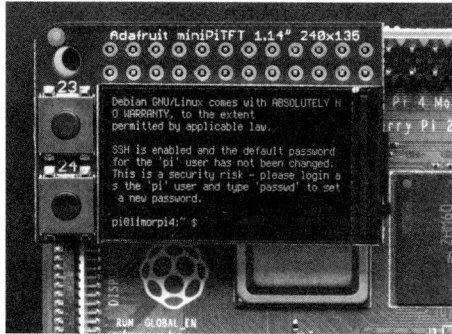

Figure 3-7: The PiTFT attached to the 2×12 header pins

The rounded corner and mounting hole should align at the top left, as shown here. Reconnect the power and boot the Pi. The PiTFT will be illuminated, but nothing should be displayed on the screen. You will notice that two tactile buttons are mounted on the circuit board on the left side of the display. These can be used to toggle states of the display or to navigate a simple user interface, as you'll explore shortly.

Attaching the LiPo Battery

The Waveshare Pi Zero UPS HAT provides regulated 5 V power output from either its rechargeable battery or a connected power supply. A built-in switching mechanism lets it automatically transition to battery power when an external power supply is unavailable. Before installing the UPS HAT on your Pi Zero, shut it down with `sudo shutdown -h now` and disconnect the power.

Connect the included 1,000 milliampere-hour (mAh) LiPo battery to the header socket on the HAT board. Remove the adhesive backing from the battery and stick it in place. As shown in Figure 3-8, the board connects to the Pi Zero via six onboard spring pogo pins, making this a no-solder affair.

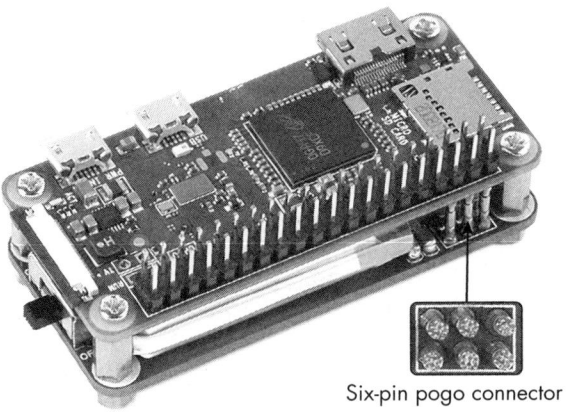

Six-pin pogo connector

Figure 3-8: The Waveshare UPS HAT's pogo pins simplify installation on the Pi Zero W.

Orient the HAT so that its pogo pin connector aligns with the Pi's 3.3 V input, 5 V power output, and ground (GND) GPIO pins. Refer to the pinout definition in Figure 3-9.

With this done, use the included mounting screws to secure the HAT in place (one in each corner, as shown in Figure 3-8). Finally, connect the Pi Zero's micro USB power supply and slide the HAT's power switch to the ON position. A red LED on the HAT will indicate its charging state.

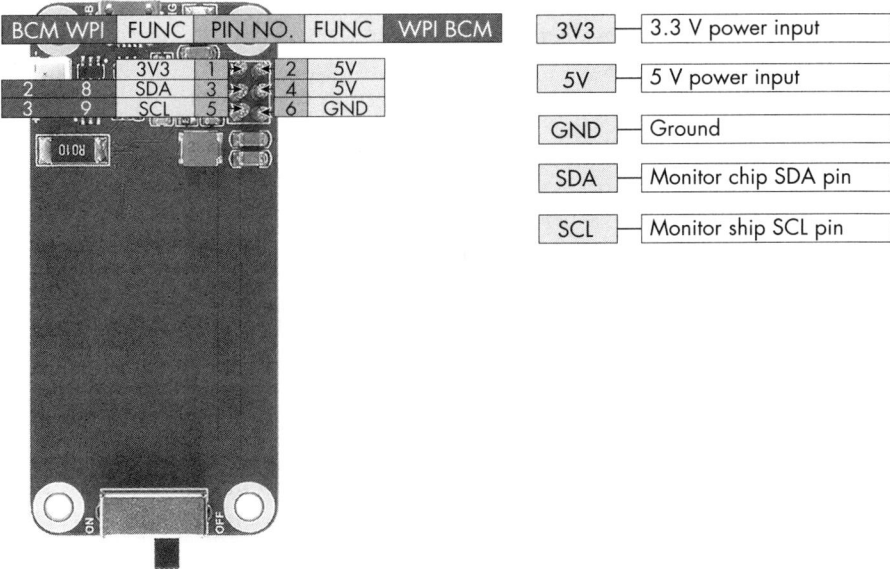

Figure 3-9: The Waveshare UPS HAT's six-pin pogo connector pinout diagram

With the hardware assembly done, you're ready to proceed with installing software to communicate with the Mini PiTFT.

Preparing the SD Card

The Pi Zero devices don't have an onboard Ethernet adapter, so they must be configured for wireless access. You can do this with the Raspberry Pi Imager tool while writing the OS to your SD card. Under **OS Customisation**, choose the **Wireless LAN** option and enter an SSID (name) and the password for your network. If the network does not broadcast an SSID publicly, enable the **Hidden SSID** setting.

Alternatively, you can rely on wpa_supplicant, as discussed in "Headless Access" on page 53. Raspberry Pi OS will move the wireless network configuration defined in */boot/wpa_supplicant.conf* to its default destination in */etc/wpa_supplicant/* the next time the system boots. Since the boot partition is accessible from any computer with an SD card reader, this offers a convenient fallback. A typical *wpa_supplicant.conf* file contains the following:

```
ctrl_interface=DIR=/var/run/wpa_supplicant GROUP=netdev
update_config=1
country=your_ISO-3166-1_two-letter_country_code

network={
    ssid="your_SSID"
    psk="your_wi-fi_password"
}
```

Replace *your_ISO-3166-1_two-letter_country_code* with your ISO country code (for example, US for the United States), *your_SSID* with your wireless network name, and *your_wi-fi_password* with your pre-shared key. Note that the ctrl_interface, update_config, and country lines are required. If they are missing, the system will fail to connect to the network.

Writing to the Display

For this recipe, you'll use Adafruit's CircuitPython library for the ST7789 chipset to send output to the display. CircuitPython is a variant of MicroPython, a stripped-down version of Python designed for microcontrollers. It adds a circuit software layer to Python that enables communication with peripherals like SPI and I^2C.

To make this work on a Raspberry Pi, you'll use the *adafruit_blinka* library, which translates CircuitPython's hardware APIs into the appropriate calls for the underlying Linux system. On the Pi, this means using the *RPi.GPIO* library for general-purpose input/output and the *spidev* Python library for SPI interfacing.

The details of how this works aren't very important at this stage, since it's all abstracted under the adafruit_blinka layer. This pattern of hiding complex implementation details while exposing only the necessary functionality of a system lets us focus on practical development without getting bogged down in the intricacies of the underlying code.

You'll use Pillow, the actively maintained fork of the Python Imaging Library (PIL), to display useful stats in one of two wireless modes: as an access point or as a wireless client. In addition to text, you can use Pillow to draw shapes, graphs, icons, and more complex images (just about anything you like, really). With refresh rates of approximately 15 frames per second (FPS), creating simple animations or videos is also possible.

Prerequisites

Begin by updating your system with the latest `apt` packages, then install Python's package manager, `python3-pip`:

```
$ sudo apt update && sudo apt upgrade
$ sudo apt install python3-pip
```

Before proceeding, a brief discussion of Python's virtual environments is warranted.

Using Python Virtual Environments

In previous versions of Raspberry Pi OS, it was possible to install libraries directly and system-wide, using Python's `pip` package installer. In newer versions, and indeed most Debian-based operating systems, this is no longer permitted. If you try to install a Python package system-wide, you'll receive an error like the following:

```
$ pip3 install adafruit-python-shell
error: externally-managed-environment

× This environment is externally managed
> To install Python packages system-wide, try apt install
  python3-xyz, where xyz is the package you are trying to
  install.

  If you wish to install a non-Debian-packaged Python package,
  create a virtual environment using python3 -m venv path/to/venv.
  Then use path/to/venv/bin/python and path/to/venv/bin/pip. Make
  sure you have python3-full installed.
--snip--
```

This error occurs because you're trying to install a third-party package into the system Python. Historically, conflicts between OS package managers like `apt` and Python-specific package management tools like `pip` have created all manner of problems for users, from Python-level API incompatibilities to conflicts over file ownership.

With the release of Debian Bookworm, packages installed via `pip` must be installed within a Python virtual environment, or venv, using venv. You can think of a virtual environment as a container that safely isolates third-party modules so they won't interfere with or break your system Python.

Creating a Virtual Project Environment

Since you'll be working from a source code repository, you can streamline the process by cloning the GitHub repo and using it as the directory for your virtual environment. Begin by installing git:

```
$ sudo apt install git
```

Next, clone the companion source code repository and change into the *mini-pitft* directory:

```
$ cd ~/
$ git clone https://github.com/wirelesscookbook/mini-pitft
$ cd mini-pitft
```

Now that you're in the directory that will hold your code and virtual environment, you can install the venv module and create the venv:

```
$ sudo apt install python3-venv
$ python3 -m venv env --system-site-packages
```

You'll need to activate the venv each time the Pi is rebooted. You can do this with the following commands:

```
$ cd ~/mini-pitft
$ source env/bin/activate
```

Note that each virtual environment is tied to a specific directory in the Linux filesystem. When the venv is active, you'll notice that the bash prompt has changed to the following:

```
(env) pi@raspberrypi:~/mini-pitft $
```

If you don't see the (env) prefix in your project directory, executing Python code that references the libraries you'll be installing will result in a ModuleNotFound error. This is a common oversight, but thankfully one that's easily remedied by repeating the activation step. You can deactivate any venv by using the deactivate command in the project directory (leave it active for now).

Automating Installation

Adafruit has created a script that automates the steps required to use the adafruit_blinka library. Using this script is recommended, as it handles most of the dependency installs for you. You can run it with the following commands:

```
$ cd ~/mini-pitft
$ pip3 install --upgrade adafruit-python-shell
$ sudo -E env PATH=$PATH python3 raspi-blinka.py
```

Alternatively, if you're installing on an earlier version of Raspberry Pi OS, such as Bullseye, you can call the script like so:

```
$ sudo python3 raspi-blinka.py
```

After a moment, the *raspi-blinka.py* script will detect your hardware and begin updating your system packages. You should see output like this:

```
This script configures your Raspberry Pi and installs Blinka

RASPBERRY_PI_ZERO_W detected.

Updating System Packages
Blinka Get:1 http://archive.raspberrypi.com/debian bookworm InRelease ...
Blinka Hit:2 http://raspbian.raspberrypi.com/raspbian bookworm InRelease
--snip--
```

When the script finishes running, you'll be prompted to reboot. Choose **Yes**, wait a couple of minutes, and then reconnect.

Checking I²C and SPI

The *raspi-blinka.py* script will enable I²C. You can confirm this by listing the contents of the following directories:

```
$ ls /dev/i2c* /dev/spi*
```

You should see output like this:

```
/dev/i2c-1  /dev/i2c-2  /dev/spidev0.0  /dev/spidev0.1
```

You can confirm that you're able to talk to the digital I/O, SPI, and I²C hardware peripherals with a simple test. In your preferred editor, create a new file called *test.py* and enter the following:

```
import board
import digitalio
import busio

print("Hello, blinka!")

# Try to create a digital input
pin = digitalio.DigitalInOut(board.D4)
print("Digital I/O okay!")
```

```
# Try to create an I2C device
i2c = busio.I2C(board.SCL, board.SDA)
print("I2C okay!")

# Try to create an SPI device
spi = busio.SPI(board.SCLK, board.MOSI, board.MISO)
print("SPI okay!")

print("done!")
```

Save the file and exit your editor, then run the test like so:

```
$ python3 blinkatest.py
```

If successful, you should see an SPI okay! response from each of the hardware peripherals.

Python Setup

With the prerequisites out of the way, you can now turn your attention to installing the Python libraries you'll need for this project. You'll be using Debian's apt package manager and Python's pip3 package installer to accomplish this.

NOTE *Adafruit's setup guide recommends installing the kernel module. This is useful if you want to draw to the framebuffer and output a mini console. However, the TFT kernel driver can't be run alongside the Python install, so if you've previously installed the kernel module, be sure to remove it prior to installing the Python library.*

Installing the Required Display Libraries

Starting from the venv home you created previously, install the required Python packages with pip3:

```
$ cd ~/mini-pitft
$ pip3 install adafruit-circuitpython-rgb-display
$ pip3 install --upgrade --force-reinstall spidev
```

Installing the FiraCode Font

Raspberry Pi OS distributions usually come with the DejaVu font preinstalled. You'll spice things up by installing FiraCode, a popular free monospaced font with programming ligatures. It's highly readable and has good support for ASCII, box drawing, and other elements commonly used in console UIs. Install it with apt like so:

```
$ sudo apt install fonts-firacode
```

Installing the Pillow Library

You'll need to install Pillow to enable drawing graphics and using text with custom fonts. Pillow relies on several system libraries, but installing it via apt gives you everything in one go. Despite the package name, this command actually installs the modern Pillow library:

```
$ sudo apt-get install python3-pil
```

Installing the NumPy Library

The Numerical Python (NumPy) library is useful for working with arrays, matrices, linear algebra, and more. A recent update to Adafruit's RGB_Display library, which you installed earlier, uses NumPy for additional speed gains. Install this with the following command:

```
$ sudo apt-get install python3-numpy
```

Running a Quickstart Test

Your device should now have all the required software to begin sending output to the display. Adafruit provides a script, *rgb_display_minipitfttest.py*, that you can run to make sure everything is set up correctly. For convenience, this script is included in the *mini-pitft* GitHub repository you cloned earlier. Execute it with the following command:

```
$ sudo python3 rgb_display_minipitfttest.py
```

With the script running, push the tactile buttons on the left side of the display. The top button should make the display light up red and the bottom button blue. Pressing both at the same time should make the display light up green. When you're satisfied that the display is working correctly, exit the program with CTRL-C.

Running the Signal Strength Monitor

The red LED that indicates your UPS HAT's charging state will be unlit when the LiPo battery is at full capacity. At that point, you may disconnect the running Pi Zero W from its power supply. Now, change into your *mini-pitft* project directory, activate the venv, and run the *stats.py* script:

```
$ cd ~/mini-pitft
$ source env/bin/activate
$ python3 stats.py
```

After a moment, the Mini PiTFT's backlight should activate. Several pieces of information related to its wireless connection will then appear on the display, updating in real time: This includes the current SSID, wireless frequency, link quality (expressed as an integer with a maximum value of

70), and signal (expressed in decibel milliwatts, or dBm). Finally, a familiar Wi-Fi signal strength bar is displayed below these stats.

You're free to move around with the Pi Zero W and its attached UPS HAT, so you can perform a Wi-Fi survey of your physical environment. Try moving into different rooms, experimenting with distance and obstructions of different material types, and changing the orientation of the Pi. The code updates the statistics at 0.1 s intervals (although in practice, the interval is slightly slower because of the overhead of writing to the display).

WHY IS LINK QUALITY EXPRESSED AS N / 70?

The source code for iw, a newer tool similar to iwconfig used by *stats.py*, contains the following comment:

The cfg80211 wext compat layer assumes a signal range of -110 dBm to -40 dBm, the quality value is derived by adding 110 to the signal level.

Adding 110 moves the minimum value to 0, to simplify the presentation of the range, and moves the maximum value to 70.

This can be a practical tool for evaluating the coverage of your wireless router, or indeed any Wi-Fi network you're able to connect to. Indoors, it could help you identify dead zones that could benefit from a wireless repeater or a secondary access point. Outdoors, you can test the maximum line-of-sight distance from your router that still yields an acceptable signal. This can help inform the placement of devices such as wireless cameras.

Use the top A tactile button to toggle the backlight display on and off to conserve battery power. Exit the running program with CTRL-C.

Examining the Monitor Code

Using the editor of your choice, open the *stats.py* file so you can look at its internals. Notice that the Linux iwconfig command is used to fetch details about the default wlan0 interface:

```
def get_wifi_info(interface='wlan0'):
    cmd = f"/usr/sbin/iwconfig {interface}"
    try:
        output = execute_command(cmd)
        essid = output.split('ESSID:"')[1].split('"')[0]
        freq = output.split('Frequency:')[1].split(' ')[0]
        quality = output.split('Link Quality=')[1].split(' ')[0]
        signal = output.split('Signal level=')[1].split(' ')[0]
        return essid, freq, quality, signal
```

The `signal` value returned by this function is used to generate the Wi-Fi signal strength bars shown on the display. If the ranges here look familiar, they should (I discussed dBm values and their perceived quality in Chapter 1):

```python
def signal_to_bars(signal):
    bars = ['\u2581', '\u2583', '\u2585', '\u2587']
    ranges = [
        (-100, -80), # 1 bar
        (-79, -67),  # 2 bars
        (-66, -56),  # 3 bars
        (-55, -30)   # 4 bars
    ]
    signal = int(signal) # cast to integer
    series = ""
    for i, (lower, upper) in enumerate(ranges):
        if signal >= lower:
            series += bars[i]
        else:
            break
    return series
```

You may, of course, modify those values to your liking, or change `get_wifi_info()` to display other properties of your wireless network.

Executing on Boot

You can automatically start the signal strength monitor after a system boot by using cron, a daemon that executes scheduled commands. Start by editing the `crontab` (the table of scheduled commands for the current user) by executing **crontab -e**.

If this is the first time you're running `crontab` on your system, you'll be prompted to select an editor. Choose your preferred editor, then enter the following line after the last comment (the line starting with # shown here):

```
# m h  dom mon dow    command
@reboot sleep 3 && /home/pi/mini-pitft/env/bin/python3 /home/pi/mini-pitft/stats.py
```

This uses cron's `@reboot` time specifier to execute your Python program after the system boots up. You first direct it to sleep for a few seconds to give the system's network interfaces time to initialize. You then specify the absolute path to the python3 executable in the *pi* user's virtual environment, followed by the absolute path to the *stats.py* program. If you've created this project with a user other than *pi*, be sure to adjust these paths.

Save and exit the editor. The system will confirm that a new crontab has been installed. As a final step, verify that the scheduled cron task works as expected by rebooting your device.

Running the Access Point Monitor

The Mini PiTFT signal strength monitor gives you wireless insights from a client perspective. In this section, you'll turn the tables and visualize data related to an operating wireless access point. Like the signal strength display, the AP monitor will update in near real time.

Thanks to its small form factor and extreme portability, the Pi Zero W is ideally suited as a Wi-Fi signal strength monitor that you can roam around with. One obvious drawback for the Pi Zero as a wireless AP is that it has only a single network interface, wlan0. You can, however, add an external Ethernet adapter. Inexpensive, pluggable micro USB to Ethernet adapters are a popular option and are widely available. If you choose to go this route, you can follow the steps in this section without modification. To simplify things, for demonstration purposes I'll use a Raspberry Pi 3B+ with integrated Ethernet and Wi-Fi.

If you've skipped to this part of the chapter, be sure to go back and read "Writing to the Display" on page 78 before proceeding. That section walks you through preparing your system with CircuitPython, a Python virtual environment, and all the related libraries you'll need to work with the Mini PiTFT display.

With your Python environment set up, you can shift your attention to creating the access point. "Software Components" on page 54 describes three ways to get an AP up and running quickly. Choose whichever method you're most comfortable with.

Confirm that the wireless access point is operating correctly by connecting a client to it. With this done, you can move on to the next section.

Starting the AP Monitor

Change into the *mini-pitft* project directory that you cloned in "Creating a Virtual Project Environment" on page 80, and activate the Python virtual environment:

```
$ cd ~/mini-pitft
$ source env/bin/activate
```

Next, execute the *stats-AP.py* Python program:

```
$ python3 stats-AP.py
```

After a moment, your Mini PiTFT's backlight should activate and output a summary of your AP's status, as shown in Figure 3-10.

Figure 3-10: The Mini PiTFT displaying access point and system statistics

The Python code displays your device's current IP address along with the status of the hotspot, current data transmission (Tx) rate, memory usage, and CPU temperature. This is a fair bit of useful information for such a small display. The program updates the display every 100 ms as long as it's running. Use the top A tactile button to toggle the backlight display on and off. Exit the program with CTRL-C.

Examining the Stats Code

With the editor of your choice, open the *stats-AP.py* file. You'll notice that several system commands are executed with their output piped (using the | character) to other Linux utilities, such as grep and awk:

```
cmd = "/usr/bin/vnstat -i wlan0 | grep tx: | awk '{printf \"Data Tx: %d %s\", $5,$6}'"
DataTx = execute_command(cmd)

cmd = "/usr/bin/free -m | awk 'NR==2{printf \"Mem: %sMB %.2f%%\", $3,$3*100/$2 }'"
MemUsage = execute_command(cmd)
```

This pattern of using several small tools in concert to accomplish a given task is common in Linux. The resulting string variables are then output to the display by using the PIL ImageDraw module.

Running at Startup

By default, your wireless AP's services will restart automatically after each system restart. If you want the Mini PiTFT display to activate at the same time, follow the steps in "Executing on Boot" on page 85. Replace the crontab entry with the following:

```
# m h  dom mon dow    command
@reboot sleep 3 && /home/pi/mini-pitft/env/bin/python3 /home/pi/mini-pitft/stats-AP.py &
```

Save your changes and exit the editor. Then reboot your device to confirm that the AP stats display on startup.

Monitoring the LiPo Battery

The Waveshare UPS HAT includes an I^2C bus interface, which makes it possible to monitor the battery voltage, current, power, and remaining capacity in real time. The I^2C kernel module is enabled by default in recent releases of Raspberry Pi OS. To confirm this, or change the setting if needed, execute **sudo raspi-config**.

Choose **Interface Options** from the top-level menu, followed by **I2C**. Select **Yes** to enable the ARM I^2C interface. Next, you'll need a package that provides bindings for the *System Management Bus (SMBus)* protocol, a subset of I^2C, which allows Python to communicate with I^2C devices:

```
$ sudo apt install python3-smbus
```

A utility program called *INA219.py* is included in the *mini-pitft* GitHub repository. Execute it with the following command:

```
$ python3 INA219.py
```

The load voltage (V), current (expressed in amperes, A), power (expressed in watts, W), and battery capacity percentage will display continuously, updated at two-second intervals. Interrupt the program with the CTRL-C keystroke. This utility is useful if you operate your Pi Zero on battery power for an extended period and want to check the remaining capacity to prevent unexpected power loss.

Going Further

A cursory glance at the Python source code in this chapter reveals a lot of potential for customization. For example, several data points are collected and written to the display in *stats-AP.py*. You could modify this program and substitute values for another service, system status, or something else entirely. The sky's the limit here, as Linux gives you many ways to explore nearly every facet of the kernel in operation.

Customizing the Signal Monitor

The signal monitoring code in *stats.py* likewise lends itself to being tweaked in various ways. Consider the example output of iwconfig wlan0 shown here:

```
$ iwconfig wlan0
wlan0    IEEE 802.11  ESSID:"Freebox-Router"
         Mode:Managed  Frequency:2.462 GHz  Access Point: 68:A3:78:D0:80:74
         Bit Rate=72.2 Mb/s    Tx-Power=20 dBm
         Retry short limit:7   RTS thr=2347 B    Fragment thr:off
         Power Management:off
         Link Quality=70/70  Signal level=-10 dBm
         Rx invalid nwid:0  Rx invalid crypt:0  Rx invalid frag:0
         Tx excessive retries:0  Invalid misc:2   Missed beacon:0
```

The individual data points we're interested in are parsed by the get_wifi _info() function, as we saw in "Examining the Monitor Code" on page 84. Think of how you might modify this function to display other properties, such as bitrate, Tx power, or mode.

For that matter, why not explore a different Linux networking utility entirely? The NetworkManager command line interface, nmcli, can be used to report on many aspects of a wired or wireless network. For example, you can list the available Wi-Fi networks (APs) in your vicinity with this command:

```
$ nmcli device wifi list
```

You can use the --fields option to display only specific columns (to see all the available fields, execute nmcli -f all dev wifi list). Given what we've covered in this section, consider ways you might parse this output and send it to the Mini PiTFT.

Customizing the AP Monitor

To give a concrete example of how you might customize the AP monitoring code, locate the following lines in *statsAP.py*:

```
cmd = "/usr/bin/top -bn1 | grep load | awk '{printf \"CPU Load: %.2f\", $(NF-2)}'"
CPU = execute_command(cmd)
```

Breaking this down, we assign a string to the variable cmd that, when executed, will perform several functions in a very Linux-like way. The system command top -bn1 fetches a list of running Linux processes, which is piped to grep to isolate the line containing the string literal load. This output is then piped to awk, which uses it to format a percentage value that we can display.

The variable cmd gets passed as an argument to the execute_command() function:

```
def execute_command(cmd):
    try:
        output = subprocess.check_output(cmd, shell=True, universal_newlines=True)
        return output
    except subprocess.CalledProcessError as e:
        print("Error:", e.output)
```

This in turn is passed to Python's subprocess module. This library has several uses, but here we're using check_output() to connect to the output pipe of the Linux shell command we've defined and store its return value.

Applying this logic, we can work backward and replace the system utility top in this example with any number of things. For instance, when monitoring an access point, we can answer questions like the following by swapping the system calls shown here for any of the existing system calls in *stats-AP.py*:

- Is the dnsmasq service running?

  ```
  $ pidof dnsmasq | wc -1
  ```

- How many bytes have been transmitted by the wlan0 interface?

  ```
  $ cat /sys/class/net/wlan0/statistics/tx_bytes
  ```

- How many client leases are there?

  ```
  $ wc -1 < /var/lib/misc/dnsmasq.leases
  ```

It's also possible to indicate CPU temperature data visually by changing the text color to match a thermal scale, for example.

Wrapping Up

This chapter introduced GPIO, pinouts, and coding with Python, including the popular CircuitPython library for microcontrollers. You attached a TFT display to your device (and, optionally, a LiPo battery HAT to enable portability), and you used CircuitPython and related libraries to parse values from the system and send output to the display.

The small software projects explored here provide different ways of visualizing various aspects of a wireless network in near real time. These projects are well suited for further customization or even complete refactoring to serve other purposes. Methods for modifying the Python code to expose the operational state of related wireless properties or services were also presented.

Most recipes in this book involve extending host devices with add-on hardware components, as you've done here. Python is also used frequently, for everything from communicating with peripherals over serial interfaces to interacting with software APIs. The foundation you've built here should give you the confidence to move forward with the projects ahead.

4

BASIC AND ADVANCED CAPTIVE PORTALS

This chapter explores a popular topic among access point owners and users: the captive portal. Understanding how this system works is valuable for anyone interested either in regulating access to a guest Wi-Fi network or simply in grasping the technology behind them.

In this recipe, you'll build two captive portals: a basic one you can get up and running quickly, and a more advanced system with encryption features and remote hosting potential. Finally, I'll guide you through implementing various methods to help you manage your clients' bandwidth usage.

Use Cases

Just about everyone has some experience with *captive portals*. Also known as Wi-Fi *splash* or *landing pages*, they generally limit access to a shared network until some verification process is completed. At a minimum, a captive portal may present the user with the network's terms of service (ToS), which they must agree to before accessing the internet. In some cases, a password or other form of authentication might be required. These measures help protect network owners from liability in the event of prohibited or malicious online behavior. Security features also add a layer of protection to guest networks. As an access point operator, a captive portal gives you more control over your users, with options such as customizable time limits and data quotas. You'll implement these and other features in this recipe.

THE CASE FOR CAPTIVE PORTALS

Most countries and ISPs place legal obligations on individuals who provide public internet access, with varying levels of enforcement depending on the location. By requiring end users to accept the ToS, a captive portal helps shift liability for any misuse from the providers onto those users.

To prove that these terms were accepted, portal owners must be able to demonstrate a chain of authorization for each client device. The portal's security must also be robust enough to prevent users from bypassing these measures. The systems you'll implement in this chapter have these features built in.

Let's start by setting some expectations. Compared with commercially available routers, a Raspberry Pi–based access point is limited in terms of network performance and the number of clients it can support. There are several reasons for this, including the Pi's onboard wireless chipset, bus speed, and overall design. Dedicated hardware routers are built with *application-specific integrated circuits (ASICs)* and optimized for computationally demanding but relatively simple networking tasks. The Raspberry Pi 4 and 5, while more powerful than earlier Pi models, rely on a general-purpose CPU and an operating system that runs *task-specific* software.

Because of these limitations, the focus here will be on smaller-scale implementations intended to support at most a dozen or so simultaneous portal users. If you're creating a portal on a local network for learning purposes or plan to operate one in a limited capacity (at a small café or guesthouse, for example), this should be sufficient. If you'd like to implement a captive portal on more performant hardware, you'll be able to apply the concepts presented here on a dedicated router running OpenWrt. The knowledge and skills you will acquire in this recipe are directly transferable.

Hardware Required

Apart from a Raspberry Pi model with onboard WLAN capabilities, no special hardware is needed for this recipe. However, an external USB wireless adapter can provide better range and enable faster 802.11ac speeds if your Pi doesn't support this mode natively.

Some adapters work out of the box, without the need to install drivers. These devices use *in-kernel* drivers, meaning the drivers are included in and maintained as part of the Linux kernel. Many such adapters, like the Netgear A6210, shown in Figure 4-1, are available at relatively low cost.

*Figure 4-1: The Netgear A6210
wireless adapter*

This is a good choice if you're looking for an ac-capable adapter with in-kernel support and good performance over short to medium distances.

Software Used

In this chapter, you'll build two captive portal implementations and integrate them with a wireless access point. The first is a rudimentary portal that requires users to accept a ToS agreement before being granted network access for a predetermined length of time. The second is a more sophisticated setup that forwards authentication requests to a web service, forming the basis for a dynamic, highly customizable captive portal.

Both of these implementations use the *open Network Demarcation Service (openNDS)*, a commercial-grade, open source captive portal solution with a small footprint. Capable of handling a high volume of client requests, it's ideally suited for dedicated routers of all kinds as well as general-purpose devices like the Raspberry Pi. openNDS is actively maintained and has a strong community behind it, with support for both OpenWrt and generic Linux distributions. Since you'll be using a Raspberry Pi for this recipe, I'll focus on the latter installation and configuration methods.

A Closer Look at Captive Portals

A wireless router usually has at least two network interfaces. On Ethernet-equipped Raspberry Pi models, these are typically named `eth0` and `wlan0`. In other router setups, a `br-lan` interface is commonly defined to bridge the wireless and wired LANs. Captive portal software like openNDS provides the "engine" that manages one of these interfaces. In this recipe, you'll configure openDNS to operate on `wlan0` only.

Let's examine how this software works in more detail. All captive portals perform two basic functions:

- Capture a client's request to access a network.
- Provide a facility (known as a portal) for clients to log in.

By default, openNDS blocks all traffic but intercepts HTTP requests on port 80. As illustrated in Figure 4-2, client devices generate initial requests on this port, either manually, when the user browses to a website, or automatically, through the device's built-in captive portal detection (CPD) process. These requests are then routed to the *default gateway* of the local network, which in this case is the interface managed by openNDS.

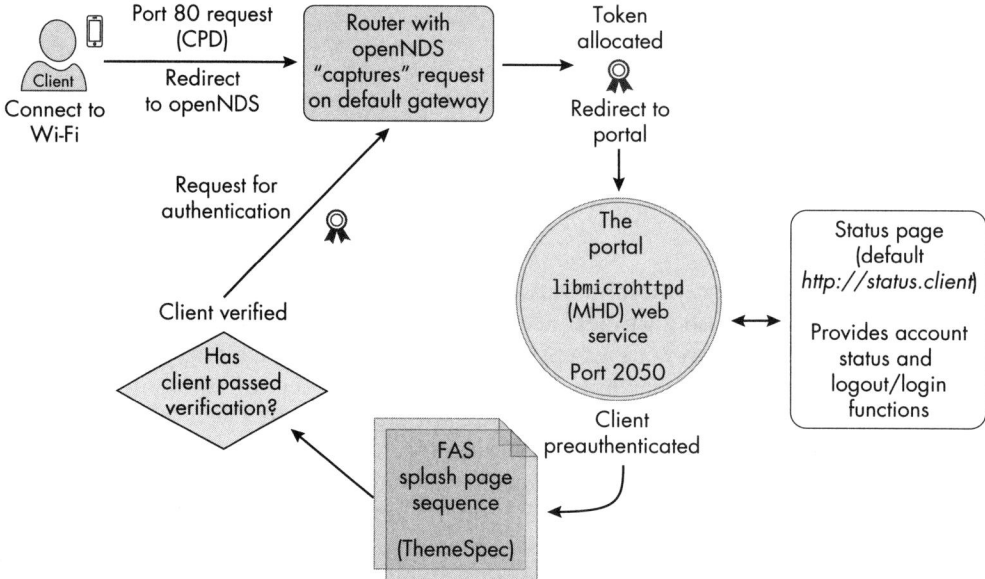

Figure 4-2: The openNDS captive portal client authentication process

When the default gateway receives an initial port 80 request, openNDS captures it, records the identity of the client device, and creates a unique token for the device. It then redirects the client's browser to the portal component of openNDS.

WHAT IS CAPTIVE PORTAL DETECTION?

All modern mobile devices, most desktop operating systems, and most web browsers have a CPD process that automatically issues a port 80 request when connecting to a network. The request is typically made to a vendor-specific URL, which the device uses to determine whether unrestricted internet access is available. Some common URLs configured for this purpose include:

- *http://captive.apple.com/hotspot-detect.html*
- *http://connectivitycheck.gstatic.com/generate_204*
- *http://detectportal.firefox.com/success.txt*

It's important to note that CPD is designed primarily for mobile devices to detect the presence of a captive portal and trigger the login page, without relying on insecure techniques like redirecting HTTPS traffic on port 443, for example, which would break SSL/TLS security.

The vast majority of devices connecting to captive portals are mobile devices. In typical guest Wi-Fi scenarios, a mobile client connects, stays online for a while, then leaves the coverage area. For this reason, most captive portals (including openNDS) have a session duration limit.

If a previously logged-in device returns to the portal's coverage area, it will recognize the known SSID and trigger the CPD process again, testing for an internet connection in the usual way. The connection remains open during the session limit defined by the portal. If the session has expired, the splash page will be displayed again.

The portal itself is a minimal web server that knows how to communicate with openNDS. It serves the splash page sequence to the client's browser. Until this sequence is completed, the client device is in a state known as *preauthentication*. During this phase, a user may be granted limited access to external services that are defined by the portal. This is commonly referred to as a *walled garden*.

The Splash Page Sequence

openNDS comes prepackaged with numerous splash page sequences that are easy to customize. Users are always expected to complete a certain action on the splash page. At the most basic level, they might be presented with the familiar Click to Continue page. You'll implement this simple version first before proceeding to a more advanced portal configuration.

The advanced portal setup uses a forward authentication service (FAS), which can be configured to use the web server embedded in openNDS, a separate web server installed on the openNDS router, a server that resides on the local network, or even an internet-hosted one. This allows you to create a highly customized and powerful captive portal, implemented in whichever programming language you prefer (such as Node.js, PHP, or Python), perhaps with a database backend or other components.

Once the user completes the required splash page actions, they are redirected from the micro web service back to openNDS.

Security Measures

For security reasons, openNDS expects to receive the same valid token it allocated when the client issued its initial port 80 request. If the token received is valid, openNDS authenticates the client device, allowing access to the internet. openNDS uses several methods to ensure this verification phase cannot be bypassed.

In the dynamic captive portal implementation, strong encryption provided by OpenSSL is used to securely encode the query string forwarded to the authentication service. As part of this setup, you'll use a system tool to generate a strong, random pre-shared key (PSK) to facilitate encryption and decryption of the data exchanged via HTTP.

In addition to these security measures, openNDS supports various post-authentication extensions. One of these is *BinAuth*, a script that allows you to override the standard client authentication flow if needed. By default, BinAuth is used to create a local log of authenticated clients.

Creating the Access Point

The first step is creating a routed wireless access point. For a basic captive portal, you can use either the NetworkManager method or the RaspAP Docker method, as described in "Software Components" on page 54. Alternatively, if you'd like to explore a more advanced captive portal setup, follow the steps in "Using the RaspAP Quick Installer" on page 61.

Before proceeding to the portal implementations, confirm that your access point is working as expected by connecting one or more clients to it. You can leave the service running while you complete the following steps.

Prerequisites

The prerequisites described here are common to both the basic and advanced captive portals. The *libmicrohttpd* library (abbreviated *MHD*) is a dependency of openNDS, so you'll compile and install it in this step. This component provides the minimal built-in web server used to serve the splash pages. For compatibility reasons, a specific version of this library is required. Download the archive to your home directory, then unpack it and change to the new directory:

```
$ cd $HOME
$ wget https://ftp.gnu.org/gnu/libmicrohttpd/libmicrohttpd-0.9.71.tar.gz
$ tar -xf libmicrohttpd-0.9.71.tar.gz
$ cd libmicrohttpd-0.9.71
```

The MHD library is written in the C programming language. With the source unpacked, you can configure and compile it by invoking the GNU make utility:

```
$ ./configure --disable-https
$ make
$ sudo rm /usr/local/lib/libmicrohttpd
$ sudo make install
$ sudo rm /etc/ld.so.cache
$ sudo ldconfig -v
```

The make command determines which pieces of a software program need to be compiled from its source. By default, the command looks for a makefile that describes the relationships between the files that make up a program. As MHD is a relatively compact library, the build and installation should take only a few moments.

You also need to install nslookup for openNDS. This is provided by the bind9-dnsutils package:

```
$ sudo apt install -y bind9-dnsutils
```

Installing openNDS

You're now ready to install openNDS. You can obtain the latest release version from *https://github.com/openNDS/openNDS/releases*. At the time of writing, this was v10.3.1; if a newer release is available, substitute that in the commands shown here.

Compile and install openNDS, and enable it so that it starts automatically at boot:

```
$ cd ~/
$ wget https://codeload.github.com/opennds/opennds/tar.gz/v10.3.1
$ tar -xf v10.3.1
$ cd openNDS-10.3.1
$ make
$ sudo make install
$ sudo systemctl enable opennds
```

You can start, restart, stop, or disable the service with the following commands:

```
$ sudo systemctl start opennds
$ sudo systemctl restart opennds
$ sudo systemctl stop opennds
$ sudo systemctl disable opennds
```

For now, leave it stopped. The next steps are important, so be sure to follow them closely; skipping them may result in a nonfunctional portal.

Configuring the Router

openNDS is designed to run on a device configured as an IPv4 router. By definition, a router will have two or more interfaces: at least one connecting to the wide area network (WAN), or source of internet connectivity, and one or more connecting to the local area network (LAN). Each LAN interface also acts as the default IP gateway for its LAN, usually serving IP addresses to client devices by using DHCP.

A *default gateway*, or *default route*, is a special routing entry that tells a device where to send network traffic when no specific route exists for the destination IP address. All routes configured for a system are summarized in a *routing table*. You can view your system's routing table by using the following command (your output will look different):

```
$ ip route
default via 192.168.1.254 dev eth0 proto dhcp src 192.168.1.49 metric 1002
10.3.141.0/24 dev wlan0 proto dhcp scope link src 10.3.141.1 metric 3003
192.168.1.0/24 dev eth0 proto dhcp scope link src 192.168.1.49 metric 1002
```

Notice that the eth0 interface has a default route configured. Metric values represent the priority associated with each route; lower metrics indicate preferred routes. The Linux kernel assigns default metric values when interfaces come online and will usually automatically select the best route based on these values.

openNDS will manage one or more of the router's interfaces. For OpenWrt routers, this is typically br-lan, the interface that bridges the wireless and wired LANs. In this case, you've configured a wireless interface (wlan0) for use as an access point. When the access point is brought up, the kernel may assign a default route to this interface so the system can direct network traffic through it to client devices. The following routing table excerpt shows an example wlan0 entry:

```
default via 10.3.141.1 dev wlan0 src 10.3.141.1 metric 3003
```

At startup, openNDS runs a check on the router in the background. If openNDS detects an improper routing configuration, it displays the message "All Upstream gateway(s) are offline or not connected." If wlan0 is configured as a default gateway, openNDS won't be able to manage it. Fortunately, this is easily resolved by simply removing the default route. Using the previous example, you can do this with:

```
$ sudo ip route del default via 10.3.141.1
```

You can execute ip route again to view the updated routing table. When no default route is configured for wlan0, openNDS uses nftables rules to direct network traffic between interfaces.

Checking Network Ports

A device's CPD process automatically issues a port 80 request upon connecting to a network. openNDS is configured to block everything except for HTTP requests on this port. If you're running a web server such as Lighttpd on the portal host, it will likely conflict with openNDS, and the portal splash pages won't be displayed.

Stop the server process by executing the following command:

```
$ sudo systemctl stop lighttpd.service
```

If you're using a different web server, such as nginx or Apache, substitute the appropriate service name in this command. Note that this change is temporary and will be effective only until your system is rebooted. If you aren't planning to complete the dynamic captive portal part of this recipe, you can disable the service permanently using:

```
$ sudo systemctl disable lighttpd.service
```

Configuring DNS

Captive portals use an access control mechanism that redirects DNS queries to a local DNS server. This ensures that when an unauthenticated client attempts to visit a web domain, the DNS query is intercepted and redirected to a fully qualified domain name (FQDN) that can be resolved only by the portal's internal DNS server.

With openNDS, a client that's connected but not yet authorized will be redirected to a client user status page. In more technical terms, this corresponds to an HTTP 511 "Network Authentication Required" response, as defined by RFC 6585. openNDS uses *http://status.client* as the default URL for this page.

Dnsmasq is a component of many Linux-based access points that combines the functionality of a DNS forwarder, DHCP server, and DHCP relay. One of Dnsmasq's configuration settings, `dhcp-option=6`, tells DHCP clients which DNS servers to use. For example, the setting

```
dhcp-option=6,9.9.9.9,1.1.1.1
```

instructs clients to use DNS servers provided by Quad9 and Cloudflare, respectively. While perfectly acceptable for a typical access point, this effectively short-circuits a captive portal's access control by preventing it from responding to DNS queries. For this reason, openNDS is explicit about avoiding the use of external DNS servers.

RaspAP uses this directive as part of its default configuration, as do many other access points. To configure it to work with openNDS, you'll need to edit the Dnsmasq configuration file for the wireless interface. Open the file in your editor with

```
$ sudo nano /etc/dnsmasq.d/090_wlan0.conf
```

and locate this section:

```
# RaspAP wlan0 configuration for wired (ethernet) AP mode
interface=wlan0
domain-needed
dhcp-range=10.3.141.50,10.3.141.254,255.255.255.0,12h
dhcp-option=6,9.9.9.9,1.1.1.1
```

Remove or comment out the `dhcp-option` line, save the file, and exit your editor. Then restart the service with:

```
$ sudo systemctl restart dnsmasq
```

This will ensure that the portal's local DNS server is able to capture clients' requests.

With your router, network ports, and DNS configured, you may now proceed with creating the captive portal.

Creating a Basic Captive Portal

The first portal implementation is a rudimentary one that makes use of pre-installed splash pages. While its functionality is limited, it's effective, quick to set up, and easy to customize. The steps you will follow here are directly transferable to the more advanced implementation in the following section. Even if you're keen to skip straight to the dynamic setup, I recommend starting here to validate the core functionality of openNDS on your system.

Configuring openNDS

In this section, you'll create a baseline setup by modifying the openNDS configuration. OpenWrt uses the Unified Configuration Interface (UCI) to define system settings. UCI configuration files consist of one or more `config` statements, called *sections*, each containing one or more `option` statements defining the actual values. Lines beginning with # are comments. The following is an example of a simple UCI configuration file:

```
config 'example'
    # A comment for the first section
    optionA    'string'      'some value'
    optionB    'boolean'     '1'
```

To begin, open the openNDS configuration file in your editor:

```
$ sudo nano /etc/config/opennds
```

The gatewayinterface option should be set to the interface your access point uses. By default, it's set to br-lan. Locate the section shown in the following listing, remove the # symbol at the start of the `option` statement, and replace br-lan with the name of your AP interface, such as wlan0. It should look like this:

```
    # GateWayInterface
    # Default br-lan
    --snip--
    option gatewayinterface 'wlan0'
```

Save the file and exit your editor. This is the only configuration change needed to enable the preinstalled splash pages provided by openNDS.

Starting openNDS

Next, start the openNDS service and check its status:

```
$ sudo systemctl start opennds.service
$ sudo systemctl status opennds.service
```

You should see output similar to the following:

```
opennds.service - openNDS Captive Portal
    Loaded: loaded (/etc/systemd/system/opennds.service; disabled; preset: enabled)
    Active: active (running) since Wed 2025-04-30 12:17:02 CEST; 10s ago
   Process: 1124512 ExecStart=/usr/bin/opennds -b (code=exited, status=0/SUCCESS)
  Main PID: 1124612 (opennds)
     Tasks: 2 (limit: 763)
       CPU: 12.044s
    CGroup: /system.slice/opennds.service
            1124612 /usr/bin/opennds -b

May 01 12:17:11 rpi3 opennds[1124612]: Preemptive authentication is enabled
May 01 12:17:12 rpi3 opennds[1124612]: Adding Serial Number suffix ...
May 01 12:17:12 rpi3 opennds[1124612]: Created web server on 10.3.141.1:2050
May 01 12:17:12 rpi3 opennds[1124612]: Maximum Html Page size is [ 10240 ] Bytes
May 01 12:17:12 rpi3 opennds[1124612]: Socket access at /run/ndsctl.sock
May 01 12:17:12 rpi3 opennds[1124612]: Click to Continue option is Enabled.
May 01 12:17:12 rpi3 opennds[1124612]: Preauth is Enabled - Overriding FAS configuration.
May 01 12:17:12 rpi3 opennds[1124612]: sha256sum provider is available
May 01 12:17:12 rpi3 opennds[1124612]: Forwarding Authentication is Enabled.
--snip--
```

There are several interesting items here. For example, you can see that a web service is running at the IPv4 address 10.3.141.1 on port 2050 and that the Click to Continue option is enabled. We'll examine the relevant openNDS internals in more detail in the next section.

A WORD ON CAPTIVE PORTAL IDENTIFICATION

Captive portal identification (CPI) is an alternative method for triggering a portal's splash page. To understand how it differs, it helps to look more closely at CPD. The CPD process is fundamentally client driven, with the user's device sending the initial port 80 HTTP request to check for internet access. Sometimes called a *canary test*, this has evolved to be a reliable de facto standard.

CPI, by contrast, is router driven. The router uses DHCP to inform the client that the network is behind a captive portal and that it will need to satisfy the portal's conditions to get internet access. The client is then served the same splash page sequence as with CPD, which it can use to complete authentication.

CPI is an evolving standard, driven by RFCs 8910 and 8908 and maintained by the Internet Engineering Task Force (IETF). As of this writing, full support by mobile device vendors is far from universal. Nevertheless, CPI shows great potential as a viable future standard for connecting to captive portals.

Connecting a Client

With the openNDS service running, you're ready to connect a client device to the wireless network you created. The CPD process will display the default ThemeSpec splash page. This HTML splash page sequence typically consists of three steps:

1. The user is presented with a "Click to Continue" dialog.
2. Next, they are asked to accept the portal's ToS.
3. Depending on the client device's CPD implementation, a third page may be displayed confirming that the user now has internet access.

This entire sequence is served by the built-in MHD web service compiled with openNDS. Click or tap **Continue** to dismiss the final page. At this stage, the client device is authenticated and granted access to the internet. As mentioned earlier, openNDS accomplishes this by manipulating nftables rules.

Behind the scenes, this event is recorded by the system journal like so:

```
rpi3 opennds[1416]: Adding 10.3.141.248 02:9d:ae:cb:29:6f token 4e8d88bd to client list
rpi3 opennds[1416]: Authenticating 10.3.141.248 02:9d:ae:cb:29:6f
```

You can find more detailed status information with:

```
$ sudo ndsctl status
==================
openNDS Status
====
Version: 10.3.0
Uptime: 9m 49s
Gateway Name: [ openNDS Node:b827eb01d76a  ]
Debug Level: [ 1 ]
Gateway FQDN: [ status.client ]
Managed interface: wlan0
Upstream gateway(s) [ online:192.168.1.254,eth0  ]
MHD Server [ version 0.9.71 ] listening on: http://10.3.141.1:2050
Maximum Html Page size is [ 10240 ] Bytes
Preemptive Authentication is Enabled
Binauth Script: /usr/lib/opennds/binauth_log.sh
ThemeSpec Core Library: /usr/lib/opennds/libopennds.sh
FAS: Secure Level 1, URL: http://status.client:2050/opennds_preauth/
--snip--
```

In the latter portion of this status output, you'll find some details about the client device you authenticated:

```
Client authentications since start: 1
Current clients: 1
```

```
Client 0
  Client Type: cpd_can
  IP: 10.3.141.248 MAC: 02:9d:ae:cb:29:6f
  Last Activity: Thu May 01 08:48:38 2025 (3m 1s ago)
  Session Start: Thu May 01 08:38:19 2025 (13m 20s ago)
  Session End:   Fri May 02 08:38:19 2025 (23h 46m 40s left)
  Token: 4e8d88bd
  State: Authenticated
  Download Rate Limit Threshold: 1024 kb/s
  Download Packet Rate Limit: 24730 packets/min
  Download Bucket Size: 250 packets
  Upload Rate Limit Threshold: 1024 kb/s
  Upload Packet Rate Limit: 148383 packets/min
  Upload Bucket Size: 250 packets
  Download quota: not set
  Upload quota: not set
  Download this session: 55 kB; Session average: 0.57 kb/s
  Upload this session: 13 kB; Session average: 0.14 kb/s
--snip--
```

Notice that the client's state is indicated as Authenticated, and its IPv4 address, MAC address, and token (4e8d88bd) are logged. In addition, some useful metrics are reported, such as upload and download rate limits, quotas, and total bytes transferred in this session. I'll revisit these in greater detail in "Setting Quotas" on page 114.

The ndsctl utility is capable of performing many administrative actions for your portal. To obtain some usage notes, simply execute ndsctl -h.

Customizing the Basic Portal

If the default captive portal pages are not to your liking, you can modify them by editing the files located in */etc/opennds/htdocs*. Here, you'll find the system's *.css* file and default splash page image. Be aware, however, that many client device CPD implementations enforce strict security measures. The following are generally prohibited in portal splash pages:

- Using <a href="..."> links
- Making references to external resources, including *.css* and *.js* files
- Executing JavaScript

As a result, all splash page resources must be local to the portal server. Also bear in mind that once the user is authenticated, many client browsers will automatically close the portal window.

Creating a Voucher System

It's common at cafés and elsewhere to give customers a voucher that they can use to access the Wi-Fi network. A community extension to the default

ThemeSpec implements exactly this: a simple voucher-based authentication system. The vouchers themselves can be generated either manually or programmatically. The extension was originally created for OpenWrt systems, but with a simple modification, it works just as well on standard Linux systems.

The required files should already be present in the archive you downloaded when installing the prerequisites for this recipe. You can install these files with the following commands (substituting your openNDS directory name if it's different):

```
$ cd ~/openNDS-10.3.1
$ sudo cp community/themespec/theme_voucher/theme_voucher.sh /usr/lib/opennds
$ sudo cp community/themespec/theme_voucher/vouchers.txt /usr/lib/opennds
```

If you don't have this archive in your home directory, you can clone the openNDS GitHub repository like so:

```
$ cd $HOME
$ git clone https://github.com/openNDS/openNDS.git
$ cd openNDS
```

Then copy the files to the openNDS system directory by using the commands shown previously.

Next, execute the following command to activate the voucher shell script:

```
$ sudo chmod 744 /usr/lib/opennds/theme_voucher.sh
```

You'll need to make a small change to the script. Open the file in your editor with

```
$ sudo nano /usr/lib/opennds/theme_voucher.sh
```

and scroll to the end. Uncomment the last two lines and set the following default values:

```
# Override the defaults to a custom location eg a mounted USB stick.
mountpoint="/usr/lib/opennds"
logdir="$mountpoint/"
```

This points the script to the location of your voucher roll, containing the example vouchers. Save the file and exit your editor.

Now, enable the voucher extension by editing the openNDS configuration. Open the configuration file in your editor by running:

```
$ sudo nano /etc/config/opennds
```

Locate the following option lines, uncomment them, and change the values to match what's shown here:

```
option login_option_enabled '3'
option themespec_path='/usr/lib/opennds/theme_voucher.sh'
```

Then restart the service to enable the voucher extension:

```
$ sudo systemctl restart opennds
```

Finally, connect a client device to your access point. You'll notice that the portal now redirects the client to a new splash page. As shown in Figure 4-3, this page requires the user to accept the ToS and provide a valid voucher number.

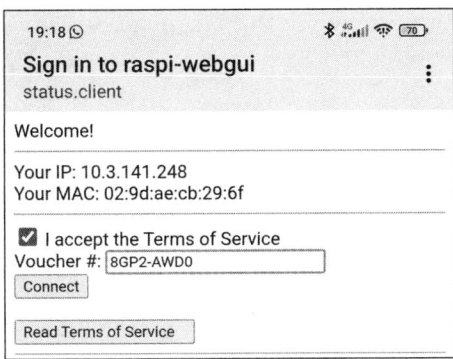

Figure 4-3: The openNDS voucher extension

Enter a voucher code from the example *vouchers.txt* file you copied, then click or tap **Connect**.

Each line in the *vouchers.txt* file contains a valid voucher code. You can manually edit this file to add or remove codes, but the extension also includes a simple voucher roll generator written in Python. To use this, copy it from the source directory to the openNDS system directory:

```
$ cd ~/openNDS-10.3.1/
$ sudo cp community/themespec/theme_voucher/voucher_generator.py \
    /usr/lib/opennds
```

You can then execute the script using the following commands (note that this will overwrite the existing *vouchers.txt* file in this directory):

```
$ cd /usr/lib/opennds
$ sudo python3 voucher_generator.py
```

The script will create a roll of 200 vouchers with fixed transfer rates and a default validity period of 24 hours.

This concludes the basic captive portal implementation with openNDS. Next, you'll create a more advanced portal that uses forward authentication.

Creating a Dynamic Captive Portal

As you saw in the preceding section, the basic "zero configuration" captive portal provided by openNDS offers fairly rich functionality. For many users, this may be entirely sufficient. However, openNDS also gives you the ability to create a more advanced portal tailored to your specific needs. In this section, you'll implement a dynamic splash page with features provided by a server-side scripting language.

The key piece behind this process is the forward authentication service. With the FAS model, client requests are forwarded to a third-party service for authentication. This allows for greater flexibility, including custom security policies, network zones, and various forms of post-processing. A FAS can be implemented in any language capable of generating dynamic web content, but PHP is commonly used on routers. openNDS includes a set of preinstalled FAS handlers written in this language, and for simplicity, we'll use those in the following sections.

Setting Up openNDS

You may now proceed by (re)configuring your captive portal. All the relevant openNDS settings are contained in the openNDS configuration file. Open this file in your editor by running:

```
$ sudo nano /etc/config/opennds
```

Locate and uncomment the following lines, and set the values as shown here:

```
option gatewayinterface 'wlan0'
option fasport '2080'
option faspath '/fas/fas-aes.php'
option fas_secure_enabled '2'
option list users_to_router 'allow tcp port 2080'
```

To encrypt the query string sent to the FAS, openNDS uses a unique key phrase called the faskey. If you leave the faskey value undefined, a strong key will be generated automatically and appended to the configuration when the openNDS service is (re)started. For security reasons, it's recommended to let openNDS generate a random faskey for you. I'll explain how to use this key in the next section.

In most cases, wlan0 should correspond to the interface of your access point. If your AP is running on a different interface, be sure to set this value accordingly. As of this writing, the last option, list users_to_router, is required. It may not be needed in a future release of openNDS, but there's no harm in defining it.

If you followed the steps in "Creating a Voucher System" on page 103 while setting up the basic portal, make sure to revert the changes you made to the openNDS configuration in that section before proceeding. If you've experimented with the login_option_enabled option, you'll also need to comment that out or set it to 0. Finally, save the file and exit your editor.

In the next section, you'll create a service to handle the forwarded authentication requests.

Implementing Forward Authentication

At this stage, you're ready to create a FAS. This implementation differs from the basic captive portal setup in several ways, notably in terms of how authentication requests are handled. The handler can reside remotely on the internet, on a LAN, or on the openNDS host itself. For this reason, encryption is used to secure user authentication tokens when forwarding them to the web service. If you're using RaspAP, you may use its preinstalled web service, Lighttpd. Alternatives are discussed in the next section.

Forward authentication is a client credential verification process. If the verification is successful, the FAS sends a request to openNDS to grant the client internet access. The fas_secure_enabled '2' configuration option you specified earlier instructs openNDS to enforce FAS with HTTP. In this scheme, several key pieces of information related to the client request are encrypted in a query string by using the faskey you've defined. The query string also contains a randomly generated initialization vector (IV) used by the FAS for decryption.

This is a common encryption approach used in many implementations, including Wi-Fi handshakes (see "Making a Connection" on page 33), where a pre-shared key is used on both ends of an encrypted channel. In this case, the FAS needs both the IV and the pre-shared faskey to decrypt the query string.

As mentioned in the previous section, openNDS will generate a strong faskey for you. To obtain this key, restart the openNDS service:

```
$ sudo systemctl restart opennds.service
```

The autogenerated faskey will be appended to the openNDS configuration file. Dump the contents of this file to the terminal with:

```
$ sudo cat etc/config/opennds
```

Locate and copy the faskey value to your clipboard for the next step.

The example FAS level 2 PHP script *fas-aes.php* is stored in the */etc/opennds* directory and is also included in the source code. Open this file in your editor with

```
$ sudo nano /etc/opennds/fas-aes.php
```

and locate the entry shown here:

```
// The pre-shared key "faskey" (this must be the same as in the openNDS
// config):
$key="49a1dfcc09a1c9e8eb20506410650137925ec9ddc600677c468f76a97167e31e";
```

Note that the value shown here is just a placeholder; the PHP key value must correspond to the faskey option you've copied from the openNDS configuration.

Before proceeding to the next step, check the openNDS status:

```
$ sudo systemctl status opennds.service
```

The status output should indicate that forward authentication is enabled with SSL. As described earlier, to get more detailed information about open-NDS's state, you can use ndsctl. The output should confirm that your FAS configuration is active, with the service web endpoint indicated:

```
$ sudo ndsctl status
--snip--
FAS: Secure Level 2, URL: http://10.3.141.1:2080/captive/fas-aes.php
```

In its current state, your system won't be able to respond to requests on this URL. You'll address this in the next steps.

Configuring the Web Service

If you've set up RaspAP by using either the Docker image or the Quick installer method, as described in "Using RaspAP" on page 56, you should already have a web service provided by Lighttpd. In this event, you may proceed to "Using Lighttpd with Stand-Alone RaspAP" on page 110. If you're hosting an access point via another method or wish to handle forward authentication on a separate server, proceed with the instructions in the next section.

WEB SERVER COMPATIBILITY

openNDS FAS has been tested with popular web servers including Lighttpd, nginx, Apache, and MHD. In addition to the web server, you'll need a way to process server-side scripts that handle incoming HTTP requests. This can be done using PHP, Python, Perl, or another scripting language. RaspAP uses PHP-CGI; however, the PHP FastCGI Process Manager (PHP-FPM) will work equally well for this application.

Installing Lighttpd

Before installing Lighttpd and PHP on your system, you can check the current PHP installation candidate for your OS by running:

```
$ apt policy php-cgi
```

At the time of writing, the latest PHP release version is 8.2. Substitute the release version reported by apt, if different, and execute the following commands:

```
$ sudo apt update
$ sudo apt install lighttpd php8.2-cgi
```

Next, enable PHP for Lighttpd, then restart the service for the settings to take effect:

```
$ sudo lighttpd-enable-mod fastcgi-php
$ sudo systemctl enable lighttpd.service
$ sudo service lighttpd force-reload
$ sudo systemctl restart lighttpd.service
```

On most Linux distributions, the PHP package includes the OpenSSL module by default. This is a requirement for the FAS to decrypt the query strings passed to it. You can verify its presence by running PHP's CLI like so:

```
$ php -i | grep -i openssl

OpenSSL support => enabled
OpenSSL Library Version => OpenSSL 3.0.15 3 Sep 2024
--snip--
```

With Lighttpd and PHP installed, deploy the FAS handler to your web server by executing the following commands:

```
$ sudo mkdir -p /var/www/html/fas
$ sudo cp /etc/opennds/fas-aes.php /var/www/html/fas
```

Now, open Lighttpd's configuration file in your editor:

```
$ sudo nano /etc/lighttpd/lighttpd.conf
```

Locate the server.port setting and modify it as shown here:

```
server.username         = "www-data"
server.groupname        = "www-data"
server.port             = 2080
```

This step is required because openNDS intercepts requests on the default port 80 with its own web service. Save the file and exit your editor, then restart the Lighttpd service:

```
$ sudo systemctl restart lighttpd.service
```

At this stage, it can be useful to see which Linux processes are actively listening on the network ports you've defined. Invoke the netstat utility and take a look at the output, which should look something like this:

```
$ sudo netstat -tulpn | grep 0.0.0.0:20
tcp       0       0 0.0.0.0:2050      0.0.0.0:      LISTEN      6836/opennds
tcp       0       0 0.0.0.0:2080      0.0.0.0:      LISTEN      949/lighttpd
```

Here, you can see that the opennds process is listening on the local port 2050, while lighttpd is listening on port 2080. In this case, the 0.0.0.0 is a wildcard value that simply indicates that each service is listening on all available network interfaces.

With your web service now configured as a FAS for openNDS, proceed to "Connecting a Client Device" on page 112.

Using Lighttpd with Stand-Alone RaspAP

This section details using Lighttpd with a stand-alone non-Dockerized RaspAP installation. Begin by verifying that Lighttpd is up and running on your system. You can do this by either opening RaspAP's web interface in your browser or checking Lighttpd's status:

```
$ sudo systemctl status lighttpd.service
```

RaspAP's installer adds the latest PHP package to your system. On most Linux distributions, the PHP package includes the OpenSSL module by default. This is a requirement for the FAS to decrypt the query strings it receives. You can verify its presence by executing this command:

```
$ php -i | grep -i openssl
```

Once you're satisfied that the web service is active and PHP's OpenSSL module is present, deploy the FAS PHP handler to your web server:

```
$ sudo mkdir -p /var/www/html/fas
$ sudo cp /etc/opennds/fas-aes.php /var/www/html/fas
```

By default, RaspAP is installed in Lighttpd's web root. If you've opted for a custom install point, be sure to specify that in these commands instead.

Next, you'll need to modify RaspAP's routing rules for Lighttpd. Open the configuration file in your editor:

```
$ sudo nano /etc/lighttpd/conf-available/50-raspap-router.conf
```

Find this line and modify it by appending |fas after |config, as shown here:

```
$HTTP["url"] =~ "^/(?!(dist|app|ajax|config|fas)).}" {
    url.rewrite-once = ( "^/(.\emph{?})(\?.+)?$"=>"/index.php/$1$2" )
    server.error-handler-404 = "/index.php"
}
```

This instructs Lighttpd to exclude files located in the *fas* directory from RaspAP's page routing functions.

Now you need to change the default port the Lighttpd web service listens on (80). For the FAS to work correctly, openNDS needs to intercept requests on port 80, encrypt them, and then forward them to Lighttpd. The trick here is to configure your web server to listen on the fasport value you defined in the openNDS configuration file. RaspAP provides an easy way to do this: On the **System ▶Advanced** tab, set the **Web Server Port** value to **2080** and choose **Save Settings** and then **Restart Lighttpd**, as illustrated in Figure 4-4.

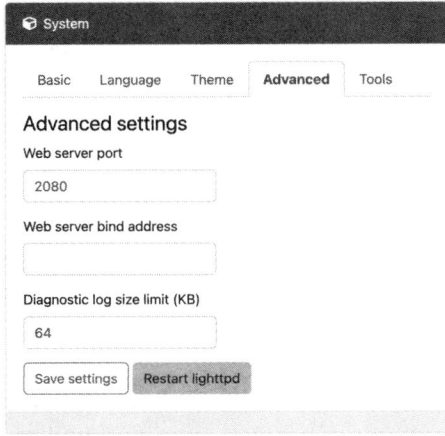

Figure 4-4: Setting a custom web server port in RaspAP

When you restart Lighttpd, the browser may time out because of the port change. Access the web UI at its new address by appending *:2080* to the hostname or IP (for example, *http://raspberrypi.local:2080*).

Alternatively, you can manually edit Lighttpd's configuration. Open the configuration file in your editor with:

```
$ sudo nano /etc/lighttpd/lighttpd.conf
```

Locate the following lines, and change the server.port value to 2080, as shown here:

```
server.username       = "www-data"
server.groupname      = "www-data"
server.port           = 2080
```

Save the file and exit your editor, then restart the Lighttpd service:

```
$ sudo systemctl restart lighttpd.service
```

As a final step, you'll need to disable authentication for RaspAP's web interface. This is required because openNDS cannot circumvent the authentication enforced by RaspAP; however, disabling authentication is clearly a security risk, as it means authenticated portal clients will be able to access and administer RaspAP. Luckily, this is an issue only if you're hosting openNDS, RaspAP, and the FAS on the same server. That setup should be used only for testing on your own network. Otherwise, a simple solution is to configure the FAS on a separate server, either on your local network or elsewhere.

To disable authentication, change to Lighttpd's web root and open the RaspAP configuration file in your editor:

```
$ cd /var/www/html
$ sudo nano config/config.php
```

This is the default installation location for RaspAP. If you've opted for a custom install point, substitute it here. In the config file, locate the following setting and change it to `false`, as shown here:

```
// Enable basic authentication for the web admin.
define('RASPI_AUTH_ENABLED', false);
```

For an additional measure of security, you can optionally place RaspAP into *monitor mode*. In this mode, the web interface remains accessible, but none of its administrative functions are available. Enable monitor mode by locating the following setting and changing it to `true`:

```
define('RASPI_MONITOR_ENABLED', true);
```

Save the file and exit your editor. You've now completed the configuration of Lighttpd to serve as a FAS for openNDS.

Connecting a Client Device

With the openNDS and FAS configuration work done, proceed by connecting a client device to your wireless access point. The CPD process on the client should identify the presence of the portal and indicate that additional authentication is needed. Behind the scenes, several events occur in sequence:

1. openNDS creates a random initialization vector, encrypts it using the AES-256-CBC cipher and the pre-shared key (the `faskey` you defined earlier), then sends the encrypted query string to the FAS.

2. The FAS decrypts the query string by using PHP's OpenSSL library.

3. The PHP handler generates a dynamic captive portal splash page. Figure 4-5 shows an example.

4. After the user provides some basic details, the client is successfully verified.

5. The FAS sends the return hash ID (`rhid`) to openNDS, notifying it that the client is authenticated.

6. openNDS permits the client device to access the internet.

7. Client data is captured and logged to the filesystem.

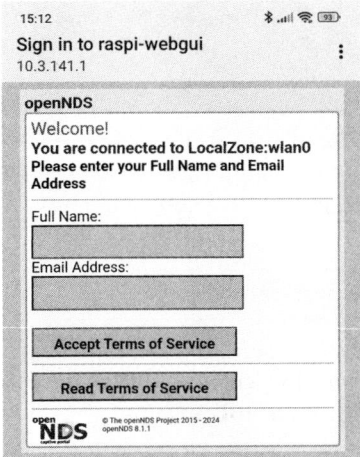

Figure 4-5: The openNDS dynamic landing page

The PHP file *fas-aes.php* handles decrypting the client authentication token and capturing basic user data. By default, this data is written to */run/ndslog/ndslog.log*, but you can modify the PHP handler to store it in a database or perform other functions instead. With the configuration you've created here, openNDS can serve as the engine for a sophisticated captive portal system. Furthermore, the openNDS forward authentication service can be hosted on a remote server and configured to respond to any number of captive portals.

Managing Clients

After authenticating one or more portal clients, you can manage them from the terminal using the ndsctl utility. Begin by executing the following command:

```
$ sudo ndsctl json
{
  "client_list_length":"1",
  "clients":{
    "02:9d:ae:cb:29:6f":{
      "gatewayname":"openNDS",
      "version":"8.1.1",
      "mac":"02:9d:ae:cb:29:6f",
      "ip":"10.3.141.248",
      "clientif":"",
      "session_start":"1714305669",
      "session_end":"null",
      "last_active":"1714305187",
      "token":"39f04072",
      "state":"Authenticated",
      --snip--
```

```
      }
    }
  }
}
```

In this example output, a list of portal clients is conveniently provided in JSON format. You can administer a client directly using its IP address, MAC address, or token value. For example, to change a client's session timeout to 60 minutes, run:

```
$ sudo ndsctl auth 10.3.141.248 sessiontimeout 60
```

For testing purposes, it may be useful to deauthenticate a client before their session expires. You can do this with the following command (substituting in a valid MAC or IP address or token value):

```
$ sudo ndsctl deauth 39f04072
Client 39f04072 deauthenticated.
```

Likewise, you can allow, trust, disallow, or block a given MAC address by using the corresponding commands. Execute ndsctl -h for details.

In the next section, I'll examine some ways you can configure data quotas with openNDS, introduce leaky buckets, and show you how to experiment with traffic-shaping techniques.

Setting Quotas

Captive portals use various methods to manage clients' bandwidth usage, with the aim of streamlining service delivery to the greatest extent possible. To this end, openNDS has built-in rate and volume quota options. In this context, a client's *data rate* (aka a *data threshold*) refers to the transfer rate calculated using a moving average, in kilobits per second (Kbps). This allows clients to burst at their maximum possible rate, limiting them only if the moving average exceeds the specified upload or download limit. By contrast, *data volume quotas* define the total amount of data a client transfers during a session, expressed in kilobytes (KB).

These settings can be defined statically in the global configuration or dynamically by a FAS, down to the individual client level. You can fine-tune these values according to the anticipated bandwidth demands on your portal.

Global Quota Settings

Global data volume quotas are defined in the openNDS configuration file. If a client exceeds the global quota, they will be deauthenticated. To continue, the client must reauthenticate with the portal.

To enable this setting, open the configuration file in your editor with

```
$ sudo nano /etc/config/opennds
```

and locate, uncomment, and define the following options:

```
# If the client data quota exceeds the value set here, the client will be forced out
# Values are in kB
# If set to 0, there is no limit
# Integer values only
option uploadquota '0'
option downloadquota '0'
```

You can also define global data rate quotas in the configuration file by uncommenting and setting these options:

```
option uploadrate '0'
option downloadrate '0'
--snip--
# The moving average window size is equal to ratecheckwindow times checkinterval
# Default 2
option ratecheckwindow '2'
```

To impose limits on global data volume and transfer rates, set the uploadquota, downloadquota, uploadrate, and downloadrate options to values other than 0. Be sure to consider the estimated number of concurrent clients and the available bandwidth when determining appropriate limits.

In addition, recent releases of openNDS include a form of network packet queuing that implements what's known as the *leaky bucket algorithm*. This allows you to define upload and download bucket ratios.

THE LEAKY BUCKET EXPLAINED

The *leaky bucket algorithm* is a mechanism that helps regulate the rate at which packets are transmitted over a network. It defines what's known as a network *queue buffer* that stores a fixed amount of data. The algorithm works by way of an analogy. Imagine a bucket with a fixed capacity that has a small hole at the bottom. Water (data packets) is poured into the top of the bucket at an irregular rate. Because of the hole, water drips out at a constant rate. In this way, "bursty" traffic is converted into smooth, fixed-rate traffic.

If the incoming flow of water (packets) exceeds the rate at which the bucket can leak, the bucket overflows: This is more than the network can handle, and the excess packets are dropped.

With this option, you define a *dynamic bucket size*, or *queue length* (in packets), that's used to buffer upload and download traffic rates. This gives clients an initial unrestricted interval during which they can burst at maximum speed. Returning to the example of a café environment, visitors will typically be using mobile devices for tasks like downloading email, using social media, or uploading photos. This sort of traffic tends to be "bursty" rather than continuous. In these scenarios, bucket ratios help enforce a fair usage policy, applying rate limiting only when a client exceeds the configured download or upload volume.

To enable this setting, locate, uncomment, and define the following options in the configuration file:

```
# If the rate is set to 0, the Bucket Ratio setting has no meaning
# and no memory is consumed.
#
option upload_bucket_ratio '1'
option download_bucket_ratio '5'
```

These options are used in conjunction with `MaxDownloadBucketSize` and `MaxUploadBucketSize`. If you're implementing bucket ratios for openNDS, it's recommended to start with the default values, do some testing, and adjust the settings as needed.

Individual Quota Settings

You performed some basic client administration tasks in "Managing Clients" on page 113. Using the `ndsctl` utility, you can also define quotas on a per-client basis.

The `ndsctl auth` command lets you set maximum upload and download rates, as well as data quotas, for individual portal users. For example, the following command sets the client session timeout to 24 hours (1,440 minutes), the upload and download rates to 300 and 1,500Kbps, respectively, and the upload and download quotas to 500,000 and 1,000,000KB:

```
$ sudo ndsctl auth 10.3.141.248 1440 300 1500 500000 1000000
```

You can also establish individual client quotas in a FAS implementation, like the one described in "Creating a Dynamic Captive Portal" on page 105. In that implementation, you deployed what's known as FAS level 2. At this level, your FAS code can invoke `ndsctl` as shown previously, with quota values passed as arguments. Alternatively, you can send custom variables to the BinAuth script to handle quota values. There's no predefined method for doing this; it's up to individual portal owners to develop their own implementations.

For many portal owners, the functionality built into openNDS may be perfectly sufficient for their needs. As you've seen in this section, openNDS supports advanced client bandwidth management, including configuration of global and per-client data rate and volume quotas, bucket ratios, FAS integrations, and more. What's more, all of this is done without external dependencies—that is, without installing any additional packages.

In the next section, I'll introduce a related technique for managing bandwidth. You may not need additional traffic shaping for your openNDS portal, but the concepts presented are nonetheless useful and worth familiarizing yourself with.

Traffic Shaping

Traffic shaping, also known as *packet shaping*, is a way of managing bandwidth to regulate the flow of certain types of network packets. To achieve this, some form of queuing and scheduling of packets is typically implemented to smooth the packet output rate.

One method for traffic shaping involves *smart queue management (SQM)*, a catchall term that includes several related network scheduling technologies. SQM aims to independently control upload and download bandwidth on a per-IP connection basis. It also helps implement *quality of service (QoS)*, a technique used to prioritize traffic and enforce bitrates lower than the physical interface's capabilities. Most ISPs use traffic shaping or policing to enforce traffic contracts with their customers. It's possible to apply the same technology to your captive portal users, albeit on a more limited scale.

You can create an SQM configuration for openNDS by using the `sqm-scripts` project, which is available for most Linux distributions. To get started, download and compile the source, like so:

```
$ cd $HOME
$ git clone https://github.com/tohojo/sqm-scripts.git
$ cd sqm-scripts
$ make
$ sudo make install
```

With `sqm-scripts` installed, copy the default configuration to the interface you want to apply SQM to (in this case, `wlan0`), then open the configuration file in an editor:

```
$ sudo cp /etc/sqm/default.conf /etc/sqm/wlan0.iface.conf
$ sudo nano /etc/sqm/wlan0.iface.conf
```

The default configuration is shown here:

```
# Uplink and Downlink values are in kbps
UPLINK=1000
DOWNLINK=85000

# SQM recipe to use. For more information, see /usr/lib/sqm/.help
SCRIPT=piece_of_cake.qos
```

You can adjust the `UPLINK` and `DOWNLINK` values as needed, depending on your available bandwidth, the wireless mode configured for your access point, and the expected number of portal users. A good compromise might be a download rate from the internet of 5,000Kbps and an upload rate of 1,000Kbps. This would, for example, allow a user to stream a YouTube video while having minimal impact on other clients browsing the web or downloading their emails.

You'll notice that `sqm-scripts` also uses recipes. By default, a basic recipe called `piece_of_cake.qos` is defined. It's a good idea to start with this simple one and experiment with more complex recipes later, so leave this as the default for now. Finally, enable and start the sqm service for wlan0:

```
$ sudo systemctl enable sqm@wlan0
$ sudo systemctl start sqm@wlan0
```

You can then check its status with the following command. You should see output similar to what's shown here:

```
$ sudo systemctl status sqm@wlan0

 sqm@wlan0.service - SQM scripts for iface wlan0
     Loaded: loaded (/lib/systemd/system/sqm@.service; disabled; preset: enabled)
     Active: active (exited) since Sun 2025-04-27 14:42:10 CEST; 4s ago
    Process: 140200 ExecStart=/usr/lib/sqm/start-sqm (code=exited, status=0/SUCCESS)
   Main PID: 140200 (code=exited, status=0/SUCCESS)
        CPU: 493ms
--snip--
```

Connect one or more clients to your access point and test a variety of applications. Next, stop the sqm@wlan0 service and repeat the test. You may want to adjust the settings and experiment with other QoS recipes.

Troubleshooting

If your captive portal behaves unpredictably or fails to start, there are some simple ways to diagnose the problem. openNDS supports three levels of debug reporting to the system log. The default setting logs errors, warnings, notices, and emergencies. You can edit this option in the configuration file after opening it in your editor with **sudo nano /etc/config/opennds**:

```
# debuglevel
# Set Debug Level (0-3)
# Default: 1
--snip--
option debuglevel '3'
```

Here, the most verbose debuglevel '3' setting is specified. This will write a substantial volume of entries to the log, which can be extremely useful when troubleshooting. Save the file and exit your editor. You can now stop and then restart the openNDS service while following the system journal output, like so:

```
$ sudo systemctl stop opennds.service
$ sudo systemctl start opennds.service; journalctl -f
```

Monitor the log output and look for any key informational items, highlighted in yellow, or critical errors, which are indicated in red. In most cases, careful examination of the openNDS service log will point you in the right direction. In my experience, nearly all the issues I encountered were the result of a misconfiguration on my part. Thankfully, the documentation for openNDS is thorough and actively maintained at *https://opennds.read thedocs.io*.

It's also a good idea to develop the habit of periodically checking your portal's operational state with `sudo ndsctl status`.

openNDS is a sophisticated captive portal engine with many moving parts, each depending on your system being properly configured for compatibility. Misconfiguration of your router, DNS settings, IP routing, ports, or web service can prevent the portal from functioning correctly. The good news is that these problems are usually solvable. I've endeavored to cover the most common pitfalls in the prerequisites and configuration sections for each portal implementation. When in doubt, refer to these sections and double-check your system's settings.

Going Further

This chapter covered basic and advanced captive portal implementations in some depth. Even so, you should regard this as merely an introduction to what's possible with openNDS. One topic you might want to explore further is walled gardens, which can be configured for your clients in various ways. These are useful if, for example, you'd like to give preauthenticated clients access to a limited set of FQDNs.

The dynamic captive portal implementation focused on a FAS that used HTTP. If you wish to add HTTPS support, you can explore this option with FAS level 3 and its associated PHP script, *fas-aes-https.php*.

In "Setting Quotas" on page 114 and "Traffic Shaping" on page 117, we explored different ways to manage bandwidth for portal clients. Gathering empirical data to compare these methods or fine-tune their settings is a logical next step. Of the tools available for this, iPerf is ideally suited to the task. See "Evaluating Performance" on page 20 for details on how to use this with your captive portal.

For simplicity, the portals detailed in this chapter manage a single interface (`wlan0` is typical) for an 802.11 wireless network with one SSID. However, openNDS also has support for *network zones*, allowing it to operate over named coverage areas. For example, in the context of a mesh network, as discussed in Chapter 10, you can configure different zones for different mesh nodes or clusters of nodes, each handling authentication for its local coverage area. You may also be interested in exploring the related openNDS `mesh11sd` project, originally designed to leverage 802.11s mesh networking at captive portal venues. For details on this mesh integration project, visit its repo at *https://github.com/openNDS/mesh11sd*.

Wrapping Up

The recipe in this chapter focused on the inner workings of a popular captive portal implementation. It's unique among the recipes presented in this book in that it requires no special hardware beyond a Raspberry Pi model with onboard WLAN, making it an ideal entry point for exploring a frequently discussed (but often misunderstood) technology commonly associated with wireless networks.

In building the portal software, you've compiled C libraries, configured various services required by a wireless router, examined system journal output, and perhaps even modified some Python and PHP code. This project involved many interrelated software components, but I hope you've been able to see the forest for the trees and gained valuable insights into how these systems function.

5

BLUETOOTH AUDIO IN TWO WAYS

In the previous recipes, you explored practical applications in the 802.11 wireless and LoRa sub-gigahertz bands. But *The Wireless Cookbook* wouldn't be complete without a Bluetooth recipe! In this chapter, we'll turn our attention to the 2.4 GHz radio band used by Bluetooth and implement some extremely popular audio applications.

Audio in Linux is a broad topic; add Bluetooth and streaming to the mix, and you're likely to encounter heated discussions about which approach is superior. The wide array of possibilities can also lead some users into a state of audio paralysis. I'll endeavor to guide you through the Minotaur's labyrinth by focusing on clear, easy-to-follow steps.

Use Cases

In this recipe, you'll use your Raspberry Pi's Bluetooth connectivity to support one of two popular and distinctly different use cases related to Linux audio (or both, if you like). I'll also present a third use case that relies on Wi-Fi. There's no best approach here; the direction you choose will depend on your specific goals. With that said, read through the following descriptions and think about which project (or projects) most closely matches your interests:

1. Use your Pi to stream audio from the Linux command line to Bluetooth speakers. This is ideal if you want to stream internet radio, play an existing audio collection (*.mp3* files, for example), or access an online streaming service with a Linux terminal client. This recipe will demonstrate how to set up audio playback from each of these sources through a Bluetooth-enabled speaker. You will not only learn the fundamentals of wireless audio in Linux but also gain experience using the terminal to manage audio collections.

2. Turn your Pi into a Bluetooth audio receiver with high-fidelity output to existing wired speakers, headphones, or home stereo equipment. This use case is a good option if you have an audio setup you'd like to upgrade with high-quality digital streaming. We'll also explore digital-to-analog converter add-ons to take your audio experience to the next level.

3. Transform your Pi into a Spotify Connect receiver on your network. Of the three use cases, this one delivers the highest-quality streaming experience to your audio equipment, suitable for discerning audiophiles. While it doesn't rely on Bluetooth, it does utilize Wi-Fi connectivity for client devices on your network.

Each of these use cases relies on Bluetooth and, optionally, Wi-Fi to stream audio from your preferred source to one of several output devices. Your available hardware, budget, and personal taste will likely determine which project appeals most to you.

Chances are, you'll be able to create at least a basic implementation with materials you have on hand. If your experiments bear fruit, the content in this chapter will equip you with the knowledge, tools, and technologies you need to tailor a bespoke setup to your needs. I can't guarantee you'll discover wireless Linux audio nirvana, but I'm hopeful this recipe will point you in the right direction.

Hardware Required

Specific hardware requirements will vary depending upon which of the use cases you're interested in. Whichever one (or ones) you choose, the hardware components for this recipe are affordable and readily available from many online retailers. You may have Bluetooth-enabled or wired speakers on hand that can be repurposed for this project. If not, it's recommended to start out with basic audio equipment, perhaps even on loan, prior to investing in a high-fidelity setup. With this in mind, a complete hardware list for each use case is presented here.

Compatible Raspberry Pi Models

Any Raspberry Pi model with integrated Bluetooth will suffice for this recipe. The Pi Zero W models can also be used; however, because they lack a 3.5 mm audio jack, you'll need to connect them to a monitor via HDMI to perform a basic audio test. If you plan to pursue the Bluetooth receiver use case, you may also need a micro USB to USB adapter. Apart from these minor considerations, the Pi Zero W models are perfectly suitable, and even recommended, for highly portable or budget applications.

Bluetooth-Ready Speaker

For the Bluetooth speaker use case (option 1), any Bluetooth-enabled audio output device will do. You needn't break the bank here, as many affordable options exist. A good approach is to start with something small and simple, and consider upgrading your Bluetooth speaker later if you wish.

Bluetooth USB Adapter

For the high-fidelity Bluetooth receiver use case (option 2), an external Bluetooth adapter can be useful to extend the range and improve the performance of the Raspberry Pi's integrated WLAN/Bluetooth module. Similar to its popular Wi-Fi adapter cousin, the Edimax BT-8500 Nano USB Adapter, shown in Figure 5-1, is an excellent choice here.

Figure 5-1: The Edimax BT-8500 is a reliable and inexpensive Bluetooth adapter.

This adapter is extremely compact, supports the Bluetooth 5.0 standard, and offers plug-and-play compatibility with Linux kernel version 5.8 and later. The adapter is widely available from online retailers for about $21.

Digital-to-Analog Converter

Although the Pi's 3.5 mm audio jack provides reasonably good sound, it's less than optimal for a high-fidelity project. For the audio output in the Bluetooth receiver and Spotify Connect use cases (options 2 and 3, respectively), you can use a *digital-to-analog converter (DAC)* to translate audio from the Raspberry Pi to your hi-fi amplifier, headphones, or speakers. There are options for every budget; I present a few here, from least to most expensive.

USB to 3.5 mm Jack Adapter

At the most budget-friendly level is an external USB to 3.5 mm jack audio adapter. These adapters include a basic integrated DAC and often provide both a headphone jack and microphone input. The latter isn't needed for this project, so given a choice, select an adapter with audio-only output, similar to the one shown in Figure 5-2.

Figure 5-2: A USB to 3.5 mm
jack audio adapter

These adapters are ideally suited for testing and can be used to validate your project before upgrading to a more sophisticated DAC, if desired. They're widely available from online retailers for about $5.

Audio DAC SHIM

At the next tier are several Hardware Attached on Top (HAT) DACs. These add-on boards mount directly to the Raspberry Pi's GPIO header. Most are friction fit and require no soldering.

The Pimoroni Audio DAC SHIM, shown in Figure 5-3, provides a simple, slim way to output digital inter-IC sound (I^2S) audio while keeping the GPIO pins conveniently accessible.

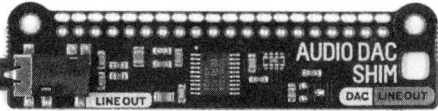

Figure 5-3: The Audio DAC SHIM (Line-Out)
by Pimoroni

SHIM in this context is an acronym for *shove hardware in middle*. It employs a header that slips over your GPIO pins and is easily removable, making it ideal for prototyping.

The Audio DAC SHIM takes high-quality digital audio from your Pi and pipes out crisp, line-level 24-bit/192 kHz stereo audio through the 3.5 mm jack. While line-level output typically requires either a separate amplifier or powered speakers, it's sufficient for earbuds or headphones with smaller drivers. This add-on is available from Pimoroni for about $15.

Raspberry Pi IQaudio DAC+ HAT

IQaudio's DAC+ has been dubbed the "de facto audiophile DAC" for the Pi, and for good reason. IQaudio was among the first companies to recognize the potential of the Raspberry Pi as a platform for high-fidelity audio. Its DACs became so popular that they were the first third-party products to be acquired by Raspberry Pi Ltd., in late 2020. Essentially unchanged apart from the color of the boards, this line of DACs continues to receive top marks under the Raspberry Pi brand.

This latest revision of the DAC+ is preprogrammed for autodetection and exposes the full Raspberry Pi GPIO header, providing access for other hardware add-ons.

The DAC+, pictured in Figure 5-4, features the Texas Instruments PCM5122 DAC chip and includes a dedicated headphone amplifier, making it a complete all-in one HD audio solution for headphone users. Volume control is built in, eliminating the need for software-based adjustments or additional audio accessories. The DAC+ is available from numerous online retailers for about $20.

Figure 5-4: The Raspberry Pi IQaudio DAC+ HAT

The DAC+ is one of four models offered by IQaudio for the Raspberry Pi. Each board has a specific purpose and feature set. These are summarized in Table 5-1.

Table 5-1: Raspberry Pi DACs

Model	Line out	Balanced out	Stereo	Mono	Headphones	AUX
DAC Pro	✓	✓			✓	
DAC+	✓				✓	
DigiAmp+			✓			
Codec Zero				✓		✓

Of course, these aren't the only DAC options; a wide range of devices is available to suit nearly every hi-fi audio setup and budget.

Home Audio Components

The high-fidelity Bluetooth receiver and Spotify Connect use cases require audio components to connect your DAC-enhanced Pi to. These might include an amplifier, a pair of quality headphones, powered speakers, or other audio hardware. As discussed previously, you needn't make a substantial investment here (unless, of course, you've already done so for an existing hi-fi setup you'd like to integrate).

Bear in mind that your home audio equipment will have an impact on which DAC you choose. Your system's inputs may include an S/PDIF digital connection, coaxial, phono (RCA), 3.5 mm AUX, passive speaker terminals, or some combination thereof. Be sure that these inputs match up with the outputs of your chosen DAC.

Software Used

Several software components are used in this recipe. In addition to libraries related to Bluetooth and Linux audio, depending on which use cases you decide to implement, you'll also need to install a few lightweight Linux clients to enable connectivity to and audio playback from various sources. I'll provide some example Python code to display audio track information in "Going Further" on page 152.

Before installing these components, let's briefly review the foundations of Linux audio that you'll be building on.

A Brief Tour of Linux Audio

By convention, computer hardware audio devices are often referred to as *sound cards*. This term harks back to the early days of computing, when machines lacked built-in audio capabilities. Sound cards were separate expansion boards that users installed in their computers. This terminology persists in today's era of integrated audio and system on a chip (SoC) architectures, and you'll often see it referenced by Linux command line tools in this section and elsewhere.

Broadly, the Linux kernel needs two things to communicate with a hardware audio device: a driver and firmware. A *driver* is an interface that implements or abstracts the internal representation of a piece of hardware. In this context, drivers enable all sound cards to effectively speak the same language. *Firmware* is the instruction set that runs on the device.

Linux audio device drivers are collected under the *Advanced Linux Sound Architecture (ALSA)* package. ALSA operates at a level of the audio stack above the hardware layer and is integrated into the Linux kernel, as illustrated in Figure 5-5.

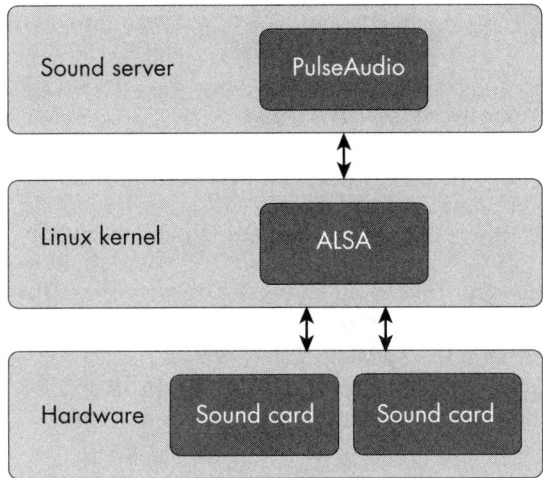

Figure 5-5: A conceptual overview of Linux audio

ALSA serves as the bridge between the hardware and higher-level systems known as *sound servers*, including PulseAudio, which I'll discuss shortly.

Since ALSA is part of the kernel, the `alsa-utils` package is preinstalled on most Debian-based distributions. You can verify its presence and check the version installed on your system by executing:

```
$ dpkg -l | grep alsa-utils
```

This package includes several utilities, such as `alsamixer`, `alsactl`, `aplay`, and `speaker-test`. You can use the `aplay` utility with the `-l` or `--list-devices` option to list all available hardware playback devices on your system:

```
$ aplay -l
  List of PLAYBACK Hardware Devices
card 0: Headphones [bcm2835 Headphones], device 0: bcm2835 Headphones
  Subdevices: 8/8
--snip--
card 1: vc4hdmi [vc4-hdmi], device 0: MAI PCM i2s-hifi-0 [MAI PCM i2s-hifi-0]
  Subdevices: 1/1
```

In this sample output, you'll notice two playback devices that are common on many Raspberry Pi models: card 0 is assigned to the headphone output, with its associated bcm2835 device driver for the Broadcom BCM 2835 SoC, while card 1 is assigned to the I^{2}S high-fidelity HDMI output.

To perform a basic Linux audio test, attach a pair of headphones to your device's 3.5 mm jack. If you're using a Pi Zero model without an audio output, you can still get digital audio via HDMI by connecting it to a monitor with speakers. Once an audio output is connected, run this command:

```
$ speaker-test -c2
```

This will play "pink" noise (random noise with equal energy in each octave) through the attached speakers, alternating between left and right channels, if available. In a separate terminal window, try executing the following command while speaker-test is running:

```
$ alsamixer
```

This graphical console utility lets you adjust the sound level up and down with the cursor keys, mute and unmute with the M key, and perform many other functions, including changing output to another available device, such as HDMI. Press ESC to exit alsamixer. Use CTRL-C in the other terminal window to stop the speaker test.

With a basic understanding of the Linux sound architecture, your next step will be installing a sound server that communicates with ALSA.

Prerequisites

Since this recipe is focused on Bluetooth connectivity and audio, you will begin by installing a common software foundation to support this. With your base established, you can then build upon it with other software packages depending on your specific requirements.

NOTE *These prerequisites apply to the first two use cases; the third "bonus" use case requires only ALSA and Wi-Fi connectivity. If you've chosen that option, you can skip this section and proceed directly to "Create a Spotify Connect Box with Spotifyd" on page 145.*

A related goal with this headless setup is to keep your install footprint lean and minimal, so you'll use a technique to reduce unnecessary desktop package support. Later, we'll examine system resource usage and compare a full-featured streaming audio client for the Linux terminal with its desktop counterpart.

Installing PulseAudio with Bluetooth

PulseAudio replaced the bluez-alsa Bluetooth audio ALSA backend as the default audio server for Raspberry Pi OS in late 2020. In addition to offering improved audio management capabilities, it simplifies and stabilizes the process of connecting Bluetooth speakers. ALSA hasn't left the building completely, however; it still acts as the intermediary between PulseAudio and your device's sound cards.

By default, PulseAudio automatically detects all sound cards on your system and manages them. It takes control of detected ALSA devices and routes audio streams through itself, making the PulseAudio daemon the central configuration point. The daemon generally works well out of the box, requiring only a few minor tweaks.

You'll begin by installing PulseAudio together with its Bluetooth module. By default, `pulseaudio` includes many X11, Wayland, and Mesa dependencies for a desktop environment. Since we're using the Lite version of Raspberry Pi OS, you can avoid loading these extra packages by adding the `--no-install-recommends` option:

```
$ sudo apt update
$ sudo apt install --no-install-recommends pulseaudio \
    pulseaudio-module-bluetooth
```

This option substantially reduces the install footprint. Next, install the official Linux Bluetooth stack, BlueZ. It provides modular support for the core Bluetooth layers and protocols:

```
$ sudo apt install bluez
```

To simplify administration, add the *pi* user to the *bluetooth* group. If you've set up a different user, replace pi with that user in the following command:

```
$ sudo usermod -a -G bluetooth pi
```

You can now proceed with configuring the packages you've just installed.

Creating a PulseAudio Service

The PulseAudio documentation correctly warns against running it as a system-wide service. This is because, in a desktop environment, each logged-in user should have their own PulseAudio instance running with that user's privileges. However, on a headless system, no regular user is logged in. There are generally two solutions here:

- Use `raspi-config` to modify the system boot options, automatically log in the *pi* user, and spawn a PulseAudio process.
- Run PulseAudio in system mode.

The second option lacks user isolation and can be problematic in a multiuser environment, but it's cleaner. Since you're using PulseAudio in a headless mode, it's perfectly acceptable to use this approach.

Debian doesn't include a system-wide PulseAudio systemd unit file, so you'll need to create your own. You can do so as follows, using your preferred editor:

```
$ sudo nano /etc/systemd/system/pulseaudio.service
```

Add the following content:

```
[Unit]
Description=PulseAudio Daemon
After=avahi-daemon.service network.target
```

```
[Service]
Type=simple
PrivateTmp=true
ExecStart=/usr/bin/pulseaudio --system --realtime --disallow-exit \
    --disable-shm --daemonize=no
ExecReload=/bin/kill -HUP $MAINPID

[Install]
WantedBy=multi-user.target
```

Save the file and exit your editor, then enable the PulseAudio service:

```
$ sudo systemctl enable pulseaudio
```

Enabling Communication with BlueZ

PulseAudio works hand-in-glove with BlueZ, although some configuration is required for PulseAudio to perform optimally. This is largely because PulseAudio communicates with BlueZ via *D-Bus*, a message bus system that applications use to exchange information. By default, D-Bus denies processes from initiating a connection unless access is explicitly granted. The solution is to add the *pulse* user to the *bluetooth* group, like so:

```
$ sudo usermod -a -G bluetooth pulse
```

Next, restart the D-Bus daemon for the change to take effect:

```
$ sudo systemctl restart dbus
```

With this done, PulseAudio will be able to talk to the BlueZ daemon.

Enabling PulseAudio Bluetooth Modules

Clients access the PulseAudio server through protocol modules that accept audio from external sources, route it through PulseAudio, and eventually direct it to a final sound output module. To enable a module, you can simply add a load-module *module-name-from-list* line to the configuration file. We're interested in Bluetooth audio devices using BlueZ, so I'll focus on these modules.

In the absence of PulseAudio user configuration files, system-wide settings from */etc/pulse/* will be applied. In keeping with its "no system mode" rule, the PulseAudio documentation advises against editing these system-wide files. However, this is again permissible in your case, as you're using a headless system. Open the PulseAudio system-mode configuration file */etc/pulse/system.pa* in your preferred editor and add the following lines to the end:

```
.ifexists module-bluetooth-policy.so
load-module module-bluetooth-policy
.endif
.ifexists module-bluetooth-discover.so
load-module module-bluetooth-discover
.endif
```

Save the file and exit the editor, then start and enable the PulseAudio service:

```
$ sudo systemctl start pulseaudio
$ sudo systemctl enable pulseaudio
```

You can then verify its status by executing:

```
$ sudo systemctl status pulseaudio
```

On subsequent system reboots, PulseAudio will start automatically. Finally, check the status of the Bluetooth daemon with:

```
$ sudo systemctl status bluetooth
```

Inspect the output of these commands for any errors or warnings. Refer to "Troubleshooting" on page 151 in the event of any anomalies.

At this stage, the prerequisites are handled and your device is configured as a Bluetooth-enabled PulseAudio server. The recipe will now fork into two paths. If connecting Bluetooth speakers to the Pi is your goal, proceed with the next section. Otherwise, skip to "Creating a Bluetooth Audio Receiver" on page 137.

Connecting Bluetooth Speakers

In this section, you'll pair your Raspberry Pi with Bluetooth speakers, test the audio output, and look at several playback options. If you haven't streamed music or managed audio libraries from the Linux terminal before, you may be in for a pleasant surprise.

Using the Bluetooth Controller

Begin by turning on your Bluetooth speaker and ensuring that it's in pairing mode. Most speakers have an audio and/or visual cue to indicate this. You'll be using an interactive Bluetooth control utility in the terminal throughout this chapter. Start the controller by running **bluetoothctl**.

The default bash prompt will change to [bluetooth] to indicate that you're acting within the interactive console. Use the following commands to set the Bluetooth agent and enable scanning mode:

```
[bluetooth]# power on
Changing power on succeeded
[bluetooth]# default-agent
```

```
Default agent request successful
[bluetooth]# scan on
Discovery started
[CHG] Controller B8:27:EB:FE:28:95 Discovering: yes
```

Depending on your local environment, you may see a number of available Bluetooth Low Energy devices appear in the scan. You can use the devices command to display a summary. Example output is shown here:

```
[bluetooth]# devices
Device F4:30:8B:38:2E:80 iPhone
Device 66:3A:70:90:D7:5E 66-3A-70-90-D7-5E
Device 33:FE:91:1F:6F:66 33-FE-91-1F-6F-66
Device 5E:CB:DB:86:28:E2 Mac
Device F4:2B:7D:22:0C:4E SoundCore mini
```

Most BLE devices broadcast small packets of data to let other devices know that they exist and they're available. The packets typically include information such as the services the device offers, a human-readable short device name, and other identifying details.

Pairing a Bluetooth Speaker

In the example output in the previous section, two unnamed devices (identified only by their MAC addresses) and three named devices appear as available for pairing. The Soundcore Mini is a Bluetooth speaker I'm using for testing purposes. Assuming you have a similar device available, you can pair with it by specifying its MAC address with the pair command. Be sure to change the MAC address to match your device:

```
[bluetooth]# pair F4:2B:7D:22:0C:4E
Attempting to pair F4:2B:7D:22:0C:4E
--snip--
[CHG] Device F4:2B:7D:22:0C:4E ServicesResolved: yes
[CHG] Device F4:2B:7D:22:0C:4E Paired: yes
Pairing successful
```

After a successful pairing, mark the device as trusted so the controller doesn't ask you for authorization each time:

```
[bluetooth]# trust F4:2B:7D:22:0C:4E
[CHG] Device F4:2B:7D:22:0C:4E Trusted: yes
Changing F4:2B:7D:22:0C:4E trust succeeded
```

Now, connect to the device:

```
[bluetooth]# connect F4:2B:7D:22:0C:4E
Attempting to connect to F4:2B:7D:22:0C:4E
Connection successful
```

The [bluetooth] console prompt will change to reflect the currently connected device. In this example, I'm connected to the Soundcore Mini Bluetooth speaker. At this point, you can turn off scanning:

```
[SoundCore mini]# scan off
Discovery stopped
```

Getting Device Properties

Use the following command to fetch some details about your connected Bluetooth speaker:

```
[SoundCore mini]# info
Device F4:2B:7D:22:0C:4E (public)
    Name: SoundCore mini
    Alias: SoundCore mini
    Class: 0x00240404
    Icon: audio-headset
    Paired: yes
    Bonded: yes
    Trusted: yes
    Blocked: no
    Connected: yes
    LegacyPairing: no
    --snip--
```

This allows you to confirm that your device is paired, trusted, and connected. The hexadecimal Class value 0x00240404 corresponds to a "Wearable Headset Device." The device I'm using definitely isn't wearable, but we'll let that slide.

Testing Audio Output

Now, you'll perform two simple tests to verify audio output through your Bluetooth speaker. Begin by using speaker-test again, this time with a *.wav* file provided by ALSA as input:

```
$ speaker-test -c2 --test=wav -w /usr/share/sounds/alsa/Front_Center.wav
```

Assuming you have stereo output, you should hear audio alternating between the left and right speakers. This is a bit more pleasant to listen to than the pink noise test performed earlier. Interrupt the output with CTRL-C. If the volume is too loud or you don't hear audio, execute **alsamixer** to adjust the sound levels, or consult "Troubleshooting" on page 151.

Streaming Internet Radio from the Console

With a basic audio test completed, you can now try streaming music from a remote source. In the process, I'll introduce playing music from the command line by using a simple open source utility. Start by installing *mpg123*, a popular MPEG audio player:

```
$ sudo apt-get install mpg123
```

This player supports streaming audio with the -@ option, making it a good choice for internet radio stations. The following command plays Soma FM's popular Groove Salad station:

```
$ mpg123 -@ http://somafm.com/groovesalad.pls
```

Bring up a handy list of terminal control keys and functions by pressing the H key. You can adjust the volume up and down with + and - respectively, pause playback, and even adjust audio levels with a built-in equalizer. When you're done listening, press Q to quit the player. If you'd like to play the station again in the future, you can create a temporary alias like so:

```
$ alias salad='mpg123 -@ http://somafm.com/groovesalad.pls'
```

Thereafter, you can simply execute **salad** from the shell to resume streaming. To make the alias permanent, you'll need to store it in your shell's configuration profile. Open the current user's *.bashrc* file in your editor:

```
$ nano ~/.bashrc
```

At the end of the file, paste the alias you created. Save your changes and exit the editor; your *.bashrc* profile will be automatically loaded in your next session.

If this stream isn't to your liking, Soma FM has playlists that cater to many tastes, including several streaming at 256Kbps. You can create aliases to suit various moods and execute them at will. If you experience audio stuttering on a slow connection, try falling back to a 128Kbps or lower bitrate.

Playing Music from an Audio Library

You can also stream your existing audio collection from the Pi to your Bluetooth speaker. One of the best terminal-based music players available is *cmus*, the C* Music Player for Linux, shown in Figure 5-6. It's open source, lightweight, fast, and packed with features. Install it with:

```
$ sudo apt install cmus
```

You can then launch the player by entering **cmus** at the command line. Adding your audio library to cmus is straightforward. Press 5 to switch to the directory browser, then use the arrow keys to navigate to any folder on your system. This can include local files, a remote network share, or any other location accessible from your Pi.

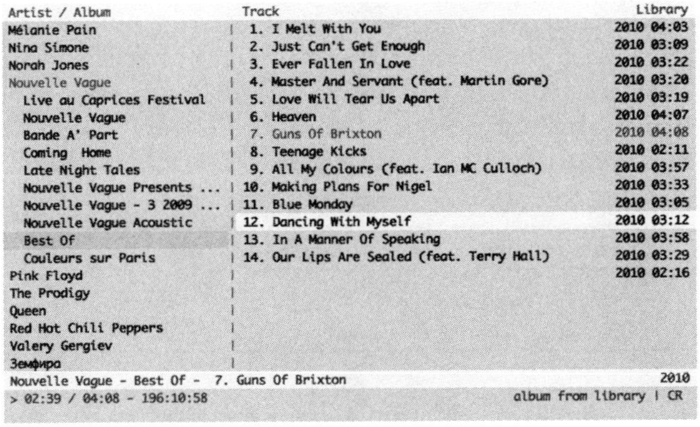

Artist / Album	Track	Library
Mélanie Pain	1. I Melt With You	2010 04:03
Nina Simone	2. Just Can't Get Enough	2010 03:09
Norah Jones	3. Ever Fallen In Love	2010 03:22
Nouvelle Vague	4. Master And Servant (feat. Martin Gore)	2010 03:20
Live au Caprices Festival	5. Love Will Tear Us Apart	2010 03:19
Nouvelle Vague	6. Heaven	2010 04:07
Bande A' Part	7. Guns Of Brixton	2010 04:08
Coming Home	8. Teenage Kicks	2010 02:11
Late Night Tales	9. All My Colours (feat. Ian MC Culloch)	2010 03:57
Nouvelle Vague Presents ...	10. Making Plans For Nigel	2010 03:33
Nouvelle Vague - 3 2009 ...	11. Blue Monday	2010 03:05
Nouvelle Vague Acoustic	12. Dancing With Myself	2010 03:12
Best Of	13. In A Manner Of Speaking	2010 03:58
Couleurs sur Paris	14. Our Lips Are Sealed (feat. Terry Hall)	2010 03:29
Pink Floyd		2010 02:16
The Prodigy		
Queen		
Red Hot Chili Peppers		
Valery Gergiev		
Земфира		

```
Nouvelle Vague - Best Of -  7. Guns Of Brixton                              2010
> 02:39 / 04:08 - 196:10:58              album from library | CR
```

Figure 5-6: The C* Music Player for Linux

For example, let's assume you have a network-attached storage (NAS) device mounted at */mnt/media*. In cmus, press L to switch to the library view, then press : to bring up the command line. Enter the command **add /mnt/media**, then press ENTER. This will add the media at that network location to your collection. Use the arrow keys to select a file, and press ENTER to play it.

You can create playlists, view albums, sort your library, and more. The cmus player includes solid reference material; the tutorial, which you can access with **man cmus-tutorial**, is a good starting point, and complete documentation is available via **man cmus**.

If you're accustomed to GUI-based music players, cmus has a learning curve, albeit not a steep one. With practice, you may even find using a terminal music player to be a liberating experience.

Playing Audio from Other Streaming Sources

Since PulseAudio assumes control of ALSA devices and redirects audio streams to itself, virtually any audio source can be sent to your Bluetooth speakers. This includes not only internet radio and local audio libraries but also podcasts and premium streaming services. All that's required is a client for the Linux terminal.

While Linux terminal clients are less common than their GUI counterparts, some excellent options exist. Among the most popular is an open source client for Spotify. I'll show you how to use that next.

Streaming Spotify from the Terminal

Spotify Premium subscribers can stream music and podcasts directly from the Linux command line. The open source, cross-platform *ncspot* project gives access to Spotify via the Linux terminal. It derives its name from the *ncurses* (new curses) library, which provides an API for developers to create text-based user interfaces in the terminal.

The ncspot player is highly efficient in terms of system resource use. Table 5-2 compares its memory footprint with that of the Spotify desktop client, measured in mebibytes (MiB) with the Python ps_mem utility on Linux during playback.

Table 5-2: System Resource Usage Comparison

Client	Private memory	Shared memory	Total
ncspot	22.1MiB	24.1MiB	46.2MiB
Spotify	407.3MiB	592.7MiB	1,000.0MiB

The ncspot player is written in the Rust programming language and can be installed in several ways. The simplest method is via a snap package.

Enabling snapd

Snaps are self-contained applications bundled with their dependencies, allowing them to run on all major Linux distributions from a single build. They update automatically and run in a containerized sandbox to avoid interfering with other system packages. Snaps are discoverable and installable from the Snap Store, an app store with a wide user base. To use them, you'll need to install snapd, the snap daemon, and the core snap on your system:

```
$ sudo apt update
$ sudo apt install snapd
$ sudo snap install core
```

Installing ncspot

To install ncspot, run:

```
$ sudo snap install ncspot
```

With the installation complete, start the player with:

```
$ ncspot
Testing for explicit PulseAudio choice...
...and PulseAudio has been explicitly chosen, so using it.
```

At startup, ncspot will automatically detect PulseAudio and select it as the default audio output. You will then be prompted to log in with your Spotify Premium account via a dialog in the terminal. The ncspot player will save your credentials so you don't need to log in each time.

As shown in Figure 5-7, the player features an intuitive top menu bar that you can navigate with the arrow keys. Find a track, album, artist, playlist, or podcast to your liking and simply press ENTER to start streaming.

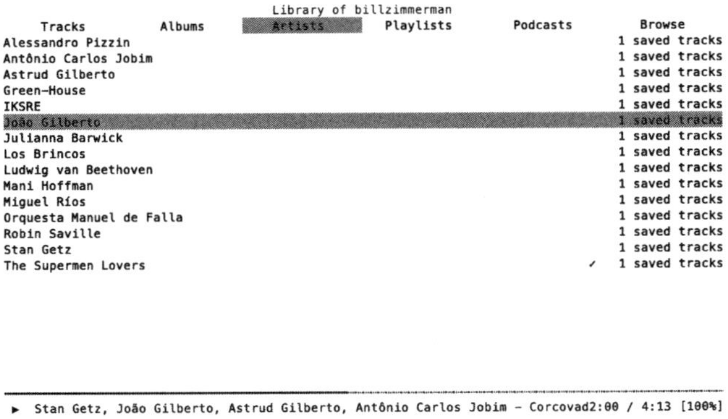

```
                           Library of billzimmerman
        Tracks          Albums       Artists       Playlists      Podcasts        Browse
Alessandro Pizzin                                                               1 saved tracks
Antônio Carlos Jobim                                                            1 saved tracks
Astrud Gilberto                                                                 1 saved tracks
Green-House                                                                     1 saved tracks
IKSRE                                                                           1 saved tracks
João Gilberto                                                                   1 saved tracks
Julianna Barwick                                                                1 saved tracks
Los Brincos                                                                     1 saved tracks
Ludwig van Beethoven                                                            1 saved tracks
Mani Hoffman                                                                    1 saved tracks
Miguel Ríos                                                                     1 saved tracks
Orquesta Manuel de Falla                                                        1 saved tracks
Robin Saville                                                                   1 saved tracks
Stan Getz                                                                       1 saved tracks
The Supermen Lovers                                                          ✓  1 saved tracks



  ▶  Stan Getz, João Gilberto, Astrud Gilberto, Antônio Carlos Jobim - Corcovad2:00 / 4:13 [100%]
```

Figure 5-7: The ncspot Spotify player for Linux

The ncspot player has key bindings to control every aspect of audio playback. Press ? to bring up a help menu and BACKSPACE to return to the player view.

At this point, you've gained practical experience with several methods for streaming music to Bluetooth speakers from the Linux command line. In the next section, you'll switch from the terminal to GUI-based client applications connected via Bluetooth.

Creating a Bluetooth Audio Receiver

The previous section focused on using your Pi to stream audio from the terminal to a Bluetooth speaker. In this section, you'll turn your Pi into a Bluetooth receiver with an integrated digital-to-analog converter for true high-fidelity output. Along the way, you'll acquire a practical understanding of how a Bluetooth sink functions.

Configuring a Bluetooth A2DP Sink

To use Bluetooth, a device must be compatible with one or more Bluetooth profiles. The *Advanced Audio Distribution Profile (A2DP)* protocol defines how audio can be streamed over Bluetooth connections from one device to another. Here, you'll configure your Pi as an A2DP sink. The sink you'll create will be capable of streaming high-quality audio wirelessly over Bluetooth connections.

Once configured and powered on, an A2DP sink enters discovery mode. A Bluetooth-compatible source device (such as a mobile phone, tablet, or laptop) can then initiate a pairing request. Depending on how it's configured, the sink may require a passkey and authorization before proceeding. When pairing is complete, the sink responds to commands sent to it by the source. You can also configure the sink to trust the source so future pairing requests are automatically approved.

The A2DP sink is responsible for several tasks, including brokering Bluetooth connections, decoding audio, responding to source commands, and ultimately sending an audio stream to an output device (such as speakers or headphones) for playback.

With a basic understanding of A2DP sinks and their roles, you'll now make your device permanently discoverable. Open the Bluetooth system configuration file in your preferred editor:

```
$ sudo nano /etc/bluetooth/main.conf
```

By default, before pairing, the sink will present itself to other devices as a generic Bluetooth device. You'll change this so it presents itself as an audio device. Near the top of this file, locate and modify the following lines:

```
Class = 0x00041C
--snip--
DiscoverableTimeout = 0
--snip--
```

The Class setting determines how the sink identifies itself. The value 0x00041C indicates that it is an audio device. The DiscoverableTimeout setting defines how long the sink remains in discoverable mode before reverting to being nondiscoverable. A value of 0 disables the timeout, making it discoverable indefinitely. With this configuration complete, save the file and exit your editor.

Using an External USB Adapter

The Raspberry Pi's onboard 802.11 WLAN/BLE chipset works well for most applications, but shortcomings may be revealed when streaming audio over Bluetooth. Using a dedicated external adapter is recommended if you experience Bluetooth connectivity issues and/or degraded audio output. I suggested an affordable option in "Hardware Required" on page 122.

NOTE *In my testing with a Raspberry Pi 3 Model B+ and its onboard WLAN/BLE chipset, I didn't observe any significant audio playback issues. If you have problems with Bluetooth connections dropping out or degraded audio, refer to "Choppy or Stuttering Audio" on page 152 for tips on how to resolve them.*

If you choose to use an external adapter, begin by disabling the onboard Bluetooth module. Open the configuration file in your editor:

```
$ sudo nano /etc/modprobe.d/blacklist-bluetooth.conf
```

Then add these lines at the end of the file (note that it may be empty):

```
blacklist btbcm
blacklist hci_uart
```

Save your changes and exit the editor. You may now connect your external Bluetooth adapter to an available USB port. Reboot your Pi with **sudo reboot** for the changes to take effect. Reconnect to the terminal via SSH, then check the Bluetooth service status and perform some basic tests to confirm the adapter is operating correctly:

```
$ sudo systemctl status bluetooth
$ hciconfig
$ sudo btmon
```

The btmon command is provided by the Linux BlueZ stack you installed as part of this recipe's prerequisites. This utility uses the Bluetooth subsystem monitor to read host controller interface (HCI) traces. Interrupt its output with CTRL-C.

If the Bluetooth service status indicates an error, or these utilities fail to produce output, your adapter likely requires a separate Linux driver—that is, it is not a plug-and-play Bluetooth device with an in-kernel driver. In this event, you must either install a driver for it or use a different adapter.

FREEING UP THE ENDPOINT

After restarting Bluetooth, you may notice a service error similar to the following:

```
SET_CONFIGURATION request rejected: Stream End Point in Use
```

This error indicates that the Bluetooth endpoint is already in use by another active connection. Usually, this occurs when the endpoint is connected to a device such as a Bluetooth speaker. If you've previously connected a device, don't worry; simply invoke the Bluetooth controller and disconnect the device. In the following example, the controller indicates that the Soundcore Mini speaker is connected. Issue the **disconnect** command to disconnect, followed by **quit** to exit the controller:

```
$ bluetoothctl
[SoundCore mini]# disconnect
Attempting to disconnect from F4:2B:7D:22:0C:4E
[DEL] Transport /org/bluez/hci0/dev_F4_2B_7D_22_0C_4E/fd2
[DEL] Endpoint /org/bluez/hci0/dev_F4_2B_7D_22_0C_4E/sep3
Successful disconnected
[CHG] Device F4:2B:7D:22:0C:4E Connected: no
[bluetooth]# quit
```

(continued)

Then restart the Bluetooth service and check its status:

```
$ sudo systemctl restart bluetooth
$ sudo systemctl status bluetooth
```

This should resolve the error related to the stream endpoint being in use. If you're still having problems, see "Troubleshooting" on page 151.

Activating the Bluetooth Sink

After these preliminary steps, you can activate the A2DP sink. Begin by starting the Bluetooth controller with **bluetoothctl**.

The default bash prompt will change to [bluetooth] to indicate that you're acting within the interactive Bluetooth console. Now, execute the **power on** and **discoverable on** commands. Sample output is shown here:

```
[bluetooth]# power on
Changing power on succeeded
[bluetooth]# discoverable on
Changing discoverable on succeeded
[CHG] Controller B8:27:EB:FE:28:95 Discoverable: yes
```

Your Raspberry Pi, identified by its default hostname, raspberrypi, should now be visible as an A2DP sink from another device. It will typically appear in the list of nearby or available devices in the Bluetooth settings of your phone or laptop. If the Raspberry Pi doesn't show up, make sure you're within Bluetooth range and restart the bluetooth.service. Also ensure that no secondary Bluetooth adapters are connected, as these can interfere with detection and pairing.

Conducting a Pairing Test

You can now perform a pairing test by connecting to your Pi. With a second device, such as a laptop or phone, choose raspberrypi (or your controller name, if different) from the list of available Bluetooth devices. The Bluetooth controller will register the pairing request. This example uses an Android phone:

```
[NEW] Device F4:30:8B:38:2E:80 POCO F3
Request confirmation
[agent] Confirm passkey 930976 (yes/no): yes
[CHG] Device F4:30:8B:38:2E:80 Bonded: yes
[CHG] Device F4:30:8B:38:2E:80 Modalias: bluetooth:v038Fp1200d1436
--snip--
[CHG] Device F4:30:8B:38:2E:80 Paired: yes
```

With the pairing done, `bluetoothctl` will prompt you to authorize the device. Enter **yes** when prompted:

```
[agent] Authorize service 0000110d-0000-1000-8000-00805f9b34fb (yes/no): yes
Authorize service
[CHG] Device F4:30:8B:38:2E:80 UUIDs: 00001105-0000-1000-8000-00805f9b34fb
--snip--
[POCO F3]#
```

The Bluetooth control prompt will now change to the name of the paired and authorized device (in this case, an Android POCO F3 handset). You can configure the device as trusted so the controller doesn't ask for authorization each time you pair with it:

```
[bluetooth]#  trust F4:30:8B:38:2E:80
[CHG] Device F4:30:8B:38:2E:80 Trusted: yes
Changing F4:30:8B:38:2E:80 trust succeeded
```

In the next section, you'll learn how to streamline this pairing process if you wish.

Configuring Automatic Pairing (Optional)

In some circumstances, you may want to bypass passkey confirmation and authorization altogether. All pairing requests will then be accepted with no interaction from the client or the A2DP sink. While this effectively throws security to the wind, it may be appropriate to streamline pairing in some situations, such as home use. If you're operating the A2DP sink in a public environment, it's advisable to skip this step.

To configure automatic pairing, you'll need to install an agent to manage incoming Bluetooth requests. The `bluez-tools` package works alongside the BlueZ stack. Install it with:

```
$ sudo apt install bluez-tools
```

Next, create a system-level unit file in your preferred editor:

```
$ sudo nano /etc/systemd/system/bt-agent.service
```

Enter the following contents. The `NoInputNoOutput` option is the key piece here:

```
[Unit]
Description=Bluetooth Auth Agent
After=bluetooth.service
PartOf=bluetooth.service

[Service]
Type=simple
ExecStart=/usr/bin/bt-agent -c NoInputNoOutput
```

```
[Install]
WantedBy=bluetooth.target
```

Now, enable the service and check its status:

```
$ sudo systemctl enable bt-agent
$ sudo systemctl status bt-agent
```

With the agent running, execute `bluetoothctl` and remove the device you paired in the previous step. Using the previous example:

```
[bluetooth]# remove F4:30:8B:38:2E:80
[DEL] Device F4:30:8B:38:2E:80 POCO F3
Device has been removed
```

Finally, repeat the Bluetooth pairing test you performed in the previous step. The client device should pair with the A2DP sink without prompting for a passkey or authorization. The `bt-agent` service you created will report pairing events from client devices.

Now that you've configured automatic pairing, you can test the Bluetooth audio output.

Conducting an Audio Test

Connect a pair of headphones or speakers to your Raspberry Pi's 3.5 mm output jack, and try playing an audio track from an application on your phone or laptop. Execute `bluetoothctl` and monitor the output.

You should hear your audio content streamed via Bluetooth through the Pi to your wired speakers. If so, the basic audio test has passed.

To adjust the output volume, run the `alsamixer` command, as described earlier. If you encounter any difficulties, check out the suggestions in "Troubleshooting" on page 151. Otherwise, I'll indulge in a brief explanation of the Pi's analog audio before we move on to integrating your DAC.

The audio quality from the Raspberry Pi's 3.5 mm jack is somewhat less than high-fidelity. While it generally suffices for casual use, its limitations quickly become evident when you connect a decent pair of headphones or full-range monitors. The sound lacks detail and can best be described as tinny, and strange audio artifacts are common.

In fact, it's quite an engineering feat that the Pi's audio doesn't sound much worse. This is because it's a digital device, producing voltages that represent streams of 0s and 1s. By contrast, headphones require an analog signal; they respond to voltage levels that vary continually with the shape of the sound waves. To accommodate this, the Pi simulates an analog signal by using a *pulse width modulation (PWM)* module. This approximates varying voltage levels by modulating incredibly quickly—on the order of 19 million times per second. An example of this modulation scheme is illustrated in Figure 5-8. Here, voltage is modulated as a series of rapid pulses that, when averaged over time, resemble a sine-like waveform.

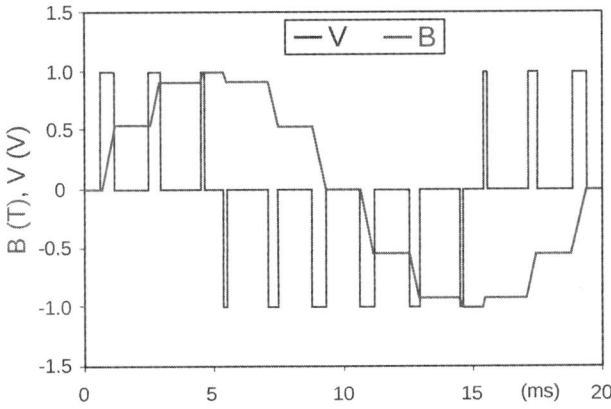

Figure 5-8: An example of PWM switching frequency

This PWM signal is then directed through a *low-pass filter*, which smooths it out into an analog waveform. The drawback is that, by design, the filter also removes much of the high-frequency content. The Raspberry Pi starts rolling frequencies off at around 7 kHz, significantly reducing harmonic detail. Moreover, the dynamic range is limited to 11 bits, which is 32 times less depth than the 16-bit audio of a CD. This further reduces detail and eliminates most subtle audio variations.

With this understanding of PWM and the Pi's analog limitations, you're now ready to integrate a DAC and vastly improve the sound output quality.

Integrating a DAC

The Raspberry Pi's built-in DAC is integrated into its audio output module. As noted in the previous section, the sound output is adequate for many applications but falls short of high fidelity. For optimal audio quality, connect your chosen DAC to the Pi, either via USB or by attaching it to the 40-pin GPIO header.

Most DAC audio boards designed for the Pi's 40-pin header come with standoffs and screws to support the circuit board. No soldering is required for normal operation, unless you're using hardwired connections for specific connectors (such as XLR connections on the DAC Pro). To mount the board, first screw the PCB spacers into the Raspberry Pi, finger-tight. Then add the audio board and secure it by attaching the remaining screws into the spacers from above.

To make your DAC sound card the primary audio device in Raspberry Pi OS, you'll need to disable the Pi's onboard audio card. To do this, simply comment out the `dtparam=audio=on` device tree parameter in *config.txt*. Open this file in your editor with:

```
$ sudo nano /boot/firmware/config.txt
```

Locate the line and place a comment character (#) at the start, like so:

```
# dtparam=audio=on
```

This will help applications automatically find the correct audio device. Next, set your chosen DAC as the default ALSA device by using the `dtoverlay` keyword to specify a device tree overlay. This value is specific to this particular DAC model and may vary from one manufacturer to the next. With these steps done, save the file, exit your editor, and reboot your system with `sudo reboot`.

Most popular DAC boards come preconfigured in Linux with the necessary EEPROM data flashed by the manufacturer, so no further user configuration is necessary. These boards are designed to be plug-and-play; Raspberry Pi OS is able to automatically detect and configure them.

Connecting the DAC to Hi-Fi Equipment

With your chosen DAC integrated with your Pi, you may now connect it to your high-fidelity components. The specifics here will depend on your exact setup. If your DAC includes a 3.5 mm line out or dedicated headphone amplifier, begin by connecting a quality headset and conducting the audio test again.

Otherwise, proceed by attaching cables from your DAC's output terminals to your audio equipment.

Initiating Audio Playback

At this stage, your Bluetooth A2DP sink should be active, and (optionally) your DAC should be integrated and connected to your audio components. All that remains is to connect to the sink from your preferred device, open an audio playback source, and begin streaming.

For your first streaming session, it's recommended to monitor the sink from the terminal during playback. You may even opt to use two terminal windows or a terminal multiplexer such as Tmux (described in "Direct Access via the Terminal" on page 42). First, start the Bluetooth controller with `bluetoothctl`. You should be familiar with the controller's basic capabilities and diagnostic output by now. To monitor the Bluetooth daemon, follow the system journal in a separate window with:

```
$ sudo journalctl -u bluetooth -f
```

If you encounter problems with audio output, note any error messages from either of these sources and refer to "Troubleshooting" on page 151 for guidance.

Controlling Volume

A Bluetooth profile known as the *Audio/Video Remote Control Profile (AVRCP)* is used for sending commands between a controller and a target device. In addition to basic remote functions such as play, pause, stop, next, previous, and volume control, AVRCP supports metadata (such as lyrics and album information) and media player states (playing, paused, stopped, and so on).

The AVRCP profile is enabled by default, but it's not automatically bound to volume control. Enabling this functionality requires some coding to monitor A2DP properties through D-Bus. Alternatively, you can simply disable the AVRCP plug-in in the Bluetooth service. This will delegate volume control to your connected device (a phone or laptop, for example), while the Pi retains basic command functions.

Start by opening the Bluetooth service file:

```
$ sudo nano /etc/systemd/system/bluetooth.target.wants/bluetooth.service
```

Find the following line and append `--noplugin=avrcp`, so it appears like this:

```
ExecStart=/usr/libexec/bluetooth/bluetoothd --noplugin=avrcp
```

Save and exit the file, then run:

```
$ sudo systemctl daemon-reload
$ sudo systemctl restart bluetooth
```

Reconnect a client device to your A2DP sink, resume playback, and confirm that volume control works as expected.

One drawback of this method is that the A2DP sink will no longer have access to metadata or the player state. This means, for example, that add-on hardware used to display album or track information will not function. I'll discuss a solution for this in "Going Further" on page 152.

Create a Spotify Connect Box with Spotifyd

In the earlier Bluetooth speaker use case, you used the cross-platform client ncspot to stream Spotify audio from the Linux terminal. In this section, you'll take a different approach and deploy the Spotifyd project to create a Spotify Connect box.

Spotify Connect streams audio over your Wi-Fi network, with control handled from the Spotify app on another device. While this may seem like a departure from the Bluetooth focus of this chapter, it aligns closely with its emphasis on DAC integration and high-fidelity audio. For those seeking a premium audiophile experience, Spotifyd offers a compelling wireless option.

Setting the Scene

With Bluetooth control via native apps on mobile devices, an audio stream is delivered to your phone through the A2DP sink, decoded, and sent to your output device. By contrast, Spotify Connect devices can receive the best-quality audio directly (via a wired Ethernet or Wi-Fi connection), encoded in Ogg Vorbis at bitrates up to 320Kbps. The audio stream is buffered and then piped through your high-fidelity DAC and out to your audio equipment. At the time of writing, Spotify Music Pro is expected to be released in late 2025, which will offer lossless streaming of up to 24 bits/44,100 Hz with Free Lossless Audio Codec (FLAC) files.

LOSSY VS. LOSSLESS

Ogg Vorbis is the best lossy format that currently exists. Hi-fi at 16- or 24-bit 44,100 Hz is better, but typically only when specialty audio equipment is used. Even then, many audiophiles would be hard-pressed to detect a difference between the two formats.

In addition to high-quality streaming audio, Spotify Connect lets anyone on your Wi-Fi network control playback without Bluetooth pairing. This is a boon for house parties, assuming you trust your friends with the controls. Spotify Connect also lets you switch between devices seamlessly. You might start a playlist from a Spotify desktop client in one room, then pick up a phone elsewhere in the house and carry on streaming without skipping a beat.

Spotifyd is a service process that runs in the background and thinly wraps the *Librespot* project, a popular open source Spotify client library. In a nutshell, Spotifyd enables applications to use Spotify's service to control and play audio directly from a Spotify Connect receiver. It's intended to be run as a Linux daemon (hence the *d* in its name) and is available as a precompiled binary for various architectures. It can also be compiled from source. Librespot, and therefore Spotifyd, requires a premium Spotify account.

Installing Spotifyd

This section will walk you through installing an instance of Spotifyd as a system-wide service, so that Spotify Connect will always be running and available on your network. For simplicity, I'll focus on using the precompiled binary for the Pi's ARM architecture.

The 32-bit Raspberry Pi OS distribution is supported with a ready-made executable. If you're using a 64-bit distribution, you have two options: build the 64-bit binary yourself, or download the 64-bit binary.

Begin by using some shell-fu to fetch the latest Spotifyd release. First, ensure that curl is installed on your system, then fetch a response from the GitHub API:

```
$ sudo apt install curl -y
$ latest=$(curl -sL "https://api.github.com/repos/Spotifyd/spotifyd/releases/latest" \
    | grep -Po '"tag_name": "\K.*?(?=")')
$ echo $latest
```

This will store a version tag in the shell variable \\$latest. Next, download the latest ARMv7 release from Spotifyd's GitHub repository to your home directory, again using curl:

```
$ cd ~/
$ archive="spotifyd-linux-armv7-slim.tar.gz"
$ curl -OL "https://github.com/Spotifyd/spotifyd/releases/download/$latest/$archive"
```

If you need arm64 support, replace armv7 with aarch64 in the archive line.

With this done, extract the archive by executing **tar xzf $archive**. In your user directory, you will now find a binary file called *spotifyd*.

At this stage, if you're using a 64-bit version of Raspberry Pi OS, you will need to install a few packages to support the 32-bit architecture. (If you're using a 32-bit distribution, skip this step and proceed with the next one.) Install these dependencies with:

```
$ sudo dpkg --add-architecture armhf
$ sudo apt update
$ sudo apt install libasound2-plugins:armhf
```

You can then execute the binary to fetch some usage notes by running **./spotifyd --help**.

Now, copy the file to */usr/sbin* to make it accessible for a later step:

```
$ sudo cp spotifyd /usr/sbin
```

With the installation complete, you can proceed with configuring the daemon.

Configuring Spotifyd

Spotifyd has many configuration options to tailor it to your specific needs. I'll focus on creating a minimal setup to get it up and running. You can then adjust these settings as needed. Begin by creating the configuration file in your home directory:

```
$ cd ~/
$ nano spotifyd.conf
```

Enter the following content, replacing the Spotify account placeholder values with your credentials:

```
[global]
username = "your_Spotify_username"
password = "your_Spotify_password"
backend = "alsa"
device = "default"
mixer = "PCM"
volume_controller = "alsa"
bitrate = 320
```

```
initial_volume = "90"
volume_normalisation = true
normalisation_pregain = -10
```

One item to note in the configuration is the device setting, which is set to default. In most cases, this value corresponds to either the Pi's analog headphone jack or its HDMI output. It's recommended to start with default, confirm audio output, then modify this setting later.

For example, if you're using an external USB audio adapter or DAC, you can obtain a list of available audio interfaces by executing **aplay --list-pcms**. Pulse code modulation (PCM) is a scheme for encoding audio signals digitally. In this context, a *PCM* refers to an interface through which audio data flows in a certain direction. This is a fundamental unit in the audio data pipeline in ALSA's user space framework. Similarly, you can list the hardware sound cards available for playback with **aplay --list-devices**.

With a basic configuration established, you're ready to create a systemd service to utilize it.

Creating a systemd Service

Spotifyd's systemd service is intended to be run in a user session and access the session D-Bus. As a result, it looks for the logged-in user's configuration, usually found in */.config*. When running Spotifyd as a system-wide service, however, it's not able to access this configuration or to communicate with the session D-Bus.

The solution in this case is to create an unprivileged *spotifyd* user with access restricted to the *audio* group. Spotifyd will then be run in this user context. Begin by creating the user:

```
$ sudo adduser --system "spotifyd" --disabled-password --group \
    --home /var/lib/spotifyd
$ sudo usermod -aG audio spotifyd
```

Next, move the Spotifyd configuration file you created previously and set permissions for the *spotifyd* user:

```
$ sudo mv ~/spotifyd.conf /var/lib/spotifyd/
$ sudo chown spotifyd:spotifyd /var/lib/spotifyd/spotifyd.conf
```

Create a new system-level unit file with your editor by using

```
$ sudo nano /etc/systemd/system/spotifyd.service
```

and enter the following contents:

```
[Unit]
Description=Spotifyd Playing Daemon
Documentation=https://github.com/Spotifyd/spotifyd
Wants=sound.target
After=sound.target
```

```
Wants=network-online.target
After=network-online.target

[Service]
User=spotifyd
Group=spotifyd
WorkingDirectory=/var/lib/spotifyd
ExecStart=dbus-run-session /usr/sbin/spotifyd \
    --config-path /var/lib/spotifyd/spotifyd.conf --no-daemon

[Install]
WantedBy=default.target
```

Note the `--config-path` option. Notice also that the `--no-daemon` option is used here; this is because systemd handles daemonizing and subsequent watching of the application.

For extra security, make the configuration readable only by the *spotifyd* user:

```
$ sudo chmod 400 /var/lib/spotifyd/spotifyd.conf
```

To make changes to the configuration in the future, you'll need to set the permissions to 644 to make the file writable again.

DISABLING PULSEAUDIO

The precompiled Spotifyd binary uses ALSA as its backend. Attempting to start it while another backend is active will result in D-Bus complaining that the audio sink is busy or already in use. You can verify this by checking the active sound devices on the system:

```
$ sudo apt install lsof -y
$ sudo lsof /dev/snd/*
COMMAND    PID USER    FD   TYPE DEVICE SIZE/OFF NODE NAME
pulseaudi 3366  pi   mem    CHR  116,3           545 /dev/snd/pcmCODOc
pulseaudi 3366  pi   mem    CHR  116,2           544 /dev/snd/pcmCODOp
pulseaudi 3366  pi   27u    CHR  116,4      0t0  546 /dev/snd/controlCO
```

In this example, PulseAudio is using the system sound card devices. The solution in this case is to stop and disable the user-level PulseAudio socket, if it exists, and then send a signal to terminate the process:

```
$ sudo killall pulseaudio
```

Disabling PulseAudio will cause your device to function as a dedicated Spotify Connect source. You can operate it as either a Bluetooth A2DP sink or a Spotify Connect box, but not both at the same time. Alternatively, if you'd prefer to run Spotifyd with the PulseAudio backend, you can compile the ARMv6 binary with it enabled as a build option.

Starting the Spotifyd Service

At this stage, you're ready to start and enable the Spotifyd service. Do so with the following commands:

```
$ sudo systemctl daemon-reload
$ sudo systemctl enable spotifyd.service
$ sudo systemctl start spotifyd.service
```

The daemon should now be up and running and will start automatically on subsequent system boots. For improved security, it runs as the unprivileged *spotifyd* user. You can check its status with:

```
$ sudo systemctl status spotifyd.service
```

If the service indicates a status of active (running), your device should be available as a Spotify Connect source on your network. While the service is running, you can follow its activity in the system journal by executing this command:

```
$ sudo journalctl -u spotifyd -f
```

Controlling Playback via the Spotify App

Spotify Connect lets you use a compatible device to remotely control playback on the host. Using this function requires all devices to be on the same network. To connect to the remote host, use the icon near the bottom of your device's screen. You can then select an available Spotify Connect device on your network. By default, the client you created in the previous step should be visible as *Spotifyd@raspberrypi*. This appears as the current device, as shown in Figure 5-9.

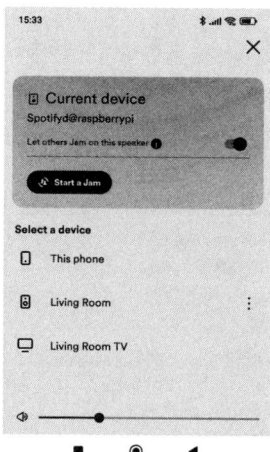

Figure 5-9: Using the Spotify app to connect to the Spotifyd network device

If your Spotifyd device doesn't appear in the list, check that it's connected to your local network. Your Raspberry Pi may be connected via Wi-Fi or Ethernet. On iPhones, you might need to give Spotify permission to access your local network: Go to **Settings ▶ Spotify ▶ Local Network** and toggle it on.

Troubleshooting

Bluetooth and audio in Linux are fascinating technologies to explore, but they are not without their pitfalls. This section, while by no means exhaustive, is intended to cover common issues that may arise and provide some potential solutions. It's organized by topic for easy reference.

No Audio Output from Speakers

Occasionally, you might start an audio client and receive no output from your Bluetooth speakers. In this event, eliminate the obvious reason by increasing the volume, either with a physical controller or by running `alsamixer` in the terminal.

If volume levels appear adequate, proceed by executing `rkfill list`. If the Bluetooth module indicates `Soft blocked: yes`, execute `rfkill unblock all` to unblock it.

Next, confirm that your speaker is connected by starting the Bluetooth controller console with `bluetoothctl`. If the console prompt is the default `[bluetooth]`, your speaker is not connected. Repeat the steps in "Using the Bluetooth Controller" on page 131 to connect to your output device.

Finally, check the Bluetooth service status:

```
$ sudo systemctl status bluetooth
```

If any failures or error messages are indicated, check the status of your Bluetooth adapter by executing `hciconfig`. If no output appears, ensure that your onboard Bluetooth adapter is enabled, or that your external adapter is compatible with your system. Refer to "Using an External USB Adapter" on page 138 for details.

Unable to Connect to the A2DP Sink

If the `bluetoothctl` console becomes unresponsive, it's possible that your A2DP sink is unable to communicate with the Bluetooth device. When this occurs, the `bluetooth.service` status will usually report an error like this:

```
src/profile.c:ext_io_disconnected() Unable to get io data for Headset unit
```

To fix the problem, you can simply restart the service by executing:

```
$ sudo systemctl restart bluetooth
```

Choppy or Stuttering Audio

In the Bluetooth receiver use case, you may observe degraded or unusable audio output. As noted in "Configuring a Bluetooth A2DP Sink" on page 137, a typical sink has many roles to fulfill. Among them, PulseAudio is one of the most processor-intensive. If you're running other software or services with high CPU utilization in parallel on the sink, audio output will likely suffer as a consequence. When in doubt, execute `htop`.

By default, the `htop` interactive process viewer displays all running processes on the system, ranked by CPU usage. Activity for each of your CPU's cores is displayed at the top as horizontal graphs, updated in real time. Press Q or F10 to exit the utility.

In most cases, simply operating the A2DP sink as a stand-alone service will resolve any audio issues. However, the PulseAudio daemon is highly customizable, and you can experiment with optimizing its settings for your needs. Open the configuration file in your preferred editor:

```
$ sudo nano /etc/pulse/daemon.conf
```

Here, you will find many optional settings that are disabled by default (prepended with a ; character). If you anticipate using your Raspberry Pi to do more than host an A2DP sink, research these settings in the PulseAudio documentation.

Depending on your Pi revision and other factors, the onboard Bluetooth module may not be optimal for this use case. The simplest solution in this event is to disable the onboard module and connect an external USB Bluetooth adapter. These adapters are very affordable and can save you significant troubleshooting time. See "Using an External USB Adapter" on page 138 for advice.

Poor-Quality or Tinny Sound Output

With better-quality audio components, the limitations of the Pi's 3.5 mm output jack will likely become evident (refer to "Conducting an Audio Test" on page 142 for an explanation). At this point, you may want to consider one of the DAC options presented in "Hardware Required" on page 122. See "Integrating a DAC" on page 143 for specifics on adding this to your system.

Going Further

As previously noted, this chapter is intended to provide an introduction to audio and wireless in a Linux context. Following this recipe should provide you with a solid base upon which to build. Here, I'll offer a few suggestions for next steps. Just as there was no one "right" use case to follow in this recipe, since your choice will be affected by factors such as your preferred media sources, available audio equipment, and physical environment, the suggestions presented here should be taken in the same spirit.

Displaying Audio Properties

Earlier in this chapter, I introduced the AVRCP service, which allows a Bluetooth device to share audio metadata (current track, album, lyrics, and so on) as well as the player state with a connected device. You also used the BlueZ library to facilitate communication with the Bluetooth stack. You can use this library, together with Python, to interact with D-Bus interfaces as well.

In "Controlling Volume" on page 144, I mentioned that AVRCP is not bound to volume control by default. Instead, it's typical for player volume properties to be monitored through D-Bus and manipulated with code. To enable volume control on an A2DP client, such as a phone, I suggested that you take the expedient measure of disabling the AVRCP plug-in.

To retrieve properties of an audio track such as the title and artist, you'll need to re-enable this plug-in. Reverse the steps described in that section, then run:

```
$ sudo systemctl daemon-reload
$ systemctl restart bluetooth
```

Now, connect a Bluetooth playback device (such as a phone or laptop) to your A2DP sink. While monitoring the output of bluetoothctl, notice that AVRCP properties are captured in the console. For example:

```
[CHG] Player /org/bluez/hci0/dev_F4_30_8B_38_2E_80/player0 Status: playing
[CHG] Player /org/bluez/hci0/dev_F4_30_8B_38_2E_80/player0 Title: She Sells...
[CHG] Player /org/bluez/hci0/dev_F4_30_8B_38_2E_80/player0 Album: Love
[CHG] Player /org/bluez/hci0/dev_F4_30_8B_38_2E_80/player0 Artist: The Cult
```

You can create a simple Python script to interface with D-Bus and capture these audio track properties. First, install the required dependencies:

```
$ sudo apt update
$ sudo apt install python3-gi python3-dbus
```

Next, create a new file called *playback-demo.py* with the following contents:

```
#!/usr/bin/env python

import dbus
from dbus.mainloop.glib import DBusGMainLoop
from gi.repository import GLib

PLAYER_PATH = "/org/bluez/hci0/dev_F4_30_8B_38_2E_80/player0"

def trackChanged(*args, **kw):
    target = args[0]
    if target == "org.bluez.MediaPlayer1":
        data = args[1].get("Track",0)
```

```
            if data != 0:
                print("Track:", data.get('Title'))
                print("Artist:", data.get('Artist'))
                print("Album:", data.get('Album'))

DBusGMainLoop(set_as_default=True)

system_bus = dbus.SystemBus()
system_bus.add_signal_receiver(trackChanged,
    dbus_interface="org.freedesktop.DBus.Properties",
    signal_name="PropertiesChanged",
    path=PLAYER_PATH)

loop = GLib.MainLoop()
loop.run()
```

Replace *PLAYER_PATH* with the player string you observed in the `bluetoothctl` output. Save the file and exit the editor, then execute the script:

```
$ python3 playback-demo.py
```

D-Bus is capable of notifying you when certain properties change. In the script, these change events are paired with the `Track` property of the `org.bluez.MediaPlayer1` target. The script will loop continuously, waiting for a track change. When you change audio tracks on your Bluetooth-connected player, the track title, artist, and album will be printed to standard output (stdout) in the terminal. Interrupt the output with CTRL-C.

Integrating with a TFT Display

The recipe in Chapter 3 demonstrates using CircuitPython to output wireless statistics to a Mini Pi-TFT hardware add-on. The Python code in that recipe is organized around functions such as `get_wifi_info()`, which returns various properties of a given wireless interface that are then output to the attached display.

Think of ways to combine the Python script in the previous section with the one from that chapter to output audio track information to the Mini Pi-TFT (or another) hardware display.

Recall also that the Mini Pi-TFT has two tactile hardware buttons mounted on the circuit board. I demonstrated some Python code to read the states of these buttons to toggle the state of the backlight. With some knowledge of Python and D-Bus, you should be able to read inputs from these buttons and implement forward and back player controls.

Wrapping Up

Bluetooth is yet another example of a transformative wireless technology that's often taken for granted. Likewise, it's easy to overlook the potential for high-quality Linux audio supported by devices like the Raspberry Pi and enabled by some highly affordable hardware add-ons.

Regardless of which use case(s) you opted to pursue here, you should now have a solid understanding of how the Linux kernel bridges sound servers like PulseAudio, how Bluetooth device discovery and pairing work in practice, and how these components can be combined to create truly useful (and perhaps even high-fidelity) Bluetooth-enabled Linux audio devices.

The audio hardware I created while developing this recipe has found a permanent home alongside my other media components. I hope that you, like me, find unique pleasure in using an audio device you've made yourself.

6

EXPLORING LONG RANGE WITH LORA

LoRa, a portmanteau of *long* and *range*, is a relatively new technology that uses spread spectrum modulation to send data over very long distances. Designed for low-bandwidth and IoT applications, LoRa is a great choice for the sub-GHz free radio spectrum. As with Wi-Fi, you effectively own the radio data path from end to end. Unlike Wi-Fi, however, LoRa isn't capable of streaming video, or indeed of handling payloads beyond short messages.

You will also need to choose a MAC layer to run on top of LoRa. LoRaWAN is the most widely used MAC layer protocol for low power, wide area networks (LPWANs), though it's certainly not the only option. The LoRaWAN protocol enables long-range communication, often between battery-operated end devices and gateways, via uplinks to network and application servers. In terms of range potential, a single LoRa-based gateway can transmit and receive signals over a distance of up to 10 miles (16 km) in rural areas. In dense urban environments, it's not uncommon for LoRa messages to travel up to 3 miles (5 km), depending on how the end devices, or nodes, are positioned.

LoRa gives you a lot of parameters to tune at the physical (PHY) layer of its modulation scheme. These can be adjusted to meet your specific requirements in terms of battery usage, range, data rates, payload sizes, and more. In fact, LoRa's flexibility is a key reason for its rapid adoption. The flip side of this flexibility is that it can make LoRa difficult for beginners to use out of the box.

In this chapter, I'll guide you through a "quick win" example project using LoRa. We'll explore the modulation scheme in detail, and I'll show you how to participate in The Things Network (TTN) by using a LoRaWAN-compatible expansion board.

Use Cases

There's no doubt that LoRa is a fascinating technology. But how is it useful in the real world? What problems does it solve? IoT networks have connected millions of devices to the internet to perform monitoring tasks, gather data, and enable remote control of systems via servos and other mechanical devices. These loosely connected, heterogeneous networks operate on various standards, including Message Queueing Telemetry Transport (MQTT), Zigbee, Wi-Fi, and cellular. LoRa and its associated network architecture, LoRaWAN, were developed in 2013 in response to the need for an LPWAN solution and saw their first real-world deployments shortly thereafter. Today, they are the most widely adopted LPWAN standards, with networks reaching hundreds of millions of devices across the globe.

LoRa is an excellent choice for battery-, solar-, or mains-powered nodes transmitting at intervals measured in minutes, in networks with low- to medium-node densities. These are typically WANs with long-range links. Other IoT communication modules are limited to a few kilometers at best and are often much more restricted in terms of range. The most common early use cases for LoRa included environmental monitoring, asset tracking, and smart metering. These days, LoRa devices and LoRaWAN networks are deployed in diverse areas ranging from smart cities and meteorology to supply chains, logistics, and agriculture.

For all its advantages, LoRa comes with trade-offs that make it less suitable for other types of projects. It's generally not well suited for applications that require high throughput, low latency, or frequent transmissions. You won't be transferring large files, using Voice over IP (VoIP), or streaming much of anything with LoRa. In terms of bandwidth, your expectations should be measured in tens of bytes rather than kilobytes or megabytes.

Hardware Required

LoRa has a relatively low barrier to entry for DIYers and enthusiasts, though costs and complexity can increase as the scope of a deployment grows. For this reason, the hardware choices for this project were made with accessibility and budget-friendliness in mind, emphasizing components that:

- Are plug-and-play with the Raspberry Pi family of devices and require little or no soldering, wiring, or use of breadboards

- Are affordable and readily available

- Use a common programming language (Python, in this case) for libraries that interface with them

- Are suitable for both rapid prototyping and deployment in real-world IoT applications

If you're interested in expanding this project by adding a LoRaWAN gateway of your own, this optional hardware is discussed in "Going Further" on page 197.

Compatible Raspberry Pi Models

Many host controller options can be used with LoRa expansion boards. In this context, a *host controller* is a hardware interface responsible for managing communication between the central processing unit (CPU) and connected peripheral devices, typically through SPI, UART, or similar interfaces. Arduino microcontrollers are among the most popular with LoRa hardware vendors and practitioners. However, several excellent LoRa expansion HATs are also available for the Raspberry Pi family of devices.

You can use any recent Raspberry Pi model for this project. I'll be using the Pi Zero 2 W, pictured in Figure 6-1, whose small form factor makes it ideally suited for this project. It's widely available from online retailers for about $15.

Figure 6-1: The Raspberry Pi Zero 2 W

The Pi Zero 2 W comes standard without a GPIO header, so you'll need to obtain a header and perform some basic soldering to attach it to the board (for details, see "Male GPIO Header" on page 231). Alternatively, you can avoid this step by purchasing a Zero 2 W with a presoldered header, usually for little extra cost.

LoRa Expansion Boards

To narrow the field, I've selected two LoRa/LoRaWAN expansion boards from different manufacturers that are a good fit for this project. Both use the standard 40-pin GPIO header and are fully compatible with the Raspberry Pi family of devices. The first node, made by Waveshare, is affordable and well suited for exploring peer-to-peer (P2P) LoRa message exchange. The second, from Pi Supply, is about twice the price but includes an integrated LoRaWAN stack that handles most of the heavy lifting involved in connecting to gateways.

Depending on your interests, budget, and desired use case, you may choose to use two Waveshare nodes, one or more Pi Supply nodes, or a combination of the two.

Waveshare LoRa/LoRaWAN Node

The SX1262 LoRaWAN Node expansion board, manufactured by Waveshare, provides an excellent and affordable on-ramp for exploring LoRa applications. It uses the newer generation of Semtech's SX1262 RF chip and communicates with the host controller via the SPI bus. The SX1262 chip provides the physical layer for LoRa communication. While Waveshare bills it as a LoRaWAN-compatible node, the implementation of the LoRaWAN protocol stack must be handled with a software library on the host. In this chapter, I'll focus on using this node exclusively for P2P LoRa applications, which it supports well out of the box. To uplink data to a LoRaWAN network server, you can configure it to communicate with a device such as the Pi Supply LoRaWAN Node, discussed in the following section.

The Waveshare SX1262 LoRaWAN Node, shown in Figure 6-2, is available in two frequency-band versions: 410 to 510 MHz and 850 to 930 MHz. Be sure to choose the correct version for use in your region.

Figure 6-2: The Waveshare SX1262 LoRaWAN
Node expansion board

This module includes an external antenna and IPEX connector adapter. It also offers an optional global navigation satellite system (GNSS) function via an onboard GPS module and rechargeable button cell for accurate location information. If your use case involves asset tracking or has other location requirements, you might consider this version. The basic expansion boards are used here, so the GNSS functions won't be covered.

The SX1262 LoRaWAN Node uses a standard Raspberry Pi 40-pin GPIO extension header and is therefore compatible with all Raspberry Pi series boards. Its form factor makes it a good match for the Raspberry Pi Zero W models. Since you'll be exploring P2P communication using LoRa modulation in this recipe, you'll need two of these expansion boards. They're available directly from Waveshare for about $16.

Pi Supply IoT LoRa/LoRaWAN pHAT

Pi Supply's IoT LoRa pHAT, shown in Figure 6-3, is a multifrequency expansion board for the Raspberry Pi. It uses the RAKWireless RAK811 node module, which is based on Semtech's SX1276 LoRa chip. Notably, the RAK811 includes an embedded LoRaWAN protocol stack that supports Class A and Class C device types. The LoRaWAN specification defines three end device classes; all LoRaWAN devices must support Class A, while Classes B and C offer extended capabilities with different downlink behaviors. Having an embedded LoRaWAN stack allows this node to streamline communication with LoRaWAN gateways: The Python library used with this node simply sends instructions to the RAK811, which then manages communication through its onboard firmware. This is useful, as timing between the module and host controller can be tricky to implement and troubleshoot.

Figure 6-3: The Pi Supply multifrequency Raspberry Pi IoT LoRa pHAT

Because this is a multifrequency board, a single version is available that you can configure for use in your region. The Pi Supply pHAT has a low-profile GPIO header that, when mounted to the Raspberry Pi Zero, sits a scant 4 mm above it, making a highly compact LoRaWAN node. A stacking header is included for use with larger Raspberry Pi models, and an inter-integrated circuit (I^2C) breakout header, visible on the board's rightmost edge in Figure 6-3, allows for easy connection of I^2C-compatible sensors and other components. The board also includes both an integrated antenna and a u.FL connector with an adapter for an external antenna. The IoT LoRa pHAT is available directly from Pi Supply for about $34.

LiPo Battery HAT

While not a strict hardware requirement, a lithium-ion polymer battery can be useful when conducting tests of LoRa's range potential. This will enable you to physically traverse your survey area with a LoRa transmitter node while gathering empirical data on the receiving node, as discussed in "Conducting Long-Range Tests" on page 180.

Given LoRa's diminutive power requirements, you've likely heard about LoRa end devices that are capable of operating for up to a decade on battery power alone. While this is possible, it should be noted that the host controller (the Raspberry Pi Zero) has significantly greater power demands. Therefore, with an attached battery HAT, you can expect a nominal operating time measured in hours. Of the many LiPo battery HATs available, Waveshare's Uninterruptible Power Supply (UPS) HAT for Raspberry Pi Zero models, shown in Figure 6-4, is both affordable and well suited for this project.

Figure 6-4: The Waveshare UPS HAT for Pi Zero models

It's available directly from Waveshare for around $24.

Software Used

You'll make extensive use of several open source Python libraries to interface with each of the LoRa node expansion boards used in this project. The first portion of this recipe will focus on peer-to-peer messaging between two LoRa nodes equipped with the SX1262 HAT. You'll use the LoRa-RF Python library for transmitting messages between these nodes. The goal here is to validate your hardware and software environment with a "quick win" LoRa demonstration. This will lay the foundation for developing a better understanding of LoRa modulation.

With a grasp of the fundamentals, you'll be ready to dive deeper into the various parameters that define a LoRa signal. After adjusting these settings with LoRa-RF, you'll conduct some tests to observe their practical effects and gather empirical data.

Then, I'll switch gears and take you through the steps of installing the RAK811 Python library that supports the Pi Supply IoT LoRa pHAT. With this done, you'll be ready to connect this node to a LoRaWAN gateway hosted by TTN, as described in "Connecting to a LoRaWAN Gateway" on page 185.

A Closer Look at the SX1262

At the core of the Waveshare HAT is the Semtech SX1262 LoRa RF chip, a LoRa transceiver module capable of both transmitting and receiving LoRa packets. It's typically used in end devices to exchange messages with other nodes or, optionally, a LoRaWAN gateway, and it's not suitable (or hardware-compatible) for use as a gateway device on its own. The SX1262 module is optimized for low power consumption, making it ideal for battery-powered sensors and IoT devices.

To fulfill the goals of this project, you will need a minimum of two HATs with SX1262 LoRa RF modules that operate on the same frequency.

If you've already completed the recipe in Chapter 3 (or some of the later recipes in this book), you'll be familiar with pinouts of hardware components that are used to extend the Pi's capabilities. You'll find references to these pins and their functions in the Python code, so it's worth acquiring a basic familiarity with them.

Looking at the pin designations in Figure 6-5, you'll notice two sets of numbers and a function name indicated for each pin.

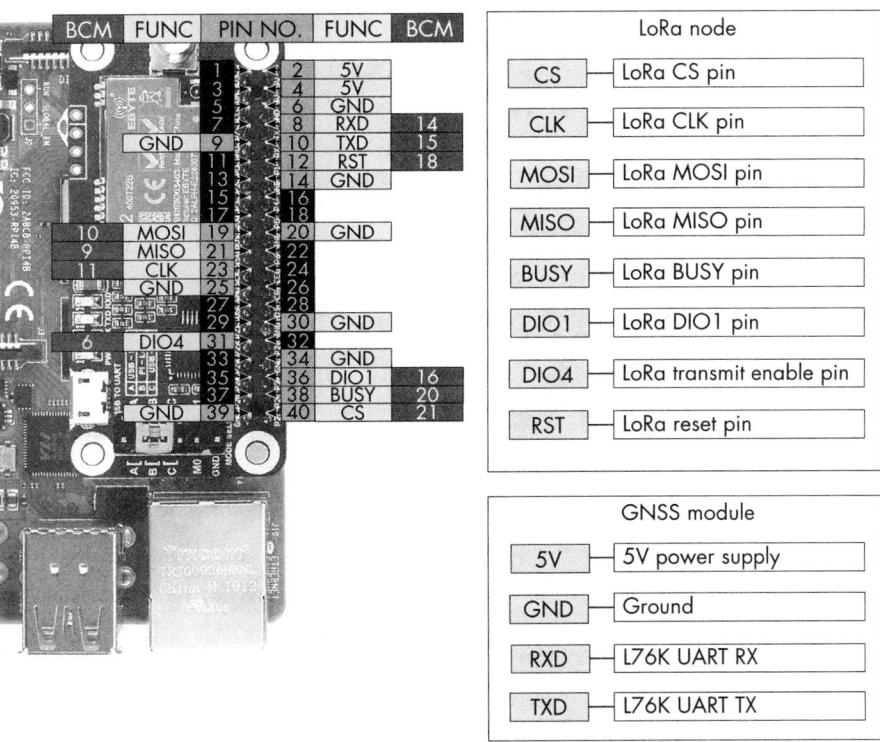

Figure 6-5: The Waveshare SX1262 LoRa expansion board pinout

The GPIO pins, sometimes referred to as *Broadcom* or *BCM* pins, are identified with "BCM" in this figure. In code, you'll often see these referenced as GPIO6, for example. These identifiers differ from the physical, or board, numbers that correspond to each pin's actual location on the header. I'll discuss the pin functions, abbreviated as "FUNC" in the pinout diagram, shortly.

Prerequisites

Before delving into the code, you'll need to configure your Raspberry Pi's serial interfaces and prepare your Python environment. I'll then guide you through the steps of building the LoRaRF Python package. Finally, you'll attach an adapter and external antenna to your SX1262 HAT.

For the initial LoRa demonstration, complete this setup on a single node. After you've verified that the project code works as expected on that node, you can repeat these steps on the second node. Later, you'll operate one LoRa node as a transmitter and the other as a receiver. Finally, you'll configure a separate node as an end device and connect it to a LoRaWAN gateway on TTN.

If you're eager to skip to the LoRaWAN portion of this chapter, I'd recommend completing the peer-to-peer demonstration first. The concepts and practical knowledge you'll acquire here are directly applicable to the latter portions of this recipe.

Enabling the SPI Port

To communicate with the SX1262 LoRa HAT, you'll need to enable the serial peripheral interface (SPI) port on your Pi. Also known as the *four-wire serial bus*, SPI lets you attach multiple compatible devices to a single set of pins by assigning them different chip select or chip enable (CE) pins. To communicate with a specific SPI device, you assert its corresponding CE pin, signaling it to become active and ready to exchange data with the main device. By default, the Raspberry Pi allows you to use SPI0 with CE0 on GPIO 8 and CE1 on GPIO 7. These appear in the bottom-right corner of the pinout diagram in Figure 6-6.

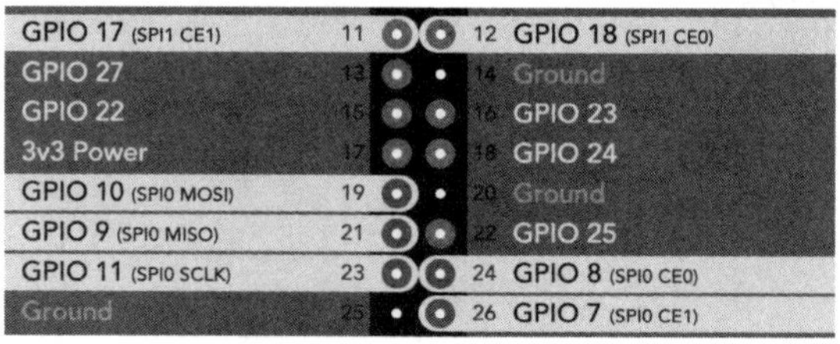

GPIO 17 (SPI1 CE1)	11	⊙⊙	12	GPIO 18 (SPI1 CE0)
GPIO 27	13	⊙ •	14	Ground
GPIO 22	15	⊙ ⊙	16	GPIO 23
3v3 Power	17	⊙ ⊙	18	GPIO 24
GPIO 10 (SPI0 MOSI)	19	⊙ •	20	Ground
GPIO 9 (SPI0 MISO)	21	⊙ •	22	GPIO 25
GPIO 11 (SPI0 SCLK)	23	⊙⊙	24	GPIO 8 (SPI0 CE0)
Ground	25	• ⊙	26	GPIO 7 (SPI0 CE1)

Figure 6-6: The SPI pins are grouped into SPI0 and SPI1 (source: https://pinout.xyz).

While you're examining this diagram, refer back to Figure 6-5. You'll see that SPI0 pins 10, 9, and 11 correspond to the LoRa HAT's MOSI, MISO, and SCLK pins, respectively. In standard SPI mode, the peripheral uses a three-wire serial protocol (MOSI, MISO, and SCLK), while the fourth wire refers to the CE pin. These SPI functions, along with their pin designations and signal names, are summarized in Table 6-1.

Table 6-1: SPI Pin Mapping

SPI function	Header pin	Broadcom pin	Signal name
MOSI	19	GPIO 10	Main out secondary in
MISO	21	GPIO 9	Main in secondary out
SCLK	23	GPIO 11	Serial clock
CE0	24	GPIO 8	Chip enable (or chip select)
CE1	26	GPIO 7	Chip enable (or chip select)

The MOSI line is used in SPI to send data from the main device to the secondary device. MISO is the corresponding line for sending data from the secondary device back to the main device. SCLK is used to synchronize data transmissions between the main and secondary devices.

SPI0 is disabled by default, but you can enable it by editing *config.txt*. While the SPI overlays typically define two chip select lines, you can combine these into one line by using `dtoverlay=spi0-1cs`. Open the configuration file in your editor with

```
$ sudo nano /boot/firmware/config.txt
```

and add the following lines at the end:

```
dtparam=spi=on
dtoverlay=spi0-1cs
```

Save the file and exit your editor, then reboot your system. To confirm that SPI0 is enabled and active, run:

```
$ ls -l /dev/spidev
crw-rw---- 1 root spi 153, 0 May 14 10:14 /dev/spidev0.0
```

You should see output similar to that shown here. You'll encounter many references to the SPI bus and these pins in this recipe's Python code, so it's worth acquiring a basic understanding of these fundamentals. With the SPI port configured on your device, proceed to the next step.

Enabling the UART Port

The Raspberry Pi has a dedicated universal asynchronous receiver-transmitter interface, which you'll use to communicate with the Pi Supply IoT LoRa/LoRaWAN pHAT. The UART and SPI interfaces use different sets of GPIO pins, so they're able to operate concurrently without pin conflicts. As shown in Figure 6-7, the UART pins GPIO 14 and GPIO 15 are used to transmit (*TXD*) and receive (*RXD*) on the serial interface, respectively.

Figure 6-7: The UART interface uses GPIO pins 14 and 15 (source: https://pinout.xyz).

The UART interface is disabled by default. To enable it, edit */boot/firmware/config.txt* again. Open the file in your editor and append the following lines:

```
enable_uart=1
dtoverlay=disable-bt,miniuart-bt
```

The second directive swaps the serial interfaces by disabling Bluetooth on the main UART and assigning the mini UART to the Bluetooth controller (for more on this, see the upcoming box on serial ports).

Save the file and exit your editor. Next, you'll need to update the boot command line. Open the kernel command line file in your editor with:

```
$ sudo nano /boot/firmware/cmdline.txt
```

Locate and remove any instance of either `console=serial0,115200` or `console=ttyAMA0,115200`. Then, add `console=tty1` to the command line to disable the terminal. This will ensure that the console doesn't interfere with UART communication and that the port remains available to the *dialout* group. Save the file, exit your editor, and reboot your system for these changes to take effect.

A BRIEF HISTORY OF SERIAL PORTS

In the not-too-distant past, writing code to use the Raspberry Pi's serial port was fairly straightforward. But with each new distribution update, the kernel evolved, with changes needed to accommodate new hardware (notably, the Raspberry Pi 3 and 4) and Broadcom's Bluetooth Low Energy (BLE) module. These days, things are a bit more complicated.

Prior to the Raspberry Pi era, developers could usually expect to find a serial interface labeled something like `COM1` on a header. On the Pi, as you saw in Figure 6-7, the equivalent interface is provided by pins 14 and 15 of the GPIO header. The corresponding Linux device file is */dev/ttyAMA0*. The Pi can use this serial port as a terminal login interface, which is handy if you don't have a network connection. By default, `ttyAMA0` is used for this purpose and managed by a software service known as *getty*.

But what if you want to use this port to communicate with an attached hardware module instead? In this section, you disabled the serial console login so that you alone can control the port. So far, so good. If you add Bluetooth to the mix, however, there's a complication: You'll find that this port has been "stolen" from the GPIO header, and an inferior */dev/ttyS0* mini UART has

---

been substituted in its place. Since you're not using Bluetooth in this project, you've explicitly swapped these ports so the high-performance /dev/ttyAMA0 can be used exclusively for communicating with the LoRa pHAT.

Getty hasn't entirely left the building, though. Your system may still attempt to spawn a serial console at boot. Fortunately, there's a simple fix for this, described next.

In some kernel versions, disabling the console by using this method or by the more traditional use of raspi-config will still result in the system spawning a serial console process at boot. For a complete explanation, refer to "Serial Console (Getty) Deactivation" on page 195. If you simply want to prevent the console from using the UART port, you can do that with:

```
$ sudo systemctl mask serial-getty@ttyAMA0.service
```

Following a reboot, you can verify that the UART interface is enabled by executing these commands:

```
$ ls -l /dev/serial
lrwxrwxrwx 1 root root 7 May 30 11:53 /dev/serial0 -> ttyAMA0
```

```
$ ls -l /dev/ttyAMA
crw-rw---- 1 root dialout 204, 64 May 31 12:07 /dev/ttyAMA0
```

```
$ ls -l /dev/ttyS
crw-rw---- 1 root dialout 4, 64 May 31 12:15 /dev/ttyS0
```

In the output shown here, /dev/ttyAMA0 is the device file that corresponds to the primary UART interface. This is the more capable UART, typically assigned to the Bluetooth module. By contrast, /dev/ttyS0 corresponds to the less capable mini UART serial interface.

Preparing Your Environment

You'll be using Python's package manager, pip, to set up a virtual environment, or venv. If you've already completed a recipe using pip, these steps will be familiar. First, update your system packages and installing python3-pip:

```
$ sudo apt update
$ sudo apt install python3-pip
```

In earlier versions of Raspberry Pi OS, it was possible to install libraries directly and system-wide using pip. In newer versions of the OS, and indeed most Debian-based operating systems, this is no longer permitted. If you attempt to install a Python package system-wide, you'll see an error like the following:

```
$ pip3 install python-dotenv
error: externally-managed-environment
```

```
x This environment is externally managed
> To install Python packages system-wide, try apt install python3-xyz,
  where xyz is the package you are trying to install.
--snip--
```

This message appears because you're trying to install a third-party package into the system Python. Historically, conflicts between system package managers like apt and Python-specific package management tools like pip have created problems for developers, including Python-level API incompatibilities, file ownership issues, and more.

To avoid this, you'll create a venv. Since you'll be working from a companion source code repository, you can clone this recipe's GitHub project and use its directory as your working environment. Start by installing git, if it isn't present on your system:

```
$ sudo apt install git
```

Next, clone the companion source code repository and change into the directory that holds your project code:

```
$ cd $HOME
$ git clone https://github.com/wirelesscookbook/lorahat-py.git
$ cd lorahat-py
```

Ensure that python3-venv is available on your system, and activate your virtual environment by executing the following commands:

```
$ sudo apt install python3-venv -y
$ python3 -m venv lora --system-site-packages
```

You'll need to activate the venv each time your system is rebooted. You can do so by running:

```
$ source lora/bin/activate
```

Note that each virtual environment is tied to a directory in the Linux filesystem. When the venv is active, you'll notice that the bash prompt has changed to the following:

```
(lora) pi@raspberrypi:~/lorawan-hat $
```

If you don't see the (lora) prefix in your project directory, executing Python code that references the libraries you'll be installing will result in ModuleNotFound errors. This is a common oversight, but one that's easily remedied by repeating the activation step. You can deactivate a venv by using the deactivate command in the project directory (leave it active for now).

Installing the Python Package

With your Python virtual environment created, you can now install the required Python package. In this recipe, you'll use a fork of the LoRa-RF Python library, which provides basic functions for sending and receiving messages using the Semtech SX126x LoRa module.

The library communicates with the LoRa module via the SPI port you configured earlier, using the GPIO pins described in "A Closer Look at the SX1262" on page 163. Your Raspberry Pi functions as the host controller, sending commands to the attached LoRa HAT and SX126x module. You can think of the LoRa-RF library as the "glue" between the host controller and the LoRa transceiver.

Ensure that you're in the project source code directory, then manually build the package:

```
(lora) $ cd ~/lorawan-hat
(lora) $ pip3 install dist/LoRaRF-1.4.0-py3-none-any.whl
```

Installing the package with pip in this way installs the rpi-lgpio and spidev libraries as dependencies. You can confirm this by checking the pip package list. You should see output similar to the following:

```
(lora) $ pip list
--snip--
LoRaRF          1.4.0
rpi-lgpio       0.6
spidev          3.5
toml            0.10.2
--snip--
```

Your package release versions may be different from these; the important thing is that they're present.

EDGE DETECTION AND DEBOUNCING

This source for this package has been forked and modified for greater flexibility and better compatibility with Debian/Raspberry Pi OS Bookworm. The principal change is replacing the RPi.GPIO dependency with the rpi-lgpio package. This package serves as a *compatibility shim* for lgpio, emulating the RPi.GPIO API.

This is important because, while RPi.GPIO is the more traditional and widely used library for handling GPIO on the Raspberry Pi, under Bookworm it has some limitations. In this project, with RPi.GPIO you'll encounter issues related to

(continued)

---

event detection, specifically when using add_event_detect() with the IRQ GPIO pin. Exceptions like the following are common:

```
GPIO.add_event_detect(irqPin, GPIO.RISING, callback=checkTransmitDone)
RuntimeError: Failed to add edge detection
```

In this context, *edge detection* refers to identifying changes in a signal's state—specifically, transitions from low to high (rising edge), high to low (falling edge), or both. Related to this is *debouncing*, the process of filtering out false or spurious signal transitions by using software or a physical hardware component, such as a resistor–capacitor circuit.

The debouncing of signals works fundamentally differently in RPi.GPIO and lgpio (the library underlying rpi-lgpio). RPi.GPIO debounces signals by tracking the last timestamp at which it saw a given edge and suppressing reports of edges that occur within a specified number of milliseconds after that. By contrast, lgpio (and thus rpi-lgpio) debounces by waiting for a signal to be stable for a specified number of milliseconds before reporting the edge. For some applications, there will be little to no difference other than rpi-lgpio reporting an edge a few milliseconds later than RPi.GPIO would.

The following diagram shows the waveform from a "bouncy" switch being pressed once, along with the positions in time where RPi.GPIO and rpi-lgpio would report the rising edge when a debounce of 3 ms is requested:

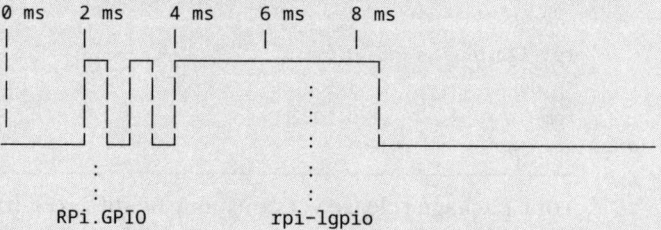

RPi.GPIO reports the edge at 2 ms, then suppresses the edges at 3 ms and 4 ms because they are within 3 ms of the last edge. By contrast, rpi-lgpio ignores the first and second rising edges (because they didn't stay stable for 3 ms) and reports only the third edge at 7 ms.

This has implications for the GPIO IRQ pin of your attached LoRa HAT. In this specific case, RPi.GPIO is unable to detect an edge from this pin to notify us (via the checkTransmitDone callback) when a LoRa message has been transmitted. The solution here is to simply let rpi-lgpio perform this detection instead. No other code changes are required.

The LoRaRF library includes support for setting frequencies, modulation parameters, transmit power, receive gain, and other RF parameters using LoRa modulation. Transmitting and receiving capabilities are achieved by using interrupt signals. You'll gain firsthand experience with these operations shortly.

Attaching the Antenna

The SX1262 HAT includes a magnetic CB-type antenna and an IPEX adapter cable. Unlike the Pi Supply IoT LoRa/LoRaWAN pHAT, which has an on-board antenna, the SX1262 HAT requires you to attach an external antenna. While you won't need it for the verification tests you'll perform in the next section, you will for the long-range operations later in this chapter.

Viewed from above with the GPIO header at the top, the board's IPEX antenna connector is located on the right-hand edge. Position the female end of the IPEX adapter cable over the connector and press down firmly to attach it.

If you chose the GNSS version of the SX1262 HAT, this will include a GPS antenna. If you like, you can connect this to the IPEX connector located just above the LoRa antenna connection point. This recipe focuses exclusively on the basic SX1262 HAT, so the GNSS functions won't be covered.

Running the LoRa Example

With the prerequisites complete, your LoRa node should be ready to run this project's Python code. The goal here is to validate that your Python environment, required modules, and SPI port are correctly configured so you can communicate with the SX1262 LoRa HAT. You can then repeat the setup steps on your second LoRa node and run the same example on it to confirm that it's also configured correctly.

Configuring the Transmitter

Start by changing to the project examples folder:

```
(lora) $ cd ~/lorahat-py/examples/SX126x/
```

If you don't see (lora) prepended to the bash prompt, activate your Python virtual environment by running:

```
$ source ~/lorahat-py/lora/bin/activate
```

I've opted to manage the LoRa project's configuration using a *Tom's Obvious Minimal Language (TOML)* file. TOML is an easy-to-read configuration format popular across many programming languages. For messages sent by a LoRa transmitter to be properly decoded, or *demodulated*, by a receiver, several modulation parameters must match. Storing these values centrally in this way means you need to edit them only once on each node. The usefulness of this approach will become clearer after you start manipulating these settings.

The TOML file contains default values for many parameters, including those defining the LoRa modulation scheme, packet length, and more. Open this file in your editor with

```
(lora) $ nano config.toml
```

and locate the frequency parameter:

```
# Set frequency to 868 MHz.
frequency = 868000000
--snip--
```

As mentioned earlier, the SX126x LoRa expansion board is available in two frequency-band versions: 410 to 510 MHz and 850 to 930 MHz. A frequency value in the latter range is used here. If you're using the lower-frequency 410 to 510 MHz band version, be sure to modify this value. For example, if you'd like to use 425 MHz, multiply that by 1,000,000 to determine the frequency setting.

At the top of the TOML file, you'll notice that the Raspberry Pi's GPIO pins are defined for the SX126x HAT. These values correspond to the Broadcom (BCM) pin values in the pinout guide (Figure 6-5). Leave these and the other parameters at their defaults for now; we'll take a closer look at these settings in the next section.

Save the file and exit the editor, then execute the demo with the following command:

```
(lora) $ python3 transmitter.py

Begin LoRa radio
Set frequency to 868 MHz
Set TX power to +22 dBm
Set modulation parameters:
    Spreading factor = 7
    Bandwidth = 125 kHz
    Coding rate = 4/5
Set packet parameters:
    Explicit header type
    Preamble length = 12
    Payload Length = 15
    CRC True
Set synchronize word to 0x3444

-- LoRa Transmitter --

HeLoRa World!  0
Transmit time: 68.36 ms | Data rate: 219.43 byte/s
HeLoRa World!  1
Transmit time: 68.62 ms | Data rate: 218.60 byte/s
--snip--
```

If you see the HeLoRa World! output and associated metrics, congratulations! You've successfully sent your first LoRa messages. There's no LoRa receiver configured to demodulate these messages yet, so the transmitter example will repeat continuously at five-second intervals. When you're satisfied that it's working as expected, you can interrupt it with CTRL-C.

You can now go back and set up your second LoRa node. Once this is done, proceed to the next section.

Configuring a Receiver

With your two LoRa transceivers prepared, you can operate one as a transmitter while the second one acts as a receiver. For the initial message test, I recommend keeping your LoRa nodes within a reasonable range of each other (say, a few meters). You'll experiment with extending the messaging range shortly.

First, ensure that the modulation parameters contained in the TOML files are in agreement on each node. The frequency, spreading factor, and bandwidth values must be identical. Again, you can stick with the defaults for now (unless you need to change the frequency). On your first LoRa transceiver, run:

```
(lora) $ python3 transmitter.py
```

The example transmitter will repeat the default HeLoRa World! message at five-second intervals. Now, run the following command on your second LoRa transceiver. You should see output similar to this:

```
(lora) $ python3 receiver.py

Begin LoRa radio
Set frequency to 868 Mhz
Set RX gain to power saving gain
Set modulation parameters:
    Spreading factor = 7
    Bandwidth = 125 kHz
    Coding rate = 4/5
Set packet parameters:
    Explicit header type
    Preamble length = 12
    Payload Length = 15
    CRC True
Set synchronize word to 0x3444

-- LoRa Receiver Continuous --

HeLoRa World!  0
Packet status: RSSI = -54.00 dBm | SNR = 11.75 dB
HeLoRa World!  1
Packet status: RSSI = -52.00 dBm | SNR = 12.25 dB
```

The LoRa radio preamble is displayed to confirm the node's settings, followed by the messages received from the transmitting LoRa node. These messages are demodulated and output along with some packet metrics. In this example, the receiver operates in *continuous mode*, meaning it requests incoming LoRa packets without entering into a sleep period. Sleep periods are typically associated with a *duty cycle*, which is the percentage of time a signal is "on" (high) versus "off" (low) during one complete cycle.

With the receiver example running, return to your transmitting LoRa node. Open the TOML file in your editor and modify the message setting as shown here, commenting out or removing the original line and adding a new one:

```
--snip--
# LoRa message to send. If set to "temperature" the transmitter's CPU
# temperature will be sent in the payload.
# message = "HeLoRa World!\0"
message = "temperature"
```

Save the file and exit your editor. Interrupt the transmitter example with CTRL-C, then start it again by executing **python3 transmitter.py**. Returning to the receiving LoRa node, you should see the current CPU temperature of the transmitter. Example output is shown here:

```
CPU temperature: 42.93°C  0
Packet status: RSSI = -57.00 dBm | SNR = 12.00 dB
CPU temperature: 43.47°C  1
Packet status: RSSI = -59.00 dBm | SNR = 12.25 dB
CPU temperature: 43.01°C  2
Packet status: RSSI = -50.00 dBm | SNR = 12.50 dB
--snip--
```

Sending CPU temperature readings is a simple example of real-time data telemetry between two LoRa nodes. It's not a stretch to imagine how this value could be replaced with something more interesting, such as GPS coordinates or readings from an environmental sensor.

Up to now, I've glossed over the modulation and packet parameters in the TOML configuration file. In the next section, we'll take a closer look at the modulation techniques LoRa uses. This will give you a practical understanding of how messages are transmitted and how to fine-tune these parameters for your specific use case.

LoRa Modulation in Detail

Depending on the broadcast frequency and power level settings, the SX1262 LoRa module draws a tiny 32 to 118 mA of current when in transmit mode. How is LoRa capable of sending messages over such great distances, while also being so power efficient? To understand this, let's start with some basics on RF modulation.

LoRa relies on *spread spectrum modulation*. You're probably familiar with AM and FM, which are modulation techniques in amplitude and frequency, respectively. These are both forms of an older analog modulation technique. Like Wi-Fi, LoRa uses digital modulation and a form of spread spectrum—but that's where the comparison ends. LoRa is derived from an existing chirp spread spectrum (CSS) modulation technology that was originally developed for radar applications in the 1940s.

Chirp pulses can be found throughout the natural world, such as those used by animals like dolphins and bats for sensing and communication. Though inaudible to us, these chirps can travel long distances and remain detectable even in noisy environments. Bird chirps, which are audible to us, have a similar property of being identifiable even when many birds are chirping at the same time.

These examples from nature translate directly to what happens on the radio spectrum with LoRa. The advantage of chirp modulation is that it allows a signal to be decoded even when it's buried in noise.

In this context, a *chirp* refers to a signal whose frequency is deliberately varied over time. That is, the signal is transmitted in short bursts, continually "hopping" between frequencies in a specific sequence. This is illustrated in Figure 6-8.

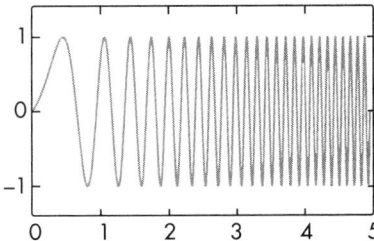

Figure 6-8: The amplitude and frequency distribution of a single LoRa chirp

Chirp modulation takes the 0s and 1s of the data you want to send and encodes them into a series of chirps. These discrete chirps are then sent in sequence on top of a fixed-frequency carrier signal. Spreading the signal in this way increases redundancy and makes the transmission more resistant to interference. To achieve the same reliability without using spread spectrum, a signal would have to be transmitted in a narrow band and with relatively high power.

To create a valid *frame*, or container of network data, a series of chirps must be assembled in a way that a LoRa radio is able to decode. Each chirp may either increase (an *up-chirp*) or decrease (a *down-chirp*) in frequency over time. These two types of chirps are illustrated in Figure 6-9.

To generate chirps, a LoRa modem modulates the phase of an oscillator. In Figure 6-9, the diagonal lines each represent a single chirp that "sweeps" over a range of frequencies. For this reason, chirps are also sometimes referred to as *sweep signals*.

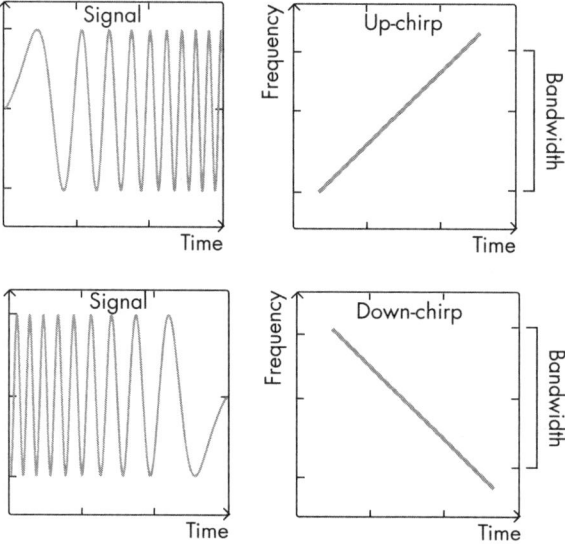

Figure 6-9: A visualization of up-chirps and down-chirps

The number of times per second the modem adjusts the phase, known as the *chip rate*, defines the modulation bandwidth. Since they appear similar, it's important to disambiguate the terms *chip* and *chirp*. In the context of spread spectrum transmission, a *chip* is the basic binary unit in a sequence of data, similar to a bit in computing. The chip rate will always be numerically equal to the selected bandwidth. For example, if the selected bandwidth is 125 kHz, the chip rate will be 125,000 chips per second.

Don't be concerned if the relationship between chirps, chips, and bandwidth is unclear at this stage. I'll break this down into manageable pieces in the next section.

Core LoRa Parameters

One of the first things newcomers to LoRa notice is the many configuration options it has. In some ways, this is not unlike what you encountered in earlier chapters while configuring Wi-Fi. However, the parameters that define LoRa's modulation scheme are quite different. Setting aside most of LoRa's complexities for the moment, I'll focus on the core modulation settings: bandwidth, spread factor, and coding rate. These three parameters are central to how a LoRa radio generates its signal. We'll take a closer look at each of them here.

Bandwidth

LoRa modulation can be configured to use a variety of RF bandwidths, defined in predetermined steps ranging from 7.8 kHz up to 500 kHz. The most commonly used channel width is 125 kHz, but 250 kHz and 500 kHz are also options. A higher (or wider) value can be used if fast transmission is required, at the expense of range. Conversely, choosing a lower (or narrower) bandwidth will result in a slower transfer rate but improved range.

There's an additional trade-off to be aware of here. The period during which a transmission occupies an RF channel, known as *airtime, dwell time,* or *time on air (ToA)*, increases as bandwidth narrows. Longer airtime means the LoRa node must spend more time actively transmitting, which leads to higher power consumption. This has obvious implications for nodes that rely on batteries.

If one thing should be obvious by now, it's that there's no free lunch with LoRa. The challenge is finding the sweet spot by selecting parameters to suit your specific requirements. Bandwidth is only the first part of the equation; we'll look at the other parameters you can use to fine-tune its modulation next.

Spreading Factor

You've seen how LoRa chirps are spread linearly in frequency. The amount of spreading applied to the original data signal is known as the *spreading factor (SF)*. LoRa supports six spreading factors, SF7 to SF12. These values affect data rate, airtime, battery life, and receiver sensitivity. As a general rule, the higher the spreading factor, the farther the signal will be able to travel and still be received without errors. A visual comparison of spreading factors is provided in Figure 6-10.

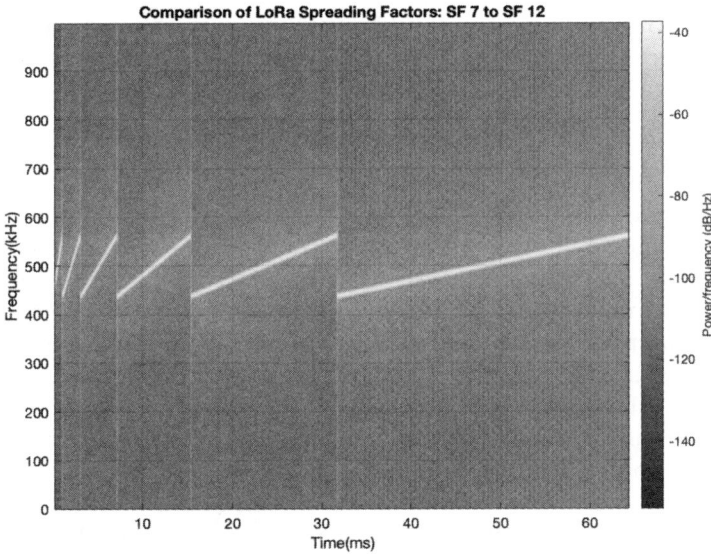

Figure 6-10: A comparison of LoRa spreading factors. Courtesy of Sakshama Ghoslya (https://www.sghoslya.com).

The spreading factor controls the chirp rate (not to be confused with the chip rate) and, by extension, the rate of data transmission. Lower spreading factors produce faster chirps and allow higher data throughput. This gives you the flexibility, through software, to trade data rate for range or power efficiency as needed. Table 6-2 shows four spreading factors (SF7–SF10) that can be used for messages on a 125 kHz channel. It also shows the relationship between chip rate, range, maximum payload size, and airtime.

Table 6-2: The Impact of Spreading Factor on LoRa Transmission Characteristics

Spreading factor	Chip rate	Range (terrain-dependent)	Max payload size	Airtime
SF10	980	8 km	11 bytes	371 ms
SF9	1,760	6 km	53 bytes	185 ms
SF8	3,125	4 km	115 bytes	103 ms
SF7	5,470	2 km	242 bytes	61 ms

The bitrate decreases as the spreading factor increases, and vice versa. At slower bitrates, the signal becomes easier for the receiver to detect in noisy environments. On the other hand, sending data slowly means it spends more time on air and keeps the devices active longer, at the cost of increased power consumption.

Finally, it's important to mention that LoRa spreading factors are inherently *orthogonal*. This means that signals modulated with different spreading factors can be transmitted simultaneously on the same frequency without interfering with one another. To a receiver, signals with mismatched spreading factors simply appear as background noise.

Coding Rate

You've seen how bandwidth and spreading factors control the physical parameters of LoRa's modulation scheme. These parameters have an effect on bitrate and range, with trade-offs in airtime, payload size, and power consumption. A third key parameter, known as the *coding rate*, controls the amount of error correction (redundant bits) added to the payload. This is expressed as the ratio of actual data to total transmitted data, with possible values being 4/5, 4/6, 4/7, or 4/8. A coding rate of 4/6 means 4 bits of data are sent with 2 bits of error correction. The LoRaWAN protocol fixes the coding rate at 4/5.

A higher coding rate will not increase range, but it will make a signal more reliable in the presence of interference. Since the coding rate does not modify the physical parameters of the modulation, LoRa transceivers using different coding rates will still be able to decode each other's signals. Applying coding rates asymmetrically is therefore useful when the receiver is located in an area of high interference, while the transmitter is not.

As you might expect, increasing the coding rate also comes at the cost of decreasing the data rate.

A Closer Look at LoRa Packets

Looking back at the transmitter example output in "Running the LoRa Example" on page 171, you'll notice that various packet parameters are reported. A LoRa modem uses two types of packet formats: explicit and implicit. The *explicit* packet includes a short header that contains information about the number of bytes, coding rate (CR), and whether a cyclic redundancy check (CRC) is used in the packet. The packet format is illustrated in Figure 6-11.

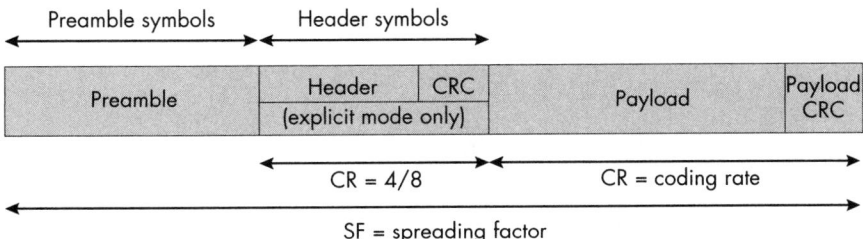

Figure 6-11: The LoRa explicit packet format

A LoRa packet starts with a *preamble sequence*, which is used to synchronize the receiver with the incoming signal. The transmitted preamble length may vary from 10 to 65,535 symbols, taking into account the fixed overhead of the preamble data. The preamble includes a *sync word*, which is a unique sequence of bits that marks the beginning of the packet and helps the receiver distinguish between noise and actual data. In the transmitter example, a sync word with the value 0x3444 is used. This corresponds to public networks such as LoRaWAN, which are commonly used with SX126x devices.

The preamble is followed by a *header* containing information about the payload that follows, such as its length and the presence of optional fields. The *payload* itself is a variable-length field that contains the actual data being transmitted. This may include things like sensor readings, instructions, or any other information relevant to an application. In the LoRa demonstration you executed earlier, your messages were contained in this payload.

Finally, an optional CRC may be appended. I touched on CRCs in "Evaluating Performance" on page 20; this is a checksum used for error detection and is common in many forms of digital communications.

An Example Packet Definition

Returning to the Python examples, you can see how these parameters are defined in practice. Open *config.toml* in your editor with

```
(lora) $ nano ~/lorahat-py/examples/SX126x/config.toml
```

and locate the following section:

```
# Packet parameters include header preamble length, payload length and
# CRC type. The explicit packet type is used by default and uses these
```

```
# parameters. The receiver can receive a packet with different coding
# rates and packet parameters in explicit header mode.
preambleLength = 12
payloadLength = 15
crcType = true
--snip--
```

Explicit header mode is used by default in the example code; the preamble and payload lengths are defined here. Finally, the CRC is enabled. Also note that a LoRa receiver is capable of decoding packets transmitted with different coding rates and packet parameters. You can experiment with this by manipulating these values on either node.

Message Size Constraints

The transmitter example uses a short message. As you saw in Table 6-2, the maximum user payload size for a LoRa packet depends on several factors, including the spreading factor, chip rate, and transmission range. However, these packets are designed to be quite small: A typical LoRa packet might have a payload size ranging from a few bytes to a few dozen bytes. The largest message a LoRa chip can send is 256 bytes, including packet overhead. This isn't a limitation imposed by a programming library or firmware, but by the chip itself. At higher spreading factors and longer ranges (up to 5 miles, theoretically), the chip rate drops considerably, and messages may be limited to just 11 bytes.

These relatively small payload sizes, coupled with power consumption (if relevant to your application), will necessarily influence the design of your data.

Conducting Long-Range Tests

The previous sections explored LoRa's modulation scheme in some detail, including the parameters used to define it as well as the composition of the packets that contain LoRa messages. We also looked at spreading factors and how they relate to range, message size, airtime, and other transmission properties. With a grasp of these fundamentals, you're no doubt ready to see what this technology is capable of.

As an example of what's possible, a new LoRa distance record was set in the summer of 2023, spanning an impressive 830 miles (1,336 km) near the Portuguese coast. LoRa beacons on the fishing vessel *Estrela de Sesimbra* and its buoys were able to exchange messages with a gateway connected to The Things Stack on the Spanish Canary Islands. The distance record was captured by the TTN mapper, as illustrated in Figure 6-12.

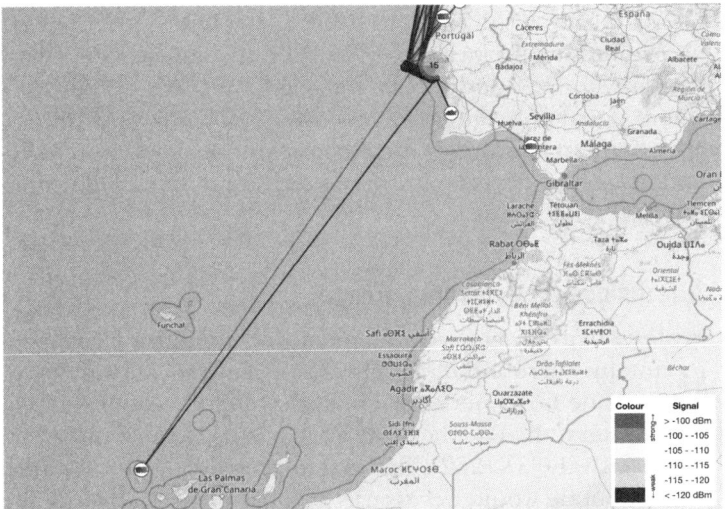

Figure 6-12: The LoRaWAN distance record established between a fishing boat and its buoys near the Portuguese coast (OpenStreetMap, CC BY-SA 2.0)

Note that this is an exceptional and rare achievement. TTN estimates that the majority of LoRaWAN devices in its network are 75 to 300 feet (25–100 meters) from the nearest gateway. Environmental factors are likely to have played an important role here, including tropospheric conditions influenced by the summer weather. Moreover, using LoRaWAN at sea level mitigates several variables introduced by varying altitudes in terrestrial applications.

Ideal Conditions

That said, you might be wondering, "What sort of effective ranges can I reasonably expect to obtain from my LoRa nodes?" Bear in mind here that your evaluation will be done with peer-to-peer communications between two LoRa end node transceivers. In other words, messages will be exchanged directly between these nodes, rather than through a LoRaWAN gateway. (I'll discuss communication uplinks between a LoRa node and a gateway in "Connecting to a LoRaWAN Gateway" on page 185.)

Let's define some test conditions. An ideal LoRa environment can be said to have the following properties:

- Fair weather (no precipitation, fog, or temperature extremes)
- A clear line of sight (an area free of obstructions such as tall trees, buildings, and so on)
- Nodes positioned at a height of approximately 8 feet (2.5 m) above the ground
- An auxiliary antenna with a gain of 2 to 5 dBi

Naturally, it's difficult to fulfill all of these conditions in real-world implementations. In fact, one of LoRa's most interesting characteristics is its ability to send and receive messages over long distances in urban areas, where signal noise and obstructions of all kinds are common. Your physical environment will largely dictate how you perform your LoRa distance evaluations. I'll discuss an evaluation technique suitable for my environment in the next section.

A Technique for Evaluating Range

My test environment is characteristically more rural than urban, with wooded mountains surrounding a valley floor. For this reason, I chose to add a UPS HAT to one LoRa node for greater mobility. With an attached 1,000 mAh LiPo battery, the Raspberry Pi Zero 2 W is capable of running for several hours with the SX1262 chip transmitting at 30-second intervals.

The node would necessarily be operating unattended, without an interactive user login. Therefore, I needed it to autostart in transmit mode on boot and write LoRa message events to a system log. A system-level systemd service fulfilled this goal. If you'd like to use it, the systemd unit file is included in the lorahat-py project in the book's GitHub repository.

To proceed with this setup, first create the logfile, set ownership and permissions, then copy and enable the systemd service:

```
(lora) $ sudo touch /var/log/lora-transmitter.log
(lora) $ sudo chown pi:pi /var/log/lora-transmitter.log
(lora) $ sudo chmod 644 /var/log/lora-transmitter.log
(lora) $ cd ~/lorahat-py
(lora) $ sudo cp lora-transmitter.service /etc/systemd/system/
(lora) $ sudo systemctl enable lora-transmitter.service
```

Note that if your username is different or you've cloned the repository into a different location, you'll need to replace pi with the name of your user in the second command and update the username and paths in the *lora-transmitter.service* file.

With that done, start and check the status of the service with the following commands:

```
(lora) $ sudo systemctl start lora-transmitter.service
(lora) $ sudo systemctl status lora-transmitter.service

lora-receiver.service - SX1262 LoRa node Python transmitter
     Loaded: loaded (/etc/systemd/system/lora-transmitter.service; enabled; preset: enabled)
     Active: active (running) since Sat 2025-05-17 09:41:25 CEST; 2s ago
   Main PID: 1057 (bash)
      Tasks: 5 (limit: 174)
        CPU: 2.526s
```

```
CGroup: /system.slice/lora-transmitter.service
        1057 /bin/bash -c "source /home/pi/lorahat-py/lora/bin/activate && python3 ...
        1058 python3 -u transmitter.py
```

Notice that the Python virtual environment is first activated, and the output of *transmitter.py* is appended to the log created in the previous step. Python's default behavior is to buffer output, so the -u option is specified here to force the stdout stream to be unbuffered.

To conserve battery power, I set sleepTime = 30 in the transmitter node's TOML configuration file. The receiving node remained at my test bench for the evaluation, with its external antenna positioned in such a way as to optimize line of sight. Running in continuous receive mode, the LoRa receiver node waits until it "hears" a transmission that matches its configured parameters. It then decodes the incoming packet and writes the message to the log, along with the packet index, RSSI, and signal-to-noise (SNR) values.

To conduct the evaluation, I started the receiver node at my test bench, disconnected the transmitter node's power adapter, and booted it with the UPS battery. It was then simply a matter of putting distance between the two nodes. This was a non-line-of-sight test, with various obstructions (buildings, vegetation, terrain) between the two nodes as I moved around. Throughout the duration of the test, RSSI and SNR values generally decreased in a nonlinear fashion as a function of distance. As range increased, and particularly when obstacles blocked the signal from the transmitter, CRC errors and dropped packets were noted in the receiver's logs.

In my testing, LoRa messages from the transmitter were successfully decoded at distances of up to 1.25 miles (2 km) at points with a clear line of sight. I was quite pleased to find that an inexpensive battery-powered LoRa node was able to successfully decode messages at ranges up to that point under these conditions.

LoRa Parameter Tuning

As you learned in "Core LoRa Parameters" on page 176, higher spreading factors typically yield longer potential ranges, at the cost of lower bitrates, smaller message payloads, and longer airtimes. My testing confirmed that increasing the spreading factor gave me greater range, at the expense of battery life because of the longer airtime. If your requirements are similar to those of most users of TTN, for example, the default parameters may well suit your needs. However, you may want to experiment with these default settings to optimize range.

Returning to the example Python project, the default LoRa modulation parameters are defined in the TOML configuration file. Open this file in your editor with

```
(lora) $ nano ~/lorahat-py/examples/SX126x/config.toml
```

and locate the parameter definitions:

```
spreadFactor = 7
bandwidth = 125000
codingRate = 5
```

The spreading factor is the one that will make or break your implementation. Finding the right setting is the key to achieving effective long-range performance in a LoRa or LoRaWAN device. As discussed earlier, the spreading factor determines how many chirps, which carry the data packets, are sent each second. A lower spreading factor (SF7, for example) corresponds to a higher chirp rate, allowing you to encode more data per second. Conversely, a higher spreading factor implies a lower chirp rate. Compared with a lower SF, sending the same amount of data at a higher SF requires a longer transmission time, or airtime. Longer airtime means the modem remains active longer, consuming more energy.

The advantage of a high SF is that the extended airtime gives the receiver more opportunities to sample the signal, resulting in better sensitivity. Increased sensitivity means the signal can be received at greater distances. Each increment in SF adds roughly 2.5 dB of receiver sensitivity, as shown in Table 6-3.

Table 6-3: The Relationship Between Spreading Factor and Receiver Sensitivity

Spreading factor	Receiver sensitivity (125 kHz fixed bandwidth)
SF7	–123 dBm
SF8	–126 dBm
SF9	–129 dBm
SF10	–132 dBm
SF11	–134.5 dBm

It's important to note here that simply increasing SF is not always the ideal solution. If you plug different values into a LoRa airtime calculator, you'll notice that it takes approximately 23 times longer (and hence 23 times more energy) to transmit a packet using SF12 than SF7. Modifying the payload size and headers for the transmission will yield different outputs, so this figure isn't cast in stone. The key takeaway is that each LoRa application is unique, so it's difficult to prescribe a one-size-fits-all set of parameters. The spreading factor that yields the lowest energy consumption for your setup won't necessarily be the highest or lowest; it will most likely be somewhere in the middle.

For this reason, you'll often find that LoRaWAN networks (such as TTN) have adopted an *adaptive data rate* option. This is an algorithm that determines the optimal spreading factor based on environmental conditions between a given LoRa node and a LoRaWAN gateway.

Take these considerations into account as you conduct your own LoRa range tests. Try starting with the default spreading factor setting (SF7), as I did, to establish a baseline. Gather data on RSSI, SNR, dropped packets, and so on as recorded by the receiver, noting the effects caused by terrain and distance. From there, modify the spreading factor and repeat your evaluation, controlling the test conditions to the greatest extent possible. You could even modify the Python code to output receiver metrics in JSON or CSV format for easier analysis.

Until now, you've examined peer-to-peer communications with the LoRa physical layer. In the next section, I'll guide you through the process of connecting a LoRa node to a LoRaWAN network.

Connecting to a LoRaWAN Gateway

You've already seen that LoRa on its own offers a great deal of utility and may even meet your requirements for peer-to-peer message exchange. Depending on the available channel bandwidth and frequency you choose, you might have significantly higher data rates than with LoRaWAN. However, in some use cases, LoRaWAN is a better fit; it's called a *WAN* for a reason! To understand LoRaWAN networks and the benefits they offer, let's first look at the technology stack.

As shown in Figure 6-13, LoRa is the physical (PHY) layer that provides the wireless modulation scheme you're already familiar with. The LoRaWAN standard defines a Media Access Control (MAC) layer designed to operate on top of the LoRa PHY.

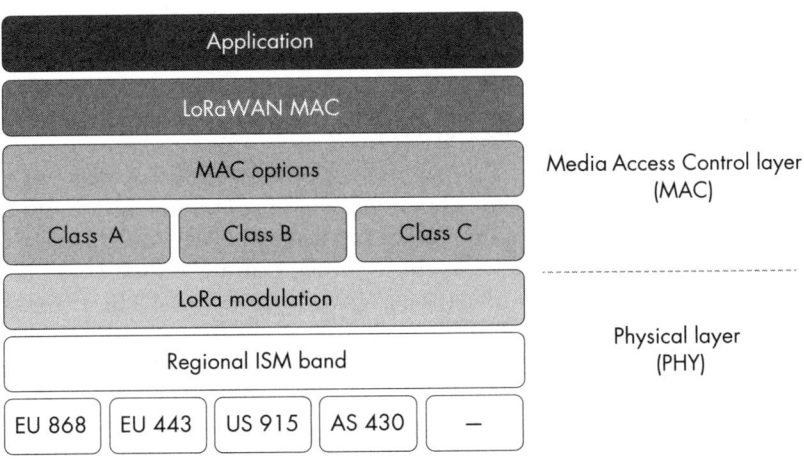

Figure 6-13: The LoRaWAN protocol stack is implemented on top of LoRa modulation.

A typical LoRaWAN architecture comprises several network elements: end devices, gateways, network servers, and application servers. End devices connect wirelessly in a star topology to a gateway, and gateways connect through IP networks to a central network server. The network server may also function as an IoT application server or connect to one or more separate application servers.

A LoRaWAN gateway listens on certain portions of the radio spectrum, decodes valid LoRaWAN packets from the signals using LoRa modulation, and forwards them to the network server via standard internet protocols such as TCP/IP. In this context, the latter protocol is known as a *backhaul*. It also transmits LoRaWAN packets from the network server back to end devices as LoRa-modulated signals.

The Things Stack is an example of a LoRaWAN network server. It runs on The Things Industries clusters that are distributed throughout the world. While there are many other regional and global LoRaWAN networks, The Things Network (TTN) is one of the largest, with thousands of active gateways worldwide. This makes it a logical choice when you want to connect a LoRa end device to a public network.

ABOUT THE THINGS NETWORK

TTN provides a global, open source LoRaWAN infrastructure with a set of tools for building and testing IoT applications. This network is actively supported by a growing community of developers and enthusiasts who volunteer their time and expertise. The TTN manifesto holds that control of global IoT networks should be distributed among as many people as possible, such that no single group, company, or nation is able to monopolize it. To that end, TTN has established itself as an open source initiative with free and open access to its infrastructure.

TTN has coverage in most large cities and is extending its reach to smaller ones. The advantage of using TTN's existing infrastructure, rather than setting up a private LoRaWAN network, is the ability to quickly scale up your IoT deployments by using a global network of community-owned gateways.

Participating in the Network

To participate in TTN, you must first create a free account at *https://www .thethingsnetwork.org*. Then launch The Things Stack Sandbox (TTSS), a crowdsourced, open, and decentralized LoRaWAN network. The TTN community currently hosts three public LoRaWAN network clusters, in Europe (eu1), North America (nam1), and Australia (au1). These are intended for non-commercial, small-scale testing and experimentation.

After logging in, specify your device location and accept the recommended cluster. Note which cluster you've selected, as you'll need this later. Next, you'll be presented with a console where you can either create an application or register a gateway, shown in Figure 6-14.

Choose **Create an Application**, enter an application ID, then specify a name and description for it. You should see a summary of your application, with several management options. There won't be any activity or live data associated with the application at this point, as there are no end devices associated with it yet.

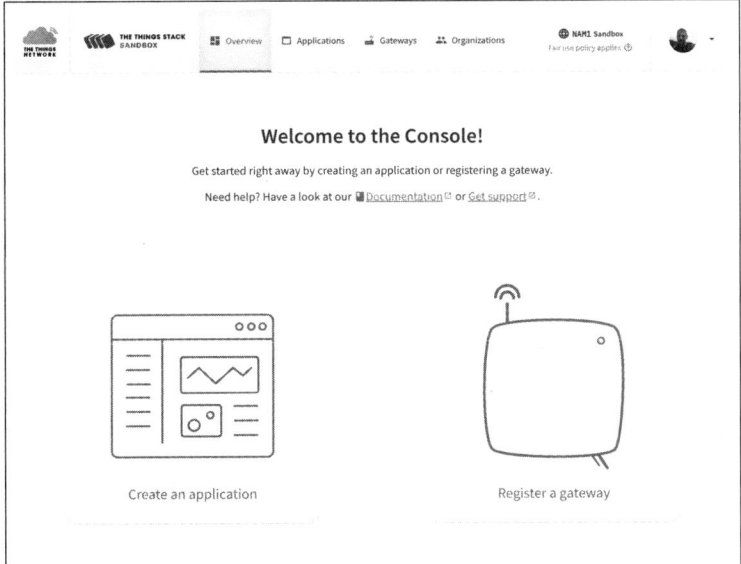

Figure 6-14: The TTSS console

Next, you'll perform one more step in the console to streamline authenticating later via the terminal. Under **API Keys** in the left-hand menu, choose **Add an API Key**. Give your key a name, accept the defaults, and click **Create API Key**. Be sure to copy the key from the dialog that appears and store it in a safe place, as you won't be able to view it again after you close the dialog.

Configuring the Pi Supply IoT pHAT

The Pi Supply IoT LoRa pHAT lets you create an inexpensive LoRa node, compatible with TTN, in conjunction with your Raspberry Pi Zero 2 W. A LoRaWAN stack is embedded in the chip, which streamlines the process of connecting to gateways. If you haven't done so already, begin by attaching your LoRa pHAT board to the Pi Zero's GPIO header, carefully aligning it with the pins. Use the mounting hardware provided to secure the board to the Pi Zero.

Selecting the External Hardware Antenna

By default, and for compliance reasons, the LoRa pHAT's internal chip antenna is connected. You may opt to use the internal antenna for testing purposes, but to maximize the board's range potential, you'll want to configure it with an external antenna. To do so, you will need to desolder the inductor on the internal (INT) pads and solder or bridge the external (EXT) pads. Viewed from above with the GPIO header at the top, these are visible on the board's leftmost edge, as illustrated in Figure 6-15.

Figure 6-15: The external (EXT) and internal (INT)
antenna solder pads on the LoRa pHAT board

Some revisions of this board ship with both pairs of antenna solder pads connected, but this significantly reduces the range of both antennas. If this is the case on your board, for the best performance, I recommend removing the inductor from the INT pads. Even if you haven't soldered before, you should find that this is a fairly simple procedure.

Next, align the thin coaxial adapter cable's connector with the u.FL connection point on the board and press down firmly. Finally, attach the external antenna. Depending on your use case, if you have a spare Waveshare SX1262 LoRa HAT, you may be able to use its longer cable and magnetic-base antenna. Connecting to the nearest LoRaWAN gateway in my area required a short drive, so I mounted the magnetic antenna to my car's roof.

Installing the RAK811 Python Library

This section presumes that you've completed the prerequisite steps already. If not, return to "Prerequisites" on page 164 and perform those steps first. Next, ensure that you've enabled the UART serial interface. Refer to "Enabling the UART Port" on page 165 for a simple method to verify this.

As with the SX1262 LoRa HAT setup, you'll need to have a Python virtual environment created and activated. For a quick review, see "Preparing Your Environment" on page 167. Clone the companion source code repository:

```
$ cd $HOME
$ git clone https://github.com/wirelesscookbook/pyrak811.git
$ cd pyrak811
```

Ensure that python3-venv is available on your system, then activate your virtual environment:

```
$ sudo apt install python3-venv -y
$ python3 -m venv lorawan --system-site-packages
```

You'll need to activate the venv each time your system is rebooted. You can do so with the following command:

```
$ source ~/pyrak811/lorawan/bin/activate
```

As mentioned earlier, each venv is tied to a directory in the Linux filesystem. When the venv is active, you'll notice that the bash prompt has changed to the following:

```
(lorawan) pi@raspberrypi:~/pyrak811 $
```

If you don't see the (lorawan) prefix in your project directory, executing Python code that references the libraries you'll be installing will result in ModuleNotFound errors.

At this point, you're ready to install the RAK811 Python library:

```
(lorawan) $ cd ~/pyrak811
(lorawan) $ sudo apt update && sudo apt upgrade
(lorawan) $ pip3 install rak811
(lorawan) $ rak811 --verbose --debug hard-reset
DEBUG:rak811.serial:Serial initialized
Hard reset complete
```

Note that the hard-reset command is needed only once, to activate the module after booting your system. The --verbose and --debug switches are useful to fetch some extra insights into how the Python library communicates with the RAK811 module.

Obtaining the RAK811 Firmware Version

With the Python library successfully installed, the next step is to determine the module's firmware version. You can do this with:

```
(lorawan) $ rak811 --verbose --debug version
DEBUG:rak811.serial:Serial initialized
DEBUG:rak811.serial:Sending: >at+version\r\n<
DEBUG:rak811.serial:Received: >OK V3.0.0.14.H<
 V3.0.0.14.H
```

The example output shows that the newer (V3) firmware is installed. For V2.0.*x* firmware, use the rak811 command and its associated Python module. For V3.0.*x*, use the rak811v3 command and the rak811_v3 Python module. I'll be using the latter tools in the subsequent steps; you should use whichever ones correspond to your firmware version.

Configuring the RAK811 Module

Now that you know your module's firmware version, you can configure it for operation as a LoRaWAN end device. Execute the following command to obtain the module's status:

```
(lorawan) $ rak811v3 get-config lora:status
```

You should see the module's current settings output to the console, as follows:

```
Work Mode: LoRaWAN
Region: US915
Join_mode: OTAA
DevEui: AC1F09xxxxxxxxxx
AppEui: AC1F09xxxxxxxxxx
AppKey: AC1F09xxxxxxxxxxxxxxxxxxxxxxxxxxxx
Class: A
Joined Network:false
```

This provides details on the work mode (LoRaWAN), region (US915), join mode, and more. The DevEui, AppEui, and AppKey values are obfuscated; be sure to safeguard these details, as a third party could use them to impersonate your device. I'll describe them in more detail shortly.

If your region is different from the default US915 value, you can change this setting like so (substituting your region value):

```
(lorawan) $ rak811v3 --verbose --debug set-config lora:region:EU868
```

Confirm the change by executing `rak811v3 get-config lora:status` again. The rest of the configuration settings can remain at their default values for now.

To join TTN with the Pi Supply pHAT node, you'll use a technique known as *over-the-air activation (OTAA)*. You'll notice that OTAA is the default authentication method, defined by Join_mode, in the RAK811 module's configuration.

You can use TTN's web interface to do this, or you can use The Things Stack CLI. The latter method will prove useful if you plan to deploy more nodes to TTN or want to automate the process, so I'll cover that next.

Installing The Things Stack CLI

While the console's web interface supports all the basic features of The Things Stack, you'll use the CLI for more advanced actions. The Things Stack CLI, ttn-lw-cli, is available on Linux as a snap package and is recommended for TTSS. I introduced snaps in Chapter 5; they're self-contained applications bundled with their dependencies, allowing them to run on most Linux distributions from a single build.

Snap packages are managed by the snapd daemon, so you'll need to have that installed and running to use snaps. Install the daemon via the apt package manager, and reboot your system. Next, install the core snap, which provides essential files and services other snaps may need to run properly. Finally, to confirm that everything is working as expected, install and execute the sample hello-world application:

```
(lorawan) $ sudo apt update && sudo apt install snapd
(lorawan) $ sudo reboot
```

```
(lorawan) $ sudo snap install core
core 16-2.61.2 from  Canonical installed
(lorawan) $ sudo snap install hello-world
hello-world 6.4 from  Canonical installed
(lorawan) $ hello-world
Hello World!
```

Now, install The Things Stack CLI with the following commands:

```
(lorawan) $ sudo snap install ttn-lw-stack
(lorawan) $ sudo snap alias ttn-lw-stack.ttn-lw-cli ttn-lw-cli
```

Execute ttn-lw-cli version to verify its operation.

Generating the Configuration File

The CLI can automatically generate a baseline configuration file for you. Substituting the regional cluster you selected when you set up your TTSS account for the placeholder value *<eu1/au1/nam1>*, run:

```
(lorawan) $ cd $HOME
(lorawan) $ ttn-lw-cli use <eu1/au1/nam1>.cloud.thethings.network
```

This will generate the CLI configuration and save it to a YAML file named *.ttn-lw-cli.yml* in your home directory. Now, make this configuration available to the CLI by executing the following command (adjust the path to the file if needed):

```
(lorawan) $ export TTN_LW_CONFIG=/home/pi/.ttn-lw-cli.yml
```

Next, verify that the configuration is being properly loaded by running:

```
(lorawan) $ ttn-lw-cli config
```

You should see the automatically generated configuration values output to the console.

Authenticating

The next step is to authenticate with the CLI by using the --api-key option. Replace the placeholder *my_api_key* value with the API key you created in "Participating in the Network" on page 186:

```
(lorawan) $ ttn-lw-cli login --api-key my_api_key
```

You're now ready to add your first LoRaWAN end device to TTSS.

Obtaining Your Device Identifiers

The first part of the process is to register your Pi Supply IoT LoRa pHAT as an end device using the CLI. The OTAA process is the most secure and preferred method for activating LoRaWAN end devices. Devices perform a join procedure with the network, during which a dynamic `DevAddr` is assigned and security keys are negotiated.

Each LoRaWAN device has a 64-bit *extended unique identifier (EUI)*, known as a `DevEUI`, that's assigned by the chip manufacturer. This is used during the join procedure to activate the end device on the network. In "Configuring the RAK811 Module" on page 189, you used the Python library to display the module's status. Execute the following command to isolate your module's unique identifiers:

```
(lorawan) $ rak811v3 get-config lora:status | grep -E 'DevEui|AppEui|AppKey'
```

Record the values returned in the console for the next step. If you receive the error message "Time out while waiting for response," confirm that you've enabled the UART serial interface, as described in "Enabling the UART Port" on page 165.

Adding an End Device

You can now add the device. In this step, you'll define several variables in the shell before passing them to TTN via the CLI. To see the available frequency plans and their LoRaWAN versions, run:

```
(lorawan) $ ttn-lw-cli end-devices list-frequency-plans
```

This will output a list, in JSON format, with details such as regional descriptions, base frequencies, and band IDs. Select a `band_id` value from this list that corresponds to the operating frequency of your LoRa pHAT hardware. Next, you'll need to define the following values related to your end device:

APP_ID The unique application ID you created in "Participating in the Network" on page 186.

DEVICE_ID A human-readable identifier for your device. This can be any descriptive tag you like, so be creative. Device IDs should be unique for each device within the same application.

DEV_EUI The `DevEui` value you obtained from the RAK811 Python library in the previous step.

APP_EUI The `AppEui` value you obtained from the RAK811 Python library in the previous step.

APP_KEY The `AppKey` value you obtained from the RAK811 Python library in the previous step. This is a device-specific 128-bit encryption key used to derive the session keys during OTAA.

You may find it easier to write out the definitions in a text editor first, then paste them into the bash shell. They should look something like this (replace the placeholder values shown here with your own values):

```
APP_ID="my-lorawan-test-application"
DEVICE_ID="lorawan-node1"
FREQUENCY_PLAN="EU_863_870"
DEV_EUI="AC1F09xxxxxxxxxx"
APP_EUI="AC1F09xxxxxxxxxx"
APP_KEY="AC1F09xxxxxxxxxxxxxxxxxxxxxxxxxxx"
```

With these values defined, run the CLI with the following command:

```
(lorawan) $ ttn-lw-cli end-devices create $APP_ID $DEVICE_ID \
    --dev-eui $DEV_EUI \
    --join-eui $APP_EUI \
    --frequency-plan-id $FREQUENCY_PLAN \
    --root-keys.app-key.key $APP_KEY \
    --lorawan-version 1.0.3 \
    --lorawan-phy-version 1.0.3-a
```

If successful, the CLI will respond with JSON output corresponding to details of the new end device.

Verifying the Device in the Console

The end device should now be listed under your application in the TTSS console. Figure 6-16 shows an example.

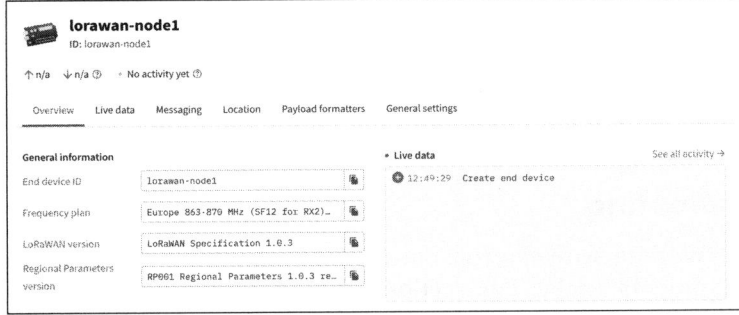

Figure 6-16: An end device displayed in the TTSS console

You'll notice that location information is currently missing for the newly added device. You can enter this manually via the console, or you can use the CLI to set the location. In the latter case, first define the LAT, LONG, and ALT variables, as shown here (substituting your own coordinates for the example values):

```
(lorawan) $ LAT="64.133542"
(lorawan) $ LONG="-21.93484"
(lorawan) $ ALT="67"
```

Then execute the following command:

```
(lorawan) $ ttn-lw-cli end-devices set $APP_ID $DEVICE_ID \
    --location.latitude $LAT \
    --location.longitude $LONG \
    --location.altitude $ALT
```

At this stage, you've successfully used The Things Stack CLI to add an end device to the console. To wrap things up, you'll join the device to the network.

Joining the Network

The RAK811 Python module provides a method for joining a device to the network in OTAA mode. Ensure that your Python virtual environment is active, then run:

```
(lorawan) $ rak811v3 --verbose join
Joined!
```

If you see the console message shown here, you've successfully joined your LoRaWAN end device to TTN. If you see an error like "RAK811 response error 99: LoRa join failed," your end device is likely not within range of a gateway. You can find the gateways nearest to your location with resources such as the TTN map (*https://www.thethingsnetwork.org/map*) or the TTN Mapper (*https://ttnmapper.org/heatmap/*). If you have a gateway within range and still fail to join the network, be sure to verify that the DevEui and AppEui values you obtained for your device agree with what's stored in the TTSS console.

If your end device has joined TTN, packets from one or more gateways should eventually be forwarded to your application. Over time, you should also see the number of sent uplinks and received downlinks for your device increment in the console.

Troubleshooting

Working with external hardware attached via the GPIO header can sometimes be tricky. This section, while not exhaustive, covers some common hiccups you may encounter when using the LoRa/LoRaWAN expansion HATs discussed in this chapter.

GPIO Edge Detection

Occasionally, you might see a Python error like this one when communicating with an attached LoRa HAT:

```
GPIO.add_event_detect(irqPin, GPIO.RISING, callback=checkTransmitDone)
RuntimeError: Failed to add edge detection
```

This occurs under Debian 12/Raspberry Pi OS Bookworm when the RPi.GPIO library is present. For a detailed explanation, see "Installing the Python Package" on page 169.

The rpi-lgpio library is a compatibility package that allows code written for the RPi.GPIO library on newer kernels that support only the gpiochip device and have removed the deprecated sysfs GPIO interface. The solution is to remove this package and replace it with the rpi-lgpio library:

```
$ sudo apt remove python3-rpi.gpio
$ sudo apt update
$ sudo apt install python3-rpi-lgpio
```

No code changes are necessary.

Serial Console (Getty) Deactivation

In some circumstances, when attempting to perform operations with the RAK811 Python library, you may encounter errors like these:

```
serial.serialutil.SerialException: [Errno 2] could not open port /dev/serial0:
rak811.serial.Rak811TimeoutError: Timeout while waiting for data
```

This usually indicates one of two things: your system's UART serial interface isn't enabled, or the serial port is being used by another process. To address the former issue, ensure that you've followed the steps in "Enabling the UART Port" on page 165. To investigate the latter, execute:

```
$ sudo fuser -v /dev/ttyAMA0
                    USER        PID ACCESS COMMAND
/dev/ttyAMA0:       root        855 F.... agetty
```

In the example output shown here, the agetty process is attached to the */dev/ttyAMA0* device file. This process is an instance of *getty*, or "get TTY," a common Unix program for managing physical or virtual terminals (TTYs). When getty detects a connection, it responds with a login prompt to authenticate a user. Login prompts on serial terminals are managed by systemd, which instantiates serial-getty@.service on the main kernel console to allow users to log in over a serial connection. The kernel console is where the kernel outputs its own log messages and is usually configured on the kernel command line in the boot loader.

You can check the status of this service with its associated ttyAMA0 serial interface, like so:

```
$ sudo systemctl status serial-getty@ttyAMA0.service
 serial-getty@ttyAMA0.service - Serial Getty on ttyAMA0
     Loaded: loaded (/lib/systemd/system/serial-getty@.service; enabled-runtime; preset: ...)
     Active: active (running) since Sun 2025-06-01 07:46:15 CEST; 6min ago
       Docs: man:agetty(8)
             man:systemd-getty-generator(8)
             https://0pointer.de/blog/projects/serial-console.html
   Main PID: 855 (agetty)
      Tasks: 1 (limit: 174)
        CPU: 8ms
     CGroup: /system.slice/system-serial\x2dgetty.slice/serial-getty@ttyAMA0.service
             855 /sbin/agetty -o "-p -- \\u" --keep-baud 115200,57600,38400,9600 - vt220

Jun 02 07:46:15 loranode2 systemd[1]: Started serial-getty@ttyAMA0.service - Serial Getty ...
```

In the example output, you'll notice that the service is active. As long as it's running, agetty will prevent access to the serial port. Stopping the service with

```
$ sudo systemctl stop serial-getty@ttyAMA0.service
```

will temporarily permit you to access the LoRa pHAT via the UART, but the usual trick of disabling the service won't prevent it from restarting at boot. This is due to systemd's use of *generators*, small binary files located in */lib/systemd/system-generators* that it executes very early in the boot process. In the service output, you'll notice a man-page link to systemd-getty-generator. To learn more about why the system spawns getty, run **man systemd-getty -generator**.

If disabling the service doesn't work, how do you prevent getty from grabbing the serial port at startup? There are various ways to achieve this, but in this case the most straightforward approach is to *mask* the service to prevent it from ever being enabled:

```
$ sudo systemctl mask serial-getty@ttyAMA0.service
```

With this done, execute **rak811 version** to validate that the Python library can communicate with the attached RAK811 module.

LoRaWAN End Device Activity

If you have access to a gateway's Live Data page and can see activity, but you don't see any activity on the application's Live Data page, this usually means TTN is receiving the data but can't parse or decrypt it. In this event, recheck your AppEUI, AppKey, and DevEUI values.

If you see join requests on the application's Live Data page but the end device never manages to complete the join procedure and start sending real data, this often indicates a gateway or network problem. The most common causes are:

- An excessive ping time between the TTN servers and your nearest gateway. Without a good ping (typically under 250 ms), replies from the network may arrive too late for the device to transmit a response. Ping times that exceed 250 ms may cause problems.

- A misconfigured or faulty gateway. If your local gateway is unable to transmit, it won't be able to service join requests. One possible culprit is the transmit power lookup table, which is commonly configurable. If the network asks for a transmit power that is not in the configured table, the gateway may refuse to transmit.

Going Further

This chapter just scratched the surface of what's possible with LoRa, LoRaWAN, and connected IoT end devices. The hardware expansion boards, software tools, techniques, and experience you've acquired here can be applied in any number of ways. This section is intended to point you toward further avenues of exploration.

Using the RAK811 Examples

The companion GitHub repository you cloned for use with the Pi Supply LoRA pHAT contains several examples. To use these examples, change to its working directory with

```
(lorawan) $ cd ~/pyrak811/examples
```

and copy the *ttn_secrets_template.py* file to *ttn_secrets.py* with the cp command. Open this file in your editor and replace the placeholder values with your TTN LoRaWAN keys. You can then experiment with the Python code for the RAK811 module V2.0.*x* and V3.0.*x* firmware versions. For example, running

```
(lorawan) $ python3 p2p_v3.py
```

executes a Python program that sends counter messages at random intervals and listens while idle. With more than one RAK811-equipped device, you can use this to observe LoRa packets flowing between the nodes. Be sure to edit the LoRa parameters in the code and verify that they are in agreement between the nodes you'd like to experiment with.

Adding IoT Sensors

The Python libraries used to communicate with each of the LoRa expansion boards discussed in this chapter transmit packets with rudimentary messages. These message payloads are intended for demonstration purposes and contain values such as a packet number or the current CPU temperature of the transmitting node. While sufficient for validating your LoRa hardware configuration, they're clearly lacking in terms of useful IoT data.

With what you know about GPIO and interfaces such as SPI, UART, and I^{2}C, you can attach an IoT sensor, GPS module, or other component to the GPIO header of a LoRa node, read values from it, and modify the existing Python code to include this data in the messages. If you've already worked through the recipe in Chapter 8, you might think of how that project could be extended to transmit sensor readings via LoRa modulation.

Countless dedicated LoRa/LoRaWAN IoT sensing devices are available commercially, but they tend to be for specific purposes. The advantage of using a general-purpose host controller like the Raspberry Pi Zero 2 W is that it lends itself to rapid prototyping. You can quickly test a solution by using a handful of low-cost components, reconfigure it as needed, and decide whether the prototype meets your requirements. This makes it ideal for evaluating a real-world IoT solution with intentions to scale, building a smaller implementation, or simply experimenting.

Building Your Own LoRaWAN Gateway

Depending on where you live, you may have several LoRaWAN gateways available for your LoRa end devices to connect to, or there may be none within range. In the latter case, you might opt to build your own LoRaWAN gateway.

Specialized hardware known as *concentrator boards* is used to build and upgrade LoRaWAN gateways. These boards are designed to handle data from many end devices across multiple channels. By contrast, the SX1262 and RAK811 modules used in this chapter are designed for single-channel operation, making them better suited as end nodes.

Popular concentrator boards include those from RAKwireless, which are equipped with Semtech's SX130x chipsets. They're available with an SPI interface and may be used with a converter board like the RAK2247 Pi HAT, which maps its pins to the Raspberry Pi's 40-pin GPIO header. Other concentrator boards, such as the iC880A-SPI, can be used directly with the Raspberry Pi.

Concentrator boards are typically more expensive than the LoRa HATs and LoRaWAN expansion boards used in this chapter. Because LoRaWAN gateways require this specialized hardware, they are not covered here. However, if you're interested in building and hosting your own gateway, the open source LoRa Basics Station (*https://github.com/lorabasics/basicstation*) provides an excellent starting point.

You can validate the gateway's operation with your RAK811-equipped end device and follow the steps in "Installing The Things Stack CLI" on page 190 to join it to TTN. In doing so, you'll contribute a gateway to extend the free, publicly accessible LoRaWAN to more IoT end devices in your area.

Wrapping Up

In this chapter, you've seen how LoRa's parameters can be adjusted to optimize for range, data rate, power consumption, payload size, and more. LoRa's inherent flexibility is one of the main reasons for its impressively fast and widespread adoption, but it can also make it tricky for new practitioners to get started with the technology.

To soften the learning curve, this recipe started with a "quick win" demonstration to validate the operation of your LoRa nodes. We then examined LoRa's spread spectrum modulation in detail, including a discussion of chirps, or sweep signals, to understand how LoRa is able to send messages over such long distances. This provided a foundation for exploring LoRa's key parameters: bandwidth, spreading factor, and coding rate. We also looked at the structure of LoRa packets, and you learned how to define them yourself using Python.

With a grasp of these fundamentals, I proposed a methodology for conducting your own long-range tests with a pair of LoRa nodes, including a technique for evaluating range, and tips for adjusting parameters to suit your local conditions and requirements. Finally, you configured a LoRaWAN IoT HAT and connected a node to a LoRaWAN gateway participating in TTN.

7

INTRUSION DETECTION WITH KISMET

Growth in public hotspots has increased exponentially since Wi-Fi was first introduced, with an estimated 1.5 billion Wi-Fi networks (both public and private) in operation worldwide at the time of writing. Their popularity should come as little surprise, given the relative ease and cost advantages of deploying wireless LANs compared to traditional wired networks. The proliferation of affordable hardware, from wireless routers to Wi-Fi–capable project boards like the Raspberry Pi and even mobile handsets, has made hosting WLANs broadly accessible to the average user.

In parallel, the rise of smart homes has introduced a wide array of wirelessly integrated IoT sensors, devices, and controllers, including thermostats, door locks, lighting, cameras, motion sensors, and appliances, to name just a few. Taking all this into account, we can expect the number of Wi-Fi networks (and devices connected to them) to continue their upward climb, following the trajectory illustrated in Figure 7-1.

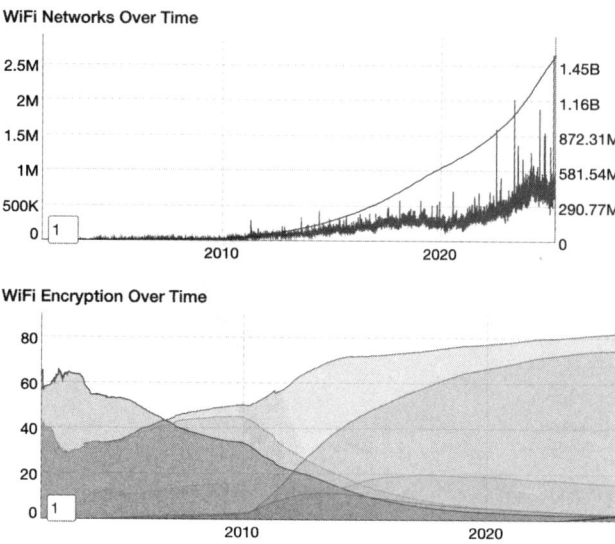

Figure 7-1: The growth of Wi-Fi networks and encryption over time. Courtesy of WiGLE (https://wigle.net).

This is all good news, right?

Not exactly. In the wireless world, there's no firm boundary between what we usually consider "inside" and "outside" the network. The nature of WLANs is such that their frequencies (or channels), broadcast on the 2.4 and 5 GHz bands, are designed to be heard by anyone with a wireless receiver within range. You can tune into a Wi-Fi network much like you would tune into a radio station. These networks commonly extend well beyond the physical borders of our private spaces, and too often, the convenience of trusting our wireless devices with internet access takes priority over the security risks they introduce.

With off-the-shelf hardware and software tools, anyone can interrogate your WLAN and quickly identify potential weaknesses. If a malicious actor gets past your AP's security, they are effectively inside your network.

Wardriving: A (Very) Brief History

As the number of Wi-Fi networks has grown over time, so too has the practice known as *wardriving*. The term evolved from *wardialing*, or finding open networks by churning through phone numbers with a modem, which itself played a central role in the popular 1983 film *WarGames*. In a similar fashion, wardriving involves scanning all wireless access points and clients that are actively broadcasting in a given area. This is usually done from a vehicle equipped with a laptop and specialized software, a GPS receiver, and one or more antennas.

Nowadays, with Arduino or similar project boards, a minimal yet effective wardriving rig can fit into a small project box. The components are all off-the-shelf and readily obtained, and many of the best scanning tools are free and open source software (FOSS). Once equipped, the scope of a wireless network survey is limited only by a wardriver's time and resources.

The resulting geospatially tagged wireless network data can be plotted on a map like the one shown in Figure 7-2, where each point represents a discovered Wi-Fi network.

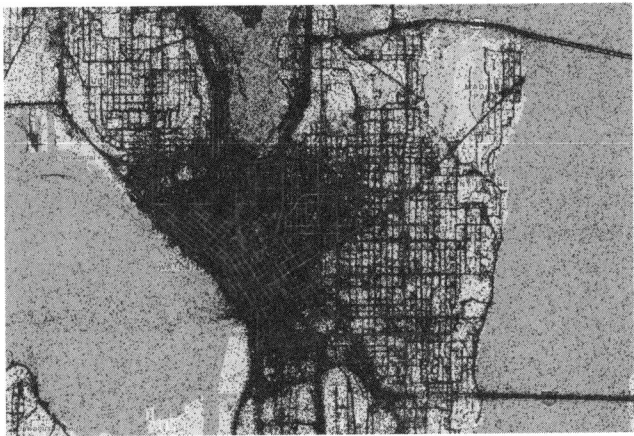

Figure 7-2: Geospatially tagged wireless network data plotted on a map. Courtesy of WiGLE (https://wigle.net).

This data can then be shared with crowdsourced mapping platforms or used for personal projects.

ETHICAL VS. MALICIOUS ACTIVITY

One might reasonably ask, is wardriving legal? Each time you scan for available Wi-Fi networks with a laptop or phone, you are essentially performing a similar function to wardriving, albeit on a much more limited scale. Collection of wireless network data on a wider scale might be done by graduate students as part of open source research. Additionally, aggregation sites such as WiGLE (https://wigle.net) use this information to inform the public about the risks of insecure wireless networks.

These surveys reveal that a significant number of WLANs use no encryption whatsoever. Some may employ other forms of protection, but this cannot be determined without more intrusive, and possibly illegal, probing. Here lies the boundary between ethical and malicious wardriving: passively detecting and recording networks versus entering the legally gray area of computer trespassing.

Armed with knowledge of a WLAN's security protocols, a bad actor who has crossed this threshold could potentially orchestrate a wide variety of attacks to gain access to a target network. We'll examine several of the main types of these attacks over the course of this chapter. First, let's look at some use cases for creating a hardware device to monitor for such intrusion attempts.

Use Cases

Security consultants often say that too many network owners, both individuals and organizations, are unaware of the threats posed by outdated or poorly secured networks. An insecure AP is a weak point that, when compromised, can grant an attacker access to all the devices connected to the internal network. Most people would cringe at the prospect of someone gaining control over the smart devices in their private spaces, but it's hardly unheard of. For example, there have been several reported cases of wireless cameras used as baby monitors being hijacked by outside parties.

A compromised AP can also open the door to other forms of remote abuse. If someone wants to commit an online crime or engage in other nefarious activities, they will usually attempt to do so in a way that ensures the events cannot be traced back to them. A poorly secured network is an open invitation for these bad actors, and one that can lead investigators straight to your door.

Malicious parties rely on the fact that the vast majority of WLAN owners are blissfully unaware of the threats they face. For this reason, part of crafting a strong security posture is understanding this threat landscape.

Even if you have a state-of-the-art wireless router with a hardware firewall, or use the latest encryption protocols and 63-character passwords on your APs, there is still intrinsic value in being aware of the wireless traffic around you and informing yourself about potential threats.

A Kismet monitoring node, like the one you'll build in this recipe, gives you an entry point into wireless intrusion detection systems (WIDS). You may decide to operate your Kismet node exclusively at home or work, or you might opt to use it for performing threat analysis at remote locations. With a second device, you can even create a WLAN security test bench to ethically practice intrusion techniques against (and validate the effectiveness of) the WIDS you'll be building.

After walking you through installing and using Kismet, I'll demonstrate how to analyze the logfiles it generates. As a bonus, in "Going Further" on page 225, I'll introduce an optional third type of device you can add to your ethical security test bench.

Hardware Required

All you'll need for this recipe is a Raspberry Pi and an external wireless adapter. If you choose a Pi Zero model, you'll also need a micro USB adapter to connect the wireless adapter to the board.

Compatible Raspberry Pi Models

A Raspberry Pi 3B+, 4, 5, or Zero 2 W will work fine for this recipe. In my testing, the original Pi Zero W proved to be underpowered in terms of CPU capabilities. Its updated, 1 GHz quad-core 64-bit ARM sibling will suffice, if you're clever about managing its 512MB of SDRAM (more on this later).

External Wireless Adapter

A key requirement for this recipe is a wireless adapter that supports *monitor mode*. Also known as *listening* or *promiscuous mode*, this feature allows the adapter to capture all types of wireless packets. The Broadcom driver for the built-in Cypress wireless chipset on Raspberry Pi models does not support this mode, but generally speaking, this isn't a showstopper. There are two ways to work around this limitation:

- Install a firmware patching framework for the Broadcom/Cypress Wi-Fi chips to enable monitor mode.

- Use an external USB wireless adapter with in-kernel support for monitor mode.

Fortunately, many low-cost USB wireless adapters are available with this capability. A perennial favorite is the Edimax EW-7811Un Nano, shown in Figure 7-3. While more powerful adapters certainly exist, the Edimax has two distinct advantages: It's inexpensive and, more importantly, it uses in-kernel Linux drivers, which means you can simply plug it in and it will work out of the box, with no need to install third-party drivers. It's widely available from online retailers from about $13.

Figure 7-3: The Edimax
EW-7811Un Nano

As mentioned previously, if you're using a Pi Zero 2 W for this recipe, you'll also need a micro USB to USB adapter to connect the Edimax to your device.

Regardless of which wireless USB adapter you choose, be sure to check that it supports monitor mode before proceeding. For example, when bound to wlan1, the Edimax EW-7811Un will output the following:

```
$ iw list
Wiphy phy1
    --snip--
    Supported interface modes:
        * IBSS
        * managed
        * AP
        * AP/VLAN
        * monitor
    --snip--
```

If your wireless adapter does not support this mode, you'll find that this recipe will quickly fall flat.

If you're interested in creating an ethical WLAN security test bench, you can use a second Raspberry Pi for this purpose. Any model will suffice, so long as it's Wi-Fi–capable.

Software Used

The software backbone of our monitoring node will be Kismet (*https://www*
.kismetwireless.net), a popular open source wireless network detector, packet sniffer, and wireless intrusion detection system framework. When used with a GPS receiver and its associated software module, it also happens to be an extremely capable wardriving tool.

Kismet works predominantly with Wi-Fi (IEEE 802.11) networks, but it can be expanded via plug-ins to handle other network types. On Linux, it works with most wireless adapters, Bluetooth interfaces, and software-defined radio (SDR) hardware. You'll be configuring it for use with a USB wireless adapter placed into monitor mode.

In addition to the Kismet framework, you'll use several Python libraries to communicate with your attached status board HAT.

A Closer Look at WIDS

In their simplest form, wireless intrusion detection systems are designed to monitor and report on network activity, or more specifically, packets exchanged between communicating nodes. To be effective, a WIDS must run online and in real time. An offline WIDS can still be useful to provide an audit trail during post-incident analysis, but it won't alert you to an attack in progress.

In the enterprise world, a WIDS may serve broader purposes than detecting break-in attempts. Network security specialists usually maintain inventories of all authorized devices on a network. They may also track access points that either shouldn't be on the network or have known security vulnerabilities. This allows the network to be scanned to identify any rogue devices (with *rogue* in this context simply meaning that the device isn't authorized, not necessarily that it's hostile).

A WIDS typically monitors a WLAN using a mixture of hardware and software called *intrusion detection sensors*. At a minimum, one or more of these sensors are positioned on an 802.11 network to examine all traffic. Network sniffing tools probe IP addresses and identify authorized and unauthorized devices. For example, a WIDS used in conjunction with a device inventory might raise an alert if it detects an unauthorized MAC address on the network during a scan.

NOTE *A WIDS is not the same as a firewall. Firewalls are outward facing and designed to limit access between networks to prevent intrusions. A WIDS, by contrast, monitors wired and wireless networks from the inside and raises alarms based on the traffic it observes.*

Security threats exist in all networks, whether wired or wireless. But with WLANs, we need to look at these threats in a different way. Network monitoring over TCP/IP doesn't always reveal which devices have Wi-Fi capabilities, and it won't catch relays that aren't directly on the network. For this reason, over-the-air sniffing is necessary as well. This can identify any APs within range and determine whether they have weak security or, worse, are impersonating a legitimate AP.

For the purposes of this recipe, you'll use a Wi-Fi adapter to monitor 802.11 wireless channels on the 2.4 GHz spectrum. By contrast, commercial WIDS tools often monitor large swaths of the RF spectrum—anywhere from 60 MHz to 6 GHz—covering a wide range of RF-enabled devices (from mobile phones, IoT devices, and hotspots to rogue Wi-Fi and other potential wireless threats).

Unauthorized access points are a common security risk. Employees might plug in personal APs on the local wired network for convenience, perhaps to connect a phone to the network (a security risk in itself). Likewise, many smart devices set up their own APs for ease of use during installation. Wi-Fi−connected printers and cameras are among the most common types of devices that do this, and they are notoriously vulnerable to attack. If no one changes the default settings, they're likely to have poor security, or even none at all.

This proved to be the Achilles' heel of many consumer-grade IoT devices that use the ARC processor, which runs a stripped-down version of Linux. The Mirai botnet scanned the internet for connected devices that used the default credentials, then infected them by logging in and copying itself over. These devices were later put into service by their controllers for coordinated distributed denial-of-service (DDoS) attacks, among other purposes.

A properly configured WIDS will alert a security specialist to rogue devices on an internal network before they become a vector for attack. For extrinsic threats, this is where over-the-air packet inspection comes into play.

A common type of extrinsic attack, often referred to as the *Evil Twin*, involves setting up a nearby rogue relay that impersonates the SSID of a legitimate access point. To be effective, it must match the real AP's password. If it does, most users won't recognize it as a fake. In fact, many devices will connect to it automatically if it provides the strongest signal for that SSID. Once connected, network traffic passes through the relay, and packets are copied and forwarded to the attacker, allowing them to collect login credentials and personal data that they can potentially use in phishing or other targeted attacks.

With this broad understanding of how WIDS are applied in the real world, let's dive in and implement a practical, Raspberry Pi−based intrusion alert system.

Configuring Headless Access

If you're using the Pi Zero 2 W for this recipe, or another Pi model without Ethernet support, you will first need to configure it for headless access. That process is described in this section; if you're using another Pi model and are connecting to it via Ethernet, you can skip this step.

Start by flashing a fresh SD card with the latest distribution of Raspberry Pi OS Lite (64- or 32-bit) from the official download page, then create an empty file named *ssh* (no extension) and save it in the boot partition of the SD card. Next, to configure wireless networking, create another file called *wpa_supplicant.conf* with the following contents:

```
ctrl_interface=DIR=/var/run/wpa_supplicant GROUP=netdev
update_config=1
country=US

network={
    ssid="your_SSID"
    psk="your_wi-fi_password"
}
```

Substitut your two-letter ISO 3166-1 alpha-2 country code for US if you're not in the United States, and be sure both your network SSID and your password (pre-shared key) are enclosed in double quotes. Copy this file to the boot partition. You'll need to complete this step before you boot the SD card for the first time, as that's the point at which the system checks for the presence of the *wpa_supplicant.conf* file.

Alternatively, you can perform this setup with the Raspberry Pi Imager tool while writing the OS to your SD card. Under **OS Customisation**, choose **Wireless LAN** and enter an SSID (name) and the password for your network. If the network does not publicly broadcast an SSID, enable the **Hidden SSID** setting.

Installing Kismet

You can install the Kismet framework on the most recent Raspberry Pi OS/Debian release (Bookworm, as of this writing) from the Kismet package repositories. This is the quickest and generally most foolproof method.

BLEEDING EDGE

If you like to be on the cutting edge, you can pull Kismet from nightly Git builds. These builds have all the latest features, but they're also the most likely to have new, exciting bugs. While it's generally fine to use them, it's not recommended for installations that require consistency or long-term support. For more details, see *https://www.kismetwireless.net/docs/*.

It's also possible to build Kismet from source, but be forewarned that the C++ compiler consumes a significant amount of the Pi's system resources. If you have a top-spec Pi (such as a Pi 4 or 5 with 4GB or 8GB RAM) and are feeling adventurous, I'll walk you through that option as well. Just note that the 32-bit Linux kernel cannot fully use 8GB of RAM, so you will need to install the 64-bit version of Raspberry Pi OS if you opt to take this route.

Using the Official Kismet Packages

The official package repositories contain the latest Kismet versions, automatically built for several Linux distributions. Before installing a packaged version of Kismet, you will need to remove any existing source-based installations. To do this, run:

```
$ sudo rm -rfv \
    /usr/local/bin/kismet* \
    /usr/local/share/kismet* \
    /usr/local/etc/kismet*
```

If you've previously installed Kismet packages from your distribution, be sure to remove those as well. Then proceed with the familiar apt update and upgrade steps, followed by a reboot:

```
$ sudo apt update && sudo apt upgrade
$ sudo reboot
```

Be sure to select the correct packages for your specific distribution. Installing packages from another distribution, or another version, *may* work in some cases, but it often results in errors related to missing library packages or similar issues.

To install the latest Kismet release for Raspberry Pi OS/Debian Bookworm (arm64), begin by fetching the key used by apt to authenticate the package, then update and install Kismet:

```
$ wget -O - https://www.kismetwireless.net/repos/kismet-release.gpg.key --quiet \
    | gpg --dearmor | sudo tee /usr/share/keyrings/kismet-archive-keyring.gpg >/dev/null

$ echo 'deb [signed-by=/usr/share/keyrings/kismet-archive-keyring.gpg] \
    https://www.kismetwireless.net/repos/apt/release/bookworm bookworm main' \
    | sudo tee /etc/apt/sources.list.d/kismet.list >/dev/null

$ sudo apt update
$ sudo apt install kismet
```

During the package install, you'll be prompted to configure kismet-core. When asked, "Should Kismet be installed with suid-root helpers?" accept the default response of **yes**.

After installing Kismet with *suid-root*, be sure to add your user to the *kismet* group:

```
$ sudo usermod -aG kismet pi
```

Group changes aren't applied automatically, so you'll need to reload the groups for your user by logging out and logging back in. Then execute **groups** at the command line and confirm that *kismet* appears in the list.

When the package installation is complete, the Kismet binary and capture tools will be located in */usr/bin/*, and you'll find the configuration files in */etc/kismet/*. Take note of these paths, as you'll be using them later.

With the installation complete, you can move on to "Configuring the Wireless Adapter" on page 212.

Building from Source (Optional)

Compiling Kismet from source is also an option, assuming your hardware is up to the task. If you previously installed Kismet using a package from your distribution, uninstall it using your package manager. Typically, packaged versions are installed under */usr/*, while source builds default to */usr/local*; leaving the packaged version installed can interfere with the build.

Likewise, if you've previously compiled Kismet from source, the safest course is to remove it manually before proceeding. However, if you didn't change the install prefix, compiling and installing a new version will overwrite the old one.

To compile Kismet, you'll need a number of libraries and development headers. Begin by updating your system packages, then install these core dependencies:

```
$ sudo apt-get update
$ sudo apt-get upgrade
$ sudo apt install build-essential git libwebsockets-dev pkg-config \
    zlib1g-dev libnl-3-dev libnl-genl-3-dev libcap-dev libpcap-dev \
```

```
libnm-dev libdw-dev libsqlite3-dev libprotobuf-dev libprotobuf-c-dev \
protobuf-compiler protobuf-c-compiler libsensors4-dev libusb-1.0-0-dev \
python3 python3-setuptools python3-protobuf python3-requests python3-numpy \
python3-serial python3-usb python3-dev python3-websockets librtlsdr0 \
librtlsdr-dev libmosquitto-dev \
libubertooth-dev libbtbb-dev
```

Next, clone the latest Kismet release from its GitHub repository:

```
$ cd $HOME
$ git clone https://www.kismetwireless.net/git/kismet.git
$ cd kismet
```

Then, run

```
$ ./configure
```

to detect your system's configuration and prepare for compilation. If you have any missing dependencies or incompatible library versions, they will be flagged at this stage.

Now for the fun part: compiling Kismet with make. On a Raspberry Pi 4 Model B with 4GB of RAM, this process takes about an hour. It's generally advisable to install Kismet with its *suid-root* capture helper enabled:

```
$ sudo make suidinstall
```

Kismet will automatically create the necessary user group and install the binaries accordingly. When the build is complete, add the *pi* user to the *kismet* group:

```
$ sudo usermod -a -G kismet pi
```

Linux groups are not updated automatically, so you will need to reload the groups for your user for this change to take effect. To do this, log out and log back in again, then verify that you are in the *kismet* group by executing **groups**. This will output a list of the Linux groups configured by default for the *pi* user; the *kismet* group should appear at the end of this list.

RESOLVING COMMON BUILD PROBLEMS

Compiling Kismet requires a *lot* of available RAM. In testing, it's very common for the Kismet build to fail on devices with insufficient RAM, resulting in cryptic errors such as:

```
g++: fatal error: Killed signal terminated program cc1plus
```

(continued)

> In these cases, the Linux kernel likely has killed the C++ compiler because of an *out-of-memory (OOM)* condition. You can confirm this by checking dmesg, the kernel's message buffer, for any oom-kill or oom_reaper messages. You can filter these messages with grep, like so:
>
> ```
> $ dmesg | grep -E 'oom-kill|oom_reaper'
> ```
>
> If you run into this issue, it's recommended to install Kismet by using the official package repositories, as described in the preceding section.

Configuring the Wireless Adapter

By the time you're done with this recipe, you'll have an operational Raspberry Pi–based Wi-Fi network scanner capable of analyzing traffic on the 2.4 GHz frequency band. Wireless intrusion detection will be implemented in the form of scripted alerts, visible in the Kismet web console.

To begin, you'll need to put your wireless adapter into monitor mode. Ensure that the Edimax EW-7811Un is connected to a USB port on your device, and list the connected USB devices with:

```
$ lsusb
Bus 002 Device 001: ID 1d6b:0003 Linux Foundation 3.0 root hub
Bus 001 Device 003: ID 7392:7811 Edimax Technology Co., Ltd EW-7811Un ...
Bus 001 Device 002: ID 2109:3431 VIA Labs, Inc. Hub
Bus 001 Device 001: ID 1d6b:0002 Linux Foundation 2.0 root hub
```

Your Edimax adapter should appear as attached to the USB bus. Next, you'll use iw to get a summary of the available wireless devices (your output may differ):

```
$ iw dev
phy#1
    Interface wlan1
        ifindex 4
        wdev 0x1
        addr 80:1f:02:9b:b0:c4
        type managed
        txpower 20.00 dBm
phy#0
    Interface wlan0
        ifindex 3
        wdev 0x100000001
        addr dc:a6:32:3d:ff:9d
        type managed
        channel 34 (5170 MHz), width: 20 MHz, center1: 5170 MHz
        txpower 31.00 dBm
```

Take note of the physical address for the adapter bound to wlan1 (phy#1, in the example output). You can inspect this device's capabilities like so:

```
$ iw phy1 info | more
--snip--
    Supported interface modes:
        * IBSS
        * managed
        * AP
        * AP/VLAN
        * monitor
        * mesh point
        * P2P-client
        * P2P-GO
```

Notice that monitor mode is included in the list of supported interface modes. Next, you'll create a new interface (I've called it mon1) and add it to the physical hardware address (phy1), specifying monitor as the type. You can do this with a single iw command:

```
$ sudo iw phy phy1 interface add mon1 type monitor
```

To confirm that the new monitor interface was created, run:

```
$ ip a | grep mon1 -A1
5: mon1: <BROADCAST,MULTICAST> mtu 1500 qdisc noop state DOWN mode DEFAULT...
    link/ieee802.11/radiotap 80:1f:02:9b:b0:c4 brd ff:ff:ff:ff:ff:ff
```

Notice that its current state is DOWN. You can bring it up with:

```
$ sudo ip link set mon1 up
```

Finally, check the wireless interfaces one more time:

```
$ iw dev
phy#1
    Interface mon1
        ifindex 5
        wdev 0x100000002
        addr 74:da:38:ed:5e:7d
        type monitor
        txpower 20.00 dBm
    Interface wlan1
        ifindex 4
        wdev 0x100000001
        addr 74:da:38:ed:5e:7d
        type managed
        channel 6 (2437 MHz), width: 20 MHz, center1: 2437 MHz
        txpower 20.00 dBm
    --snip--
```

In the output, you'll notice that a new monitor interface, mon1, has been successfully added to your `wlan1` interface. With your wireless adapter configured, you can now instruct Kismet to use this as your data source.

Monitoring Traffic

Before starting Kismet, you'll need to specify your `wlan1` interface as the data source for wireless traffic. If you've installed Kismet from the official package repositories, you can open its configuration file for editing with:

```
$ sudo nano /etc/kismet/kismet_site.conf
```

Alternatively, if you compiled Kismet from source, run:

```
$ sudo nano /usr/local/etc/kismet_site.conf
```

Add the line

```
source=wlan1:name=Edimax
```

to the configuration file, then save the file and exit your editor.

KISMET'S MONITOR INTERFACES

It's also possible to specify the monitor interface you added to wlan1 as the data source. Kismet will use this interface successfully. However, in testing with the latest Raspberry Pi OS Linux kernel (version 6.6.28, as of this writing), I found that Kismet raised source errors as this interface cycles repeatedly between connected and disconnected states. For this reason, I recommend that you stick with specifying the parent interface.

Kismet Startup

You can now start Kismet from the command line by executing the binary with no options, then use the web interface to administer it:

```
$ cd $HOME
$ kismet
KISMET - Point your browser to http://localhost:2501
(or the address of this system) for the Kismet UI
INFO: Edimax telling NetworkManager not to control interface 'wlan1': you
      may need to re-initialize this interface later or tell
      NetworkManager to control it again via 'nmcli'
```

```
INFO: Edimax found existing monitor interface 'mon1' for source interface
      'wlan1'
INFO: Edimax monitor interface 'mon1' already exists for capture interface
      'wlan1', we'll use that.
INFO: Edimax bringing down parent interface 'wlan1'
INFO: Edimax finished configuring mon1, ready to capture
INFO: Data source 'wlan1:name=Edimax' launched successfully
```

Upon starting, Kismet will show a text-based display of recent output from the server. Since you're running Kismet on dedicated hardware, you'll need to connect to the address of the device. In most cases, this will be *http://raspberrypi.local:2501* (substitute your device's IPv4 address or hostname for *raspberrypi.local*, if different). This will be the same address you use to connect to Kismet with ssh.

If in doubt, you can execute the following command to get your device's current IP address:

```
$ hostname -I
```

Paste the result into your browser's location bar, appending Kismet's web service port (*:2501*).

The first time Kismet is started, you'll be prompted to set your username and password, as shown in Figure 7-4. These credentials will be saved in the configuration file *$HOME/.kismet/kismet_httpd.conf*, located in the home directory of the user who started Kismet (the *pi* user, by default).

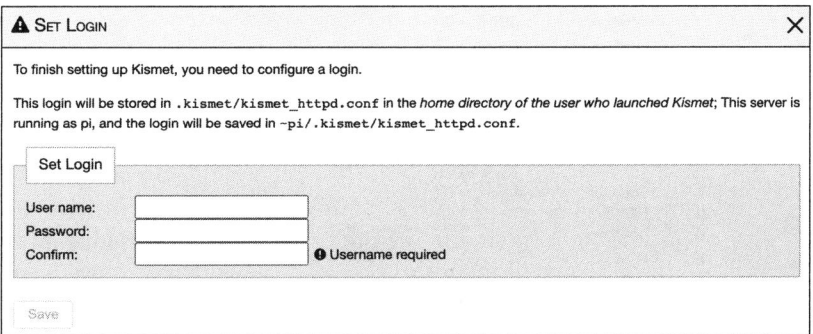

Figure 7-4: Kismet's initial login screen

With this done, you should see Kismet's web interface begin populating with nearby Wi-Fi access points, devices, and related data, as shown in Figure 7-5. Click or tap on any of the listed devices to open a dialog with detailed information, including packet frequency distribution, packet types, and more.

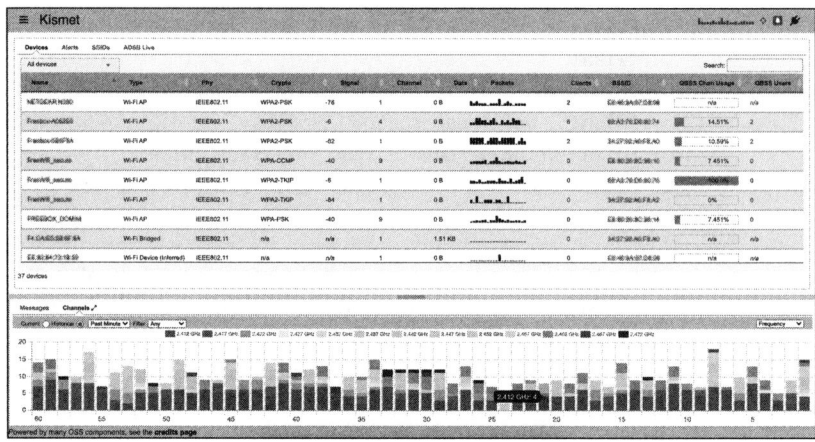

Figure 7-5: Kismet's dashboard showing a continuous scan of the local wireless neighborhood

From the top-left menu, select **Data Sources** to open a dialog showing the state of your Edimax adapter. The summary includes details on interface hardware, received packets, activity, and active channels. In Figure 7-6, notice that the physical adapter wlan1 and its associated mon1 interface are indicated as the data source.

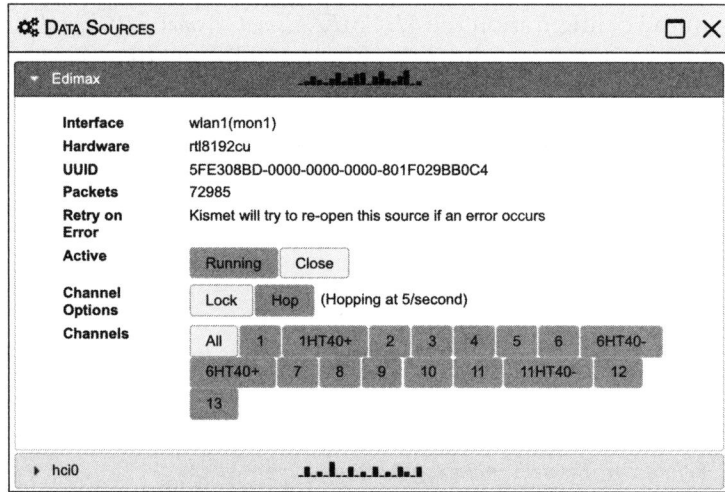

Figure 7-6: Kismet's Data Sources dialog displaying the Edimax USB adapter bound to wlan1

Note that the channels listed here are restricted to the 2.4 GHz band, reflecting the device's hardware capabilities. You can selectively enable or disable monitoring on any of the available channels or deactivate the data source entirely from this dialog, if you wish.

Bluetooth Sources

Bluetooth uses a frequency-hopping system with dynamic MAC addresses and other oddities, which makes monitoring it less straightforward than capturing Wi-Fi traffic. Kismet includes support for the Linux Host Controller Interface to perform Bluetooth discovery, using a generic Bluetooth adapter to scan for discoverable Bluetooth Classic and BLE devices. This is an active scan, not passive monitoring, and it reports device attributes and advertised information, not raw packets as with Wi-Fi.

If your Raspberry Pi model has integrated Bluetooth, you may be able to use it as a data source as well. In the dialog shown in Figure 7-6, the Pi 4's Bluetooth 5.0 device appears as hci0 below the Edimax data source. Expand this entry and select **Enable Source**, and Kismet will add Bluetooth discovery data from this interface to the network scanner.

Packet Capture

In addition to its real-time packet-scanning capabilities, Kismet also stores packets as binary data for later analysis. By default, Kismet uses its own log format, which combines all the data it captures: packets, devices, alerts, system messages, non-packet data, and more. You can view or modify Kismet's log settings by editing its configuration:

```
$ sudo nano /etc/kismet/kismet_logging.conf
```

Kismet's default packet capture (often abbreviated *PCAP*) location is the directory it was launched from. If you started Kismet from the *pi* user's home directory, you will find one or more **.kismet* logfiles there, along with a *.kismet-journal* file.

You can do several things with these PCAP files, including replaying them within Kismet. This can be useful for demos, testing, debugging, or reprocessing a network scan. To use a PCAP file as a kismetdb data source, specify it when running Kismet, like so:

```
$ kismet -c $HOME/my-logfile.kismet
```

PCAP files are commonly generated by tools like tcpdump, Wireshark, and Kismet itself. If you'd like to use tools such as these to perform your own packet analysis, Kismet includes a command line tool, kismetdb_to_pcap, to convert its logs to the standard *.pcap* or *.pcapng* formats. For example, to convert a Kismet log to a standard *.pcapng* file, you can use a command like:

```
$ kismetdb_to_pcap --in some-kismet-log.kismet --out some-pcap-log.pcapng
```

The *.pcapng* file type contains the most information and is generally the preferred format for tools like Wireshark.

Alerts and WIDS

You've seen how, with very basic hardware, you can create a powerful WLAN monitoring and packet capture framework using Kismet. Next, we'll explore how Kismet can be put into service as a WIDS with alerting capabilities.

Kismet allows you to configure alerts for various types of fingerprint- and trend-based monitoring. A fingerprint alert may be triggered when a known-hostile behavior is detected, such as AP spoofing (recall the Evil Twin attack discussed earlier). By contrast, trend-based monitors detect unusual patterns of activity over time, such as denial-of-service attacks or flooding with certain packet types. For example, they would allow you to detect a *deauth flood* attack, which involves spoofing the deauthentication packets that typically are used to disconnect clients from a network in order to disrupt service or force clients to connect to a rogue AP.

Configuring Alerts

By default, Kismet comes preconfigured with a wide range of alerts mapped to common intrusion signatures. These are defined in the *kismet_alerts.conf* file. If you installed Kismet from the official package repositories, you can open this file in your editor by running:

```
$ sudo nano /etc/kismet/kismet_alerts.conf
```

It's generally recommended to retain Kismet's default alert settings when you're first getting started, with one exception. If you host a Wi-Fi access point, you may want Kismet to alert you in the event of an APSPOOF, or Evil Twin, attack. To enable this, locate and edit the following lines in the *kismet_alerts.conf* file, replacing the placeholder values with your AP's SSID and MAC address:

```
apspoof=Foo1:ssid="Foobar",
validmacs="00:11:22:33:44:55,aa:bb:cc:dd:ee:ff"
```

Replace *Foo1* with a descriptive name for the rule, such as Spoofed Wi-Fi Router. If you aren't sure of your AP's MAC address, start Kismet while the AP is active, then inspect its entry in the network scan. The next time you start Kismet, it will alert you when it detects an SSID that appears to be trying to impersonate, or spoof, one from your authorized inventory. You can add any number of authorized APs to this list.

You can fine-tune Kismet's alert subsystem by controlling how often each alert is reported, or whether it's reported at all. You can configure throttle values to specify the maximum number of alerts allowed in a given time frame (in seconds or minutes), as well as a burst value to control how many alerts can occur in quick succession. For example, the configuration

```
alert=DEAUTHFLOOD,5/min,2/sec
```

allows at most two DEAUTHFLODD alerts per second and no more than five per minute.

After reviewing the alert settings, save the file and exit your editor. Once you've operated your WIDS for a while, you may decide to adjust some of the alert reporting thresholds, or to ignore certain alerts altogether. To disable reporting for a specific alert, simply comment out its line in the configuration file.

Don't be too concerned at this stage if Kismet's alerts appear cryptic. When an alert is triggered, a detailed description will appear on the Alerts tab of the Kismet web interface when it's generated. You can also find documentation for each alert type on the Kismet website.

Operating the WIDS

Kismet is most effective as a WIDS when deployed in a stationary location (that is, in a non-wardriving role). Generally speaking, it's best to install your Kismet-enabled device in a fixed position and allow it to operate continuously over the course of several hours, days, or even longer. This gives it time to build a comprehensive profile of nearby wireless activity and detect anomalies more reliably.

WATCH KISMET'S PCAP FILES

Bear in mind that Kismet's packet capturing is enabled by default. These binary logfiles can become quite large, so be sure you have adequate space on your device's SD card. If you're planning to operate your WIDS over an extended period of time, consider limiting which items are logged or disabling logging altogether.

Depending on your environment, the amount of ordinary or expected wireless traffic around you will vary considerably. In a city center, for example, you can expect to have a greater density of WLANs and many wireless devices passing in and out of range of your WIDS, and therefore a greater likelihood of alert activity.

Even if you're located in an area with relatively few wireless networks, you may be surprised by the amount of benign "background" traffic you observe with your monitoring node. Left running for a few hours in a quiet neighborhood, Kismet might detect things like an Amazon Ring doorbell, a person walking by with a phone, or a passing car. Any of these devices might be broadcasting APs, possibly unbeknownst to their owners. Quite often, the device's make and model will be advertised. Don't be surprised if, for example, you catch an Audi using Apple CarPlay in your list of detected SSIDs.

Creating a WLAN Security Test Bench

There is, of course, another way to validate the effectiveness of your WIDS that doesn't require waiting for a malicious actor or less-than-ethical wardriver to wage an attack. With a second Wi-Fi–capable device, such as a Raspberry

Pi, you can create a WLAN test bench to generate alerts on your WIDS and validate your setup.

By default, Kismet will generate alerts for several trend-based and stateful behaviors observed in access points over time. Some of these may reflect ordinary configuration changes in an AP, while others might indicate something more serious, such as a spoofing attack. To test these alerts, you'll need access to an AP that you can manipulate.

The user interface provided by RaspAP simplifies the process of manipulating the AP settings to test Kismet's alert system. Referring back to "Using RaspAP" on page 56, choose the method that you find most suitable and follow the steps to create an instance of RaspAP.

Once you have a functional access point running on a second device, you're ready to explore techniques for triggering AP spoof alerts on your Kismet monitoring node.

NOTE *The examples here will describe using RaspAP's web interface to manipulate your access point. If you wish to see how the* hostapd *configuration is modified behind the scenes, execute the following command after you save settings via the web interface:*

```
$ sudo cat /etc/hostapd/hostapd.conf
```

Generating Alerts

In its default configuration, RaspAP will create a routed wireless AP on the 2.4 GH band, broadcasting the SSID RaspAP. The default security type used is WPA2, and the encryption is CCMP.

To trigger a Kismet AP spoof alert, navigate to the **Hotspot ▶ Security** tab in the web interface and change the encryption type to **TKIP+CCMP**. Next, choose **Save Settings** and then **Restart Hotspot**. Shortly after, Kismet should generate a trend-based ADVCRYPTCHANGE spoof alert, as shown in Figure 7-7. This alert is triggered whenever an SSID changes the encryption options it advertises, whether because of a routine configuration change, as in this case, or as a sign of a potential AP spoofing attempt.

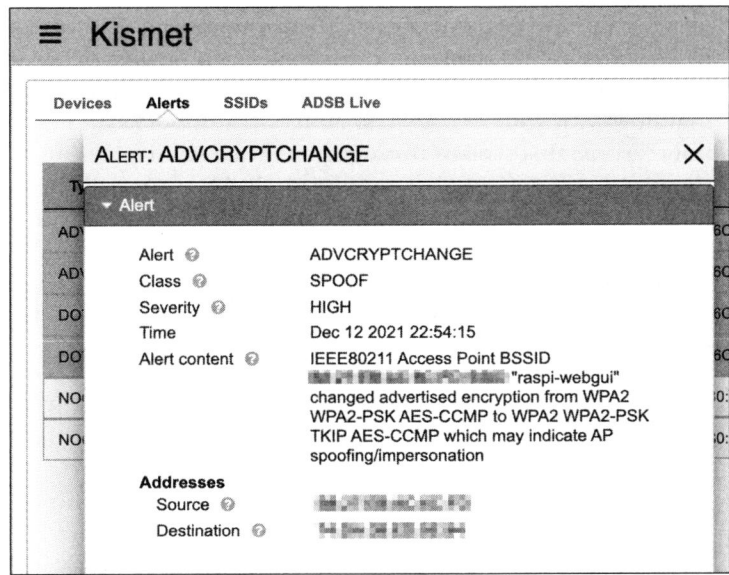

Figure 7-7: Generating an AP spoofing/impersonation alert by using the WLAN test bench

Next, you can try raising a BEACONRATE alert. To do this, change the **Beacon Interval** value on the **Hotspot ▶ Advanced** tab (any value other than the default is fine), then select **Save Settings** followed by **Restart Hotspot**. The corresponding Kismet alert is shown in Figure 7-8.

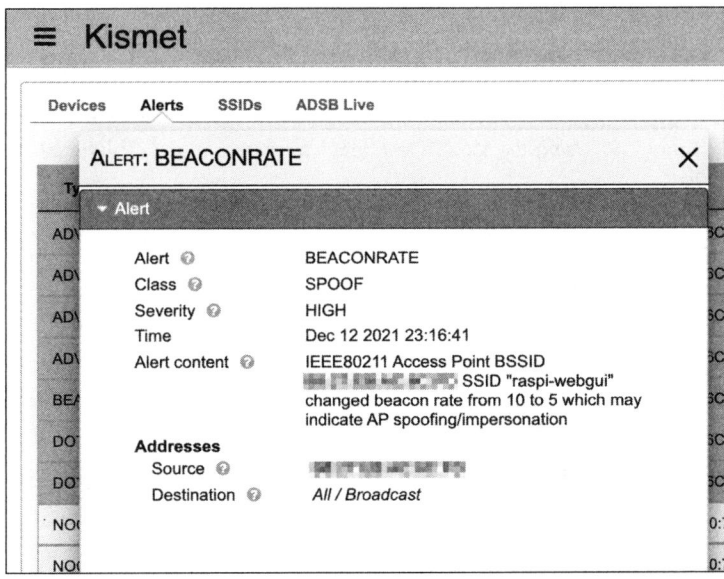

Figure 7-8: An example beacon rate change alert raised by the WLAN test bench

Finally, for your *pièce de résistance*, you can try generating a convincing Evil Twin, or `APSPOOF`, alert. If you've defined an authorized AP in *kismet _alerts.conf*, as described in "Configuring Alerts" on page 218, you can use that now with your WLAN test bench. It's important to note that, for ethical reasons, this type of testing should be performed only with an AP that you own. Impersonating someone else's AP is generally regarded as bad-mannered, at the very least, and could potentially land you in hot water.

Make note of your authorized AP's SSID, then place this value in the **SSID** field on RaspAP's **Hotspot ▶ Basic** tab. Next, choose **Save Settings** and then **Restart Hotspot**. Kismet should immediately raise an alert matching the `APSPOOF` rule you defined, as shown in Figure 7-9.

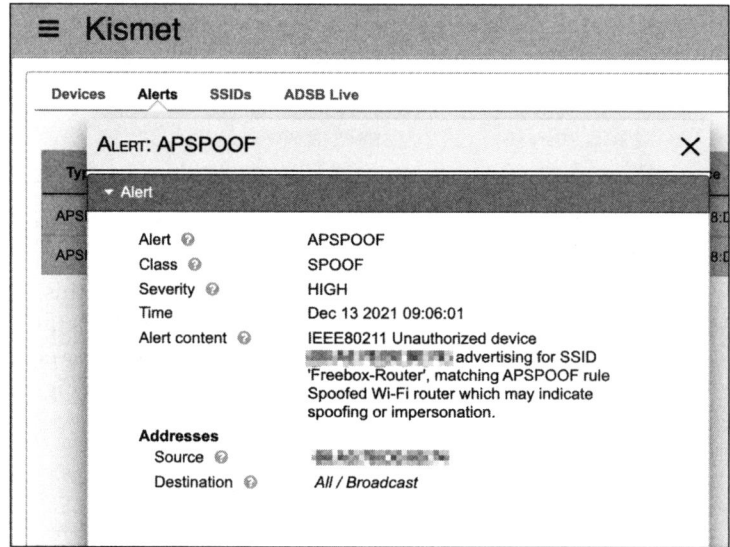

Figure 7-9: Using the WLAN test bench to generate an Evil Twin (APSPOOF) alert

If the password of your fake AP is the same as the authorized one, and it has a better signal strength, you may find that some client devices will connect to it automatically. To avoid this, after you've completed this alert test, be sure to change your spoofed SSID back to something unique.

REAL-WORLD EVIL TWIN ATTACKS

Spoofed or impersonated APs are difficult to mitigate through software or similar means. In most cases, the only effective way to deal with a spoof is through a "boots on the ground" approach. Security specialists typically begin by disabling the AP that's being spoofed, then use a Wi-Fi scanner to measure the signal strength of the rogue AP from multiple locations. This process, while time-consuming, helps triangulate the device's physical location so appropriate actions can be taken to remove or disable it.

Continuing Your Tests

With your WLAN test bench and the help of RaspAP, you've demonstrated
that your WIDS is capable of detecting several common AP spoofing techniques. This is only the beginning, though. Many other tools exist to practice cracking both WEP and WPA2-PSK Wi-Fi passwords, deploy deauth
attacks, and much more. A survey of these tools and their usage is beyond
the scope of this recipe, but the concepts introduced here should put you
on the right path. Just be sure that your WLAN security journey takes place
within the ethical confines of your local test bench.

When you're done with your current monitoring session, use CTRL-C to
safely shut Kismet down.

Parsing Kismet's Logs

After Kismet exits, it unlocks the logfile generated during the last session.
As described previously, Kismet uses a unified log format that combines
packets, non-packet data, devices, locations, data source records, system
messages, trends, and nearly everything else it tracks in a common *.kismet*
file. This is in contrast to the legacy approach, where multiple logfiles were
generated, and eliminates the need to correlate data from multiple logs to
get a complete view of the capture history.

By default, Kismet writes logfiles to the directory from which it was
launched. If you've followed the steps in this recipe, this will be the logged-
in user's *$HOME* directory. Logs generated by Kismet are stored using a
SQLite3 database format. However, this database is not designed as a traditional, strictly normalized relational database. Instead, to support the wide
variety of data collected, spanning different PHY layers and any plug-ins
that may have been loaded, the log contains a few normalized fields (such
as location, timestamps, and device identifiers), with the majority of the data
stored as serialized JSON objects or raw binary packet data.

Using Kismetdb Statistics

Kismet's unified kismetdb logs are stored as binary files. To examine a previous Kismet monitoring session, select a *.kismet* file for parsing with the
kismetdb_statistics tool. Execute the tool with the --in option, specifying
the path to the *.kismet* logfile you wish to parse. In this example, I'm using a
logfile from my last session:

```
$ kismetdb_statistics --in Kismet-20240701-12-02-37-1.kismet
* Cleaning database 'Kismet-20240701-12-02-37-1.kismet'...
  KismetDB version: 8

  Packets: 51552
  Non-packet data: 0

  Devices: 401
```

```
Devices seen between: 2024-07-01 12:02:40 (1719835360) to ...
1 datasources
  Edimax wlan1  5FE308BD-0000-0000-0000-74DA38ED5E7D linuxwifi
    Hardware: rtl8192cu
    Packets: 51157
    Hop rate: 5.000000/second
    Hop channels: 1, 1HT40+, 2, 3, 4, 5, 6, 6HT40-, 6HT40+ ...
--snip--
```

Alternatively, you can have kismetdb_statistics output the data in JSON format by appending the --json option.

If the statistics from a previous session appear interesting, you may want to examine them more closely. In most cases, the best way to do this is by converting them to the widely used packet capture format. You can then analyze the capture with a tool that supports processing of PCAP logs, such as tcpdump, Wireshark, or any number of other utilities made for this purpose.

Converting to PCAP Files

Kismet includes tools for converting its native logfiles to both the legacy *.pcap* format and the newer *.pcapng* (PCAP next generation) format. The more modern format supports multiple data sources, such as Wi-Fi and Bluetooth, and retains information about which source each packet came from.

As you're using a single capture device for this project, the legacy format will suffice. To convert an existing *.kismet* file to *.pcap* format, use a command like the following:

```
$ kismetdb_to_pcap --in my-kismet-log.kismet --out my-kismet.pcap --old-pcap
```

Replace *my-kismet-log.kismet* with the name of your Kismet logfile and *my-kismet.pcap* with the name of the PCAP file you wish to output.

With the resulting PCAP file, you can now use a tool such as tcpdump in the terminal to view the packets in a human-readable form. Install the package, then execute it with the following options:

```
$ sudo apt install -y tcpdump
$ tcpdump -qns 0 -X -r my-kismet.pcap | less
```

Again, replace *my-kismet.pcap* with your Kismet *.pcap* file. The -X flag tells tcpdump to display the packet data in both hexadecimal and ASCII formats. The output is piped to less so it can be paged a screenful at a time.

You can also securely transfer PCAP files from your Kismet node to another device, using sftp for more detailed analysis with a graphical tool such as Wireshark.

Going Further

At this stage, you have a feature-rich wireless network scanner capable of both monitoring packets in real time and capturing them for later analysis. You've also seen how Kismet's powerful wireless intrusion detection capabilities can alert you to potential exploits targeting access points, by modifying the settings of an AP that's part of your WLAN security test bench. However, there's another class of alert that Kismet can detect, which you may not have observed yet. To trigger this type of alert, you can add a third device to your testing environment.

Of the recipes presented in this book, there's perhaps no better pairing than Kismet and Pwnagotchi. The recipe in Chapter 9 guides you through building this analog (or perhaps antagonist) to Kismet: a device that automates the collection of Wi-Fi handshakes by various means. With the aid of its sophisticated AI engine, Pwnagotchi employs two primary strategies to capture handshakes: by deauthenticating client stations and by sending crafted association frames. For a detailed explanation of these methods, see "Collecting Handshakes" on page 292.

With Kismet and a target access point running in your WLAN security test bench, power up a Pwnagotchi unit and ensure it's within range of your networks. After a few moments, you can expect Pwnagotchi to begin launching deauthentication attacks against nearby access points. As Kismet detects these events, it will raise a DEAUTHFLOOD alert like the following in the web interface and also report it to the console:

```
ALERT: DEAUTHFLOOD Deauth/Disassociate flood on E0:46:9A:FF:00:00
```

This alert type is enabled by default in Kismet's configuration. Given enough time, you may observe Pwnagotchi initiating several of these attacks against non-whitelisted access points within its range. Additionally, Kismet will log the association frames generated by Pwnagotchi. While not strictly treated as alerts, the captured association frames can still be examined in the PCAP logs. To view them with Wireshark, open the *.pcap* file generated by Kismet and apply the display filter wlan.fc.type_subtype == 0x00.

Wrapping Up

In this chapter, we took a deep dive into the world of wireless intrusion detection systems and explored some of the most common WLAN vulnerabilities. With the rapid proliferation of wireless networks worldwide, threats against them have surged. It's no surprise, then, that wireless security has become one of the fastest-growing specializations in cybersecurity.

Armed with the software tools presented here and some inexpensive hardware, you now have the components of a robust WLAN security test bench. You can test real-world exploits on your own network, perform advanced analysis of the resulting PCAP files, and much more. You might also choose to participate in mapping Wi-Fi networks in your area. Kismet supports logging in a format compatible with WiGLE, making it easy to join the global wardriving movement, if you wish.

The WLAN security field is constantly evolving, as researchers uncover new vulnerabilities and practitioners work to develop countermeasures and mitigate threats in the wild. With the foundational skills you've acquired here, you're now well equipped to not only protect your own networks but also guide others through the ever-shifting wireless landscape.

8

WIRELESS AIR QUALITY MONITORING

The proliferation of Internet of Things technologies and the availability of low-cost sensors have created enormous opportunities for makers. A compelling example is the democratization of air quality monitoring (AQM). Once the domain of research institutions and government bodies, such efforts are now well within the reach of individuals. With ever-increasing concerns about pollution levels and their health impacts, especially in urban areas, this area of citizen science is more vital now than ever, and in this chapter I'll demonstrate how you can participate in it.

If you have an interest in IoT hardware, environmental sensing, and data visualizations, prepare to roll up your sleeves. In this recipe, you'll delve into the science of AQM and use a wireless uplink to transport sensor data from your monitoring station to your local network and, optionally, to the cloud. The project requires some very basic soldering skills, but if you prefer, you can avoid this altogether by starting with a presoldered board and simply plugging the components together.

Use Cases

The science and practice of measuring air quality accelerated in the 1980s with the introduction of monitoring networks and instrumentation capable of detecting airborne pollutants. Although sophisticated for its time, the technology was fairly limited and prohibitively expensive, with its cost placing it beyond the reach of the average citizen. Monitoring stations of this era were almost exclusively managed by governments, universities, and grant-funded researchers.

Today, with the advent of affordable sensors and devices like the Raspberry Pi, air quality monitoring is more precise, faster, and available to nearly anyone with an interest in the science. Several of these technologies are related to the IoT practice of sensing and measuring various phenomena in the world around us. While the quality of these sensors varies, some are approaching the performance of professional monitoring equipment, at a tiny fraction of the cost.

In this recipe, you'll create a station built around the Pi Zero 2 W that records two key pieces of air quality data with a high degree of precision: PM2.5 (fine particles smaller than 2.5 micrometers) and PM10 (coarse particles smaller than 10 micrometers). This data will be accessible from a visual dashboard on your local network, similar to the one shown in Figure 8-1.

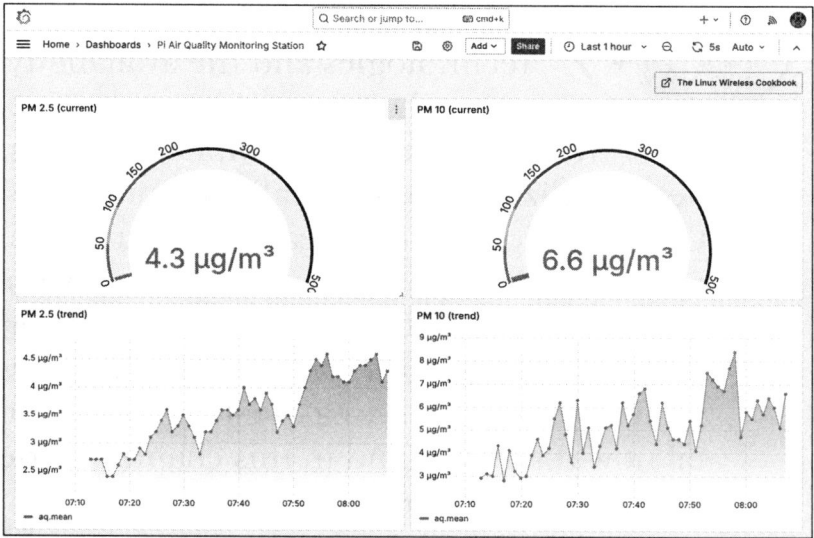

Figure 8-1: A sophisticated air quality–sensing dashboard powered by inexpensive components

In the process, you'll explore not only IoT concepts but also sending your data to a cloud-based IoT feed. I'll wrap up by demonstrating how to assemble the components used for this project into a weatherproof, purpose-built 3D-printed enclosure designed for mounting the station outdoors.

Before we get to the hardware requirements, a word on air quality standards is warranted. Different countries have their own air quality indices, corresponding to their own national air quality standards. Many countries, including the United States, South Korea, India, and China, use a scale from 0 to 500 that measures the amount of airborne pollution and maps these values to human health concerns. This is also the scale used by the World Air Quality Index (AQI) project (*https://waqi.info*), which is the standard I've adopted for this recipe. The AQI scale is shown in Table 8-1.

Table 8-1: The Air Quality Index Scale

AQI	Pollution level	Health implications	Cautionary statement (for PM2.5)
0–50	Good	Air quality is considered satisfactory, and air pollution poses little or no risk.	None.
51–100	Moderate	Air quality is acceptable; however, for some pollutants there may be a moderate health concern for a very small number of people who are unusually sensitive to air pollution.	Unusually sensitive individuals should consider limiting prolonged outdoor exertion.
101–150	Unhealthy for sensitive groups	Members of sensitive groups may experience health effects. The general public is not likely to be affected.	Active children and adults, and people with respiratory disease, such as asthma, should limit prolonged outdoor exertion.
151–200	Unhealthy	Everyone may begin to experience health effects; members of sensitive groups may experience more serious health effects.	Active children and adults, and people with respiratory disease, such as asthma, should avoid prolonged outdoor exertion; everyone else, especially children, should limit prolonged outdoor exertion.
201–300	Very unhealthy	Health warnings of emergency conditions. The entire population is more likely to be affected.	Active children and adults, and people with respiratory disease, such as asthma, should avoid all outdoor exertion; everyone else, especially children, should limit outdoor exertion.
301–500	Hazardous	Health alert: Everyone may experience more serious health effects.	Everyone should avoid all outdoor exertion.

Air quality is seldom distributed equally across a region. Pollution has a tendency to accumulate in isolated areas, due to inputs such as industry or transportation, and is influenced by factors like local weather conditions and topography. It's difficult to draw conclusions about how air quality varies from place to place if you have a limited set of data points to work with. This is where citizen science plays an important role. With the right tools, you too can contribute more information to fill these gaps.

You may live in a region with persistent or seasonal air quality issues. Perhaps your nearest monitoring station is too distant to provide reliable data for your locality. Maybe you're curious about the quality of the air you and the people around you breathe, interested in participating in a global citizen science project, or simply looking for an excuse to use your Pi to gather data from your environment. If any of these motivations apply, this project is for you.

Hardware Required

This recipe makes use of an affordable, state-of-the-art sensor, plus some smaller components to connect everything together. At a minimum, you can complete this project using only a Pi Zero 2 W and the Nova SDS011 particle sensor. Alternatively, you may choose to expand your implementation with an additional sensor, a 3D-printed enclosure, and perhaps a different means of providing the required data uplink.

In addition to these hardware components, you'll need some basic tools (namely, a soldering iron, screwdriver, and hot glue gun) that you may already have or be able to borrow. A complete hardware list with optional components is provided in this section.

Raspberry Pi Zero 2 W

The Pi Zero 2 W, shown in Figure 8-2, works especially well for this project because of its diminutive form factor. The CPU demands are minimal, so processing power isn't a concern.

Figure 8-2: The Pi Zero 2 W is ideally suited for this project.

This model is available from various online retailers for about $15.

Male GPIO Header

Unlike other Raspberry Pi models, the Pi Zero range does not come standard with a presoldered GPIO header. This is partly to reduce cost, but also to make it easier to embed these devices into small spaces. Consequently, you'll need to attach a 40-pin GPIO header.

An adapter with a 2×20-pin connector, as shown in Figure 8-3, is the standard way to add GPIO pins to your Pi Zero 2 W. Many options are available here, including some color-coded ones. They're inexpensive (typically about $1, so if ordering one, you may as well stock up on several. You'll need basic soldering equipment as well, to attach the header to the board.

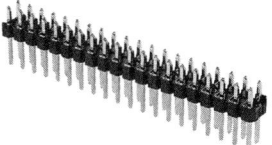

Figure 8-3: A GPIO header

Alternatively, if you'd prefer to avoid soldering or don't have the equipment on hand, several online retailers offer Pi Zero 2 Ws with presoldered GPIO headers. These are usually not significantly more expensive.

Nova SDS011 Particle Sensor

The Nova SDS011 laser-based PM2.5/PM10 particle sensor, pictured in Figure 8-4 and available from online retailers for about $30, is a relatively recent air quality sensor and among the best available in terms of accuracy for its size. It uses a fan to draw in air for sampling, with the sensor itself using a laser light scattering principle to measure suspended dust particles.

Figure 8-4: The Nova SDS011

The Nova sensor ships with a ribbon cable suitable for connecting it to the Pi's GPIO header, plus a USB-to-UART converter. This recipe assumes you'll be using GPIO. You may use the USB-to-UART converter instead if you prefer, but note that it communicates with the Pi Zero on a different serial interface than the one you'll be using here (ttyUSB0 is typical).

Bosch BME680 Sensor (Optional)

You can further extend your station's capabilities with an additional sensor. A popular option is the Bosch BME680 Breakout, shown in Figure 8-5, or the updated BME688 Breakout. This four-in-one sensor provides temperature, pressure, humidity, and indoor air quality measurements in a tiny package.

Figure 8-5: The BME680
four-in-one sensor

Both Pimoroni and Adafruit produce breakout board versions of this Bosch sensor, available for about $21. The sensors were recently updated to be Qwiic/STEMMA QT–compatible, meaning they can be connected via a cable without any soldering. The model shown in Figure 8-5 requires soldering a 1×5-pin header. I'll discuss adding this sensor in "Going Further" on page 258.

3G–4G/LTE Base HAT (Optional)

If you anticipate placing your monitoring station in a location outside the range of your Wi-Fi router's coverage, a popular option for data connectivity is a stackable 3G/4G cellular HAT, such as the one shown in Figure 8-6. Sixfab makes a compact 3G–4G/LTE Base HAT that gives 40-pin GPIO devices like the Raspberry Pi a bridge to mini PCIe cellular modems. You'll need to add a modem (not shown) to enable cellular connectivity, but with this inserted into the Base HAT, your Pi-based projects will have access to 3G/4G data networks all around the world.

Figure 8-6: The Sixfab 3G–4G/LTE
Base HAT

This is just one example of a connectivity option to provide a wireless uplink for your station; you're free to investigate other solutions. The Sixfab 3G–4G/LTE Base HAT is available for about $45 and is compatible with all Raspberry Pi models. More information is available from *https://sixfab.com*.

3D-Printed Enclosure (Optional)

An enclosure is recommended to weatherproof your monitoring station for outdoor use. If you're going to use it only indoors, you won't need an enclosure.

I'll walk you through creating the enclosure in "Creating an Outdoor Enclosure" on page 251. Many affordable on-demand 3D printing services are available, so you needn't worry if you don't have access to a 3D printer. I had an enclosure made by a local 3D printing service for about $30, and it arrived in just a few days.

If you decide to use an enclosure, you'll need some small fasteners, such as self-tapping screws, to assemble the 3D-printed parts. A hot glue gun is also handy for affixing the Pi Zero 2 W to the enclosure; just be sure to use it sparingly.

Software Used

Several pieces of Python code are used in this project to communicate with the attached sensor. In addition, you'll use two powerful open source packages for recording and displaying air quality data (more on this in "Gathering Sensor Data" on page 239). Finally, you'll use `wpa_supplicant` to provide a wireless 802.11 data link for your monitoring station. I'll also discuss some ways to extend the reporting range of your station up to several miles, or anywhere in the world where 3G/4G mobile network connectivity exists.

Prerequisites

A key open source software component you'll be using to create the dashboard requires arm64, the 64-bit extension of the ARM architecture. For this reason, be sure to begin with the latest 64-bit version of Debian/Raspberry Pi OS Lite.

For the purposes of this recipe, I'll assume you're using the Pi Zero 2 W in headless mode. You may, of course, choose to access it via an attached monitor and keyboard, but the steps described here will be performed in the Linux terminal. If you've opted to use VS Code for development, you can run these commands from the terminal built into the IDE.

Configuring Headless Access

Flash a fresh SD card with the latest distribution of Raspberry Pi OS Lite (64-bit) from the official download page, then create an empty file named *ssh* (no extension) and save it in the boot partition of the SD card. Next, to configure wireless networking, create another file called *wpa_supplicant.conf* with the following contents:

```
ctrl_interface=DIR=/var/run/wpa_supplicant GROUP=netdev
update_config=1
country=US

network={
    ssid="your_SSID"
    psk="your_wi-fi_password"
}
```

Substitute your two-letter ISO 3166-1 alpha-2 country code for US if you're not in the United States, and be sure both your network SSID and your password (pre-shared key) are enclosed in double quotes. Copy this file to the boot partition as well. You'll need to complete this step before you boot the SD card for the first time, as that's the point at which the system checks for the presence of the *wpa_supplicant.conf* file.

Alternatively, you can perform this setup with the Raspberry Pi Imager tool while writing the OS to your SD card. Under **OS Customisation**, choose **Wireless LAN** and enter an SSID (name) and the password for your network. If the network doesn't broadcast an SSID publicly, enable the **Hidden SSID** setting.

Completing this step ensures that all interactions with your Pi will be performed wirelessly. Eject the SD card, insert it into the Pi Zero 2 W, connect it to power, and boot it up. Check your router's admin interface for connected devices on your network. Your Pi should appear in the list with an assigned IPv4 address. Connect to your Pi via SSH, substituting your device's IP address or hostname, if necessary:

```
$ ssh pi@raspberrypi.local
```

With this done, you can set some parameters in the Linux kernel.

Preparing the Serial Port

To use the Nova sensor via GPIO, you must first ensure that no other serial communication is taking place. The Linux kernel accepts a command line of parameters during boot. On Raspberry Pi OS, this is defined in a file in the boot partition called *cmdline.txt*.

Open this file in your editor with

```
$ sudo nano /boot/firmware/cmdline.txt
```

and append the following parameters to the existing line:

```
plymouth.ignore-serial-consoles ipv6.disable=1
```

Then save the file and exit the editor. If the Plymouth module is enabled, it can prevent boot messages from appearing on any serial console that's present. This flag tells Plymouth to ignore all serial consoles. IPv6 can safely be disabled, as no applications or services rely on it for this project.

Next, you'll ensure that UART is enabled. This is discussed in more detail in the following section. For now, open the *config.txt* file in your editor by running

```
$ sudo nano /boot/firmware/config.txt
```

and append the following lines:

```
# Enable UART
enable_uart=1
```

Save this file and exit your editor. Next, run `raspi-config` in noninteractive mode to configure two serial interface settings directly:

```
$ sudo raspi-config nonint do_serial_hw 0
$ sudo raspi-config nonint do_serial_cons 1
```

The first command enables the hardware serial port, while the second one disables shell and kernel messages on the serial connection.

Finally, update the system packages to their latest versions and reboot:

```
$ sudo apt update && sudo apt upgrade
$ sudo reboot
```

Now you're ready to connect your sensor to the Pi's GPIO header pins.

Getting to Know the GPIO

If you've previously worked through the some of the earlier recipes in this book (particularly, Chapter 3), you'll already be familiar with the Pi's general-purpose input/output pins. Like most Raspberry Pi boards, the Pi Zero 2 W provides a 40-pin GPIO header (though it's not presoldered). This gives you an interface to extend the Pi Zero with other electronic components, such as the Nova sensor used in this chapter.

Recent distributions of Raspberry Pi OS include a built-in utility called `pinout`. This tool queries your Pi's GPIO configuration and outputs a helpful schematic along with some specs. Example output of this utility on the Pi Zero 2 W is shown in Figure 8-7.

```
pi@pizero2w:~ $ pinout
Description       : Raspberry Pi Zero2W rev 1.0
Revision          : 902120
SoC               : BCM2837
RAM               : 512MB
Storage           : MicroSD
USB ports         : 1 (of which 0 USB3)
Ethernet ports    : 0 (0Mbps max. speed)
Wi-fi             : True
Bluetooth         : True
Camera ports (CSI) : 1
Display ports (DSI): 0
```

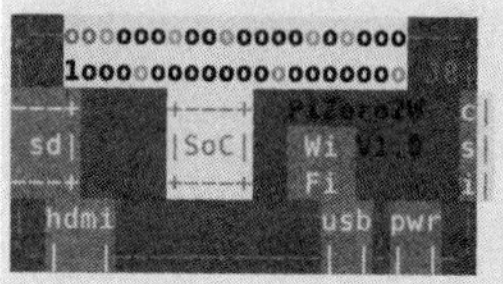

```
J8:
    3V3  (1) (2)  5V
  GPIO2  (3) (4)  5V
  GPIO3  (5) (6)  GND
  GPIO4  (7) (8)  GPIO14
    GND  (9) (10) GPIO15
 GPIO17 (11) (12) GPIO18
 GPIO27 (13) (14) GND
 GPIO22 (15) (16) GPIO23
    3V3 (17) (18) GPIO24
 GPIO10 (19) (20) GND
  GPIO9 (21) (22) GPIO25
 GPIO11 (23) (24) GPIO8
    GND (25) (26) GPIO7
  GPIO0 (27) (28) GPIO1
  GPIO5 (29) (30) GND
  GPIO6 (31) (32) GPIO12
 GPIO13 (33) (34) GND
 GPIO19 (35) (36) GPIO16
 GPIO26 (37) (38) GPIO20
    GND (39) (40) GPIO21
```

Figure 8-7: The output of the pinout utility on a
Pi Zero 2 W

As you can see, the GPIO interface includes several types of pins. For
the purposes of this project, we'll focus on the three broad categories discussed in the next sections: power pins, UART pins, and ground pins.

Power Pins

The Pi Zero board includes two 5V pins, two 3V3 pins, and nine ground
pins (0V), all of which are nonconfigurable. The 5V pins deliver the 5-volt
supply coming from the power adapter. They can be used to power up the
Raspberry Pi Zero directly, or to provide power to other 5 V devices. In
this project, you'll use one of the Pi Zero's two 5V pins to power the Nova
SDS011 sensor. The 3V3 pins provide a stable 3.3-volt supply to power
smaller components, such as test LEDs and breakout boards.

UART Pins

The Raspberry Pi has a dedicated universal asynchronous receiver-transmitter
interface, which you'll use to enable communication between two microcontrollers. The transmitter pin (abbreviated *TX* or *TXD*) transmits serial data,
while the receiver pin (*RX* or *RXD*) receives serial data from a connected

device. A GPIO receiver pin reads incoming voltage signals sent by the device. The Pi interprets voltages between 1.8 V and 3.3 V as high (logical "one") and voltages below 1.8 V as low (logical "zero"). This allows serial data to be exchanged in binary form.

For this project, you'll use two UART pins for communication with the Nova SDS011 sensor: GPIO 14 and GPIO 15, shown in the bottom-right corner of Figure 8-8.

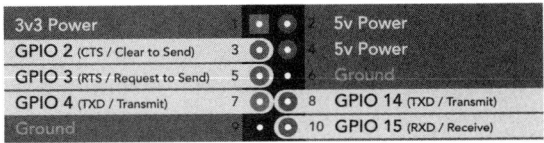

Figure 8-8: The UART pins used for communication with the Nova SDS011 sensor (source: https://pinout.xyz)

UART is also commonly used on the Pi as a convenient way to control it over GPIO or to access kernel boot messages via the serial console.

Ground Pins

The ground pins, commonly abbreviated *GND*, serve as a reference point for voltage measurements and are used to complete electrical circuits. The ground pins are all electrically connected on the Raspberry Pi boards, so using a specific one when connecting a power supply isn't necessary. Ground pins are included at various locations on the GPIO header to facilitate connecting things in a tidy, convenient way. The Nova sensor happens to use ground pin 6 in its connector.

Programming Language

There are many ways to program the GPIO interface and several languages to choose from. If fast execution or high-speed control of externally connected hardware is required, the C programming language is a common choice. This is also generally true when timing in an application is critical.

For the purposes of this recipe, however, performance is not a major concern, as you'll be reading sensor data on a human time scale. For this reason, we'll use Python instead. Python is often described as an interpreted language, but it actually combines elements of both compiled and interpreted languages. When Python code is executed (either in interactive mode or by running a file with a *.py* extension), it's first compiled into *bytecode*. This is a low-level, intermediate representation of the source code, but it's not the same as the binary machine code produced by a C compiler; you can think of it as a set of instructions to be executed by the Python Virtual Machine (PVM). This process is illustrated in Figure 8-9.

Figure 8-9: A high-level view of Python code execution, from source to the PVM

Although there are some important differences, this approach is similar to that used by Java. It's even possible to translate Python programs into Java bytecode for execution on the Java Virtual Machine (JVM) by using *Jython*, a pure Java implementation of Python that allows Python code to run in a Java environment.

Nova SDS011 Connection

With some basic knowledge of GPIO, you can now proceed with connecting your Nova SDS011 sensor. Be sure the power is disconnected from your Pi Zero 2 W, then attach the four-wire ribbon cable from the Nova SDS011 to the GPIO header, as shown in Figure 8-10.

Figure 8-10: Attaching the Nova SDS011 sensor's ribbon cable to the Pi Zero 2 W's GPIO header pins

Note that the ribbon connector block has an empty slot at the top. This connection uses one 5V pin, one GND pin, and GPIO pins 14 and 15. For clarity, a 1×6 male GPIO header is shown instead of a 2×20 header.

Now, connect power to the Pi Zero 2 W and allow it to boot. At this point, you should hear the Nova SDS011's fan spin up. If not, don't worry; this often results from an incomplete solder connection between the header and the Pi's 5V GPIO pin. Inspect your solder joints carefully, reflow them if needed, and try again.

Gathering Sensor Data

At this stage, you may be thinking about how to handle the data you'll receive from the sensor. One simple approach is to persist the data to a file somewhere on the Pi's filesystem. This could be useful if you want to display a single, near-real-time particulate reading on a web page or hardware display, for example. However, it's often more insightful to look at data trends over different periods of time (hourly, daily, weekly, and so on). While this is technically possible with structured file formats such as JSON, there are more efficient ways to go about it.

Installing InfluxDB and Grafana

InfluxDB is an open source time-series database ideally suited for this purpose. It provides the ability to handle large volumes of timestamped data produced by sensors like the Nova SDS011. With your sensor data stored in InfluxDB, you'll have the foundation for creating an effective air quality analytics dashboard.

To achieve this, you'll need another component capable of translating the raw InfluxDB data into a human-digestible form. This is where Grafana really shines. An open source analytics and visualization platform for the web, Grafana can be configured to use InfluxDB as a data source to create highly customizable visual dashboards.

These two packages work so well together that you will often hear them mentioned in the same breath. Start by installing InfluxDB via the apt package manager:

```
$ sudo apt update
$ sudo apt install influxdb influxdb-client
```

Grafana provides official builds for the arm64 processor family. As of this writing, the latest Grafana release is 10.4.2. The musl standard arm64 C library is a dependency. Install these packages with:

```
$ sudo apt install musl adduser libfontconfig1
$ wget https://dl.grafana.com/oss/release/grafana_10.4.2_arm64.deb
$ sudo dpkg -i grafana_10.4.2_arm64.deb
```

As mentioned previously, Python will be your language of choice for reading sensor data. If you've completed the recipe in Chapter 3, you'll already be familiar with Python virtual environments. If not, take a moment now to read through "Using Python Virtual Environments" on page 79.

Creating a Virtual Project Environment

You'll be working from a source code repository for this project, which provides a convenient working directory for your virtual environment. Begin by installing git, if it isn't present on your system, then clone the companion

GitHub repository into your home directory and change into the directory that holds the project code:

```
$ sudo apt install git
$ cd $HOME
$ git clone https://github.com/wirelesscookbook/py-airq.git
$ cd py-airq
```

Next, ensure that `python3-venv` is available on your system and activate the virtual environment:

```
$ sudo apt install python3-venv
$ python3 -m venv env --system-site-packages
```

To run this project, you'll need to activate the virtual environment each time you reboot your system. You can do so manually with:

```
$ cd ~/py-airq
$ source env/bin/activate
```

Alternatively, you can open your *.bashrc* file in your preferred editor by running

```
$ sudo nano ~/.bashrc
```

and add the following line to the end:

```
source ~/py-airq/env/bin/activate
```

This will ensure that the venv is activated automatically each time the system reboots.

Note that each virtual environment is tied to a directory in the Linux filesystem. When the venv is active, you'll notice that the bash prompt has changed to the following:

```
(env) pi@raspberrypi:~/py-airq $
```

If you don't see the (env) prefix in your project directory, executing Python code that references the libraries you'll be installing will result in `ModuleNotFound` errors. This is a common oversight, but thankfully one that's easily remedied by repeating the activation step. You can deactivate a venv by using the `deactivate` command in the project directory (leave it active for now).

Installing pySerial

With your virtual environment active, you may now install Python's package manager, `pip`, and use this to install pySerial for serial communication support, together with the `influxdb` Python package:

```
(env) $ sudo apt update
(env) $ sudo apt install python3-pip
(env) $ pip install pyserial influxdb
```

Next, start the InfluxDB service, enable it to launch at startup, and verify that you're able to connect to it:

```
(env) $ sudo systemctl enable influxdb.service
(env) $ sudo systemctl start influxdb.service
(env) $ influx
Connected to http://localhost:8086 version 1.6.7~rc0
InfluxDB shell version: 1.6.7~rc0
>
```

At the InfluxDB prompt (>), you'll enter commands to create a database for storing your sensor readings. In the following example, the database name pistation is used. You can change this to any name you like, but be sure to keep a note of it as you'll use it in a later step.

By default, InfluxDB retains data indefinitely, which can become problematic on systems with limited storage. To avoid this, define a custom retention period, verify that it's been applied, and then exit the InfluxDB shell:

```
> CREATE DATABASE pistation
> CREATE RETENTION POLICY one_month ON pistation DURATION 30d REPLICATION 1 DEFAULT
> SHOW RETENTION POLICIES on pistation
name       duration shardGroupDuration replicaN default
----       -------- ------------------ -------- -------
autogen    0s       168h0m0s           1        false
one_month  720h0m0s 24h0m0s            1        true
> exit
```

Here, one_month is the name of the retention policy. You can modify this policy to suit your own needs. For example, you might create a policy called one_week with a DURATION value of 7d. The REPLICATION directive is relevant only for clustered systems but is still a required parameter.

Obtaining Your Geohash

Next, you'll define a few arguments that are required by the py-airq project you cloned. One of these is a geohash value. A *geohash* is a compact alphanumeric string that represents a geographic location. It works by interleaving the binary representations of latitude and longitude in a bitwise fashion to produce a single value. To create your geohash, first determine your latitude and longitude coordinates, then use a converter to encode them. You can use any level of precision you like, depending on your needs.

Starting the Sampler

With your geohash in hand, choose a descriptive name for your monitoring location (home is used here, but you might want to use the name of your town or street). You'll also need to specify the InfluxDB server location (localhost, in this case) and the name of the database you created earlier (here, pistation). Since you're using the Pi Zero's GPIO UART, the --port value will be set to /dev/ttyS0. Finally, the --sds011_measurement argument lets you define a data series for the measurements stored in InfluxDB. This example uses the abbreviation aq, for air quality.

You can now execute the Python module with the -m switch, passing each of these arguments:

```
(env) $ python -m sampler --port /dev/ttyS0 --influx localhost \
    --database pistation --sds011_measurement aq \
    --location home --geohash ge2kv5h
```

Note that all these parameters have default values defined in the code, so you can also run the module without any arguments, like so:

```
(env) $ python -m sampler
```

Still, it's important to know how to override these defaults. If you examine the module's source code, you'll see how these arguments are parsed, along with their default values. You'll also notice that there are two additional arguments, which control the sensor's warm-up and sampling intervals. At each sampling interval, the sensor's microcontroller will start up the fan and draw a sample of air into a small metallic chamber. Inside this chamber, a laser passes through the air and measures the scattering value of suspended dust particles. From this, the sensor can determine the concentration of different sizes of suspended particles in the sample.

MEASURING PARTICLE SIZES

Light scattering is a technique used in physics to determine the size distribution of small particles in suspension or polymers in a solution. Scattering occurs when particles pass through the laser beam in the detection area. The scattered light is transformed into electrical signals, which are amplified and processed. The number and diameter of particles can be sensed to a reasonably high degree of precision because of the way signal waveforms relate to particle diameter.

You should hear the Nova SDS011 sensor's fan whirring for several seconds as it warms up, followed by some output in the terminal, like so:

```
Warming up SDS011...
SDS011: PM2.5 8.4; PM10 12.4
SDS011: PM2.5 7.4; PM10 11.0
SDS011: PM2.5 9.8; PM10 14.4
```

```
SDS011: PM2.5 10.2; PM10 16.9
SDS011: PM2.5 10.5; PM10 17.4
SDS011: PM2.5 10.9; PM10 17.4
SDS011: PM2.5 11.1; PM10 17.8
SDS011: PM2.5 11.1; PM10 18.6
SDS011: PM2.5 11.4; PM10 17.2
SDS011: PM2.5 11.5; PM10 19.3
SDS011: PM2.5 11.2; PM10 18.6
SDS011: PM2.5 10.9; PM10 18.8
--snip--
```

Between sampling runs, the sensor will be put into sleep mode. The laser diode in the Nova sensor has a rated service life of 8,000 hours under continuous operation, so using sleep mode helps extend its lifespan. As there's no practical need to sample continuously, you'll "wake" the sensor at intervals (every 60 seconds is the default setting), take a measurement, and put it to sleep again. The ratio of the time the circuit is on compared to the total sampling interval is known as the *duty cycle*.

Verifying Sample Data

After you've collected some sample data, interrupt the Python program with a CTRL-C keystroke. The code will detect the keyboard interrupt and place the sensor back into sleep mode. Now, verify that the data returned by the sensor was stored successfully by InfluxDB. Start the service and enter the commands shown here at the > prompt. You should see output similar to the following:

```
(env) $ influx

Connected to http://localhost:8086 version 1.6.7~rc0
InfluxDB shell version: 1.6.7~rc0
> show databases
name: databases
name
----
_internal
pistation
> use pistation
Using database pistation
> select * from aq
name: aq
time                 geohash location pm100 pm25 sensor
----                 ------- -------- ----- ---- ------
1638395321083829000 ge2kv5h home     12.4  8.4  sds011
1638395381474917000 ge2kv5h home     11    7.4  sds011
1638395441833658000 ge2kv5h home     14.4  9.8  sds011
1638395502192707000 ge2kv5h home     16.9  10.2 sds011
```

```
1638395562558894000 ge2kv5h home      17.4  10.5 sds011
1638395622903462000 ge2kv5h home      17.4  10.9 sds011
1638395683253459000 ge2kv5h home      17.8  11.1 sds011
1638395743639090000 ge2kv5h home      18.6  11.1 sds011
1638395804006308000 ge2kv5h home      17.2  11.4 sds011
1638395864326085000 ge2kv5h home      19.3  11.5 sds011
--snip--
> exit
```

The example output confirms that time-series particulate sensor data has been recorded to InfluxDB. After creating a service to automate the sampler's operation, you'll make this data much more accessible and visually appealing.

Enabling the Service

To have the Nova SDS011 sampler start automatically when the system boots, you can enable its service. The GitHub source code repository you cloned for this project includes a systemd unit file made for this purpose. Open the service file in your editor by running

```
(env) $ cd ~/py-airq
(env) $ nano py-airq.service
```

and locate this line:

```
Environment="GEOHASH=ge2kv5h"
```

Replace ge2kv5h with the value you created in "Obtaining Your Geohash" on page 241, save the file, and exit your editor.

Next, copy the systemd unit file to the directory where system-wide services are defined, instruct systemd to scan for new or changed units, and enable the service:

```
(env) $ sudo cp py-airq.service /lib/systemd/system/
(env) $ sudo systemctl daemon-reload
(env) $ sudo systemctl enable py-airq.service
```

Finally, start the service and check its status:

```
(env) $ sudo systemctl start py-airq.service
(env) $ sudo systemctl status py-airq.service
```

With these steps completed, your sensor will begin sampling automatically each time your system boots. You can stop the service with

```
(env) $ sudo systemctl stop py-airq.service
```

or disable it with:

```
(env) $ sudo systemctl disable py-airq.service
```

Building the Dashboard

Thus far, you've succeeding in collecting data from the Nova SDS011 sensor and storing it in an InfluxDB database. This is where Grafana, which you installed earlier, takes center stage. Begin by enabling, starting, and checking the status of the Grafana server:

```
(env) $ sudo systemctl enable grafana-server.service
(env) $ sudo systemctl start grafana-server.service
(env) $ sudo systemctl status grafana-server.service

grafana-server.service - Grafana instance
    Loaded: loaded (/lib/systemd/system/grafana-server.service; enabled)
    Active: active (running) since Wed 2025-05-07 10:54:21 GMT; 7s ago
      Docs: http://docs.grafana.org
  Main PID: 5053 (grafana-server)
     Tasks: 8 (limit: 871)
       CPU: 1.812s
    CGroup: /system.slice/grafana-server.service
```

Behind the scenes, Grafana has started up its own web service running on port 3000, which you can access from your device's hostname or IP address. In my case, this URL is *http://raspberrypi.local:3000* (yours may differ, depending on the IP address or hostname assigned to your device).

After a moment, you should see a Welcome to Grafana page appear with a login dialog. The default login is `admin` for both the username and password. Enter these values and click **Log In**. You'll be prompted to change the default password after your first login.

Adding a Data Source

If this is your first time using Grafana, locate and select the **Add Your First Data Source** widget on the dashboard. Alternatively, you can choose **Connections ▶ Data Sources** in the left vertical sidebar. In the list of time-series databases, choose InfluxDB, then click **Add New Data Source** (see Figure 8-11).

Figure 8-11: Adding a new InfluxDB data source

The InfluxDB HTTP service runs on port 8086 by default. In the **URL** field in the **HTTP** section of the data source configuration page, enter **http://127.0.0.1:8086** for the InfluxDB URL, as shown in Figure 8-12.

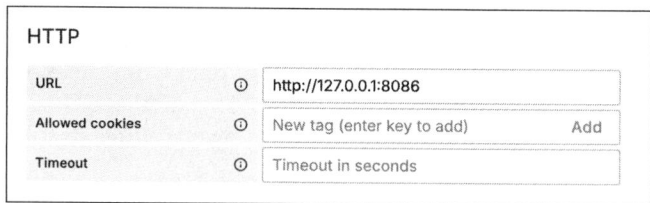

Figure 8-12: The Grafana HTTP options for an InfluxDB data source

At the bottom of the page, under **InfluxDB Details**, enter **pistation** in the **Database** field. Leave the fields for the database login credentials empty, as shown in Figure 8-13.

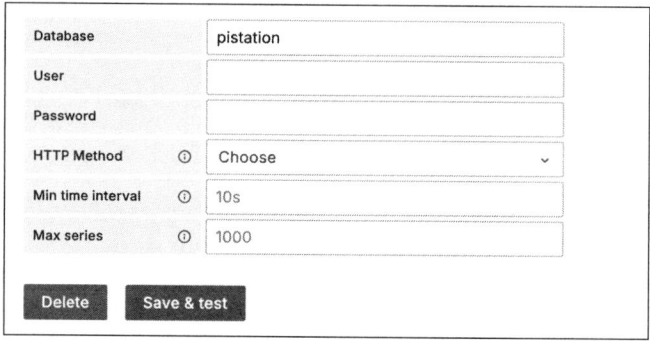

Figure 8-13: The Grafana InfluxDB database settings

Finally, choose **Save & Test**. You should see a green check mark with a message indicating "Datasource is working. 1 measurements found."

Importing the Model Dashboard

At this stage, you can proceed with loading a preconfigured dashboard to use as a starting point. Choose **Dashboards** in the left vertical sidebar, followed by **Create Dashboard**. Next, choose **Import Dashboard** from the list of available options. Grafana gives you several ways to import a dashboard definition, as shown in Figure 8-14.

You can upload a dashboard JSON file, paste in a Grafana.com dashboard URL, or import the dashboard JSON directly into the text area. The py-airq repository includes a prebuilt dashboard that you can use. The URL to the dashboard JSON file is *https://raw.githubusercontent.com/wirelesscookbook/ py-airq/master/dashboard.json*.

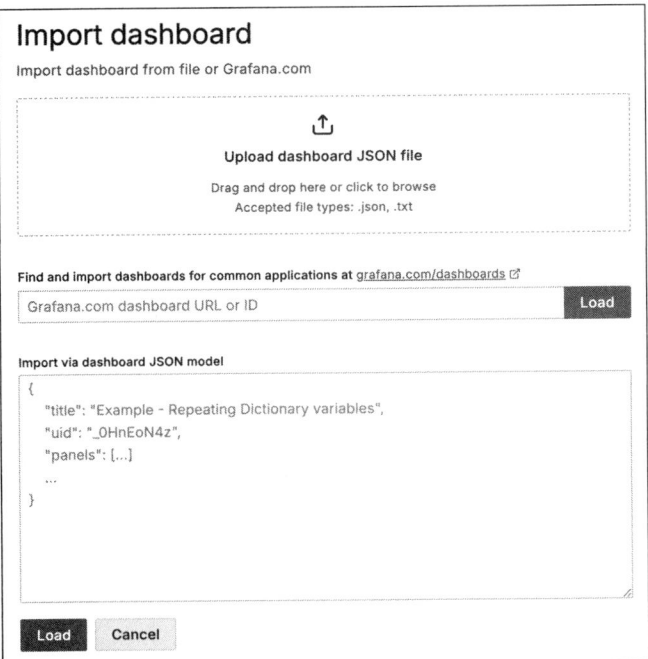

Import dashboard

Import dashboard from file or Grafana.com

⬆

Upload dashboard JSON file

Drag and drop here or click to browse
Accepted file types: .json, .txt

Find and import dashboards for common applications at grafana.com/dashboards ↗

Grafana.com dashboard URL or ID `Load`

Import via dashboard JSON model

```
{
    "title": "Example - Repeating Dictionary variables",
    "uid": "_0HnEoN4z",
    "panels": [...]
    ...
}
```

`Load` Cancel

Figure 8-14: Options for importing a JSON dashboard into Grafana

There are two ways to import this file:

- Enter this URL into a browser, save the file to your local filesystem as *dashboard.json*, then drag and drop it into the **Upload Dashboard JSON File** area and choose **Load**.

- Enter this URL into a browser and copy the source JSON to the clipboard. Then paste it into the **Import via Dashboard JSON Model** input and choose **Load**.

With either method, the dashboard name "Pi Air Quality Monitoring Station" should appear in the next dialog. You can change this name to anything you like. For the **Folder** option, select the default **Dashboards** value, and finally choose **Import**.

Using the Dashboard

At this stage, the Pi Air Quality Monitoring Station dashboard should load in Grafana's main window. The model dashboard you imported contains many default settings, primarily geared around visualizing the PM2.5 and PM10 data series collected by the Nova SDS011 sensor. Four dashboard widgets are defined: one for each data series, to display both current and trending sensor values. The dashboard is automatically refreshed at a default interval of 10 seconds. You can change this interval value under **Settings ▶ General**, and you can manually refresh the dashboard at any time using the controls at the upper right.

Depending on the time span covered by your data, you may want to examine it over longer or shorter periods. You can view data collected during any absolute time range, such as a 12-hour window starting at noon yesterday. This can be useful if you suspect an air quality event has occurred in your region and want to review the data captured by your station during the relevant period. Grafana is highly customizable in this regard.

Another useful feature of Grafana's trendline widgets is the ability to annotate specific data points. To do so, simply click a point in a trend graph and choose **Add Annotation**. Enter a description and click **Save**, and your annotation will appear directly on the trendline.

Editing the Dashboard

You can customize the dashboard layout by repositioning or resizing any of the four panels. To move a panel, click and drag its title bar. To resize it, click and drag the lower-right corner.

Editing the data series behind a panel is just as straightforward. For example, hover over the **PM 2.5 (Current)** panel and press E to enter edit mode. Below the panel, a visual query editor where you can adjust query terms will appear, as shown in Figure 8-15.

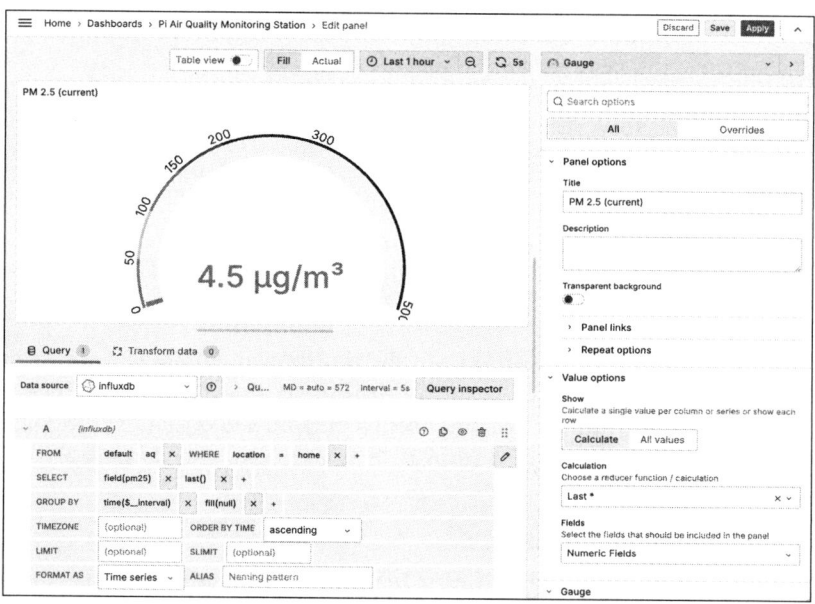

Figure 8-15: Grafana's query editor allows you to visually construct a data query.

Clicking the pencil icon will switch you to raw query mode. Try this with the PM2.5 data series. You should see the InfluxDB Query Language (InfluxQL) statement used to provide data to this panel:

```
SELECT last("pm25") FROM "aq" WHERE ("location" = 'home')
AND $timeFilter GROUP BY time($__interval) fill(null)
```

In the panel editor (on the right side of Figure 8-15), you'll find many properties for formatting the panel. Scroll to the bottom to see how the Thresholds editor maps data values to AQI ranges and colors. Feel free to modify these thresholds as you see fit.

Creating Alerts

One of Grafana's most powerful features is its ability to define *alert rules*. For example, you can configure an alert to inform you (or someone else) when an air quality reading exceeds a certain threshold over a specified period. Grafana implements this by periodically querying your data sources and evaluating the condition defined in the alert rule. If the condition is met, an *alert instance* fires. Notification policies then route these alerts to specific contact points.

Create your first alert by expanding the left-hand menu and selecting **Alerting ▶ Alert Rules**. You can manage all your alerts from this page. Click **New Alert Rule**, and enter **PM 2.5 concern** as the name. In the **Define Query and Alert Condition** section, you'll see an interactive query builder. First, confirm that **InfluxDB** is selected as the data source. In the `FROM` clause, specify `aq` as the measurement. Next, in the `SELECT` clause, choose `pm25` from the `field (value)` list. You can leave all the other fields at their default values. Your query should look similar to the example in Figure 8-16.

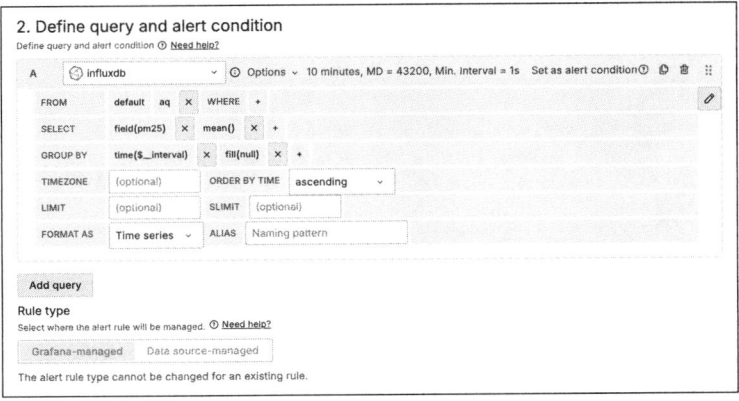

Figure 8-16: Defining a query for an alert

Now, you'll create the expression that raises an alert condition. Start by removing the default expressions, if any are present, by clicking their corresponding trash can icons. Next, choose **Classic Condition** from the **Expression** drop-down menu. Using the query editor, specify `WHEN max()` `OF A IS ABOVE 50`, as shown in Figure 8-17.

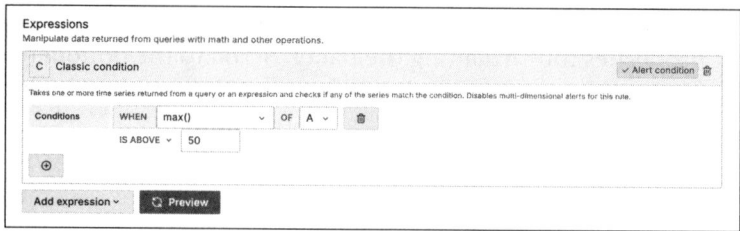

Figure 8-17: Defining the expression used for an alert

A is a reference to the query you created in the previous step. This expression tells Grafana to evaluate the maximum value of your pm25 query and trigger an alert if it exceeds 50. You can adjust the IS ABOVE threshold to correspond to your desired AQI level, if it's different. When you're done, click **Preview** to test the condition, then select **Set as Alert Condition**.

Before saving the rule, you'll need to define how and when it will be evaluated. In Grafana, *evaluation groups* are containers for alerting rules. Each group has a defined evaluation interval, defining how often its rules are checked. Start by clicking **New Folder** to create a place to store your rule. Then select **New Evaluation Group** to create a group. By default, all rules in the selected group are evaluated every five minutes, as shown in Figure 8-18.

3. Set evaluation behavior

Define how the alert rule is evaluated. ⓘ Need help?

Folder
Select a folder to store your rule.

| PM2.5 alerts | ∨ | or | + New folder |

Evaluation group
Rules within the same group are evaluated concurrently over the same time interval.

| My group | ∨ | or | + New evaluation group |

All rules in the selected group are evaluated every 5m. ✎

Pending period
Period in which an alert rule can be in breach of the condition until the alert rule fires.

| 5m |

⬤ Pause evaluation ⓘ

Figure 8-18: Configuring evaluation behavior

Finally, the *pending period* defines how long a condition can be breached before the alert rule fires. In this case, if PM2.5 values stay over 50 for a full 5-minute period, the alert instance is fired. Accept these defaults for now; you can always adjust them later. To save your new alert rule, choose **Save Rule and Exit**.

Testing Alerts

With an alert rule defined, test the alert condition with your monitoring station. You can manually trigger an alert with a source of airborne particulates. In my case, extinguishing a match near the station's sampling input did the trick: At the next sampling interval, the Nova SDS011 sensor detected a spike in both PM2.5 and PM10 readings. The PM2.5 value exceeded the threshold by wide margin, and Grafana's alert instance was triggered, as shown in Figure 8-19.

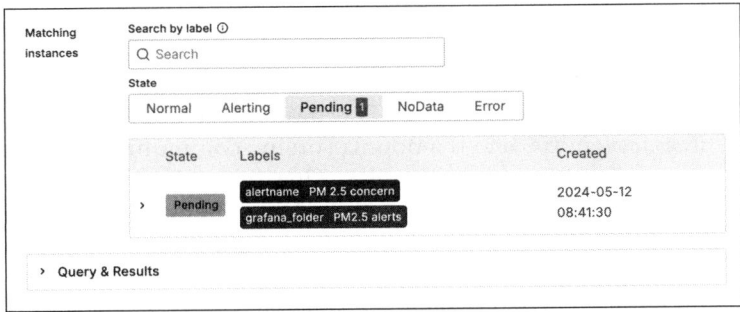

Figure 8-19: The PM 2.5 concern alert instance as seen in Grafana

The dashboard indicates a "Pending" state for the alert, which is to be expected given the 5-minute pending period defined for the alert condition. If the PM2.5 value were to remain above the specified threshold for longer than five minutes, the state would change to "Alerting." At this stage, your configured contact points would receive notifications about the alert. Grafana supports many delivery methods, including Grafana OnCall, Discord, Slack, Telegram, and email, which you can configure under **Alerting ▶ Contact Points**.

This section demonstrated creating an alert related to a single air quality data series. You can, of course, create any number of alerts for various thresholds. You might then escalate alerts to evaluation groups correlated with the cautionary values defined by the AQI, for example.

FINAL THOUGHTS ON GRAFANA

There's a lot you can do with Grafana. I encourage you to try modifying the dashboard included in this recipe, or building your own dashboard completely from scratch. Grafana has a versioning system for its dashboards, so you can save, restore, and export them without concern for breaking things. You can even compare versions by fetching detailed history lists and examining what changes you've made.

If you're unsure where to find a particular menu item or setting, use the CMD-K keystroke to search or jump to a page. Press ESC to return to your dashboard from any settings page.

Creating an Outdoor Enclosure

You now have a high-performance air quality monitoring station, complete with a real-time graphical dashboard accessible via Wi-Fi. For indoor applications, you might leave it at that. However, this project is designed to gather dynamic, real-world environmental data. To do this effectively, you'll need to think about equipping your station for outdoor deployment. The Nova SDS011 sensor will need to be in an appropriate location to perform its sampling function, while the computing module (the Pi Zero 2 W) remains protected.

Enter the Thingiverse

This is one use case where 3D printing really shines. Thingiverse (*https:// www.thingiverse.com*) is a popular online community dedicated to sharing user-created digital design files. These are primarily free, open source hardware designs licensed under the GNU General Public License or Creative Commons licenses. This means that in most cases you can freely "collect" a thing, modify it as needed, and either print it with your 3D printer or send it off to an on-demand 3D printing service.

As luck would have it, a design specifically made to fulfill this recipe's requirements already exists. A mechanical and electrical engineer named Roland Sautner has created a clever 3D-print design for a complete outdoor monitoring station. There's space for a custom board, which could be equipped with a voltage regulator or another component, and an integrated slot perfectly sized for the Bosch BME680 four-in-one sensor (more on this later). Vents on the underside allow effective sampling by the sensors, which can optionally be protected by adding small pieces of fly screen. Details of the design are available at *https://www.thingiverse.com/thing:2993515*. The station, complete with its weatherproof enclosure, is shown in Figure 8-20.

Figure 8-20: The air quality station with weatherproof top enclosure, ready for placement outdoors

This 3D project is also included in the companion GitHub repository you cloned earlier. If you use this design, please consider tipping (or at the very least crediting) the creator for his design work.

In the next sections, you'll assemble your components and identify a suitable location for your station.

Assembly Tips

It bears mentioning here that the 3D-printed parts require some basic assembly. Self-tapping screws work just fine for this task. You'll notice that the Nova SDS011 sensor mounts perfectly in the underside of the chassis, and there's even an inlet port to draw air through for sampling. You may wish to connect a short length of tubing to the sensor and extend it to the base of the chassis, although in my testing this didn't make an appreciable difference in sample readings. The assembled station with the 3D-printed enclosure is shown in Figure 8-21.

Figure 8-21: The air quality station fully assembled and mounted in a 3D-printed chassis

You have a few options for mounting the Pi Zero 2 W to the top of the chassis. One expedient (and quite effective) method often favored by makers is to place a small dab of hot glue under each corner of the Pi and attach it this way. If you choose this method, just be sure to use the glue sparingly in case you need to unmount the Pi later.

Siting Considerations

In deciding where to mount your station, think about nearby pollution sources that could impact your readings. Hyperlocal pollution sources may release brief but high concentrations of pollutants. Barbecues, building exhausts, chimneys, and dusty roads are all possible sources of pollution. This might be interesting for testing or calibrating your station's sensor, but it can complicate measurement of local air quality conditions.

A good rule of thumb is to install your station about 3 to 6 feet (1–2 m) above the ground. This results in the station sampling air around where a person might breathe and isolates it from potential ground effects. Evaluate nearby obstructions, such as fences or buildings, that might inhibit the free flow of air to the sensor.

Power and wireless communications are obvious siting considerations as well. You may wish to place your station within range of your wireless router. If you need to extend your existing Wi-Fi network to provide coverage to your station, consider creating a wireless repeater. There are many ways to go about this, such as the method described at *https://docs.raspap.com/repeater/*.

Battery Power

For truly remote, off-grid applications, the Pi Zero can be configured to draw power from an attached lithium-ion polymer (LiPo) battery bank and a solar panel. Data connectivity can be provided by a stackable 3G/4G cellular HAT, such as the one described in this recipe's hardware requirements. The Sixfab 3G/4G & LTE Base HAT is compatible with all Raspberry Pi models.

If you choose to go down this route, you'll need to modify the 3D-printed outdoor enclosure to accommodate the additional HAT. This is a great opportunity to develop your 3D modeling skills and contribute something back to the Thingiverse community.

Publishing Your Data

You can choose from many available platforms to share your data. I'll demonstrate this with *Adafruit IO*, an online service for storing and visualizing data. In many respects, it functions like a cloud-based version of your local InfluxDB server and Grafana dashboard. Adafruit IO is able to consume and visualize multiple data feeds. You can then share your dashboard with the world, if you wish.

Start by creating a free account on the Adafruit IO website, *https://io .adafruit.com*. Be sure to record your Adafruit IO username and key, as you'll need these in the code you'll be working with shortly.

One minor point to be aware of is that, at the free tier, Adafruit IO stores data for only 30 days. This matches the data retention policy you defined for InfluxDB, however, so this shouldn't be an issue if you're using the default policy. If you need historical data beyond this threshold, consider upgrading your Adafruit IO plan or using another data source.

Creating Data Feeds

Feeds are the core of Adafruit IO. They hold both the data you'll upload and the metadata about the values your sensors push to Adafruit IO. The data sources in this case are the PM2.5 and PM10 air quality measurement series stored in InfluxDB. The metadata includes location information, settings for whether the data is public or private, what license the stored sensor data falls under, and a human-readable description of the data.

Creating a new Adafruit IO feed is straightforward. Choose **Feeds** ▶ **New Feed** and enter **pistation10** as the feed name. Then repeat the process, entering **pistation25** as the name. These will be used to receive your real-time sensor data. Note that the names you use here must match the identifiers defined in the Python code.

Sending Data with Python

With the feeds in place, you have a destination at Adafruit IO ready to receive your sensor data. Next, you'll need a Python package to facilitate communication with the platform. Ensure that you're in the project directory and that the Python virtual environment is active, then install the package:

```
(env) $ cd ~/py-airq
(env) $ pip install adafruit-io
```

You'll need just a handful of additional lines of code to start sending your data to Adafruit IO. Begin by opening __*main*__.*py* in your editor:

```
(env) $ cd ~/py-airq/sampler
(env) $ nano __main__.py
```

Locate and uncomment the following lines:

```
from Adafruit_IO import Client
ADAFRUIT_AIO_USERNAME = "my-aio-username"
ADAFRUIT_AIO_KEY      = "my-aio-key"
aio = Client(ADAFRUIT_AIO_USERNAME, ADAFRUIT_AIO_KEY)
```

Be sure to replace the *my-aio-username* and *my-aio-key* placeholder values with your Adafruit IO username and key. Keep the file open in your editor and proceed to the next step.

If you plan on making your Adafruit IO dashboard public, for privacy reasons you may want to limit map coordinate information to your city or town, rather than your precise location. The example coordinates used here are for Reykjavik, Iceland. Determine the map coordinates you'd like to use, making a note of the latitude, longitude, and elevation.

In the same file, locate and uncomment the following lines of code, and update location_meta with your latitude, longitude, and elevation (ele):

```
# set up location metadata
location_meta = {
    "lat": 64.1334735,
    "lon": -21.922653,
    "ele": 12,
    "created_at": ts
}

# send sds011 results to Adafruit IO
aio.send('pistation25',pm25,location_meta)
```

```
aio.send('pistation10',pm100,location_meta)
--snip--
```

Save the file and exit your editor. If py-airq.service is running, restart it so the changes take effect:

```
(env) $ sudo systemctl restart py-airq.service
```

Alternatively, if you've opted to start the sampler manually, you can do so with the following command. Ensure that you replace the geohash example value with the one you obtained previously:

```
(env) $ python -m sampler --port /dev/ttyS0 --influx localhost \
    --database pistation --sds011_measurement aq \
    --location home --geohash ge2kv5h
```

After a few moments, the live sensor data should appear in your Adafruit IO account overview, as shown in Figure 8-22.

```
Live Data (newest data at top)
2024/05/12 07:17PM   pistation10      5.6   64.1335,-21.9227
2024/05/12 07:17PM   pistation25      2.0   64.1335,-21.9227
2024/05/12 07:16PM   pistation10      6.4   64.1335,-21.9227
2024/05/12 07:16PM   pistation25      2.1   64.1335,-21.9227
```

Figure 8-22: Live sensor data appearing in Adafruit IO's feeds

If you receive an error from the Adafruit client module, check that the feed names in __main__.py correspond to the ones you entered in your Adafruit IO profile. Once you've verified your Adafruit IO feed data, the next step is to create a dashboard to consume the linked feeds.

Creating an Adafruit IO Dashboard

Dashboards are a feature integrated into Adafruit IO that allow you to visualize your data feeds. Dashboards are private by default, but you can easily change this to make your visualizations and data feeds available to the public. Begin by creating a new dashboard from your Adafruit IO profile with the name **Pi Air Quality Station**. Adafruit IO's dashboards are composed of blocks, similar to Grafana's panels. You'll add several new ones to your dashboard: a map block, two gauges, and two line charts. For each one, select the option to **Connect a Feed**. For the map block, you may select either of the sensor data feeds, as each contains location metadata. Connect each of the two feeds to a gauge and a line chart.

You can use the dashboard layout in Figure 8-23 for guidance, or create something entirely original.

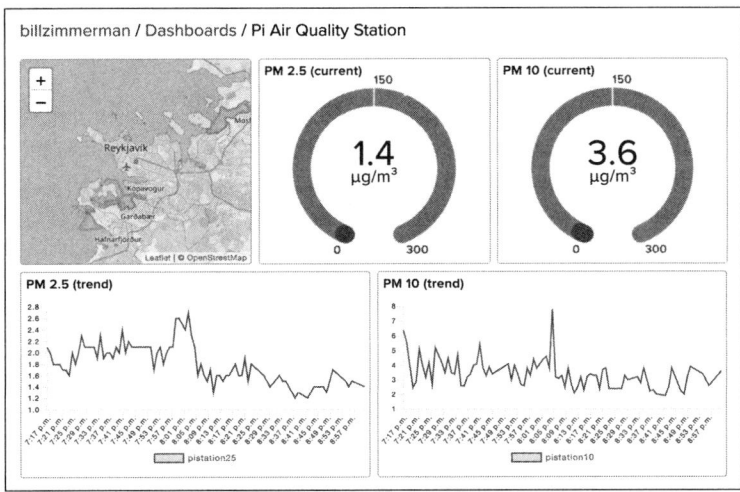

Figure 8-23: An Adafruit IO dashboard powered by Python data feeds

Similar to the alert rules in your Grafana dashboard, Adafruit IO lets you define warning values. If either of your air quality sensor readings exceeds these values, the corresponding gauge will change color.

Troubleshooting

In some cases, running the Python code to read from the Nova SDS011 sensor may result in output like this:

```
Warming up SDS011...
No response from SDS011 sensor
```

This indicates that communication over your device's GPIO UART port (/dev/ttyS0) is working, but the sensor isn't responding. Most often, this is caused by a poor physical connection between the sensor and the GPIO header. In my case, an incomplete solder joint on one of the pins was preventing contact; a quick solder repair resolved the issue.

Occasionally, the Python code may return the error "SerialException: device disconnected or multiple access on port." This usually indicates that the serial port has timed out or another process is using it. To investigate this, install the lsof package and use it to list any processes that currently have the serial port /dev/ttyS0 open:

```
$ sudo apt install lsof -y
$ sudo lsof /dev/ttyS0

COMMAND PID USER   FD   TYPE DEVICE SIZE/OFF NODE NAME
agetty  827 root   0u   CHR  4,64   0t0      130  /dev/ttyS0
--snip--
```

In this case, the output shows that the agetty process is using the serial port. This is an instance of *getty*, a program that manages terminal or console logins in Linux. If you run into this problem, ensure that you've followed the steps in "Preparing the Serial Port" on page 234.

Going Further

I've covered a lot of ground in this project, but there are still ways to expand your monitoring station's capabilities and broaden your understanding of this citizen science domain. I'll conclude here by discussing fine-tuning your alerts based on what you consider "safe" air quality levels, calibrating your station, and integrating an optional four-in-one sensor.

Adjusting Alert Thresholds

Now that you're monitoring PM2.5 and PM10 air quality levels, a logical next question is: What should you look out for? The World Health Organization Air Quality Guidelines stipulate that annual mean PM2.5 exposure should not exceed 5 micrograms per cubic meter ($\mu g/m^3$), with a 24-hour mean no higher than 15 $\mu g/m^3$. For PM10, the annual mean should not exceed 15 $\mu g/m^3$, and the 24-hour mean should be no more than 45 $\mu g/m^3$.

However, even these levels might not be safe. Some peer-reviewed studies suggest a correlation between increased health risks with each 5 $\mu g/m^3$ increase in PM2.5, at any level of air quality. Do your own research and, optionally, set alert thresholds in your dashboards that correspond to your acceptable safety levels.

Calibrating Your Station

In all sciences, accurate measurements are key to making reliable observations. How confident are you in the accuracy of the air quality data from your station? The best way to answer this is to calibrate your station against what's commonly known as a *reference monitor*. With an attached USB battery pack or other power source, take your monitoring station to your nearest air quality reference station. Reconfigure its wireless connection to use a mobile hotspot, or run it in offline mode and observe the raw data output in the console. Compare these observations to the local station's data.

Alternatively, citizen-powered networks of open source air quality data can provide you with benchmarking values for your locality. One example is OpenAQ, an environmental tech nonprofit that advocates for publicly accessible air quality data and aggregates ground-level ambient air quality data on a centralized platform. Their open datasets include readings from reference-grade monitors around the world, which you can use to test the accuracy of your sensor.

Adding Sensors

If you'd like to extend your station's capabilities beyond air quality monitoring, you can add other sensors. A popular option is the Bosch family of BME680 and BME688 Breakout sensors. To use one of these with the

Pi Zero 2 W, you'll first need to ensure that I^2C is enabled. You can do this by executing **sudo raspi-config** in the shell and navigating to **Interface Options ▶ I4 I2C**. Enable I^2C, exit, and reboot. Another way to achieve the same result is by executing Pimoroni's one-line configuration script (note that this script requires root privileges, so the curl output is piped to sudo here):

```
(env) $ curl https://get.pimoroni.com/i2c | sudo bash
```

Recall that the Nova SDS011 sensor used the Pi Zero's UART pins (GPIO 14 and 15). The BME680 is connected to the two adjacent I^2C pins: GPIO 2 (I2C1 SDA) and GPIO 3 (I2C1 SCL). In place of a 5V pin, this sensor uses a 3V3 pin for power.

With I^2C enabled, you can use another script by Pimoroni to install the prerequisites needed for the BME680. Execute it like so:

```
(env) $ cd ~/py-airq
(env) $ curl https://get.pimoroni.com/bme680 | bash

This script will install everything needed to use
BME680 Breakout

--snip--
Note: BME680 Breakout requires I2C communication
Do you wish to continue? [y/N] y
--snip--

All done. Enjoy your BME680 Breakout!
```

With the dependencies and sample code installed, move the newly created examples to your project directory:

```
(env) $ mv ~/Pimoroni ~/py-airq
```

Now, execute the following commands to verify that the BME680/688 is functioning correctly:

```
(env) $ cd ~/py-airq/Pimoroni/bme680/examples
(env) $ python read-all.py
read-all.py - Displays temperature, pressure, humidity, and gas.

Press Ctrl+C to exit!
--snip--
Polling:
17.25 C,881.74 hPa,29.29 %RH,5684.846331497602 Ohms
17.29 C,881.74 hPa,29.29 %RH,5684.846331497602 Ohms
17.33 C,881.73 hPa,29.26 %RH,5684.846331497602 Ohms
17.37 C,881.73 hPa,29.24 %RH,5684.846331497602 Ohms
--snip--
```

This outputs all of the sensor's readings continuously: temperature, pressure, humidity, and gas resistance values. You can interrupt the program with CTRL-C. On first use, it's recommended to "burn in" the sensor by running it for at least 20 minutes. The sensor's readings, especially the gas resistance values, will drift gradually and then stabilize after a while. This drift will occur each time you start taking readings, but after the initial burn-in, they should stabilize fairly quickly (usually after a couple of minutes).

To log the sensor values to a text file, simply redirect the program's output, like so:

```
(env) $ python read-all.py > bme680-data.txt
```

You'll notice that the data returned by the sensor is neatly formatted into comma-separated values, not unlike the data collected by the Nova SDS011 sensor. You could import these values into a spreadsheet, for example, and plot them fairly easily. Given what you've done in this recipe, you might also think about modifying the Python sampler code to push this data to InfluxDB and then to your Grafana dashboard.

You have the basic building blocks to integrate the BME680, or perhaps even another sensor, into your monitoring station.

Wrapping Up

In this recipe, you assembled hardware components to facilitate near-real-time environmental data collection, used Python to communicate with them via their UART or I^{2}C interfaces, and persisted this data to InfluxDB via its associated Python package. You also practiced using this as a data source to build a highly customizable Grafana dashboard. This pairing of InfluxDB and Grafana is common in many software implementations, making this a valuable skill on its own.

For simplicity, an 802.11 wireless uplink was used to make the air quality monitor accessible from your local network and, optionally, a cloud-based IoT service. I discussed two possible methods for extending the range of your monitoring station: by configuring a Wi-Fi repeater or using an LTE cellular modem HAT. For truly remote applications, I'll leave you with a third option: With the material covered in Chapter 6, this project could be modified to incorporate a LoRaWAN node HAT and publish sensor data to The Things Network.

The Nova SDS011 sensor has relatively high power demands compared to LoRaWAN devices, which can potentially operate for months or years. If you want to run it off-grid, you'll need a solar-powered station and perhaps a larger battery. Alternatively, several other laser-based PM2.5/PM10 particle sensors are available with lower power requirements. If you choose to pursue a LoRaWAN implementation, consider how the code in this recipe might be repurposed to read data from a LoRaWAN source and populate your dashboard.

9

PWNING WI-FI WITH PWNAGOTCHI

Pwnagotchi has, justifiably, attracted a devout following among the network security community and hobbyists since its release in 2019. Its name combines the traditional hacker term for gaining control over a system, *pwning*, with a nostalgic reference to the Tamagotchi digital pets that were a cultural touchstone for a generation of kids.

Similar to the original electronic pet, Pwnagotchi needs to be "fed" to keep it happy. It evaluates nearby wireless networks and, using deep learning, adapts its capture parameters to maximize the data it extracts from its environment. Each Wi-Fi vulnerability it finds is added to the Pwnagotchi's list of pwned networks.

Despite its popularity among ethical hackers and security enthusiasts, I'm often surprised to discover that technology-savvy friends and colleagues (at least, the ones who aren't regulars at DEF CON) have never built one and may not even be familiar with the project. This recipe aims to change that with a modern, up-to-date guide that examines the Pwnagotchi's technology stack in depth. If you're interested in the ways that your own wireless networks might be at risk or want to learn more about encryption, security, and AI, these disciplines are combined here into a rewarding (and eminently portable) project. Once it's built, you may even find it difficult to leave your Pwnagotchi at home.

Use Cases

As wireless networks and IoT devices become increasingly pervasive, it's more important than ever to understand the risks associated with operating and using them, and how to safeguard against potential threats. All Wi-Fi networks have inherent vulnerabilities, and the first step toward properly securing them is learning how these networks work and how they can be attacked. If you're interested in cybersecurity of information security (InfoSec), there are few better ways to acquire hands-on experience than by using a Pwnagotchi to demonstrate practical Wi-Fi attacks and defenses. With its ability to automate different types of attacks and capture WPA key material from wireless handshakes, it's an invaluable tool.

Pwnagotchi's utility extends well beyond its primary use case as an automated handshake collection tool. It's an excellent learning platform, providing an on-ramp to building practical, real-world applications with neural networks and deep reinforcement learning. Its extensibility and open source ethos have attracted a global community of enthusiasts dedicated to improving the software with third-party plug-ins, new features, and support for the latest hardware. Many users have made their first open source contributions to the Pwnagotchi project.

In terms of potential for experimentation, this project is largely plug-and-play, but it lends itself to customization by integrating other components in various ways. The hardware presented here can be considered the required building blocks for a "classic" Pwnagotchi design, but you can deploy it on a wide range of devices, using different displays, external antennas, and more.

The Pwnagotchi unit you'll build here excels at capturing Wi-Fi handshakes. But that's not the end of the story; I'll also demonstrate how to analyze the packet capture files it collects. Since this is a common question, I'll note up front that this will all be performed in an ethical manner (see "Processing PCAP Files" on page 295).

Hardware Required

Building a Pwnagotchi requires a few basic hardware components, all of which are widely available from online vendors. If you're planning to implement this project experimentally, you can get started with nothing more than a Raspberry Pi and a micro USB data cable. Alternatively, you can connect your phone to a Pwnagotchi via Bluetooth tethering and use it as the unit's display. This minimal setup is enough to run Pwnagotchi and Bettercap's software, and you can access their web interfaces from a host computer or mobile device.

Of course, Pwnagotchi's portability and ASCII-based facial expressions are a large part of its appeal. To enable these features, you'll need some additional modestly priced hardware components.

Compatible Raspberry Pi Models

Pwnagotchi can run on several Raspberry Pi models, but the Pi Zero 2 W, available from various online retailers for about $15, is favored among the community and continues to be the gold standard for new builds. Its small footprint mates perfectly with the recommended e-ink display as well as the battery module used for this project. The Pi Zero also has much lower power requirements than its larger model 3, 4, and 5 siblings.

The Pi Zero 2 W comes standard without a GPIO header, so you'll need to obtain a 40-pin header and perform some basic soldering to attach it. Alternatively, you can avoid soldering by purchasing a model with a presoldered header, as shown in Figure 9-1.

Figure 9-1: A Pi Zero 2 W with a presoldered 40-pin GPIO header

Several retailers offer these, usually at little extra cost.

External Battery Module

Pwnagotchi is designed to be taken out into the world to discover new and interesting Wi-Fi environments, so you'll need to provide it with external battery power. Your choice of battery module will depend on your plans: A small battery may suffice if you'll be out for only a couple of hours, but if you intend to be out exploring the wireless wilderness all day, you'll likely need something bigger.

How do you know how much power you'll need to keep your Pwnagotchi running? The Pwnagotchi community has done extensive field testing and compiled benchmarks using some popular battery options. One of the more common choices is the PiSugar 2, which provides 1,200 mAh of power. With Pwnagotchi running in AI mode (more on this later), this battery has an observed runtime of just under five hours of continuous operation. It strikes a good balance between size, capacity, and cost.

The PiSugar 2 is easy to use, requires no soldering, and doesn't conflict with other add-on HATs. As shown in Figure 9-2, it also perfectly matches the size of the Pi Zero 2. The battery module uses small spring pins (sometimes called *pogo pins*) to power the Pi Zero from its back side. 5 V power is delivered via the two bottom pads on the Pi Zero, eliminating the need for an external cable: Simply affix the battery module to the back of the board using the screws provided.

Figure 9-2: The PiSugar 2 battery for
Raspberry Pi Zero models

The PiSugar 2 has two other notable advantages: an onboard real-time clock (RTC) and a software plug-in ready for use with Pwnagotchi. These are discussed in "Installing the PiSugar Plug-in" on page 286. The PiSugar 2 battery module is available directly from PiSugar for about $36.

E-Ink Display Module

Among Pwnagotchi's more interesting features are its two built-in web interfaces. These can be accessed from a separate device (a laptop or phone) when you're using USB Ethernet gadget mode or tethered via Bluetooth. However, most users prefer to walk around with their Pwnagotchi and watch its expressions change as it pwns Wi-Fi networks in the wild. Many small-form-factor displays are available for this purpose, including both color and monochrome e-ink varieties. A drawback to be aware of with color e-ink displays is their slow refresh rate (in some cases, up to 15 seconds).

All the e-ink-type displays with official support from the project use the serial peripheral interface (SPI). The most commonly used model in Pwnagotchi builds is the Waveshare 250×122, 2.13-inch E-Ink display HAT, shown in Figure 9-3, which fits the Raspberry Pi Zero perfectly.

Figure 9-3: The Waveshare 2.13-inch E-Ink
display HAT

First-generation (V1) Waveshare E-Ink displays had issues with image ghosting, but these have largely been superseded by newer V2 and V3 models. These later versions are fully supported by the Pwnagotchi software and usually "just work" straight out of the box. The Waveshare 2.13-inch E-Ink display is available directly from Waveshare for about $15.

As of this writing, Waveshare has recently released the 2.13-inch E-Paper HAT+, shown in Figure 9-4, as an update to its popular display. Notably, this module eliminates the eight-pin connector for a more compact stack height. In addition, it includes a real-time clock and adds mounting holes that were missing in earlier generations.

Figure 9-4: The Waveshare 2.13-inch E-Paper HAT+

If giving your Pwnagotchi some bling is a priority, the HAT+ uses a gold immersion process, presumably for better anti-oxidation and electrical properties. It's available from Waveshare for around $16.

Micro USB Cable

In most cases, you'll access your Pi Zero 2 W wirelessly via its onboard WLAN chipset. With Pwnagotchi, however, a custom driver is compiled for the Broadcom WLAN chipset to enable *monitor mode*, which allows the adapter to monitor all traffic received on a given wireless channel. With your Wi-Fi adapter operating in this mode, you'll need to access your device by an alternative method. Fortunately, the software preconfigures access to the system via USB Ethernet gadget mode. This means you'll need to attach a micro USB to USB-C or similar cable between the Pi Zero's USB connector and your host computer.

Poor-quality or otherwise unsuitable cables have been the source of frustration for users in the past, so it's worth investing a few dollars in a decent-quality cable that's rated for data transfer, like the one shown in Figure 9-5.

Figure 9-5: A decent-quality micro USB
cable that allows data transfer

These items are widely available from online vendors for under $10.

3D-Printed Case (Optional)

If you're running your Pwnagotchi in headless mode (that is, without an attached e-ink display) and using its web interface, any generic case for the Pi Zero will suffice. Alternatively, your device might be a component of a dedicated home Wi-Fi test bench. If so, you might choose to forgo a case completely. Many users opt to take their Pwnagotchis on the road, though. If this is your intent, housing the components in a case will protect them and prevent electrical shorts across the exposed GPIO pins.

Once again, the Pwnagotchi community has stepped up with countless open source case designs, all ready to be used with your 3D printer or sent to an on-demand 3D printing service. Personal taste will likely guide your decision here. Personally, I find the case design by Sarah Kastrau, shown in Figure 9-6, to be both highly functional and attractive.

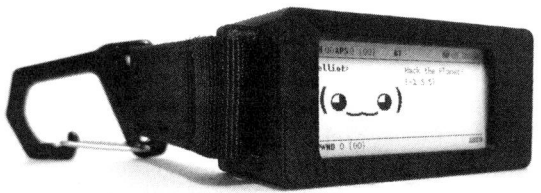

Figure 9-6: A functional and handsome 3D-printed
Pwnagotchi case designed by Sarah Kastrau

This particular design is made for the Waveshare UPS HAT, but it will also accommodate the PiSugar with some minor modifications to the design files. The STL files for the case are available directly from the designer for free (*https://www.sarahkastrau.com/pwnagotchi-battery-case/*), although a small donation is recommended.

Assembling the Components

If your Pi Zero 2 W doesn't have a presoldered GPIO header, begin by soldering this component to the board. Next, attach the external battery module to the underside of your device. The PiSugar and Waveshare modules use similar pogo-style connectors to connect with the 5V power and ground

(GND) pins. Note that the PiSugar's mounting holes are protected with a thin plastic film; you'll need to remove this prior to attaching the battery module. Affix the module with the provided mounting screws.

The PiSugar's micro USB port should be used for charging with an official 5.1 V power supply. With power connected, an LED indicator will indicate the module's charging state: Blue is charging, while green indicates a fully charged battery. The PiSugar has a micro power switch and a programmable button located along the board's edge, next to the micro USB socket.

To attach the Waveshare 2.13-inch E-Ink display to the Pi Zero's GPIO header, simply align the board's socket with the header pins and press down. No screws or other mounting hardware is required. The display communicates with the host controller via the SPI interface by using 3V3 power and six GPIO pins, as illustrated in Figure 9-7.

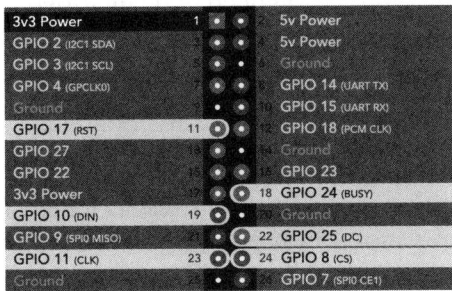

Figure 9-7: The Pi's SPI pins (source: https://pinout.xyz)

With the hardware as supplied out of the box, the attached e-ink display will stand off from the Pi Zero's circuit board with a noticeable, but not considerable, gap. Some users prefer to create a cleaner "short stack" design. The process to achieve this is described in the next section.

Creating a Short Stack

If you'd like to create a more compact unit (sometimes referred to as a *Slimagotchi*), you can, with care, desolder the display's eight-pin connector. Use a desoldering wick braid together with flux to absorb the solder and prevent bridging the pads or damaging other components. If you have a soldering iron with temperature control, set it to between 300 and 325°C. It should be hot enough to flow solder into the wick. With the pins desoldered and the connector body removed, apply a piece of Kapton polyimide film tape to the back of the board to prevent it from shorting against the Pi Zero's components.

The most common GPIO header pin height (from the shroud base to the pin top) is 0.24 inches, or 6.13 mm. For a shorter stack height, your options are to find a shorter 40-pin male GPIO header or cut down an existing one. For the latter approach, a Dremel-type tool with a cutting wheel will provide cleaner, faster, and more accurate cuts than other methods. This permits the e-ink display module to mount flush with the header's base. The end result is a reduction of the unit's overall height by several millimeters. A completed unit configured in this way is shown in Figure 9-8.

Figure 9-8: A Pwnagotchi short stack unit

If you plan to use a short hardware stack like this with a 3D-printed case, bear in mind that the design files will need to be modified accordingly. For Sarah Kastrau's case design, a variant customized for the short stack with the PiSugar battery module is available in this chapter's companion GitHub repository. You can obtain it by cloning the repository, like so:

```
$ git clone https://github.com/wirelesscookbook/pwnagotchi.git
```

The STL design files are located in the */casefiles* folder. Depending on the final height of your compact Pwnagotchi, you may want to add a piece of nonconductive material to the case's interior to ensure a snug fit.

Software Used

Rather than following a monolithic application design, Pwnagotchi is built around a suite of software components, several of which provide APIs to enable interoperability between them. Pwnagotchi itself is developed in Python, which handles its core functionality, including packet capture, AI, and user interactions. In many ways, Pwnagotchi's friendly exterior belies the sophisticated technology stack operating beneath its surface. In the following sections, we'll explore the roles these components play and how they work together to create Pwnagotchi's moods.

TensorFlow and Keras

TensorFlow is an open source platform for machine learning (ML) built around data flow graphs. Initially developed by the Google Brain team to conduct research into ML and deep neural networks (DNNs), it has since grown into a system that is general enough to be applied across many practical domains. DNNs and deep learning are a subset of machine learning that involve analyzing large amounts of unstructured data at scale.

TensorFlow derives its name from the way it operates on multidimensional arrays of data, known as *tensors*. Broadly, it preprocesses data, builds a model, and then trains that model to make predictions. It achieves this by creating a computational graph that describes the nodes, their mathematical operations, and the connections between them. The edges of the graph represent tensors flowing between the nodes. In this way, the architecture permits machine learning algorithms to be described as a graph of connected operations.

As shown in Figure 9-9, unlike a scalar value, one-dimensional vector, array, or two-dimensional matrix, a tensor can have *n* dimensions. In the TensorFlow Python library, the term *shape* refers to the dimensionality of the tensor.

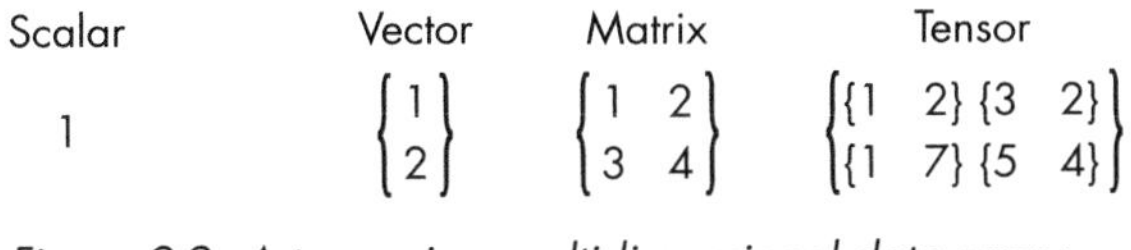

Scalar   Vector   Matrix   Tensor

$$1 \qquad \begin{Bmatrix} 1 \\ 2 \end{Bmatrix} \quad \begin{Bmatrix} 1 & 2 \\ 3 & 4 \end{Bmatrix} \quad \begin{Bmatrix} \{1 & 2\} \{3 & 2\} \\ \{1 & 7\} \{5 & 4\} \end{Bmatrix}$$

Figure 9-9: A tensor is a multidimensional data array.

One of the factors behind TensorFlow's popularity is that it provides a convenient Python frontend API for building applications while executing operations in high-performance, optimized C++. Together with Keras, its associated high-level API, TensorFlow is a key component of Pwnagotchi's AI framework. This is arguably one of the most fascinating pieces of Pwnagotchi's technology stack, and it plays a central role in giving the device its unique personality. I'll examine this in greater detail in "A Closer Look at Pwnagotchi's AI" on page 275.

Bettercap

A portable framework written in the Go programming language, Bettercap is a versatile Swiss army knife–type tool for attacking Wi-Fi networks and scanning both BLE devices and Ethernet networks. Its capabilities include network reconnaissance, real-time manipulation of HTTP and HTTPS traffic, network sniffing, spoofing, and various types of man-in-the-middle attacks. Bettercap's API runs as a service in the background and is used to communicate with Pwnagotchi. However, it also boasts both an interactive CLI and a highly usable web interface, making it extremely useful as a standalone network security tool. We'll explore it further in "Using Bettercap" on page 289.

Nexmon Firmware

Nexmon is a C-based patching framework for Broadcom/Cypress Wi-Fi chips that enables the creation of firmware patches. It's mainly used to enable monitor mode and frame injection on many popular WLAN chipsets.

Wi-Fi firmware consists of a read-only portion stored in the ROM of the wireless chip and a second portion that's loaded into RAM by the driver. On the Raspberry Pi, this firmware logic is executed by the ARM Cortex-R4 (ARMCR4) core within the wireless chip. According to the Cypress datasheet, adapted in Figure 9-10, the chip contains 704KB of ROM for firmware code, plus 800KB of RAM for data processing and storing firmware patches.

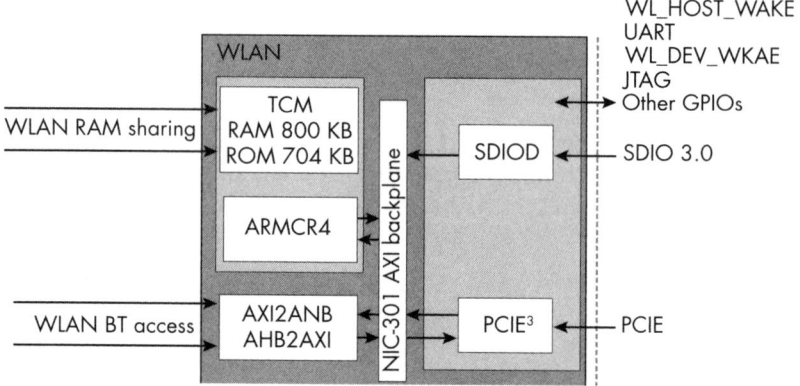

Figure 9-10: The ARM Cortex-R4, adapted from the Cypress chipset datasheet

To begin inspecting the code running on the ARM core, its contents must first be extracted from the ROM. The data that's loaded into RAM can then be located and extracted.

Extracting firmware data from the ROM and RAM is somewhat tricky. Locating the data loaded into the ARM core's RAM requires reading the initialization code in the host's driver. Nexmon isolates the file whose contents are uploaded to RAM by the driver. But what about the ROM's contents? Fortunately, Broadcom provides a powerful command line utility called dhdutil that can communicate with the chip. To dump the ROM directly, you need to know its location and size. On Wi-Fi chips with an ARM Cortex-R4, you can then use dhdutil to extract the ROM, like so:

```
$ dhdutil membytes -r 0x0 0xA0000 > rom.bin
```

Nexmon includes a simple Dhdutil.java class that wraps this utility and captures its results from the console:

```java
public class Dhdutil {
    protected static Dhdutil instance;
    private String dhdutilPath;

    protected Dhdutil() {
        this.instance = this;
        dhdutilPath = Assets.getAssetsPath(MyApplication.getAppContext(), "dhdutil");
    }
    --snip--
    public String dumpConsole() {
        List<String> out = Shell.SU.run(dhdutilPath + " consoledump");
        StringBuilder sb = new StringBuilder();
        for(String str : out) {
            sb.append(str);
            sb.append("\n");
        }
        return sb.toString();
```

```
}
}
```

With both the ROM and RAM portions of the firmware extracted, a flash patch for a specific firmware version can be created. In this context, a *flash patch* is a modified instruction set that rewrites the firmware to fix bugs, enable new features, or modify the behavior of a device. With Pwnagotchi, network monitoring and packet injection are the key features enabled by Nexmon.

Once the patched firmware is compiled, the `brcmfmac` module is removed from the Linux kernel and replaced with the modified version. You can verify its new capabilities by running:

```
$ iw phy0 info | grep "Supported interface modes" -A8
    Supported interface modes:
        * IBSS
        * managed
        * AP
        * monitor
        * P2P-client
        * P2P-GO
--snip--
```

In this output, `monitor` now appears as a supported interface mode.

The Nexmon project supports many Broadcom/Cypress Wi-Fi chipsets, including those used not only in the Raspberry Pi family but also in mobile devices made by Samsung, Apple, and Google.

Hcxtools and Hashcat

The Wi-Fi handshake packets extracted by Bettercap, enabled by the patched Nexmon firmware, are stored in packet capture (PCAP) files. Hcxtools is a collection of tools used to capture and convert wireless traffic that's particularly useful for working with WPA handshakes. Its primary use is to identify weak points within Wi-Fi networks under your control by analyzing the hashes contained in these PCAP files. Potential vulnerabilities in the AP or client are found by using common word lists or a weak password generation algorithm.

You can use Hashcat, a popular password-cracking tool, in conjunction with Hcxtools to attempt to crack captured WPA handshakes. It's important to note that these tools should be used only on networks that you have permission to audit. I'll walk you through a practical example of their use in "Processing PCAP Files" on page 295.

Preparing the SD Card

Like many popular open source projects, Pwnagotchi has evolved with the times. Since its initial release, new hardware, firmware, and OS distributions have become available, while software dependencies have followed their own trajectories. Open source project maintainers are often burdened with the task of keeping up with these changes while simultaneously fixing bugs and otherwise supporting a growing community of users.

Today, the Pwnagotchi community has largely taken up the reins from EvilSocket to ensure that the project remains healthy. The original source has been forked and improved in many ways. Notably, this includes compatibility with recent releases of Debian/Raspberry Pi OS and newer hardware, including the Raspberry Pi 5. This means several third-party Pwnagotchi images are available, many of which improve on the original with updated dependencies, crash prevention, more default plug-ins, reduced CPU utilization, and numerous other refinements.

As of this writing, the most actively developed fork and corresponding image is maintained by GitHub user Jayofelony. This fork is the primary Pwnagotchi source for the original Pi Zero W (32-bit), Pi Zero 2 W (64-bit), and Pi 3, 4, and 5. While it's possible to build an image from this repository by compiling its components from scratch, this is a fairly time-consuming process. If my experience is any indication, you may end up bricking your Pwnagotchi while experimenting with a custom build. For this reason, I recommend using a ready-made image so you can achieve a "quick win" and focus on exploring Pwnagotchi's functionality, rather than recompiling software and driver files.

Begin by downloading the latest release at *https://github.com/jayofelony/ pwnagotchi/releases/latest*. A cross-platform image-writing tool such as balena-Etcher or the Raspberry Pi Imager is the generally the easiest way to write the image to your SD card. If you're using the latter, be sure to skip the OS customization options.

Alternatively, you can use the dd utility in Linux or macOS. Run the following command, replacing the path to the image file you downloaded and the path to your SD card device (*/dev/sdcard* is used here) if necessary:

```
$ dd if=/path/to/pwnagotchi-2.9.5.3-64bit.img of=/dev/sdcard \
    bs=1M status=progress
```

Some imaging software will automatically eject the SD card when it's done writing. In this case, reinsert the card before proceeding with creating an initial configuration.

Configuring Pwnagotchi

After preparing your SD card with the prebuilt Pwnagotchi image, you'll need to create an initial configuration for its first boot. If you've completed the recipe in Chapter 6, you'll already be familiar with the TOML configuration language. The simplest method here is to create a configuration called *config.toml* in the boot partition of the SD card. This partition should be accessible from any computer, regardless of its operating system.

Use the following template as a starting point. Assign a unique name for your unit, set your preferred language, define any networks you want to whitelist (specified by SSID or MAC address), and indicate the display type. As of this writing, Waveshare has introduced the fourth revision (V4) of its 2.13-inch E-Ink display. The module I used for my build is a V3. Be sure to check the manufacturer's version information for yours and set it correctly in the `ui.display.type` property, as shown here:

```
main.name = "pwnagotchi"
main.lang = "en"
main.whitelist = [
  "EXAMPLE_NETWORK",
  "fo:ob:ar:be:fo:od"
]

ui.display.enabled = true
ui.display.type = "waveshare_3"  # Modify this to match your display
ui.display.color = "black"
ui.invert = true
ui.fps = 1
```

It's advisable to start with a basic configuration like this one. When you're done editing, save this file and exit your editor. At first boot, the software will install the file to */etc/pwnagotchi/config.toml* and remove it from the boot partition. Thereafter, you can edit your configuration at this location.

First Boot

Remove your SD card and insert it into the Pi Zero 2 W. If you're using the PiSugar 2 battery module, connect 5.1 V power to its micro USB port, then boot your device using the power switch. If you don't have a battery add-on, simply connect power to the micro USB port labeled PWR IN on the Pi Zero.

If you're not using the default *pi* user, you'll need to create a symlink to the *pi* user in the */home* directory to ensure that everything works properly. To do this, run:

```
$ ln -s /home/USER /home/pi
```

After a few moments, Pwnagotchi's interface will appear with a "Generating keys, do not turn off" message. Once this process is complete, a randomly selected startup message will appear with the version number. If the Waveshare E-Ink display appears grainy or exhibits image ghosting, don't worry; this is common at startup, and it will usually appear normal after it's refreshed a few times.

Pwnagotchi operates in one of three modes that govern how it behaves. When connected to the USB power port, its default mode is AUTO. In this mode, your unit will begin performing attacks and sniffing Wi-Fi handshakes by using its default personality settings.

The second mode, AI, is enabled by default in the configuration. Pwnagotchi will automatically transition to this mode, illustrated in Figure 9-11, after several minutes.

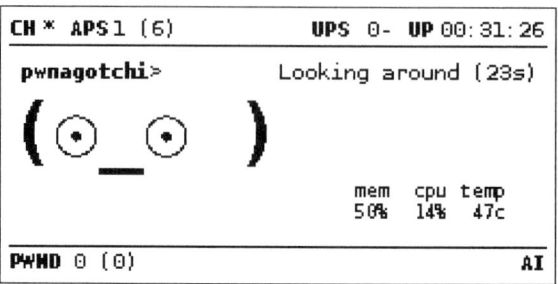

Figure 9-11: A Pwnagotchi unit operating in AI mode

On first boot, the software will load all of the AI module's dependencies and initialize the neural network. With the dependencies in place and the */root/brain.nn* file populated, AI mode will select an optimal set of parameters in real time. The parameter set is dependent on how long the unit has been trained in the specific environment it is observing.

Depending on the `laziness` configuration parameter, Pwnagotchi's AI will periodically enter a "training" phase during which it explores a wider range of settings to determine their effects on its reward. During what are known as *inference epochs* (periods when the unit is not learning, but rather selecting parameters based on previous knowledge), the AI tends to be more conservative, using narrower ranges of settings that are known to work in that situation.

We'll explore the inner workings of the AI further in "A Closer Look at Pwnagotchi's AI" on page 275. We'll look at the third mode, MANUAL, in "Using USB Ethernet Gadget Mode" on page 279.

A Brief Tour of the Interface

Pwnagotchi's expressions and status messages are mostly self-explanatory. There are, however, several interface elements that may not be obvious at first use. These are illustrated in Figure 9-12.

In the upper-left corner of Pwnagotchi's display, you'll find the channel the unit is currently operating on. When a Pwnagotchi unit is performing Wi-Fi reconnaissance and hopping around on all channels, it will display CH * in place of a channel number. During this phase, it will record the number of APs found on each channel. APS *x* indicates the number of access points found on the current channel, and the total number of recorded APs across all channels (found during the last recon) is displayed after this in parentheses. This unit has the optional Bluetooth tethering (`bt-tether`) plug-in enabled, which indicates its current state as connected (C). Likewise, the optional PiSugar 2 battery monitor plug-in is enabled and is displaying its charge status (I'll cover configuring the plug-in for this battery module in "Installing the PiSugar Plug-in" on page 286). Next to this is the unit's uptime since the last boot.

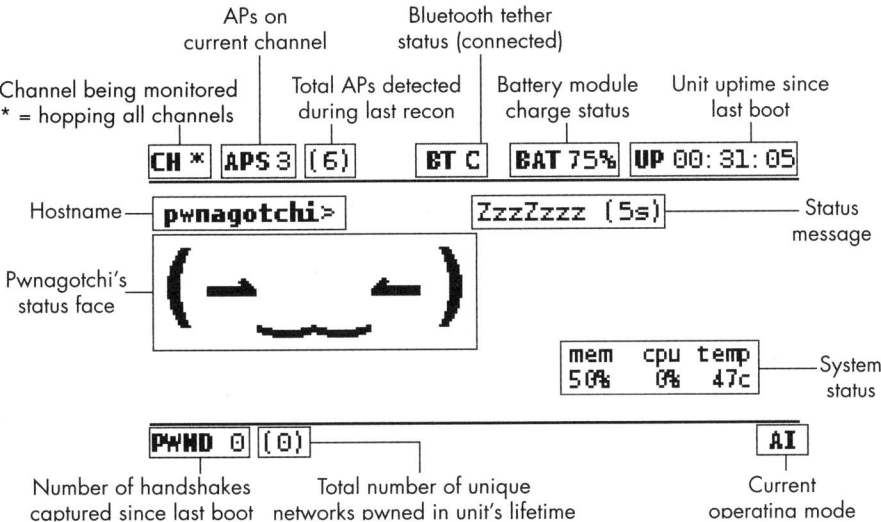

Figure 9-12: A Pwnagotchi unit's interface elements

In the main display area, you'll find the unit's hostname and status message, followed by Pwnagotchi's trademark expressions. The latter can be customized to your liking, as described in "Going Further" on page 302.

Below this are some basic system statistics. The bottommost row displays the number of Wi-Fi handshakes captured during the current session, expressed as PWND *x*. This is followed by the number of unique networks your Pwnagotchi has "eaten" since the beginning of its life, in parentheses. Finally, the current operating mode is shown, as described in the previous section.

The Pwnagotchi unit shown in Figure 9-11 has just begun operating. Once your unit starts capturing handshakes, it will display the SSID of its most recently acquired handshake in the bottom row. The main display will also indicate when another Pwnagotchi unit is detected nearby.

A Closer Look at Pwnagotchi's AI

Beneath Pwnagotchi's approachable exterior, advanced deep reinforcement learning is at work. *Reinforcement learning (RL)* is a subfield of machine learning that trains software agents to acquire optimal behaviors in complex environments. Broadly stated, this is achieved through trial and error combined with feedback from the environment. Many techniques have been developed to approach this problem. Pwnagotchi uses an algorithm called *Advantage Actor–Critic (A2C)*. To understand how this works, let's first consider the world a Pwnagotchi unit operates in and the challenges it faces.

Pwnagotchi's target environment is a highly dynamic, constantly changing wireless spectrum. To capture handshakes, it must learn continuously by observing the real world, which is varied and unpredictable. In real time, its ARM CPU needs to scan the entire Wi-Fi spectrum in its environment and make decisions about its findings, a process that can take microseconds or

several minutes. Crucially, and unlike many reinforcement learning environments, this process can't be replayed. Pwnagotchi must use the observations
it receives to form policy decisions, which in turn influence future observations and subsequent policies. It's an enormous engineering task with limited computing resources to bring to bear.

The author of Pwnagotchi, Simone Margaritelli (better known by his
online moniker, EvilSocket), saw the challenge laid out before him. There
were no existing code examples, use cases, or guides for integrating the algorithms needed to pull this off. He knew the ideal algorithm would need to
do the following:

1. Gather observations from the environment (such as access points,
   client stations, and other signals).

2. Make decisions based on these observations and its current status
   on how to adjust its parameters.

3. Iteratively repeat this process each time new observations became
   available.

In abstract terms, this was not unlike playing a video game: Observations made while controlling an onscreen character would determine the inputs that should be sent to the controller. As it happened, the technology to
solve this type of problem already existed; state-of-the-art examples ranged
from classic Atari titles and more ancient games like Go to popular console
games like *Super Mario Bros.* and *Sonic the Hedgehog*.

The Actor–Critic Process Loop

Imagine that you're playing a new video game while a friend observes
and critiques your moves. In this scenario, you assume the *actor* role, and
your friend is the *critic*. At first, you're unfamiliar with the gameplay, so you
try various moves at random. The critic observes your decisions and provides feedback. As you learn from this feedback, you adjust your strategy,
gradually improving your ability to play the game. Meanwhile, your friend
refines the way they provide feedback, such that it also becomes more effective over time.

Conceived of this way, the actor–critic approach comprises two neural
networks. The actor uses what's known as a *policy function*, which determines
how the agent (your video game character) behaves. By contrast, the critic
uses a *value function* that measures the success or failure of the agent's decisions. These two functions run in parallel. Since two models are being
trained, different weights must be optimized for each.

Returning to the video game example, at each time step, the current
state (s) of the game (the environment) is passed as input to both the actor
and the critic. The actor's policy function reads this state and returns an
action (a) for the agent to carry out. The effectiveness of the action is evaluated, and a *reward (r)* value is returned. The critic computes the value of
the action taken in that particular state as an *advantage*, or a measure of how
much better or worse the action was compared to the average action from

that state. The actor then updates its policy parameters based on this value. The advantage value calculated by the critic completes the A2C algorithm. This cycle is repeated continuously, as illustrated in Figure 9-13.

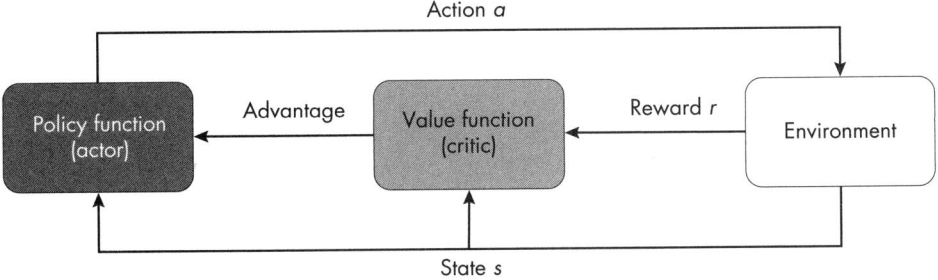

Figure 9-13: A conceptual view of the Advantage Actor–Critic process loop

Pwnagotchi creates two neural networks with TensorFlow, one each to represent the actor and the critic. Its learning cycles are divided into *epochs*, or loops of the main algorithm when new observations become available. The actor and the critic together evaluate the current state of the environment in terms of reward potential (the number of handshakes). They then use this input to determine the best policy (set of parameters) for the actor to use in order to maximize its reward potential. These parameters are defined in *pwnagotchi/pwnagotchi/ai/gym.py*:

```
import pwnagotchi.ai.featurizer as featurizer
import pwnagotchi.ai.reward as reward
from pwnagotchi.ai.parameter import Parameter

class Environment(gym.Env):
    metadata = {'render.modes': ['human']}
    params = [
        Parameter('min_rssi', min_value=-200, max_value=-50),
        Parameter('ap_ttl', min_value=30, max_value=600),
        Parameter('sta_ttl', min_value=60, max_value=300),
        Parameter('recon_time', min_value=5, max_value=60),
        Parameter('max_inactive_scale', min_value=3, max_value=10),
        Parameter('recon_inactive_multiplier', min_value=1, max_value=3),
        Parameter('hop_recon_time', min_value=5, max_value=60),
        Parameter('min_recon_time', min_value=1, max_value=30),
        Parameter('max_interactions', min_value=1, max_value=25),
        Parameter('max_misses_for_recon', min_value=3, max_value=10),
        Parameter('excited_num_epochs', min_value=5, max_value=30),
        Parameter('bored_num_epochs', min_value=5, max_value=30),
        Parameter('sad_num_epochs', min_value=5, max_value=30),
    ]
    --snip--
```

Pwnagotchi's actor–critic process loop works continuously to optimize these parameters in order to achieve the best possible reward. Sharp-eyed readers will notice that gym is referenced in this file. This is the open source Gym toolkit, originally developed by OpenAI for researchers to test and evaluate their reinforcement learning agents.

The Reward Function

After each iteration of the main loop, a score (the reward) is computed that represents how well Pwnagotchi's parameters performed during that epoch. This reward value is derived in the following way (excerpted from *pwnagotchi/ai/reward.py*):

```
# state contains the information of the last epoch
# epoch_n is the number of the last epoch
tot_epochs = epoch_n + 1e-20 # 1e-20 is added to avoid a division by 0
tot_interactions = max(state['num_deauths'] + state['num_associations'], \
    state['num_handshakes']) + 1e-20
tot_channels = wifi.NumChannels


# ideally, for each interaction we would have a handshake
h = state['num_handshakes'] / tot_interactions
# small positive rewards the more active epochs we have
a = .2 (state['active_for_epochs'] / tot_epochs)
# make sure we keep hopping on the widest channel spectrum
c = .1 (state['num_hops'] / tot_channels)
# small negative reward if we don't see aps for a while
b = -.3 (state['blind_for_epochs'] / tot_epochs)
# small negative reward if we interact with things that are not
# in range anymore
m = -.3 (state['missed_interactions'] / tot_interactions)
# small negative reward for inactive epochs
i = -.2 (state['inactive_for_epochs'] / tot_epochs)

reward = h + a + c + b + i + m
--snip--
```

Through the process of optimizing this reward value, the AI learns over time how to find the best set of parameters for the current environmental conditions. The continuous reinforcement learning logic is influenced by a *laziness* factor, which determines whether the next epoch will be used for training. When Pwnagotchi is in training mode, it uses the next 50 epochs for deep reinforcement learning. Initially, the laziness factor is set to a low value so that younger units learn more quickly. As units gain experience and mature over time, a higher laziness factor can help prevent them from unlearning adaptive behaviors.

How does all this work in practice? Depending on the density of your Wi-Fi environment, you can observe a new Pwnagotchi unit adjusting itself to focus on the channels where it "sees" the highest reward potential. It will also adjust its timeout values based on whether the unit is static (sitting on a desk) or moving through space, allowing it to determine how long it should spend trying to acquire a new target.

With an understanding of the technology behind Pwnagotchi's AI, you can now explore its "brain" at a deeper level by connecting your unit in MANUAL mode.

Using USB Ethernet Gadget Mode

Up to this point, all your interactions with Pwnagotchi have been in AUTO or AI mode. The third mode, MANUAL (abbreviated MANU in the interface), is enabled when the unit is connected via its micro USB port, also known as USB Ethernet gadget mode. In this mode, the USB On-The-Go port functions as a Remote Network Driver Interface Specification (RNDIS) peer-to-peer wired Ethernet device. This is achieved by enabling the *dwc2* overlay and loading its corresponding module in the boot `cmdline`. These settings are already defined in the prebuilt Pwnagotchi image, so there's no need to edit the boot *config.txt* or *cmdline.txt* files. Conveniently, the usb0 interface is also preconfigured with a static IPv4 address.

To access Pwnagotchi in this mode, connect a data cable to the micro USB port labeled DATA on your Pi Zero 2 W, then to your computer, and wait for the system to boot. After a few moments, your computer should recognize the Pi Zero as a new network device. The way you configure this device will vary according to your host OS; examples for macOS, Windows, and Linux are described in the following sections.

Configuring the Device on macOS

On macOS systems, open **System Preferences** and go to the **Network** panel. You should see a new RNDIS/Ethernet Gadget service available in the list of networking options. Its initial state will indicate a self-assigned IP address. Open the details panel for this service, select **TCP/IP**, and change the **Configure IPv4** setting from DHCP to **Manually**. Then, configure the settings to match what's shown in Figure 9-14.

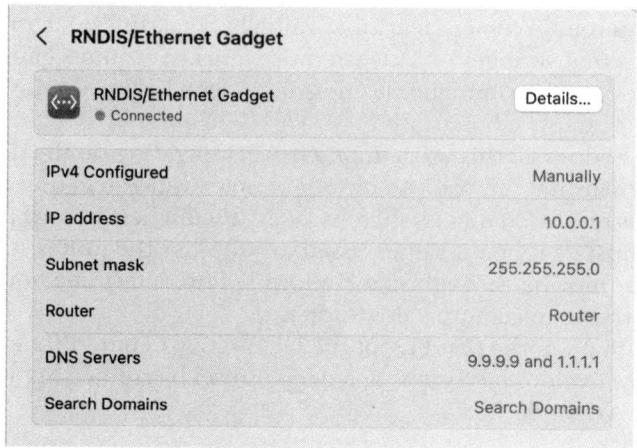

Figure 9-14: An RNDIS/Ethernet Gadget detected in the macOS
Network panel

Upon saving these settings, the service status should change to "Connected," as shown here.

You may find that your internet access is disrupted while this service is active. To remedy this, expand the Network options with the **Action** pop-up menu (**...**), then choose **Set Service Order** and drag the interface you use for internet connectivity to the top of the list. Drag the **RNDIS/Ethernet Gadget** service to the position just below this.

Configuring the Device on Windows

On Windows, open your network settings and confirm the presence of a new Ethernet connection with the type RNDIS. Right-click it, select **Properties**, then choose **Internet Protocol Version 4 (TCP/IPv4)** and click **Properties** again. In the dialog that appears, select the **Manual** option and enter the values for the IP address, subnet mask, and DNS servers shown in Figure 9-14. The gateway value corresponds to the IP address of your router. Save your changes and close these windows.

Configuring the Device on Linux

Linux desktop environments vary between distributions, so I'll cover this process by using the terminal. Begin by listing the available USB devices on your system:

```
$ lsusb
--snip--
Bus 001 Device 011: ID 0525:a4a2 Netchip Technology, Inc. Linux-USB
   Ethernet/RNDIS Gadget
```

In the example output shown here, the connected Pi Zero appears as a `Linux-USB Ethernet/RNDIS Gadget`. To obtain a list of the available network interfaces on your system, run:

```
$ ip -o link show | awk -F': ' '{print $2}'
lo
eth0
wlan0
usb0
```

Here, the RNDIS gadget interface is designated usb0. If your system uses predictable network interface naming, the interface may have a prefix like enp or enx. You can confirm that it's the right one by checking the detailed description of the interface with:

```
$ sudo ethtool -i usb0
```

This will provide additional information about the specified interface, including its driver. The driver value will usually be rndis_host, which indicates it's an RNDIS gadget.

Before a connection can be established, you'll need to configure the link. If your host system uses DHCP, you can append an entry like the following to */etc/dhcpcd.conf*:

```
interface usb0
static ip_address=10.0.0.1/24
```

Save the file and exit your editor, then restart the DHCP daemon with:

```
$ sudo systemctl restart dhcpcd.service
```

Alternatively, you can configure the link by using */etc/network/interfaces*. This method is deprecated and may disrupt other network interfaces, so use it with caution. Logged in as the root user, or using sudo, create a new file called */etc/network/interfaces.d/usb0* with the following contents:

```
auto usb0
allow-hotplug usb0
iface usb0 inet static
address 10.0.0.1
netmask 255.255.255.0
gateway 10.0.0.1
```

Save the file and exit your editor. Then restart the interface to enable the new static IP:

```
$ sudo ifdown usb0
$ sudo ifup usb0
```

Finally, run

```
$ ip a | grep usb0
```

to confirm that the usb0 interface has been assigned its new fixed IP address.

Sharing Internet Connectivity

Each host OS has its own method for sharing internet access with devices connected via different services, including RNDIS/Ethernet gadget mode. When it comes to networking, I generally prefer using the terminal over graphical interfaces that abstract these configurations. Here, I'll outline the steps that worked for me. In essence, the goal is to use network address translation (NAT) to route traffic from the host computer's primary interface to the connected RNDIS/Ethernet gadget (that is, your Pwnagotchi).

First, you'll need to identify the interfaces on your host computer that you'll be working with. You can do this by running `ifconfig` in the terminal. However, if your system is anything like mine, this will dump several screenfuls of output. If you know your host computer's IPv4 address, you can filter this output by using grep. In this example, I'm using my laptop's IP address, 192.168.1.11:

```
$ ifconfig | grep 192.168.1.11 -B4
en0: flags=8863<UP,BROADCAST,SMART,RUNNING,SIMPLEX,MULTICAST> mtu 1500
--snip--
```

Replace this with your computer's IPv4 address. Note that my host interface's name is en0; yours may differ. Next, repeat this process for the static IPv4 address you've assigned to the RNDIS/Ethernet gadget:

```
$ ifconfig | grep 10.0.0.1 -B4
en10: flags=8b63<UP,BROADCAST,SMART,RUNNING,PROMISC,ALLMULTI,SIMPLEX,MULTICAST> mtu 1500
--snip--
```

Here, the interface name en10 is assigned to this device; again, yours may be different. With the interface names known, you may now manipulate packet forwarding and NAT rules to allow routing between them, using the sysctl and pfctl utilities:

```
$ sudo sysctl -w net.inet.ip.forwarding=1
$ sudo pfctl -e
$ echo "nat on en0 from en10:network to any -> (en0)" | sudo pfctl -f -
```

Be sure to replace the en0 and en10 values with your own interface names if they're different. Note that sudo is required to use these networking tools if you're not logged in as root. You'll see how to confirm that internet connectivity is shared between your host machine and the connected Pwnagotchi in "Using MANUAL Mode" on page 283.

Connecting via SSH

With the usb0 RNDIS configuration established on your host system, you should now be able to access the Pwnagotchi via this interface's static IPv4 address. Confirm this by pinging it:

```
$ ping 10.0.0.2
PING 10.0.0.2 (10.0.0.2): 56 data bytes
64 bytes from 10.0.0.2: icmp_seq=0 ttl=64 time=1.056 ms
64 bytes from 10.0.0.2: icmp_seq=1 ttl=64 time=1.234 ms
--snip--
```

You should receive a ping response from 10.0.0.2. At this stage, you may proceed by connecting to your device:

```
$ ssh pi@10.0.0.2
```

The prebuilt Pwnagotchi image uses the default *raspberry* password. You should change this after your first login by executing the **passwd** command and choosing a strong passphrase. If you want to log in directly without using a password, securely copy your SSH public key to the unit's list of authorized keys:

```
$ ssh-copy-id -i ~/.ssh/id_rsa.pub pi@10.0.0.2
```

Thereafter, you may log in without being prompted for a password.

Using MANUAL Mode

Each time you log in to your Pwnagotchi, you'll be greeted by its *message of the day*. This contains the installed version, some pointers to configuration files, plus some general usage notes:

```
(●‿‿●) pwnagotchi

    Hi! I'm a pwnagotchi 2.9.2, please take good care of me!
    Here are some basic things you need to know to raise me properly!

    If you want to change my configuration, use /etc/pwnagotchi/config.toml
    All plugin config files are located in /etc/pwnagotchi/conf.d/
    --snip--
```

If you followed the steps in "Sharing Internet Connectivity" on page 282, you can conduct a ping test like so:

```
$ ping pwnagotchi.ai
PING pwnagotchi.ai (172.67.162.248): 56 data bytes
64 bytes from 172.67.162.248: icmp_seq=0 ttl=57 time=36.624 ms
64 bytes from 172.67.162.248: icmp_seq=1 ttl=57 time=40.432 ms
--snip--
```

In MANUAL mode, your Pwnagotchi will read the log of the previous session and report some statistics on the display. This is the mode you'll use to exchange data with your unit, install third-party plug-ins, examine its logs, and more. A unit operating in this mode is shown in Figure 9-15.

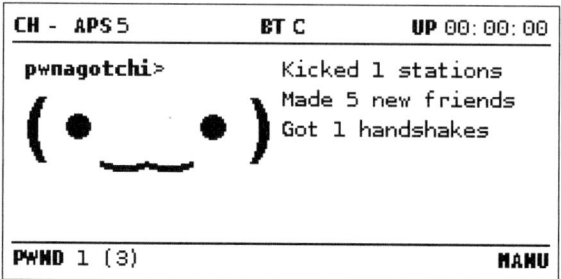

Figure 9-15: A Pwnagotchi unit operating in MANUAL mode

In this mode, you'll also be able to access the Pwnagotchi and Better-cap web interfaces from your computer. Start by configuring access to Pwnagotchi's web interface by editing its configuration:

```
$ sudo nano /etc/pwnagotchi/config.toml
```

The default username and password for Pwnagotchi's web interface are both *changeme*. It's good practice to modify these. Append the following lines to the end of this file, replacing the *my_new_username* and *my_new_password* placeholder values with your own login credentials:

```
ui.web.username = "my_new_username"
ui.web.password = "my_new_password"
```

Save this file, exit your editor, then restart Pwnagotchi's systemd service:

```
$ sudo systemctl restart pwnagotchi.service
```

Pwnagotchi's display will reinitialize as the service restarts. Next, open a web browser on your host computer and navigate to *http://10.0.0.2:8080*. On the login page, enter the credentials you specified in the configuration file. The web interface should then load in your browser. In addition to Pwnagotchi's primary display, the web interface has navigation items located at the top and bottom.

Under the Profile tab, you'll find the name you assigned your unit, along with its unique identifier and a QR code. The grid_version number corresponds to the installed Grid API, or *pwngrid*, release:

```
Name
pwnagotchi
Fingerprint
5844e420db6903639c5fd09f7fb88f2b14e4116beba55a1cf331b483d58c6c8b
```

```
Data
{
  "grid_version": "1.11.4",
  "identity": "52f64e631e7b046473a24cac10fceee667693dab895ee573437857165b2ba970",
  "name": "pwnagotchi",
  "session_id": "9c:7e:00:bd:a5:63"
}
```

Your Pwnagotchi's fingerprint may be shared with other users, or used to look up your statistics on the pwngrid leaderboard.

Using Plug-ins

The Plugins tab contains a list of active and available plug-ins that can be used to extend or modify Pwnagotchi's capabilities. You can change the active state of any plug-in by sliding the toggle beneath it. If you prefer to use the terminal, Pwnagotchi's CLI also has a `plugins` subcommand that you can use to manage them:

```
$ pwnagotchi plugins -h
usage: pwnagotchi plugins [-h] {search,list,update,upgrade,enable,disable,
    install,uninstall,edit} ...
```

Plug-ins are written in Python and utilize a rich set of *callbacks*, or functions that are passed as arguments to other functions. These are commonly used for asynchronous operations and event handling. Table 9-1 shows a subset of Pwnagotchi's available callback functions.

Table 9-1: Plug-in Callback Functions

Callback	Description
on_ai_training_end	Called when the AI is done training
on_channel_hop	Called when the agent is tuning in a specific channel
on_deauthentication	Called when the agent is deauthenticating a client station from an AP
on_epoch	Called when an epoch is over
on_excited	Called when the status is set to excited
on_free_channel	Called when a nonoverlapping Wi-Fi channel is found to be free
on_ready	Called when everything is ready and the main loop is about to start
on_sleep	Called when the agent is sleeping for *t* seconds
on_ui_update	Called when the UI is updated
on_wait	Called when the agent is waiting for *t* seconds
on_wifi_update	Called when the agent refreshed its access points list

The plug-in architecture and callbacks have led to the development of many third-party plug-ins for Pwnagotchi. User plug-ins can be placed anywhere as Python files; their containing folder is then defined in *config.toml*, in the `main.plugins` setting. In the next section, I'll demonstrate installing a third-party plug-in to enable a battery meter for the PiSugar 2.

Installing the PiSugar Plug-in

A plug-in is available to show the PiSugar 2's battery percentage on a Pwnagotchi's display. To enable this plug-in, begin by creating a directory to store it (if you're using the prebuilt Pwnagotchi image, this directory should already be present):

```
$ sudo mkdir -p /usr/local/share/pwnagotchi/custom-plugins
```

Next, download the installer for the PiSugar's management software and execute it:

```
$ cd $HOME
$ wget https://cdn.pisugar.com/release/pisugar-power-manager.sh
$ bash pisugar-power-manager.sh -c release
```

After the installer unpacks the power manager's files, a dialog will appear where you can specify your PiSugar model. Select your model and choose **OK**, then enter your login credentials for the PiSugar server. When the installer completes, the power manager's web interface will be available at *http://10.0.0.2:8421*. Enter this into your host computer's browser and log in with the credentials you've defined. Since you're connected in USB gadget mode, the battery module isn't active, and therefore its status won't appear. You can, however, synchronize the PiSugar's onboard real-time clock.

With the PiSugar's power manager installed, download the plug-in and its supporting library:

```
$ git clone https://github.com/PiSugar/pisugar2py.git
$ git clone https://github.com/PiSugar/pwnagotchi-pisugar2-plugin.git
```

Now, create a symbolic link to make the plug-in library accessible to your Python environment:

```
$ sudo ln -s ~/pisugar2py/ \
    /usr/local/lib/python3.11/dist-packages/pisugar2
```

A symbolic link (or *symlink*) acts like a shortcut, pointing from one location to another. In this case, you're creating a shortcut so Python can find your pisugar2py library. If your installed Python version isn't `python3.11`, be sure to adjust this in the path.

Next, install the user plug-in:

```
$ sudo ln -s ~/pwnagotchi-pisugar2-plugin/pisugar2.py \
    /usr/local/share/pwnagotchi/custom-plugins/pisugar2.py
```

Finally, open your Pwnagotchi's configuration file in your editor with

```
$ sudo nano /etc/pwnagotchi/config.toml
```

and append the following lines:

```
main.custom_plugins = "/usr/local/share/pwnagotchi/custom-plugins/"
main.plugins.pisugar2.enabled = true
main.plugins.pisugar2.shutdown = 5
main.plugins.pisugar2.sync_rtc_on_boot = true
```

Execute a safe shutdown by running:

```
$ sudo shutdown -h now
```

Then disconnect the USB data cable from your unit and power it on via the PiSugar's micro switch. When the unit starts up, a BAT indicator should appear in the top row of Pwnagotchi's display, followed by a percentage value, as you saw in Figure 9-12.

In addition to the plug-in CLI, you may have noticed that Pwnagotchi includes a web-based plug-in administration interface, accessible by default at *http://10.0.0.2:8080/plugins*. The new PiSugar2 plug-in should appear here and indicate its Enabled status.

Saving and Restoring a Configuration

As the previous sections have illustrated, Pwnagotchi is highly configurable, with parameters to control its appearance, AI, plug-ins, and much more. After spending some time customizing your unit, you may want to back up its configuration. Before making substantial changes to your system, it's also advisable to create a backup that you can restore later if things don't go as planned.

The files located in */etc/pwnagotchi* contain Pwnagotchi's TOML configuration, the RSA key pair generated at first boot, logfiles, and more. To back up and archive this directory to */root*, run:

```
$ sudo tar -czvf /root/pwnagotchi_config.tar.gz /etc/pwnagotchi/
```

To restore a configuration later, use the following commands:

```
$ cd /root
$ sudo tar -xzvf pwnagotchi_config.tar.gz
```

This will extract the contents of the archive in the current */root* path. With this done, move the files back to the original configuration path:

```
$ sudo mv ./etc/pwnagotchi/* /etc/pwnagotchi
```

It's wise to also store a copy of this configuration on a host computer in case your Pwnagotchi becomes inaccessible. The simplest method to do this securely is with sftp. From your host computer, execute the following commands:

```
$ sftp pi@10.0.0.2
Connected to 10.0.0.2.
sftp> cd /root
sftp> get pwnagotchi_config.tar.gz
Fetching /root/pwnagotchi_config.tar.gz to pwnagotchi_config.tar.gz
sftp> exit
```

The compressed configuration archive will be stored in your local directory.

Performing a Full Backup and Restore

The steps described in the previous section are effective for capturing Pwnagotchi's configuration, keys, and related files. However, it's possible to go a step further and perform a complete backup of your unit's AI brain, captured handshakes, peers, SSH keys, bash profile, and more. This allows you to restore your Pwnagotchi to its last backed-up state, including its AI, capture history, and configuration. This may be desirable if you've been using your Pwnagotchi for a while and would like to clone it.

Conveniently, EvilSocket provides backup and restore shell scripts for this purpose. On your host computer, open a terminal, create a directory to store your backups, and change into it. I've called mine *pwnagotchi_backup*:

```
$ mkdir pwnagotchi_backup && cd pwnagotchi_backup
```

Now, download the scripts and set their execute bits by running:

```
$ wget https://raw.githubusercontent.com/evilsocket/pwnagotchi/master/scripts/backup.sh
$ wget https://raw.githubusercontent.com/evilsocket/pwnagotchi/master/scripts/restore.sh
$ chmod +x *.sh
```

You can obtain usage notes for either script by using the -h (help) option, like so:

```
$ ./backup.sh -h
Usage: backup.sh [-honu] [-h] [-u user] [-n host name or ip] [-o output]
```

The scripts will use the default 10.0.0.2 IPv4 address configured for the Ethernet gadget interface on the host. You can override this by specifying a different hostname or IP address with the -n switch. To use the default settings and back up your unit, run the *./backup.sh* script. The script will report the files it's archiving and generate a compressed *.tar* file with a unique name. To restore a backup, run **./restore.sh** *_filename_*, replacing the *filename* placeholder with the name of the backup file you created.

Note that custom plug-ins are not included in the backup. This is because many third-party plug-ins, including the one provided by PiSugar, rely on dependencies installed elsewhere in the system. You'll need to manually reinstall these plug-ins, repeating the steps you used earlier.

Using Bettercap

I only scratched the surface of Bettercap's capabilities in the "Software Used" section on page 268. Given its usefulness as a stand-alone network security tool, and the fact that it forms the backbone of Pwnagotchi, it deserves a closer examination.

Bettercap can be used in a variety of ways: by entering commands in an interactive terminal session, by scripting with *caplets* (self-contained script files with a *.cap* extension), or through its web interface. You'll gain experience with each of these methods in this section. The examples presented here assume you're connected to your Pwnagotchi in MANUAL mode.

Starting an Interactive Session

With Bettercap's powerful interactive terminal, you can execute commands, enable modules, set session parameters, and more. Before starting an interactive session, you'll need to determine the interface configured for monitor mode. You can do this by running:

```
$ iwconfig | grep Monitor
wlan0mon  IEEE 802.11  Mode:Monitor  Frequency:2.412 GHz
```

In this example, the output shows that `wlan0mon` is operating in monitor mode. You can then start Bettercap, specifying this interface with the `-iface` option:

```
$ sudo bettercap -iface wlan0mon
```

At the interactive terminal prompt, type `wifi.recon on` and press ENTER. You should see a stream of events in the console, such as `wifi.ap.new` and `wifi.client.probe` messages, as Bettercap discovers and probes nearby base stations. Nothing malicious is occurring during this initial reconnaissance; it's roughly analogous to what many devices, like your phone, do when looking for available Wi-Fi networks to connect to. After a few moments, type `wifi.show` followed by ENTER. You should see a table summarizing nearby access points, sorted by RSSI, with various details including the number of connected clients (if available).

This is merely an entry point into Bettercap's capabilities with the `wifi` module. At the prompt, type `help wifi` followed by ENTER for a complete list of commands related to this module. When you're done, type `quit` and press ENTER to exit the interactive session.

Scripting with Caplets

Caplets provide a way of chaining Bettercap commands together to perform sophisticated actions. Conditional logic can also be included using

JavaScript. To create your first caplet, start from the logged-in user's home directory and create a new file called *example.cap*:

```
$ cd $HOME
$ nano example.cap
```

Enter the following contents:

```
net.probe on
clear
ticker on
```

Save this file and exit your editor. Then run Bettercap with the -caplet option and specify your caplet:

```
$ sudo bettercap -caplet example
```

This simple caplet initiates a probe of Pwnagotchi's local network, clears the display, and starts a ticker. The probe will continue until you choose to interrupt it, producing output like the following:

IP ▲	MAC	Name	Vendor	Sent	Recvd	Seen
10.0.0.2	16:a1:a9:20:xx:xx	usb0		0 B	0 B	14:43:29
10.0.0.1	36:84:81:5d:xx:xx	gateway		50 kB	370 kB	14:43:29

```
↑ 281 kB / ↓ 1.2 MB / 18272 pkts
10.0.0.0/24 > 10.0.0.2   »
```

To stop the probe, type **quit** followed by ENTER.

Notice that in this example, the caplet was loaded by name without a path or extension. When the -caplet switch is specified, Bettercap looks for the requested caplet with the following search order:

1. In *./example.cap* (that is, in the current directory)
2. In *./caplets/example.cap* (in a subfolder called *caplets*)
3. In any folder in the environment variable $CAPSPATH (values are separated by :, as with $PATH)
4. In */usr/local/share/bettercap/caplets/example.cap* (the default path where caplets are installed)

Incidentally, you can achieve the same result this caplet produces by concatenating commands with the ; operator and passing them as an argument with the -eval switch, like so:

```
$ sudo bettercap -eval 'net.probe on; clear; ticker on'
```

This is a very basic example; caplets may include external JavaScript files and other caplet files to script complex actions using any of Bettercap's modules. I recommend looking in the default caplet install path (indicated in the preceding list) to familiarize yourself with what's possible with caplets.

Accessing the Web Interface

Bettercap's interactive terminal and caplets are an incredibly powerful combination. They do, however, have a learning curve (though not a particularly steep one). Arguably, the easiest way to get started with Bettercap is by using its official web user interface.

To run Bettercap and the web UI simultaneously, you'll use the `http-ui` caplet, which starts the `api.rest` and `http.server` modules. You'll need to make a few modifications to this caplet's parameters, so start by opening it in your editor with:

```
$ sudo nano /usr/local/share/bettercap/caplets/http-ui.cap
```

As you'll be accessing the interface from your host computer's browser, locate the following parameters and edit them so they have the values shown here:

```
set api.rest.address 10.0.0.2
set http.server.address 10.0.0.2
set http.server.port 8000
```

Next, choose a username and strong password, and substitute these for the *user* and *pass* placeholder values shown in the following lines:

```
set api.rest.username user
set api.rest.password pass
```

Save the caplet and exit your editor. Before starting Bettercap with the `http-ui` caplet, you'll need to stop the running `bettercap.service`. This is enabled to start automatically at boot, which binds the `api.rest` module to port 8081. You can stop the service temporarily with:

```
$ sudo systemctl stop bettercap.service
```

Finally, execute Bettercap, specifying the caplet and the monitor interface. Be sure to replace `wlan0mon` if your monitor interface differs:

```
$ sudo bettercap -caplet http-ui -iface wlan0mon
```

An interactive Bettercap session will begin, indicating that both the API server and the web interface have started. Copy or note the `http.server` address, usually *http://10.0.0.2:8000*, and open it in your host computer's browser. Bettercap's login screen should appear; enter the credentials you specified in the previous step and click **Login**.

Initially, there won't be many events reported in Bettercap's web interface. This is expected. Select **Advanced** from the right end of the top toolbar. On the left side, active Bettercap modules will appear highlighted, while the inactive ones are grayed out. Choose the `ble.recon` module near the top, then, under the **Commands** section, select `ble.recon on`. The BLE device discovery module's status will change to "Running." Repeat this for the `wifi` module, then return to the Events view. Bettercap's web interface should now be recording some interesting event activity.

Now, choose **Caplets** from the top navigation. You'll notice that Bettercap's installed caplets are activated by default and ready for use, including the `example` caplet you created earlier. You can edit, save, and execute any of the installed caplets via this interface.

Most users, upon discovering Bettercap's web interface, proceed to spend an extended period of time exploring its capabilities. When you emerge from the rabbit role, I'll guide you through processing Bettercap's packet capture files.

Collecting Handshakes

You've now gained some insight into Pwnagotchi's AI system based on TensorFlow and deep reinforcement learning, and you've seen how Bettercap can be used to capture Wi-Fi handshakes. To understand why it's valuable to train an AI to "eat" these handshakes, it's helpful to review how they work.

Before a client device can securely send and receive data from a wireless access point, a *four-way handshake* must occur. This process, which is a central feature of the WPA/WPA2 protocols, generates the WPA keys used to encrypt traffic between a client (such as a phone) and an AP. As discussed in "Making a Connection" on page 33, during this process, four packets are exchanged between a client device and the AP. The steps are illustrated in Figure 9-16; refer back to Chapter 1 for a detailed explanation of this diagram.

Once the packets have been successfully exchanged and the keys generated, the client device is authenticated and can begin securely communicating with the wireless AP. However, there's a catch: All four packets can be *sniffed* from the radio spectrum by a third party monitoring the exchange. An attacker can then use a dictionary or brute-force attack to crack the handshake and recover the original Wi-Fi passphrase. Importantly, note that capturing all four packets isn't necessary for a successful recovery.

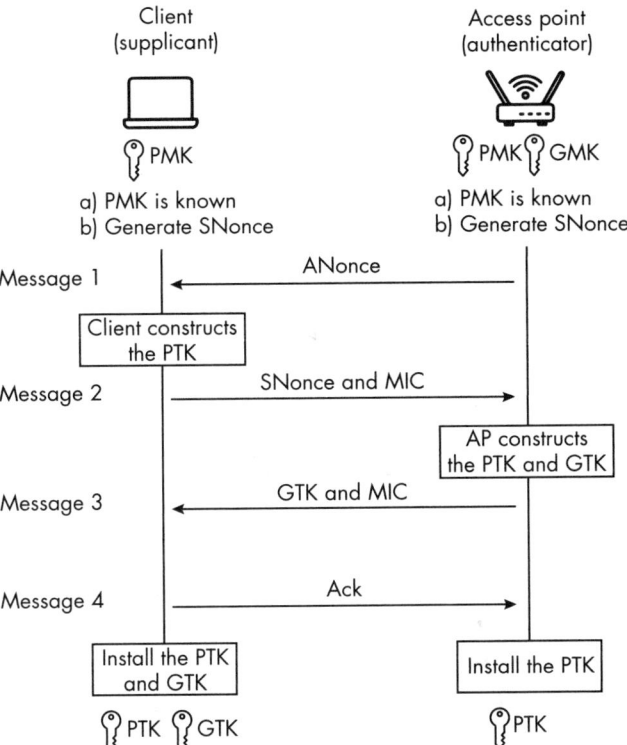

Figure 9-16: The steps involved in a four-way wireless handshake

Pwnagotchi employs two primary strategies to collect as many handshakes as possible:

Deauthenticating client stations

If you've observed Pwnagotchi over any length of time, you've probably noticed it deauthenticating (or "kicking") devices from the access points it has detected. When this happens, a device must reauthenticate by repeating the four-way handshake process. This gives Pwnagotchi another opportunity to sniff the handshake packets and collect more potentially crackable data.

Sending association frames

Rather than requiring a client to be connected to an access point, this method sends association frames directly to the access points themselves. It involves sending a single packet to a target AP, in an attempt to force it to leak what's known as a *pairwise master key identifier (PMKID)*. As it happens, many modern routers append an optional field to the first frame sent by the AP when a client is associating with it. This field, the *Robust Security Network (RSN) Information Element*, may include the PMKID value. As shown in Figure 9-16, the pairwise master key (PMK) is known by both the client and the access point. With the PMK and PMKID values in hand, Hashcat has all it needs to derive the passphrase.

All the handshakes captured by Pwnagotchi are collected as PCAP files on its filesystem, with one file per access point. These handshakes can later be analyzed with the proper hardware and software.

Creating a Target Network

To facilitate handshake collection with Pwnagotchi, you can create additional access points with WLAN-capable Raspberry Pis. On modern Debian-based systems, the simplest method to achieve this is by using NetworkManager. First, start the service and check its status:

```
$ sudo systemctl start NetworkManager
$ sudo systemctl status NetworkManager
```

Then execute the following command to create an AP with a weak passphrase:

```
$ sudo nmcli d wifi hotspot ifname wlan0 ssid pwnagotchi-target \
    password 12345678
```

NetworkManager should report that device wlan0 was successfully activated. To confirm this, run:

```
$ sudo nmcli dev wifi show-password
SSID: pwnagotchi-target
Security: WPA
Password: 12345678
--snip--
```

You can also use the following `nmcli` command to verify that the access point is up and available:

```
$ nmcli device wifi
IN-USE  BSSID                SSID               MODE   CHAN  RATE       SIGNAL  BARS  SECURITY
        B8:27:EB:01:xx:xx    pwnagotchi-target  Infra  6     65 Mbit/s  100     ▂▄▆█  WPA2
```

To provide Pwnagotchi with a rich target environment, you may choose to operate one or more APs simultaneously by using this method, or rotate SSIDs and passphrases as it obtains handshakes from them. Note that the tools you'll be using in the next section are capable of using large *word lists*, or precompiled lists of potential passphrases, so you may choose more complex passwords than the one used in the previous example.

Processing PCAP Files

After you've successfully captured handshakes from your target networks, you can analyze the resulting PCAP files with the aid of some additional software. Connected in MANUAL mode, the Pwnagotchi unit shown in Figure 9-17 is reporting statistics derived from the log of its last session. A total of 23 access points (*friends* in Pwnagotchi-speak) were surveyed, from which 14 clients were deauthenticated (or *kicked*), resulting in 4 handshakes being collected.

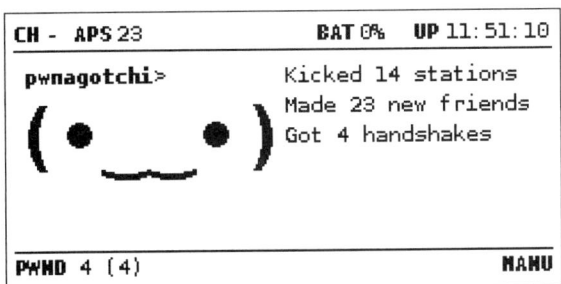

Figure 9-17: A Pwnagotchi unit indicating its collected handshakes

This is a reasonably good haul from my test bench, and certainly enough crackable WPA material to warrant a closer look. Prior to extracting data from your *.pcap* files, you may wish to examine the files' contents. PCAP files are binary, but you can use `tcpdump` in the Linux terminal to view the packets in a human-readable form. If it's not present on your system, install it with:

```
$ sudo apt install -y tcpdump
```

Then execute it with the following options:

```
$ tcpdump -qns 0 -X -r my-target-network.pcap | more
```

Replace *my-target-network.pcap* with the name of your *.pcap* file. The -X switch displays the packet data in both hexadecimal and ASCII formats. The output is piped through more for paging a screenful at a time. The following output is from a PCAP file obtained from my pwnagotchi-target:

```
reading from file pnwagotchi-target.pcap, link-type IEEE802_11_RADIO (802.11 plus radiotap ...
19:31:26.748488 51449071us tsft 2437 MHz -86dBm signal EAPOL key (3) v1, len 95
        0x0000:  0103 005f 0200 8a00 1000 0000 0000 0000  ..._............
        0x0010:  01d4 a7ce e12f 75e5 e343 795b 18a7 4f14  ...../u..Cy[..O.
        0x0020:  1ceb 046d 2b3e dbc5 d139 6704 14ee 3caf  ...m+>...9g...<.
        0x0030:  fd00 0000 0000 0000 0000 0000 0000 0000  ................
        0x0040:  0000 0000 0000 0000 0000 0000 0000 0000  ................
        0x0050:  0000 0000 0000 0000 0000 0000 0000 0000  ................
        0x0060:  0000 0073 49e7 f0                         ...sI..
```

This portion of the PCAP file includes an Extensible Authentication Protocol over LAN (EAPOL) key frame: specifically, an EAPOL key message 3. To derive the pre-shared key (PSK) for this AP with a dictionary attack, an EAPOL key message 2 is also required.

AN ETHICAL APPROACH TO PASSPHRASE CRACKING

It's important to note that the handshake PCAP files used here all belong to access points under my direct control. To facilitate PCAP processing, I configured several APs at my test bench with deliberately weak passphrases, using the nmcli method described in "Creating a Target Network" on page 294. Use of software like Hcxtools or Hashcat to crack passphrases for Wi-Fi networks that you don't own can expose you to legal consequences.

In the United States, the *Computer Fraud and Abuse Act (CFAA)* makes it illegal to intentionally access a computer without authorization, or by exceeding your authorized level of access. Wi-Fi networks fall under this category, and cracking a wireless passphrase with the intent of accessing someone else's network could land you in hot water. The European Union, various individual European nations, the United Kingdom, many Asian countries, and Australia all have similar legal frameworks in place.

If Pwnagotchi collects handshakes from Wi-Fi networks outside your control, you should understand the risks associated with manipulating these files. Bottom line: Play it safe and obtain consent from the network owner before conducting any security surveys, including deauthentication attacks. Be sure to adhere to ethical hacking practices and use the tools presented here responsibly.

Hashcat, a free and open source software project, is the gold standard for password recovery tools. It boasts support for hundreds of hash types and has loads of features. Recent versions of Hashcat include a dedicated hash mode specifically tailored for cracking WPA/WPA2 PSKs, better known as Wi-Fi passphrases. Before using Hashcat, you'll need to preprocess your PCAP files. You'll use a utility provided by Hcxtools, hcxpcapngtool, to convert the captured packets to the hash format expected by Hashcat.

The Hcxtools package should already be installed on your prebuilt Pwnagotchi image. You can confirm this, or install it on another system, by running:

```
$ sudo apt install -y hcxtools
```

Pwnagotchi saves the handshakes it collects in the */root/handshakes/* directory. Change into this directory and list the available PCAP files:

```
$ cd /root/handshakes
$ ls -la *.pcap
```

Recall that PCAP files are named and organized according to each access point's SSID. In the following examples, I'll be working with *pwnagotchi-target.pcap*. Replacing this filename with the name of your own *.pcap* file, run:

```
$ sudo hcxpcapngtool pwnagotchi-target.pcap -o candidates.hc22000
```

The hcxpcapngtool will display a detailed summary of the capture file, including the number of packets it contains, association requests, EAPOL messages, and more. Importantly, it converts the *.pcap* file into an output file called *candidates.hc22000*. This is the file that will be used with Hashcat.

Using Hashcat

You now have a *candidates.hc22000* file that's suitable for the next processing step. Hashcat benefits from powerful CPUs and, more importantly, GPUs. It requires a minimum of 2GB of system RAM, though more is recommended for larger hash lists and complex attacks. While it's technically possible to install Hashcat from the Debian package repositories on a Pi Zero 2, you won't get very far with it. Even if you configure a swapfile twice the size of the Zero's available RAM, Hashcat will report that it doesn't have enough allocatable memory to run.

USING HASHCAT WITH GRAPHICAL PROCESSING UNIT ACCELERATION

A variant of this tool, hashcat-nvidia, is capable of using the more powerful graphical processing unit (GPU) acceleration of dedicated Nvidia graphics cards to process large volumes of data (word lists and preprocessed capture files, in this case). If you have access to a computer with this hardware, you may opt to install this package and perform a benchmarking test. Start the test with **hashcat -m 22000 --benchmark**.

Fortunately, Hashcat is available for most operating systems, including x86-based ones and macOS. I opted to use a Raspberry Pi 5 with 4GB of RAM, which proved to be a stable performer. You can install Hashcat and its associated dependency with:

```
$ sudo apt install -y hashcat hashcat-data
```

The hashcat-data package contains Hashcat's supporting files, including word lists, salts, and various Python helper tools. If hashcat-data isn't available on your system, this chapter's companion GitHub repository contains a *wordlist.txt* file that you can use with Hashcat. Download the compressed archive and unpack the word list by executing these commands:

```
$ cd $HOME
$ wget https://github.com/wirelesscookbook/pwnagotchi/raw/master/wordlist.txt.gz
$ gunzip wordlist.txt.gz
```

Transfer the *candidates.hc22000* file from your Pwnagotchi's filesystem to the computer you've chosen for running Hashcat. Alternatively, you can copy the unprocessed *.pcap* files, install hcxtools on that system, and repeat the extraction step you performed earlier. I opted to use sftp to securely move the *candidates.hc22000* file from one device to another over my network. My working directory is located at *$HOME/candidates*; you may choose whichever location you prefer.

With your environment prepared, you're ready to execute Hashcat against the extracted handshake data. I copied the *example.dict* word list to my working directory before running the following commands, for convenience. You can replace *example.dict* with *wordlist.txt* or another word list:

```
$ cd $HOME/candidates
$ cp /usr/share/doc/hashcat-data/examples/example.dict .
$ hashcat -m 22000 candidates.hc22000 example.dict --status --status-timer=3
```

This instructs Hashcat to run in hash mode 22000, which is used for cracking WPA/WPA2 PSKs. The --status option enables continuous status updates, while --status-timer=3 sets the interval between status messages to three seconds. You can adjust this value to your preferred interval. As it processes the word list, Hashcat will display its progress along with several statistics. When it's done processing, you can check whether any passphrases were successfully recovered by running:

```
$ hashcat -m 22000 candidates.hc22000 --show
```

With the target access point I created, Hashcat produced the following output:

```
12345678::B8:27:EB:01:xx:xx:pwnagotchi-target
```

This result indicates that Hashcat has successfully cracked the hash entry, which it displays in a human-readable form. The output follows the format *passphrase::BSSID:SSID*.

Troubleshooting

This section covers a few of the more common issues that users have encountered with their Pwnagotchi units. While far from exhaustive, it will nonetheless hopefully point you in the right direction should things go awry. For problems not covered here, the original Pwnagotchi GitHub repository at *https://github.com/evilsocket/pwnagotchi* and the fork used in this chapter both contain many reported user issues with detailed histories. While locating a relevant thread may require a bit of patience, you should be able to find a solution or workaround for just about any issue you encounter.

Local Network Conflicts

As you saw in "Using USB Ethernet Gadget Mode" on page 279, Pwnagotchi's default configuration assigns the static IPv4 address 10.0.0.2 to your Ethernet gadget interface. If your local network also uses the 10.0.0.0/24 subnet, your Pwnagotchi may conflict with other devices on the network. To remedy this, you can change the IP address assigned to your Pwnagotchi. Connect to it in MANUAL mode via SSH and open the */etc/network/interfaces.d/usb0-cfg* file in your preferred editor. Replace its contents with the following:

```
allow-hotplug usb0
iface usb0 inet static
  address 192.168.0.2
  netmask 255.255.255.0
  network 192.168.0.0
  broadcast 192.168.0.255
  gateway 192.168.0.1
  metric 20
```

This assigns a different IPv4 address, 192.168.0.2, to your device. Naturally, ensure that no other devices are using this Class C private address range on your network; if so, choose something different. Save this file and reboot your Pwnagotchi. Then repeat the steps in "Using USB Ethernet Gadget Mode" with this new static IP address.

GPIO Faults

This is seldom an issue when using a prebuilt Pwnagotchi image, as the required serial port configurations are handled for you, but you may encounter GPIO errors when building your own image from scratch or when working with add-on hardware that attaches to the GPIO header. The methodology outlined here is a general troubleshooting process to identify and resolve the source of many GPIO faults.

If Pwnagotchi's display fails to start on boot, you can start the software directly from the terminal in MANUAL mode. Before doing so, ensure that the systemd pwnagotchi.service is stopped. Then launch the Pwnagotchi service with the --debug option:

```
$ sudo systemctl stop pwnagotchi.service
$ sudo pwnagotchi --debug
--snip--
File "/usr/lib/python3/dist-packages/lgpio.py", line 458, in _u2i
    raise error(error_text(v))
lgpio.error: 'GPIO busy'
```

Here, the debug output indicates a problem with the Python lgpio library: specifically, that the GPIO is reporting a "busy" state. If you keep reading, you'll see the following:

```
KeyError: PinInfo(number=11, name='GPIO17', names=frozenset({'J8:11', 17,
  'BCM17', 'GPIO17', 'WPIO', 'BOARD11', '17'}))
```

In this case, the output indicates that GPIO Broadcom (BCM) pin 17 is reporting a frozen state. This corresponds to the reset pin used by the Waveshare display. Next, you can use the gpioinfo tool to identify the used and unused GPIO pins:

```
$ gpioinfo
--snip--
    line  16:    "GPIO16"        unused  input   active-high
    line  17:    "GPIO17"          "lg"  output  active-high [used]
    line  18:    "GPIO18"          "lg"  output  active-high [used]
--snip--
```

This output shows that GPIO pins 17 and 18 are both in use. This usually indicates one of two possibilities: Either your system's serial peripheral interface isn't enabled, or the serial interface is being used by another process. To investigate the latter, run:

```
$ sudo fuser -v /dev/serial0
                USER        PID ACCESS COMMAND
/dev/ttyS0:     root        570 F....  agetty
```

This output shows that the agetty process is attached to the */dev/ttyS0* device file. This process is an instance of *getty*, a common Unix program for managing physical or virtual terminals (TTYs). When getty detects a connection, it responds with a login prompt to authenticate a user. Handling of login prompts on serial terminals is done by systemd, which will instantiate a serial-getty@.service on the main kernel console. The kernel console is where the kernel outputs its own log messages and is usually configured on the kernel command line in the boot loader.

You can check the status of this service with its associated /dev/ttyS0 serial interface like so:

```
$ sudo systemctl status serial-getty@ttyS0.service
```

As long as it's running, agetty will prevent access to the serial port. Stopping the service with

```
$ sudo systemctl stop serial-getty@ttyS0.service
```

will temporarily permit you to use the Waveshare E-Ink display, but you'll run into the same problem the next time you reboot, because the service will restart. This is due to systemd's use of *generators*, small binary files located in */lib/systemd/system-generators* that it executes very early in the boot process. You can learn more about why the system spawns getty by running `man systemd-getty-generator`.

So how do you prevent getty from grabbing the serial port at startup if disabling the service doesn't work? There are various ways to achieve this, but the preferred method is to edit the system boot firmware at */boot/firmware/cmdline.txt*. First, remove the `console=serial0,115200` or `console=ttyAMA0,115200` portion from the line contained in this file. Next, add `console=tty1` to inhibit the serial terminal service. This will prevent `agetty` from starting at the next boot.

An expedient alternative approach is to mask the service to prevent it from ever being enabled:

```
$ sudo systemctl mask serial-getty@ttyS0.service
```

Reboot Pwnagotchi and confirm that your attached display hardware works as expected.

Internet Connection Sharing Failure

The steps described in "Sharing Internet Connectivity" on page 282 should, in most scenarios, allow your Pwnagotchi to share your host's internet connection. However, I've noted the occasional loss of Internet Connection Sharing (ICS) when connected to a Windows host computer in MANUAL mode. In this event, repeat the steps to identify your network interfaces with `ifconfig` and execute the NAT and IP forwarding commands again. In my case, the en0 interface didn't change; however, the interface name assigned to your USB gadget may be reassigned following a reboot of the host OS. While many find them useful, I generally don't execute the connection sharing scripts provided in the Pwnagotchi GitHub repo, but rather adapt their contents to manual steps in the terminal.

If you're using Windows as your host OS, ensure that the RNDIS drivers are installed. It may sound obvious, but also be sure that you're using a micro USB cable that's rated for data transfer. The majority of cheaper cables are suitable only for providing power. Even with a data-rated cable, I occasionally noticed that a poor connection at the Pi Zero's micro USB port, or at my laptop's USB-C port, was at fault. Other times, I've noticed a loss of ICS when my local network connection (Wi-Fi or Ethernet) was disrupted while the Pwnagotchi unit was connected via RNDIS. When this occurs, rebooting the unit restores ICS.

If your ICS problems persist, many users find Bluetooth tethering and connection sharing from an Android or iOS device to be a viable alternative solution.

Nexmon Driver Blindness

Occasionally, you may see your Pwnagotchi report that it's "blind," meaning that it's unable to see access points on any available channel. This usually results from a known issue with the Nexmon driver, as reported in the system logs:

```
brcmfmac: brcmf_cfg80211_nexmon_set_channel: Set Channel failed: chspec=4099, -110
```

Previously, the only workable solution in this event was a system reboot. The mon_max_blind_epochs parameter exists for this purpose. In the past, a third-party watchdog plug-in would automatically reboot Pwnagotchi when this parameter reached a threshold value. However, with the prebuilt Pwnagotchi image used in this recipe, this is largely a solved issue.

Error messages thrown by brcmfmac may still be present, although in all cases that I've observed, the plug-in is capable of reinitializing the wlan0mon interface. Pwnagotchi should continue to monitor APs and handshakes as before without a restart.

Going Further

With its open and extensible design, Pwnagotchi lends itself to being modified and extended in any number of ways. Thanks to an active community supporting the project with third-party plug-ins, hardware integrations, and more, you're unlikely to feel constrained by a lack of possibilities. So, you can consider the basic unit you've built in this chapter could be a blank canvas of sorts.

Rather than attempt to cover the broad classifications of all the various mods available for Pwnagotchi, I'll instead highlight here a few customizations I find particularly interesting. I'll also present a few tips and tricks for streamlining your data collection efforts that I hope you'll find useful as you continue to explore what this project has to offer.

Customizing Personality and Expressions

Among Pwnagotchi's many customizations, two of the most accessible involve changing its default personality settings and expressions, or faces. You can override any of the default configuration values defined in the *pwnagotchi/defaults.toml* source file. In the prebuilt Pwnagotchi image, you'll find this file at */usr/local/lib/python3.11/dist-packages/pwnagotchi/defaults.toml*. You can also download the file from EvilSocket's GitHub repository and examine it like so:

```
$ cd $HOME
$ wget https://raw.githubusercontent.com/evilsocket/pwnagotchi/master/pwnagotchi/defaults.toml
$ nano defaults.toml
```

The personality settings, a subset of which are shown here, can be adjusted to override Pwnagotchi's default behavior:

```
--snip--
personality.hop_recon_time = 10
personality.min_recon_time = 5
personality.max_interactions = 3
personality.max_misses_for_recon = 5
personality.excited_num_epochs = 10
personality.bored_num_epochs = 15
personality.sad_num_epochs = 25
personality.bond_encounters_factor = 20000
--snip--
```

Similarly, you can override any of the standard expressions by defining a ui.faces value for a corresponding mood in your */etc/pwnagotchi/config.toml* file. A subset of the default faces is shown here:

```
--snip--
ui.faces.look_r = "( ☉_☉)"
ui.faces.look_l = "(☉_☉)"
ui.faces.look_r_happy = "( ◕‿◕)"
ui.faces.look_l_happy = "(◕‿◕ )"
ui.faces.sleep = "(⇀‿‿↼)"
ui.faces.sleep2 = "(≖_≖)"
ui.faces.awake = "(◕‿‿◕)"
ui.faces.bored = "(-__-)"
ui.faces.intense = "(°▇▇°)"
ui.faces.cool = "(⌐■_■)"
--snip--
```

After editing the configuration file, to see your changes, save the file and exit your editor, then restart Pwnagotchi's systemd service with:

```
$ sudo systemctl restart pwnagotchi.service
```

Third-party plug-ins are available that replace Pwnagotchi's ASCII-based faces with graphical ones. You can use these as is, or use them as a starting point to create your own. If you followed the steps described in "Installing the PiSugar Plug-in" on page 286, this process should be familiar.

Mapping Handshakes with GPS

One of the more interesting hardware modifications involves adding a GPS module to your Pwnagotchi unit. The prebuilt image used in this chapter has a gps plug-in that can be activated and used for this purpose. With a GPS module and this plug-in enabled, you'll be able to create a map of the handshakes Pwnagotchi captures in your wireless environment. This is often referred to as *warwalking*, in contrast to *wardriving* (discussed in "Wardriving: A (Very) Brief History" on page 202).

With an associated geospatial data layer, annotating a map like the one shown in Figure 9-18 with captured handshake locations is straightforward.

Figure 9-18: A Google map annotated with a Pwnagotchi unit's handshake capture locations

Combined with PCAP time-series data, you could also create an animated version to replay the results of your warwalk. There's even a third-party Wardriver plug-in for Pwnagotchi that saves all networks surveyed by Bettercap, not just the ones that handshakes are collected from. With a valid API key for WiGLE, you can then upload your sessions to *https://wigle.net*, along with your global statistics.

Leveling Up with Experience

Pwnagotchi already has lots of gamification features built into it by default. A creative third-party user plug-in takes this to the next level (pardon the pun). To install it, first download the plug-in's Python source to your home directory, then move it to the custom plug-ins location:

```
$ cd $HOME
$ wget \
  https://raw.githubusercontent.com/GaelicThunder/Experience-Plugin-Pwnagotchi/master/exp.py
$ sudo mv exp.py /usr/local/share/pwnagotchi/custom-plugins
```

Enable the plug-in by adding the following lines to your */etc/pwnagotchi/config.toml* file. You can adjust the placement of the level and experience values on the display by modifying their x- and y-coordinates, if needed:

```
main.plugins.exp.enabled = true
main.plugins.exp.lvl_x_coord = 0
main.plugins.exp.lvl_y_coord = 81
main.plugins.exp.exp_x_coord = 38
main.plugins.exp.exp_y_coord = 81
main.plugins.exp.bar_symbols_count = 12
```

Save the file and exit your editor, then restart the Pwnagotchi service with:

```
$ sudo systemctl restart pwnagotchi.service
```

Your display will now indicate the Pwnagotchi unit's current level and experience, as determined by several metrics that you can customize. The result is shown in Figure 9-19.

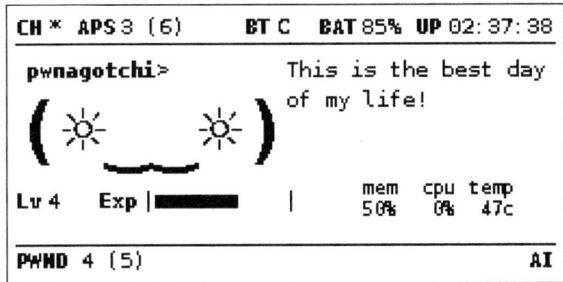

Figure 9-19: A Pwnagotchi unit with the experience plug-in enabled

The level and experience values are computed from the number of lifetime AP associations, successful deauthentications, handshakes captured, and best rewards achieved. The plug-in also includes a custom face that appears when the unit successfully levels up.

Testing with Kismet

Are you curious to see how Pwnagotchi's attacks appear to a target network? If you've completed the recipe in Chapter 7, you already have one of the best tools available for precisely this: Kismet. With a Pwnagotchi unit, a separate device running Kismet, and (optionally) a computer to access Kismet's web interface, you have all the basic elements of a Wi-Fi security test bench.

Like Pwnagotchi, Kismet requires a WLAN adapter that supports monitor mode. In the Kismet recipe, an external adapter is used to fulfill this requirement. With both systems running, Kismet will raise an alert each time it detects one of Pwnagotchi's deauthentication attacks. You should also observe it sending association frames to nearby APs.

Another similarity to Pwnagotchi is that Kismet also stores packets captured from its monitored wireless interface as *.pcap* files. You can use tcpdump, as described in "Processing PCAP Files" on page 295, for preliminary analysis of these files. Alternatively, you can use popular GUI-based network analysis tools like Wireshark. With timestamped PCAP files from the attacker and the target network, you have the raw material to examine these exploits from both sides, down to the individual packet level.

Streamlining Your Data Collection

If you're like me, you'll probably repeatedly take your Pwnagotchi for a walk, return home, connect to it in MANUAL mode, and examine its findings. With practice, you'll acquire a greater familiarity with its log output, file locations, and so on. I've compiled these quick tips to help streamline this process.

Default Folder Locations

When working with Pwnagotchi in MANUAL mode, it can be helpful to know the locations of certain files and folders. The more common ones are summarized in Table 9-2 for easy reference.

Table 9-2: Default File and Folder Locations

Folder	Location
Default plug-ins directory	/usr/local/lib/python3.11/dist-packages/ pwnagotchi/plugins/default/
Custom plug-ins directory	/usr/local/share/pwnagotchi/custom-plugins/
Configuration directory	/etc/pwnagotchi/
Neural network	/root/brain.nn
Details about neural network	/root/brain.json
Primary logfile	/etc/pwnagotchi/log/pwnagotchi.log
Peers history	/root/peers/
Handshakes captured	/root/handshakes/

Note that, with the exception of the plug-ins (which you'll need to reinstall manually), backing up these files will enable you to effectively clone your Pwnagotchi unit. A related restore script will permit you to re-create your unit with a fresh SD card. For details, see "Performing a Full Backup and Restore" on page 288.

Bash Aliases

After experimenting with Pwnagotchi for some time, you may find it useful to have an uncluttered view of the log messages it generates. You can enable this by adding an alias to *.bashrc*, the user configuration file for the bash shell. Open the logged-in user's bash configuration in your editor with

```
$ nano ~/.bashrc
```

and append the following lines:

```
LOG_FILE=/etc/pwnagotchi/log/pwnagotchi.log
alias pwnlog='tail -f -n300 $LOG_FILE | \
    sed --unbuffered "s/,[[:digit:]]\{3\}\]//g" | cut -d " " -f 2-'
```

Save the file and exit your editor, then reload *.bashrc*'s settings by sourcing the file with **source ~/.bashrc**. Thereafter, executing **pwnlog** at the terminal prompt will follow (or tail) Pwnagotchi's log activity in a human-readable format. Interrupt the log output with CTRL-C.

Wrapping Up

A big part of Pwnagotchi's popularity stems from its relative ease of assembly and the ability to personalize nearly every aspect of its design. As a result, no two Pwnagotchi units are alike, and each is a reflection of its owner. Likewise, it has broad appeal for both casual users and those who prefer to dig deep into its internals.

In this chapter, you examined in detail the sophisticated technology stack behind Pwnagotchi's friendly exterior. This includes TensorFlow, the machine learning framework used in its predictive modeling, and its associated API, Keras. For those with an interest in deep reinforcement learning, you learned how the Advantage Actor–Critic algorithm works with TensorFlow to optimize search parameters in a complex, ever-changing wireless environment.

On the security side, you saw how Bettercap is effective as a stand-alone utility for reconnaissance of both wired and wireless networks and explored how it's used to conduct various types of attacks on Wi-Fi networks, such as deauthenticating client stations and sending association frames. On the firmware end, you learned how the Nexmon patching framework is used to enable monitor mode in popular WLAN chipsets.

Finally, you learned how Wi-Fi handshakes captured by Bettercap, stored as PCAP files, can be analyzed with tools such as tcpdump, Hcxtools, and Hashcat. When used within an ethical framework, these tools provide the means to recover, or crack, Wi-Fi passphrases from networks discovered by Pwnagotchi, making it a valuable platform for exploring and understanding modern Wi-Fi security.

10

EXPLORING MESH NETWORKING

As you learned in Chapter 1, Wi-Fi networks operate in one of two ways: infrastructure or ad hoc mode. The vast majority of wireless networks we interact with operate in infrastructure mode, where all devices communicate through a single access point. Ad hoc mode, by contrast, doesn't rely on a centralized router but rather distributes control to individual peers in the network.

Mesh networking, as its name implies, is meant to work via a large number of short-haul connections without any sort of centralized control. This is in contrast to traditional networks that follow a hub-and-spoke topology, where all devices connect to a central router or Wi-Fi base station. A proper mesh network should configure itself dynamically, responding to the addition and removal of nodes and changes in connectivity. In a well-functioning mesh, networking "just happens" without high-level coordination.

Mesh networks have earned a reputation as being difficult for do-it-yourself enthusiasts to implement. In this chapter, I'll dispel this myth by demonstrating a clear, methodical approach to building a resilient and scalable mesh network with inexpensive, off-the-shelf components. This recipe will work with two or more Raspberry Pi devices. Once you've successfully connected two nodes by using the ad hoc wireless routing protocol, the only limitation is available hardware: You can apply the same configuration steps to subsequent nodes and expand the mesh with ease.

A Brief History

The decentralized and ad hoc nature of mesh networks affords them many advantages. A network of this type is often described as *self-healing*, meaning that if one node fails or becomes unavailable, data packets can still be routed through alternate paths. This redundancy and fault tolerance implies that mesh networks should, in theory, be very difficult to disrupt.

It should perhaps come as no surprise that the origins of wireless mesh networks can be traced back to military applications. Among the earliest known wireless mesh networks was the Packet Radio Network (PRNET) project initiated by the Defense Advanced Research Projects Agency (DARPA) in the late 1970s. This project involved the development of protocols and algorithms for routing data through a network of wireless nodes, paving the way for today's modern mesh networks.

MIT's Roofnet project in the early 2000s was an initiative to deploy a large-scale wireless mesh network to provide internet access to residents in Cambridge, Massachusetts. Roofnet's technology later formed the basis for Meraki, a mesh networking startup spun off by several MIT engineers. Meraki was subsequently acquired by Cisco Systems and is still in use today.

Around the same time in Europe, the Freifunk Paderborn project was started to deliver free and open wireless mesh connectivity to residents in the city of Paderborn, Germany. Participants install open source firmware on their wireless routers, which allows them to share a portion of their internet connection with others in the community. The Freifunk mesh network has been in operation continuously since 2002 (a section of the network is illustrated in Figure 10-1).

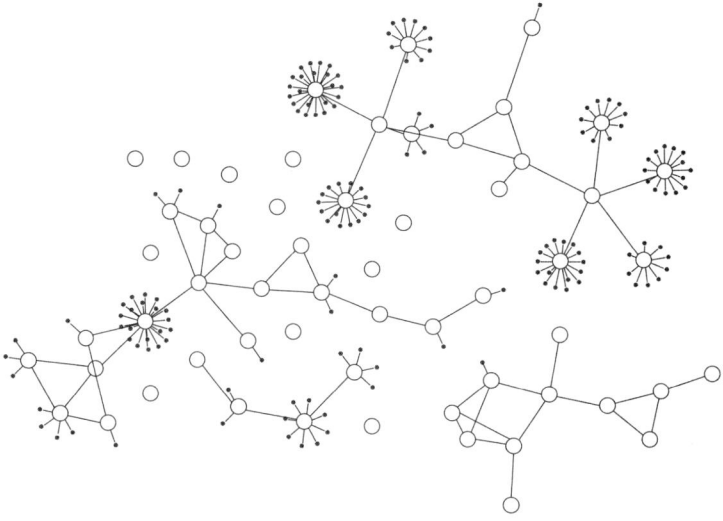

Figure 10-1: A small section of the Freifunk Paderborn wireless mesh network simulation

Since its introduction, Freifunk has grown into a global movement promoting community-driven mesh networking with open source software.

Use Cases

Initiatives like Freifunk are among the most popular examples of practical, community-based mesh network applications. These types of networks have also proven to be essential in providing communication lifelines when traditional networks have been either destroyed or severely disrupted. Since they can be deployed quickly, mesh networks have been used in the aftermath of numerous natural disasters in recent years, including earthquakes, hurricanes, floods, and wildfires.

Today, many commercial product offerings aim to replace your home Wi-Fi base station with a small constellation of wireless mesh nodes. A key value proposition to consumers is that these systems, while somewhat pricier on average than traditional home network router setups, require very little knowledge to deploy. A home user needn't know anything about what's happening under the hood; the mesh nodes dynamically and continuously adjust their routing parameters to optimize coverage and throughput.

Owing to the relatively small size, weight, and power requirements of wireless mesh hardware, NASA has identified this technology for use in both human and robotic space exploration. One recent area of practical research at NASA has focused on the Orion spacecraft's camera system. In fact, the mesh protocol evaluated by NASA is the very same one you'll be using in this chapter.

Hardware Required

This recipe can be implemented with any number of available Raspberry Pi devices. If my experience is any indication, you may find yourself eager to press additional devices into service after the mesh is up and running, making this recipe ideally suited as a group project.

Compatible Raspberry Pi Models

It's certainly possible to build a proof-of-concept mesh network with just two devices. However, things become more interesting as more nodes are added to the network. The only strict requirement is an available USB port that can accept an external wireless adapter. In addition, at least one device on your mesh network should be equipped with an Ethernet port, for reasons that will be discussed in the implementation steps.

You can use any Raspberry Pi model for this project, but its affordability and small form factor make the Zero 2 W an ideal choice. If you opt to use this model, bear in mind that you'll need a micro USB to USB-C adapter to connect an external wireless adapter, as the onboard WLAN chipset does not support the required mesh mode.

The Pi Zero 2 W is widely available from online retailers for around $15. It comes standard without a GPIO header, as pictured in Figure 10-2, so you'll need to obtain a 40-pin header and perform some basic soldering to attach it.

Figure 10-2: A standard Pi Zero 2 W

Alternatively, you can avoid soldering by purchasing a model with a presoldered header. Several retailers offer these, usually at little extra cost.

Mesh-Capable Adapter

If you've followed the recipe in Chapter 7, you'll already be familiar with the Edimax EW-7811Un Nano. This inexpensive yet capable USB wireless adapter, shown in Figure 10-3, has everything you need to begin exploring mesh networking, including in-kernel Linux driver support.

Figure 10-3: The Edimax EW-7811Un USB wireless adapter

At minimum, your Pi-based mesh network will comprise two nodes, so plan on budgeting for an equal number of these adapters. The Edimax adapter is available from various online retailers from about $13.

Squid RGB (Optional)

You'll acquire hands-on experience with several software tools for monitoring your mesh network in this chapter, but it can be quite useful to have at-a-glance visual indicators of network packet traffic on your mesh nodes. As an optional component, the Pi Hut's Squid RGB is an excellent addition to this project; you can pick up one for each node you want to monitor in this way.

As shown in Figure 10-4, the Squid RGB has separate leads that control the red, green, and blue channels of the attached LED.

Figure 10-4: The Squid RGB from
the Pi Hut

The Squid RGB's lead sockets fit directly onto the Pi's GPIO header, so no soldering is required. It's available directly from the Pi Hut for about $6.

Uninterruptible Power Supply HAT

Optionally, you may choose to equip one or more of your Raspberry Pi Zero 2 Ws with an add-on battery HAT. This isn't strictly necessary, but you can often gain great insights if one or more of the nodes in your mesh network is completely untethered and free to move around a given service area. This is an excellent way to evaluate the self-healing nature of your mesh and to observe how a phenomenon known as *hopping* occurs in practice.

Many affordable options exist for the Raspberry Pi Zero and other models. A favorite in my testing lab is the Waveshare UPS HAT, shown in Figure 10-5.

Figure 10-5: The Waveshare UPS HAT for
Raspberry Pi Zero

It's available directly from Waveshare for about $24.

Software Used

The primary software component you'll be using for this recipe is the Better Approach to Mobile Ad hoc Networking (BATMAN) protocol. A BATMAN mesh is made up of a set of *originators*, which communicate via network interfaces such as standard wireless adapters. Periodically, each originator broadcasts an originator message (OGM) to all its neighbors to announce its presence. Each neighbor makes a note of the presence of the originator and rebroadcasts the message to its own neighbors. The net effect is that, over time, every node in the mesh receives the OGM (possibly via multiple paths) and learns both that the originator exists and which of its neighbors provides the best path to reach it. Each node maintains a routing table that lists every node it has ever heard of, along with the best next hop to reach that node.

This protocol has the advantage of building and updating the routing tables on the fly, with no central coordination needed. It should also find near-optimal routes to each node. If a node goes offline, the routing tables will reconfigure themselves to maintain connectivity in its absence. In all but the smallest networks, no single node has a complete view of how the mesh is constructed; each node knows only which of its neighbors are available and which is the best next hop to get to a given node. This decentralized approach adds to the security and robustness of the mesh.

Implemented in Linux as the `batman-adv` kernel module, the BATMAN protocol has been part of the official kernel since version 2.6.38, released in early 2011. This module operates at Layer 2 of the OSI network model (the Data Link layer, discussed in the box titled "The OSI Network Model Explained" on page 322). As the module is already present in most Linux kernels, you shouldn't need to install it from scratch.

Because `batman-adv` operates in kernel land, a tool to manage the module and debug the network is required. The `batctl` utility was created to fill that role and has proven an indispensable companion to `batman-adv`.

KERNEL VS. USERLAND

In this context, *kernel land* (or *kernel space*) refers to the privileged area of virtual memory where the operating system's kernel is stored and executed. Modern operating systems, including Linux, use this separation to protect the kernel from malicious or errant software and to isolate hardware access.

By contrast, *userland*, also known as *user space*, is the area of memory where code that runs outside the operating system's kernel (such as application software, libraries that interact with the kernel, and some drivers) resides. This division is depicted in the following illustration, which shows a typical Linux operating system architecture.

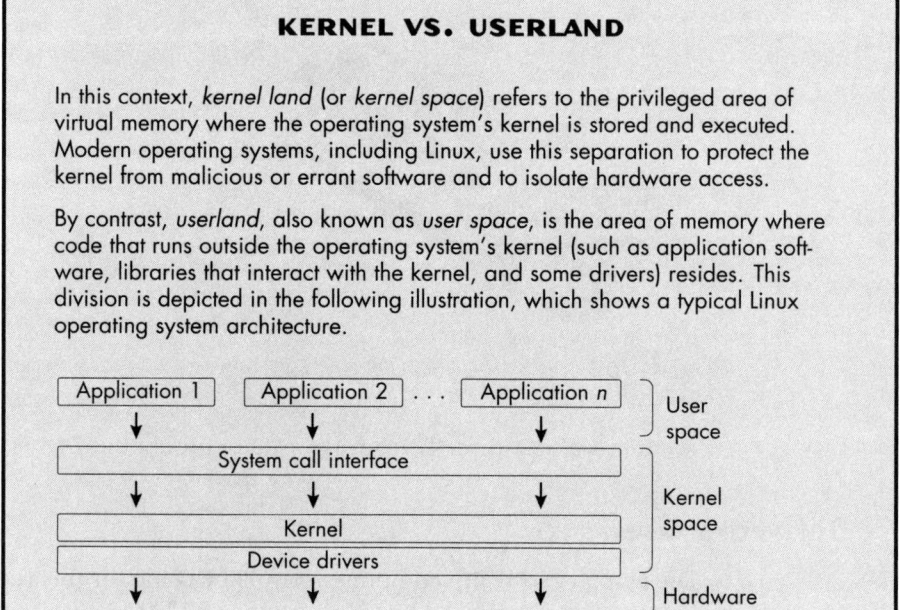

Naturally, this recipe wouldn't be a complete without a dash of Python. Once you delve into the wilds of mesh networking, you'll likely want to add more devices to your network, and you'll want to be able to monitor their status at a glance. While not required for operation of the mesh network, you can use a bit of Python code to flash an LED attached to your Pi. This will give you a simple mesh network traffic indicator.

This recipe will walk you through creating the mesh network step-by-step, so you can gain hands-on experience with the tools and processes involved. After that, you'll use a simple bash script to help you automate this process.

All the source code for this recipe is available at *https://github.com/ wirelesscookbook/pi-mesh*.

Preparing the Nodes

To maximize the flexibility of your setup, you'll configure your mesh network nodes to operate without an Ethernet connection from the outset. With the nodes untethered by a network cabling, you'll be better able to move them around to test the resiliency of your mesh. You can, of course, make them entirely wireless by trading the power supplies for attached battery modules. Later, I'll discuss configuring one node as a gateway to provide internet connectivity to the rest of the network.

There is no hard-and-fast rule about using `wpa_supplicant` instead of Ethernet here. If you prefer to access your devices with `eth0` rather than a wireless interface, the outcome of the recipe will be the same.

For ease of setup later on, leave your Edimax EW-7811Un USB wireless adapter disconnected at this stage. You'll perform some basic configuration steps later to assist with streamlining the build process.

You'll need a minimum of two devices to create a basic mesh network. As noted in "Hardware Required," on page 311, you can use any Raspberry Pi model capable of supporting a USB wireless adapter. Repeat the steps described here for each device you plan to deploy on your network.

Begin by preparing the SD card. For this recipe, you'll use a legacy version of Raspberry Pi OS, Bullseye Lite (64- or 32-bit). The Bookworm distribution's kernel drivers for the wireless chipset used here require additional work to fully support the mesh networking mode, but Bullseye includes well-tested drivers that are known to work reliably with this recipe's hardware.

Flash a fresh SD card with Raspberry Pi OS (Legacy) Lite, available on the official download page, then create an empty file named *ssh* (no extension) and save it to the card's boot partition.

You'll use `wpa_supplicant` to connect to your existing wireless network. The built-in wireless interface will handle connecting your device to the network, while the interface provided by the USB wireless adapter will be used to create the mesh network. Using your preferred editor, create a file called *wpa_supplicant.conf* with the following contents:

```
ctrl_interface=DIR=/var/run/wpa_supplicant GROUP=netdev
update_config=1
country=US

network={
    ssid="your_SSID"
```

```
    psk="your_wi-fi_password"
    key_mgmt=WPA-PSK
}
```

Substitute your two-letter ISO 3166-1 alpha-2 country code for US if you're not in the United States, and be sure both your network SSID and your password (PSK) are enclosed in double quotes. Copy this file to the card's boot partition. You'll need to complete this step before you boot the SD card for the first time, as that's the point at which the system checks for the presence of the *wpa_supplicant.conf* file.

Alternatively, you can perform this configuration step with the Raspberry Pi Imager tool while writing the OS to your SD card. Under **OS Customisation**, choose the **Wireless LAN** option and enter an SSID (name) and the password for your network. If the network doesn't broadcast an SSID publicly, enable the **Hidden SSID** setting.

Finally, ensure that your Pi is within range of your wireless router, then insert the SD card and connect it to power.

Creating the Mesh Network

At this stage, I'll assume that your required minimum two devices are booted and accessible on your WLAN. As with the previous section, repeat the steps described here for each device you plan to configure for your network.

The batman-adv driver is already present in the Linux kernel, but you'll need to install its companion userland tool, batctl. This will provide you with a full set of tools for creating, monitoring, and troubleshooting a single mesh node or the entire network. You'll also install git to support a later step. Since you're starting with a clean OS, begin with a full upgrade to be sure you have the latest kernel and packages, then install these prerequisites and reboot:

```
$ sudo apt update && sudo apt full-upgrade
$ sudo apt install batctl git
$ sudo reboot
```

You'll need to instruct the DHCP client daemon, dhcpcd, to ignore wlan1 when discovering new interfaces. To do this, use dhcpcd's denyinterfaces pattern. Open *dhcpcd.conf* in your editor with

```
$ sudo nano /etc/dhcpcd.conf
```

and add this directive to the end of the file:

```
denyinterfaces wlan1
```

Next, instruct dhcpcd to configure the wlan0 interface with wpa_supplicant. Append the following below the line you added previously:

```
interface wlan0
wpa-conf /etc/wpa_supplicant/wpa_supplicant.conf
```

Save the file and exit your editor. With these steps done, restart the dhcpcd service for the changes to take effect:

```
$ sudo systemctl restart dhcpcd.service
```

If you're using NetworkManager, use the following modification to stop it from managing the Wi-Fi adapter:

```
$ sudo touch /etc/network/interfaces
$ sudo echo "iface wlan1 inet manual" > /etc/network/interfaces
```

Now, connect your Edimax EW-7811Un wireless adapter to one of the Pi's USB ports. By connecting it after boot, you can more reliably have it bound to wlan1, which leaves it unused by wpa_supplicant and ready to be put into service as a mesh point. With the adapter connected to your device, run lsusb to confirm that it's recognized by the OS. You should see information such as the device ID, manufacturer, model name, and chipset.

If this is a fresh install, ensure that Wi-Fi isn't blocked by rfkill:

```
$ sudo rfkill unblock wlan
```

At this point, you can use iw to list the available wireless devices. For clarity, I'll refer to this first node as *Mesh-Pi #1*. Example output is shown here (yours may differ):

```
$ iw dev
phy#1
    Interface wlan1
        ifindex 4
        wdev 0x100000001
        addr 80:1f:02:9b:b0:c4
        type managed
        txpower 20.00 dBm
phy#0
    Interface wlan0
        ifindex 3
        wdev 0x1
        addr dc:a6:32:3d:ff:9d
        ssid Home-Router
        type managed
        channel 11 (2462 MHz), width: 20 MHz, center1: 2462 MHz
        txpower 31.00 dBm
```

Take note of the physical address (phy#1, in this example) for the adapter bound to the wlan1 interface. You can inspect this wireless device's capabilities by running:

```
$ iw phy1 info | grep "Supported interface modes" -A10
    Supported interface modes:
        * IBSS
```

```
* managed
* AP
* AP/VLAN
* monitor
* mesh point
* P2P-client
* P2P-GO
--snip--
```

Notice that the Edimax adapter's mesh point mode is listed as an available option. Since you know the physical address (phy#1) and the interface (wlan1), you may now use iw to reconfigure this interface as a mesh point. Begin by removing the existing interface so you can define its type:

```
$ sudo iw dev wlan1 del
```

Now, redefine this interface as a mesh type, like so:

```
$ sudo iw phy phy1 interface add wlan1 type mesh
```

You can confirm the change by checking the output of iw again:

```
$ iw wlan1 info
Interface wlan1
    ifindex 5
    wdev 0x100000002
    addr 80:1f:02:9b:b0:c4
    type mesh point
    wiphy 1
    txpower 20.00 dBm
```

Next, use ip to set the MTU value for the interface, then call iw to join it to the pi-mesh network (you can change this name if you like, just be sure to use it consistently):

```
$ sudo ip link set mtu 1532 dev wlan1
$ sudo ip link set wlan1 up
$ sudo iw dev wlan1 mesh join pi-mesh
```

Now, you'll use batctl to instruct the batman-adv kernel module to create the new virtual bat0 mesh interface:

```
$ sudo batctl if add wlan1
$ sudo ip link set up dev bat0
```

These commands will typically not produce any output in the terminal. However, you can use dmesg to view these events in the kernel's ring buffer by executing the following command:

```
$ dmesg | grep batman_adv
[  145.630607] batman_adv: B.A.T.M.A.N. advanced 2022.3 loaded
```

```
[  145.635757] batman_adv: bat0: Adding interface: wlan1
[  145.635886] batman_adv: bat0: Interface activated: wlan1
```

Each `batman-adv` node maintains a list of all single-hop neighbors it detects. Whether a single-hop neighbor is routed to directly or via another neighbor is determined based on the link quality. You can view the current node's neighbor table with:

```
$ sudo batctl neighbors
[B.A.T.M.A.N. adv 2020.4, MainIF/MAC: wlan1/80:1f:02:9b:b0:c4
(bat0/66:24:2a:20:a2:71 BATMAN_IV)]
IF              Neighbor             last-seen
```

At the moment, no other nodes are visible because you haven't yet enabled mesh support on your other devices.

Working with MTU Values

In TCP/IP networking, the *maximum transmission unit (MTU)* refers to the size, in bytes, of the largest datagram that a given layer of a communications protocol may pass in a single transaction. A large MTU value requires less overhead, while a smaller MTU has less delay. This value will vary depending on the most appropriate size for a given application.

The default MTU size for most Ethernet networks is 1,500 bytes. You can check the MTU setting for the interfaces on your device by running:

```
$ ip a | grep mtu
1: lo: <LOOPBACK,UP,LOWER_UP> mtu 65536 noqueue state UNKNOWN group default
2: eth0: <BROADCAST,MULTICAST,UP,LOWER_UP> mtu 1500 state UP group default
3: wlan0: <BROADCAST,MULTICAST,UP,LOWER_UP> mtu 1500 state UP group default
4: wlan1: <BROADCAST,MULTICAST,UP,LOWER_UP> mtu 1532 state UP group default
6: bat0: <BROADCAST,MULTICAST,UP,LOWER_UP> mtu 1500 state UNKNOWN group default
```

The Linux module `batman-adv` will advise you, via `dmesg`, when the MTU setting of your configured mesh interface falls outside its recommended range. For example, you may see a message such as:

```
The MTU interface wlan1 is too small (1500) to handle the transport of
batman-adv packets. Packets going over this interface will be fragmented
on layer2 which could impact performance. Setting the MTU to 1532 would
solve the problem.
--snip--
```

The MTU value is reflected in your configuration for the Edimax EW-7811Un wireless adapter's `wlan1` interface. If you receive an error such as "MTU greater than device maximum," this usually indicates a limitation of the wireless adapter hardware. Helpfully, `ip` will report the minimum and maximum supported MTU values for a given interface. Use the `-d` or

-details option with `ip` and pipe it through `grep` to get detailed information about the interface:

```
$ ip -details link list | grep wlan1 -A1
5: wlan1: <BROADCAST,MULTICAST,UP,LOWER_UP> mtu 1532 bat0 state UP mode DEF...
    link/ether 74:da:38:ed:5e:7d... promiscuity 0 minmtu 256 maxmtu 2304
```

These values appear as `minmtu` and `maxmtu` in the output.

Adding More Nodes

To add more nodes to your mesh network, repeat the steps in the preceding section on your other device(s). When you're done, execute the following commands on each device to view the interface status and neighbor table, respectively. On Mesh-Pi #1, you should see output similar to this:

```
$ sudo batctl interface
wlan1: active

$ sudo batctl neighbors
[B.A.T.M.A.N. adv 2020.4, MainIF/MAC: wlan1/80:1f:02:9b:b0:c4
(bat0/d6:43:53:6c:61:88 BATMAN_IV)]
IF          Neighbor              last-seen
wlan1       74:da:38:ed:5e:94     0.570s
```

Now, execute the same commands on Mesh-Pi #2. Take note of the different MAC addresses:

```
$ sudo batctl interface
wlan1: active
$ sudo batctl neighbors
[B.A.T.M.A.N. adv 2020.4, MainIF/MAC: wlan1/74:da:38:ed:5e:94
(bat0/0e:36:d1:d2:dc:28 BATMAN_IV)]
IF          Neighbor              last-seen
wlan1       80:1f:02:9b:b0:c4     0.290s
```

As you can see, the MAC addresses of each device in the mesh is visible to the other node.

In these examples, the `batman-adv` interface `bat0` is used as a default parameter. You can specify the interface to use with the `meshif` option, and you can use the abbreviated form of the `neighbors` command, `n`, if you prefer:

```
$ sudo batctl meshif bat0 n
```

Diagnosing Mesh Network Connectivity

Most wireless routing protocols operate at Layer 3 of the OSI network model (see the box titled "The OSI Network Model Explained" on page 322 for a brief overview). This means they exchange routing information by sending UDP packets and make routing decisions by manipulating the kernel routing table. By contrast, `batman-adv` operates entirely at Layer 2, meaning it handles not only the routing information but also the data traffic itself. In practice, `batman-adv` encapsulates and forwards all traffic until it reaches its destination, effectively emulating a virtual network switch with all nodes participating. This is illustrated in Figure 10-6.

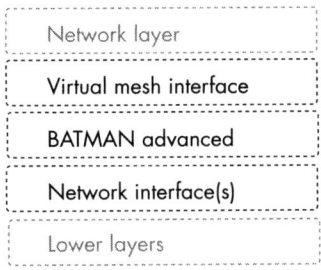

Figure 10-6: The batman-adv encapsulation structure

For this reason, all nodes appear to be *link-local* and are unaware of the network's topology. Similarly, mesh nodes are unaffected by changes within the network.

LINK-LOCAL ADDRESSES

In this context, *link-local* refers to addresses on a TCP/IP network that interfaces can automatically adopt if an address has not been manually configured for them or assigned by DHCP. These addresses are often used for automatic address configuration or neighbor discovery within a single link, or when no router is present. They also enable direct communication between nodes on the same network segment.

Traditional network debugging tools based on the Internet Control Message Protocol (ICMP), such as `ping` and `traceroute`, won't work as expected with `batman-adv`. This is because all traffic in the mesh is transported to its destination transparently at Layer 2, so higher-layer protocols have no visibility of hop counts or path details.

This transparency is one of the main reasons you can roam around without breaking your connection. To provide comparable diagnostic tools, `batman-adv` includes its own version of ICMP, which is integrated directly into the protocol. Here, I'll demonstrate using `batctl ping` to inject IMCP packets that behave very similarly to their Layer 3 network counterpart.

Execute the following command on Mesh-Pi #1, replacing the MAC address with the one for your own device. Your output will differ, but it should have a similar format to the example output shown here:

```
$ sudo batctl ping 74:da:38:ed:5e:94
PING 74:da:38:ed:5e:94 (74:da:38:ed:5e:94) 20(48) bytes of data
```

```
20 bytes from 74:da:38:ed:5e:94 icmp_seq=7 ttl=50 time=12.99 ms
20 bytes from 74:da:38:ed:5e:94 icmp_seq=8 ttl=50 time=18.18 ms
```

You can also perform this ping test on Mesh-Pi #2:

```
$ sudo batctl ping 80:1f:02:9b:b0:c4
PING 80:1f:02:9b:b0:c4 (80:1f:02:9b:b0:c4) 20(48) bytes of data
20 bytes from 80:1f:02:9b:b0:c4 icmp_seq=1 ttl=50 time=6.01 ms
20 bytes from 80:1f:02:9b:b0:c4 icmp_seq=7 ttl=50 time=13.71 ms
```

Interrupt ping with CTRL-C. This is just a basic network connectivity test. In the sections that follow, I'll show you additional steps you can use to verify the integrity of your new mesh network.

THE OSI NETWORK MODEL EXPLAINED

The *Open Systems Interconnect (OSI) model* is a conceptual framework that breaks down networking into seven layers, each with its own role and responsibilities. These layers help engineers visualize what's going on in their networks and pinpoint where issues occur. For our purposes, we're primarily concerned with Layers 3 (Network), 2 (Data Link), and 1 (Physical). Here's a brief overview of each:

Layer 3 (Network) At the Network layer, you'll find most of the routing functionality that networking professionals and hobbyists work with. In its most basic sense, this layer is responsible for packet forwarding, including routing traffic through different routers.

Layer 2 (Data Link) The Data Link layer provides node-to-node data transfer between directly connected devices and handles error detection and correction from the Physical layer. It has two sublayers: the Media Access Control (MAC) layer and the Logical Link Control (LLC) layer. In the networking world, most switches operate at Layer 2; however, some also operate at Layer 3 to support virtual LANs that span more than one switch subnet, which requires routing capabilities.

Layer 1 (Physical) At the bottom of the OSI model is the Physical layer, which represents the electrical and physical hardware. This can include everything from radio frequencies (as in a Wi-Fi network) and voltages to cables, hubs, repeaters, and other physical assets. When a networking problem occurs, engineers commonly start at the Physical layer, checking that all the hardware is properly connected and no components have lost power.

Creating Mesh Hostnames

Until now, you've referred to your mesh devices by their MAC addresses. Here, you'll create a file called */etc/bat-hosts* and define hostnames for each device. This step is not required, but it can make common tasks easier to perform and help clarify diagnostic output, as the symbolic names will be used instead of the MAC addresses in the output of many batctl commands.

Create the file with

```
$ sudo nano /etc/bat-hosts
```

and define your mesh hostnames as shown here, replacing the MAC addresses with those of your devices:

```
80:1f:02:9b:b0:c4    mesh-pi1
74:da:38:ed:5e:94    mesh-pi2
```

You can use different names if you prefer; they don't need to match the device hostnames or be consistent with DNS or any other naming schemes. When you're done, save the file and exit your editor. The next time you execute a batctl command, you should see the mesh node MAC addresses replaced with symbolic names. For example:

```
$ sudo batctl meshif bat0 neighbors
[B.A.T.M.A.N. adv 2022.3, MainIF/MAC: wlan1/74:da:38:ed:5e:7d
  (bat0/66:52:d4:22:36:67 BATMAN_IV)]
IF        Neighbor          last-seen
wlan1     mesh-pi2          0.820s
```

This can be helpful for tracking and diagnosing issues with individual nodes, particularly in larger mesh networks. You may even want to consider affixing physical labels to your devices that correspond to these symbolic names.

Running at Boot

The steps you've used to configure each mesh node will need to be performed each time the device is rebooted. To streamline this process, you can combine them into a bash startup script that you can run after a reboot. Begin by cloning the companion GitHub repository for this project:

```
$ cd $HOME
$ git clone https://github.com/wirelesscookbook/pi-mesh.git
```

At the next device boot, reconnect the Edimax adapter to a USB port if necessary, then run **iw dev** to confirm that it's available for use. With the presence of the wlan1 interface verified, execute the startup script as shown here. The output should appear similar to the following:

```
$ cd $HOME/pi-mesh
$ ./startup.sh wlan1
Configuring wlan1 as mesh point
Physical wlan1 address is phy#1
Loading batman-adv kernel module
Releasing wlan1 interface
Adding wlan1 as mesh interface
Setting MTU value for batman-adv and joining pi-mesh
```

```
Adding wlan1 to batman-adv and bringing it up
Diagnostic output from batctl...
wlan1: active
[B.A.T.M.A.N. adv 2022.3, MainIF/MAC: wlan1/80:1f:02:9b:b0:c4
(bat0/ee:f8:60:47:7c:8a BATMAN_IV)]
IF          Neighbor              last-seen
wlan1       74:da:38:ed:5e:94     0.360s
```

If your mesh point interface is not `wlan1`, be sure to specify it when invoking the startup script. Otherwise, your device may become inaccessible when the interface is reconfigured. The script will automatically detect the physical interface, execute each of the required manual steps, and finish by performing a diagnostic with `batctl`, as indicated in the output, to check the status of the mesh interface and any connected nodes.

If you'd like this script to run automatically each time your mesh node boots, a *pi-mesh.service* systemd unit file is included in the GitHub repository. Begin by opening this file in your editor. If the path to *startup.sh* is different from */home/pi/pi-mesh*, be sure to adjust it accordingly in the unit file. Likewise, this service is configured to run as the *pi* user, but you can change this if necessary. When you're satisfied with the configuration, install and enable the service with:

```
$ sudo cp $HOME/pi-mesh/pi-mesh.service /etc/systemd/system/
$ sudo systemctl daemon-reload
$ sudo systemctl enable pi-mesh.service
```

Following a reboot, you can check its status with:

```
$ sudo systemctl status pi-mesh.service
```

You may have noticed that the `oneshot` type is defined in the systemd service unit file. This is used for services that perform a one-time task, then exit. In this case, the service handles initialization of the `wlan1` interface, brings up `bat0`, and joins the `pi-mesh` network. There's no need for the service to remain running in the background, so it appears as `inactive (dead)`. This is expected; you should see the status (`code=exited, status=0/SUCCESS`) returned in the output to indicate that it executed successfully.

Extending the Mesh Network

If you have additional devices to add to the mesh, repeat the previous steps for each one in turn. Verify each step, checking the kernel message log with `dmesg` to see if an error is thrown at any stage. Filtering kernel messages for `batman-adv` can be helpful for diagnosing problems. Example output is shown here:

```
$ dmesg | grep batman_adv
batman_adv: B.A.T.M.A.N. advanced 2022.3 (compatibility version 15) loaded
batman_adv: bat0: Interface deactivated: wlan1
```

```
batman_adv: bat0: Removing interface: wlan1
batman_adv: bat0: Adding interface: wlan1
batman_adv: bat0: Interface activated: wlan1
```

When you're satisfied with the state of your mesh network, move on to the next section, where you'll configure a gateway device to allow traffic to be routed to and from the internet.

Configure a Gateway and Allow Access

In the previous steps, you configured two or more Raspberry Pis to create a mesh network by using the batman-adv protocol. In this section, you'll ensure that you can access the devices forming the mesh and provide internet connectivity to them. To do this, you'll add a *gateway* node that allows mesh traffic to reach the internet, while maintaining a level of isolation and privacy for the mesh network itself. A visual representation is presented in Figure 10-7.

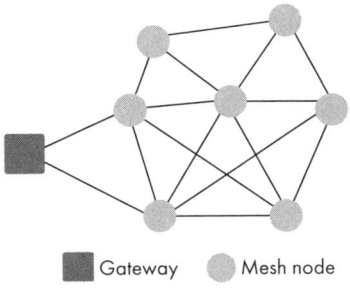

Gateway ● Mesh node

Figure 10-7: A conceptual view of a wireless mesh network with a single gateway

To make the internet uplink available to the mesh network, batman-adv lets you enable a so-called gateway mode. In this mode, the user-defined internet uplink bandwidth is propagated throughout the network. Since the gateway functionality is based on DHCP, as you'll see shortly, the protocol assumes that each gateway operates its own DHCP server and each client runs a DHCP client. When a DHCP client starts, it broadcasts a DHCP request to the entire network. Every available DHCP server sends a reply back to the client, which then chooses one of the responding DHCP servers as its gateway.

Depending on its topology, a mesh can have more than one gateway. Here, I'll demonstrate how to configure a single gateway for your mesh, but you can repeat the same process for any number of devices.

Adding a Gateway

To create a gateway, you'll need to select one device from your mesh network and configure it accordingly. For simplicity, connect this device to your external network via Ethernet, so it can be accessed via eth0. The other devices in your mesh can remain connected via wpa_supplicant, if you opted to go with a fully wireless setup.

Since you're using IP routing to selectively move traffic between the mesh and your external network, you'll need to define a unique address range. The steps outlined here assume the following network details:

```
Gateway address 192.168.99.1
Subnet mask     255.255.255.0
Address range   192.168.99.50 - 192.168.99.150
```

In the previous section, you used the DHCP client daemon, dhcpcd, to configure the wireless interfaces for individual nodes in your mesh. batman-adv doesn't assign IP addresses itself; to do this, you'll need to host a DHCP server on your gateway. A separate software package called dnsmasq will handle automatic IP address assignment within the mesh. Installing it is straightforward:

```
$ sudo apt update
$ sudo apt install dnsmasq iptables
```

With the dnsmasq package installed, you can configure it to provide IP addresses to client nodes on the bat0 mesh interface. To do this, you'll define a pool of available addresses for DHCP to draw from and set a lease time of 12 hours. This ensures that DHCP leases for devices that are no longer active on the network are freed, or released, after a predefined time. This helps make your mesh network more efficient, particularly if it's a dynamic one where nodes frequently go into and out of range.

Rather than editing the default dnsmasq configuration file (located at */etc/dnsmasq.conf*) directly, you can drop in a stand-alone configuration to keep things neater. Create the file in your editor with

```
$ sudo nano /etc/dnsmasq.d/bat0.conf
```

and add the following contents to it:

```
interface=bat0
dhcp-range=192.168.99.50,192.168.99.150,255.255.255.0,12h
```

Save the file and exit your editor. Next, you'll need to use a modified version of the startup script you created earlier for the gateway node. Examine the contents of this file by running:

```
$ cat $HOME/pi-mesh/startup-gw.sh
--snip--
iface=${1:-wlan1}
networkid="pi-mesh"

echo "Configuring ${iface} as mesh point..."

# get physical address of wlan1 adapter
addr=$(iw dev ${iface} info | awk '$1=="wiphy"{print $2}')
echo "Physical ${iface} address is phy#${addr}"

# load the module
echo "Loading batman-adv kernel module"
sudo modprobe batman-adv
--snip--

# tell batman-adv this is a gateway node
sudo batctl gw_mode server

# enable port forwarding
sudo sysctl -w net.ipv4.ip_forward=1
sudo iptables -t nat -A POSTROUTING -o eth0 -j MASQUERADE
sudo iptables -A FORWARD -i eth0 -o bat0 -m conntrack --ctstate RELATED,
  ESTABLISHED -j ACCEPT
sudo iptables -A FORWARD -i bat0 -o eth0 -j ACCEPT
--snip--
```

The key changes here are using `batctl` to tell `batman-adv` that this is a gateway node, assigning a static IP address to the gateway interface, and defining some NAT rules (as described earlier) with `iptables`. To ensure the `iptables` rules persist across reboots, install the following package:

```
$ sudo apt install iptables-persistent
```

At this point, your mesh node has all the required components to function as a gateway for the network. All that's left to do now is reboot the nodes and verify that IP addressing and internet access are working across your mesh network.

Rebooting the Mesh Network

Rebooting your gateway and the other nodes in the mesh will ensure that IP addressing and NAT are functioning as they should. Check that the gateway node is connected to your router via Ethernet, then reboot each of the Pis in your mesh network, starting with the gateway. Next, access the gateway node via `ssh` and run:

```
$ cd $HOME/pi-mesh
$ ./startup-gw.sh wlan1
--snip--
Configuring wlan1 as mesh point...

Physical wlan1 address is phy#0
Loading batman-adv kernel module
Releasing wlan1 interface
Adding wlan1 as mesh interface
Setting MTU value for batman-adv and joining pi-mesh
Tell batman-adv this is a gw_mode server
Enabling IP forwarding and NAT
net.ipv4.ip_forward = 1
Adding wlan1 to batman-adv and bringing it up
```

If you've installed the `pi-mesh` systemd service, you can skip the following step. Otherwise, connect to each of the other nodes via `ssh` and execute the "normal" (non-gateway-enabled) startup script:

```
$ cd $HOME/pi-mesh
$ ./startup.sh wlan1
```

When this process is complete, your mesh should be fully formed, and each node on the network should have an IP address assigned by the gateway. You'll confirm this in the next section.

Verifying Your Mesh

There are many tools and techniques you can use to verify the integrity of your mesh network. I'll demonstrate several of these here, starting with the gateway node. To begin, connect to the gateway via ssh and execute ip to inspect the configured network interfaces. The bat0 interface is isolated here for clarity:

```
$ ip a
--snip--
bat0: flags=4163<UP,BROADCAST,RUNNING,MULTICAST>  mtu 1500
      inet 192.168.199.1  netmask 255.255.255.0  broadcast 192.168.199.255
--snip--
```

Notice that the bat0 interface is configured with the gateway's static IP address, which you defined earlier. You should also see the eth0 interface configured with an IP address assigned by your router.

Next, use batctl to check the status of neighboring nodes as seen by the gateway:

```
$ sudo batctl neighbors
[B.A.T.M.A.N. adv 2022.3, MainIF/MAC: wlan1/80:1f:02:9b:b0:c4
(bat0/5e:26:41:3e:fd:7e BATMAN_IV)]
IF              Neighbor              last-seen
wlan1           mesh-pi#2             0.930s
wlan1           mesh-pi#3             0.070s
wlan1           mesh-pi#4             0.610s
wlan1           mesh-pi#5             1.780s
wlan1           mesh-pi#6             0.820s
```

The example output shows that several new mesh nodes have been added (symbolic names have been mapped to their MAC addresses in */etc/bat-hosts*, as discussed earlier).

Now, verify the nodes in your mesh. Choose one of the mesh-pi nodes and connect to it via ssh. Then use ip to inspect its bat0 interface, as you did with the gateway node:

```
$ ip a | grep bat0
bat0: <BROADCAST,MULTICAST,UP,LOWER_UP> mtu 1500 qdisc noqueue state
inet 192.168.99.133/24 brd 192.168.99.255 scope global dynamic noprefixroute bat0
--snip--
```

Notice that this node's bat0 interface has been assigned an IP address, 192.168.99.133, from the range you defined in the gateway node's dnsmasq service. If the bat0 interface doesn't have an IP address assigned, you can run dhclient bat0 to request one. Make note of this address for a later step.

Next, using the batctl commands you explored earlier, try inspecting the batman-adv interface status and neighboring mesh nodes.

Up to this point, you've been accessing your nodes via the onboard wireless interface, `wlan0`, configured with `wpa_supplicant`. The wireless connection to your router provides internet access in this configuration. To verify connectivity within your mesh and to the wider internet via the gateway, you can disable this interface. First, list your configured wireless devices:

```
$ iw dev
phy#1
    Interface wlan1
        ifindex 5
        wdev 0x2
        addr 74:da:38:ed:5e:94
        type mesh point
        channel 1 (2412 MHz), width: 20 MHz (no HT), center1: 2412 MHz
        txpower 20.00 dBm
phy#0
    Interface wlan0
        ifindex 3
        wdev 0x1
        addr dc:a6:32:3d:ff:9d
        ssid Home-Router
        type managed
        channel 11 (2462 MHz), width: 20 MHz, center1: 2462 MHz
        txpower 31.00 dBm
```

Note that bringing down the interface you're currently connected to via `ssh` will cause your terminal session to freeze. Don't worry; this is expected. I'll demonstrate an alternative method to access your device remotely.

In the preceding output, you can see that the `wlan0` interface is connected to `Home-Router`. Execute the following command to bring down this interface:

```
$ sudo ip link set down dev wlan0
```

At this point, your `ssh` session will become unresponsive because your device is no longer connected to your home network. Reconnect to your gateway node via `ssh`, using the IP address you noted earlier in place of `192.168.99.133`:

```
$ ssh pi@192.168.99.133
pi@192.168.99.133 password:
--snip--
```

If your username is different, you'll also need to replace `pi` with the name of your user. If you've set up key-based authentication, as described in "Key-Based Authentication" on page 44, you should now be connected remotely to this node over the mesh network via `ssh`. To verify that the gateway is providing internet access via IP forwarding and NAT, you can perform a basic ping test:

```
$ ping nostarch.com
PING nostarch.com (104.20.17.121): 56 data bytes
64 bytes from nostarch.com (104.20.17.121): icmp_seq=1 ttl=47 time=21.9 ms
64 bytes from nostarch.com (104.20.17.121): icmp_seq=2 ttl=47 time=14.6 ms
--snip--
```

Interrupt the ping test with CTRL-C. You may also want to use ip again to check the status of this mesh node's interfaces:

```
$ ip a
--snip--
2: eth0: <NO-CARRIER,BROADCAST,MULTICAST,UP> mtu 1500 qdisc pfifo_fast state DOWN
    group default qlen 1000
    link/ether b8:27:eb:f9:39:a8 brd ff:ff:ff:ff:ff:ff
3: wlan0: <BROADCAST,MULTICAST> mtu 1500 qdisc pfifo_fast state DOWN
    group default qlen 1000
    link/ether b8:27:eb:ac:6c:fd brd ff:ff:ff:ff:ff:ff
5: wlan1: <BROADCAST,MULTICAST,UP,LOWER_UP> mtu 1532 qdisc mq master bat0 state UP
    group default qlen 1000
    link/ether 74:da:38:ed:5e:94 brd ff:ff:ff:ff:ff:ff
    inet6 fe80::76da:38ff:feed:5e94/64 scope link
    valid_lft forever preferred_lft forever
6: bat0: <BROADCAST,MULTICAST,UP,LOWER_UP> mtu 1500 qdisc noqueue state UNKNOWN
    group default qlen 1000
    link/ether be:54:cb:4a:34:d8 brd ff:ff:ff:ff:ff:ff
    inet 192.168.99.133/24 brd 192.168.99.255 scope global dynamic noprefixroute
--snip--
```

Notice that the eth0 and wlan0 interfaces appear as DOWN, while the wlan1 interface is UP and associated with the virtual bat0 interface. Congratulations! Your node is successfully communicating on the mesh network, with internet connectivity provided by the gateway. While you're connected, you may also execute any of the batctl commands covered earlier to monitor the status of the mesh.

Managing Nodes with the Gateway

You may have noticed that the gateway is the only node that's directly accessible from your external network. The other mesh nodes remain hidden behind it. To access them, simply log in to the gateway node; you can then manage these nodes from the command line or access them directly via ssh. Bear in mind, however, that any external services that rely on network broadcast traffic, such as media servers or wireless printers, won't be passed through to the mesh network.

There are several ways you can survey nodes on the mesh, apart from using batctl and the batman-adv protocol. One method is to use the mesh gateway's dnsmasq service to check the active DHCP leases. You can do this by inspecting the contents of the leases file, like so:

```
$ cat /var/lib/misc/dnsmasq.leases
1640415313 be:54:cb:4a:34:d8 192.168.99.133 raspberrypi 01:be:54:cb:4a:34:d8
--snip--
```

Recall that you've set leases to expire after 12 hours, so this may not accurately reflect all active nodes. Another handy utility for this scenario is nmap (or *network mapper*), a staple in every network administrator's toolbox. Install it and use it to explore your mesh network by executing the following commands:

```
$ sudo apt install nmap -y
$ sudo nmap -sn 192.168.99.0/24
Starting Nmap 7.80 ( https://nmap.org ) at 2021-12-24 20:18 GMT
Nmap scan report for 192.168.99.133
Host is up (0.0014s latency).
--snip--
```

Here, the -sn option tells nmap to list available hosts that respond to discovery probes, without performing a port scan. Often called a *ping scan*, this will provide you with a list of all the active IP addresses belonging to nodes on your mesh network. As a reminder, these services and tools operate at Layer 3 of the mesh. You can, of course, inspect the single-hop mesh neighborhood at the protocol (Layer 2) level with sudo batctl neighbors periodically as well, and compare the results.

batman-adv will proactively do all the dynamic packet routing and "dead node" detection in your mesh for you. You can monitor all aspects of the network by using the suite of tools available from batctl, including tcpdump, traceroute, and more, as well as analyzing logfiles and debug tables, if needed. Execute **batctl -h** for a complete list of options.

In most cases, a batman-adv wireless mesh will optimize itself without your intervention as nodes enter and leave the network. There are still ways you can tweak it to better suit your specific requirements, however. These are discussed in "Pointers on Fine-Tuning" on page 333.

A Closer Look at the Protocol

The batman-adv algorithm works by dispersing knowledge about the optimal end-to-end paths between nodes in the mesh across all participating nodes. Each node maintains information only about the best next hop to every other node, making global knowledge about network topology unnecessary. This might sound like voodoo, but the inner workings of the algorithm will become clearer as you explore it further.

On a practical level, each node in a batman-adv mesh periodically broadcasts a *hello* signal, also known as an *originator message*, or *OGM*, to inform neighboring nodes of its existence. An OGM consists of an originator address, a sender address, and a unique sequence number. When a node receives an OGM, it changes the sending address to its own address and rebroadcasts the message according to specific rules. The sequence number is used to identify which of a pair of messages is newer. Through this process, each node in the network becomes aware of its own direct, or single-hop neighbors. At the same time, a node also learns about other nodes that aren't in range through a direct link but can be reached by hopping through a neighbor.

While node *A* is moving through the mesh, the route between *A* and *B* should recover as fast as possible. This process is illustrated in Figure 10-8, where *N1* and *N2* are intermediate nodes.

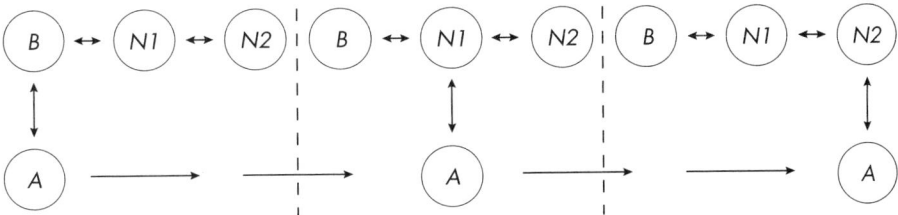

Figure 10-8: A visual representation of node mobility and hopping in a mesh network

OGMs that follow a path where the quality of wireless links is poor or where links are saturated will suffer from packet loss or delays on their way through the mesh. OGMs that travel along better routes will propagate faster and more reliably. The routing algorithm uses this information when selecting which neighbor to use as the next hop and updates its routing table accordingly.

Pointers on Fine-Tuning

Given this high-level view of how OGMs are used to build mesh routing tables, let's consider some scenarios in which you might tweak the network configuration to better suit your needs. To reduce the overhead of discovering all participants in the mesh, batman-adv can aggregate OGMs into a single packet rather than sending several smaller ones. This feature is enabled by default because it's helpful in the vast majority of setups. However, if you're operating batman-adv in a highly mobile environment (such as a fleet of vehicles, unmanned aerial vehicles, or robots), you may want to disable it, as it introduces a slight delay while updating the network. You can check and modify this setting as follows:

```
$ sudo batctl meshif bat0 aggregation
enabled
$ sudo batctl meshif bat0 aggregation 0
disabled
```

A related setting you can adjust for mobile environments is the *hop penalty*, which influences batman-adv's preference for multihop versus direct routes. This value is applied to each forwarded OGM. A higher hop penalty makes it less likely that other nodes will choose this node as an intermediate hop to any given destination, while a lower hop penalty may result in longer routes because retransmissions are not penalized.

The default hop penalty of 15 is a good balance for most mesh configurations and in most cases may be left as is. In mobile deployments, you might choose a higher value (up to a maximum of 255) to discourage other nodes from routing traffic through certain nodes. To view the current setting on any mesh node, run:

```
$ sudo batctl meshif bat0 hop_penalty
```

To change it, add the new value after the `hop_penalty` option. For example, to make sure a mobile node won't be chosen as a router, you might use:

```
$ sudo batctl meshif bat0 hop_penalty 255
```

As you saw in the previous section, a `batman-adv` node can operate in a gateway server mode in which it shares its internet connection with the rest of the mesh. One of the features of a gateway is its ability to announce its available internet bandwidth. The default gateway bandwidth is 10Mbps for downloads and 2Mbps for uploads. You can confirm this setting by running the following command on your gateway node:

```
$ sudo batctl meshif bat0 gw_mode
server (announced bw: 10.0/2.0 MBit)
```

As your mesh grows, it can be advantageous to configure more than one gateway. In these scenarios, gateways can adjust their announced bandwidth to more accurately represent their capabilities. To do this, enter the desired numbers separated with a forward slash (/), optionally followed by `kbit` or `mbit`):

```
$ sudo batctl meshif bat0 gw_mode server 20mbit/5mbit
```

The protocol will propagate these values throughout the mesh, allowing client nodes to select the best gateway based on criteria such as link quality and announced bandwidth.

These are a few of the common settings you can use to fine-tune your mesh network. Of course, `batman-adv` offers many more configuration options not covered here. If you'd like to make further adjustments to your mesh, a good practice is to establish a baseline by measuring latency between nodes (using the tools we've explored), then modify the settings on one or more nodes and observe how your metrics change.

For insights into additional mesh tuning parameters, visualized in real time, see "Using LED Activity Indicators" on page 336.

A Word on Security

One of the most common questions asked about `batman-adv`, and about wireless mesh networks in general, is: "How do I secure the mesh?" The short answer is, it depends on the type of security you need. Security is a broad topic. Most often, it involves authentication, encryption, or (probably) some combination of both. The environment in which you deploy your mesh will also shape its security requirements. In real-world implementations, achieving strong security always involves trade-offs, and even the most secure systems usually have vulnerabilities. You might opt for making your community wireless mesh secure enough for most clients to join, or for use in an emergency, but not so bulletproof that the system becomes unusable. After all, the plug-and-play nature of mesh networks is one of their greatest selling points.

In the case of authentication, the lack of central infrastructure in an ad hoc wireless mesh presents special challenges when it comes to establishing trust between nodes. Contrast this to the public internet, where we can use a public key infrastructure (PKI) with certificates and keys to secure data transfers between a client device, such as a web browser, and a server.

In the context of community wireless projects, the lack of a central authority in a self-organizing mesh means that it's often simpler to forgo encryption at the Wi-Fi link layer and implement security at higher layers. This means using encrypted channels with tools such as ssh and sftp rather than insecure protocols like telnet, for example.

One proposed approach for mesh authentication is to use special public key certificates called proxy certificates, combined with a neighbor trust mechanism. Together, these allow authentication and access control to be managed in a secure manner.

Monitoring the Mesh Network

You should now have a minimum of two active mesh nodes in your network. You may also have configured a third node as a gateway to provide internet connectivity to the network and to give you an entry point to manage your mesh nodes. If you haven't set up a gateway, you can continue to provide WLAN connectivity to your nodes via the onboard wireless adapter's wlan0 interface.

As noted in "Diagnosing Mesh Network Connectivity" on page 320, because batman-adv operates at Layer 2, traditional ICMP-based tools like ping and traceroute aren't able to provide their usual insights within the mesh. However, several other network tools can help you monitor the activity and overall health of your mesh nodes. These generally work by observing the flow of network packets transmitted and received over the mesh interface, then collecting and displaying various metrics. In addition to these terminal utilities, this section will demonstrate a monitoring technique that uses an optional hardware component and accompanying Python source code.

Using the Terminal

There are many command line tools you can use to monitor traffic over a batman-adv mesh interface. Several of the more popular utilities are described here. The one you choose will largely depend on your specific network diagnostic goals, as well as personal taste.

One popular tool is iftop, a real-time bandwidth monitor for the terminal. It listens to network traffic on a specific interface, or on the first interface it can find if none is specified. By default, iftop counts all IP packets that pass through its filter and tracks their direction as they transit the interface. It then displays a summary of current bandwidth usage. To install and run iftop on the bat0 interface, use the following commands:

```
$ sudo apt install iftop -y
$ sudo iftop -i bat0
```

After a few moments, you should see traffic between your node's bat0 interface and other nodes in the mesh. Note the directional traffic indicators (=> and <=) between the hosts. To exit the monitor, press Q.

Another popular tool is bmon (bandwidth monitor), which can be used to monitor network traffic over a mesh interface and its associated wireless interface simultaneously. Install it with:

```
$ sudo apt install bmon -y
```

Then launch it, specifying the bat0 and wlan1 interfaces for monitoring:

```
$ bmon -p bat0,wlan1
```

You can use the up and down arrow keys to toggle between the interfaces. To exit bmon, press Q.

The final network monitor tool I'll mention is slurm. Install it with:

```
$ sudo apt install slurm -y
```

Then run it, specifying the bat0 mesh interface with the -i option. The -L option enables software-based transmit/receive LED indicators:

```
$ slurm -i bat0 -L
```

Exit the program with a Q keystroke. In the next section, you'll implement a hardware-based monitoring technique.

Using LED Activity Indicators

Another way of visualizing how network traffic propagates through your mesh is by adding LED indicators to your nodes. This can be done with one or more Squid RGB add-ons and a dash of Python. As you saw in "Hardware Required" on page 311, this component provides a single LED with several fully controllable color channels.

Begin by connecting the Squid RGB to the GPIO header of the mesh node (or nodes, if you have multiple Squids) you want to monitor. If you're unsure of the GPIO pin numbering, execute **pinout** from the terminal for a handy reference. The black lead serves as a ground; connect this to one of the GND pins on the header. The GND pin between GPIO pins 18 and 23 is most convenient, as it permits you to connect the Squid's leads in a series. Next, connect the color-coded leads as follows:

- Red Squid lead to GPIO 18
- Green Squid lead to GPIO 23
- Blue Squid lead to GPIO 24

With that done, access the node and install the necessary dependencies:

```
$ sudo apt install python3-rpi.gpio python3-pip python3-psutil
$ pip3 install psutil
```

If you haven't done so already, clone this chapter's companion GitHub repository to your home directory. Then change to the project directory and open *netactivity.py* in your editor:

```
$ cd $HOME
$ git clone https://github.com/wirelesscookbook/pi-mesh.git
$ cd pi-mesh
$ nano netactivity.py
```

The *netactivity.py* Python script uses the Squid class, which provides a convenient interface to the standard RPi.GPIO library. Each of the Squid RGB's three color channels is controlled by a separate GPIO pin. These pins and their corresponding colors are defined in the following code sample:

```
from squid import Squid, RED, GREEN, OFF
from time import sleep
import psutil
import time
import sys

# GPIO pins for RED, GREEN, BLUE channels (BCM numbering)
RED_PIN = 17
GREEN_PIN = 27
BLUE_PIN = 22

led = Squid(RED_PIN, GREEN_PIN, BLUE_PIN)

# Default network interface
interface = 'wlan1'

def flash(color):
    led.set_color(color)
    time.sleep(0.01)  # Flash duration
    led.set_color(OFF)
```

```
try:
    while True:
        net_io = psutil.net_io_counters(pernic=True)
        interface_io = net_io.get(interface)
--snip--
```

Inside the main `while` loop, the `psutil` (process and system utilities) Python package is used to fetch information on system utilization—in this case, network I/O, or input and output, statistics. By comparing the current number of bytes sent and received over the selected interface to their previous values, the script can flash the corresponding LED color to indicate activity. This is handled by `flash(GREEN)` and `flash(RED)`, respectively. A short `time.sleep()` interval is added so each flash is visible. Execute the script with:

```
$ python netactivity.py wlan1 &
```

You can omit the `wlan1` argument if you like, as this is the default interface. If your mesh interface is something other than `wlan1`, be sure to specify it here.

Appending an ampersand (&) to the command line instructs the shell to run the command as a background process. The shell will respond with the process ID (PID) of the running program, followed by a message indicating the monitored interface. Pressing ENTER will return you to the bash command prompt, allowing you to perform other operations while the Python script is running. At any time, you can use the `jobs` command to view a list of background jobs. Use `fg %n` to bring a background job (job number *n*) to the foreground. To exit the Python script, press CTRL-C.

The first thing you may notice upon running the script is that the LED flashes green (send, or transmit) on your mesh nodes at regular intervals. This activity corresponds to the *hello* originator messages sent to inform neighboring nodes of their presence, as discussed in "A Closer Look at the Protocol" on page 332. You can determine the current setting for this interval by running:

```
$ batctl meshif bat0 orig_interval
```

The default interval value is 1,000 ms (1 s). This is generally suitable for small, relatively stable mesh networks. In larger or highly dynamic networks (where nodes move frequently or change often), decreasing this interval can help the network adapt more quickly to topology changes. However, bear in mind that this also increases overhead. To adjust the interval, specify a new parameter value in milliseconds:

```
$ sudo batctl meshif bat0 orig_interval 500
```

After making this change, restart the *netactivity.py* script and check that the green send LED flashes to confirm that it has taken effect. As you tune your mesh, monitor the network's performance using `batctl` and the command line tools discussed in the previous section. A good rule of thumb is to make incremental, rather than drastic, changes while fine-tuning the network.

Troubleshooting

If a node isn't able to join your mesh network, start by verifying that the `batman-adv` module is loaded. Then check the installed version using `batctl`, like so:

```
$ lsmod | grep batman_adv
$ batctl -v
batctl debian-2020.4-2 [batman-adv: 2022.3]
```

The example output indicates that the installed `batman-adv` version is 2022.3. In practice, different minor versions usually interoperate without issues, but major version differences (for example, 2020.1 versus 2023.1) can cause protocol compatibility problems. To ensure a stable and reliable mesh, I recommend that all nodes run the same version of the protocol.

If you suspect a node has lost connectivity to the mesh, a best practice is to begin by conducting basic ping and traceroute tests. As mentioned in "Diagnosing Mesh Network Connectivity" on page 320, you'll need to use `batctl`'s versions of these tools. You can identify a node by its MAC address or hostname, using commands like the following:

```
$ sudo batctl ping node_mac_address
$ sudo batctl traceroute hostname
```

Make sure to substitute the actual MAC address or hostname of the node you want to test in place of the placeholder values. If your node responds to these tests, you can further examine your mesh with these `batctl` diagnostics:

```
$ sudo batctl neighbors
$ sudo batctl originators
$ sudo batctl gateways
```

As a next step, you can check the global translation table with:

```
$ sudo batctl transglobal
```

This table maps client MAC addresses to the appropriate mesh nodes and ensures that packets are correctly routed to their destination nodes within the network. This routing information is especially vital in dynamic environments where nodes frequently change position. If your mesh is highly dynamic, consider tuning the `orig_interval` parameter value as described in "Using LED Activity Indicators" on page 336.

All `batman-adv` error messages, warnings, and information messages are written to the kernel log. To see these messages in the system logs, use the following commands:

```
$ journalctl -xe | grep batman
$ dmesg | grep batman
```

As a last measure, restarting a node will often permit it to rejoin the network. The mesh node startup scripts described in "Running at Boot" on page 323 are useful here.

Going Further

In the previous sections, you looked at several methods to verify and monitor connectivity between nodes in your mesh network, including optionally integrating an LED activity indicator. In terms of where to go from here, the direction you choose will be guided by your (or your future mesh community's) specific requirements, goals, and ambitions. Mesh networks afford many unique possibilities that set them apart from typical Wi-Fi networks. To provide some inspiration, I'll describe a few popular use cases drawn from existing mesh implementations.

The Freifunk Paderborn project, discussed at the beginning of this chapter, is one of the best-known and most successful community-based mesh networks worldwide. This project, which is part of the larger Freifunk ("free Wi-Fi") initiative in Germany, has the egalitarian aim of providing free and open internet access to its members and visitors. The project's open source ethos has inspired and enabled the growth of mesh-based free wireless connectivity in many other regions. Organized in a grassroots manner, local communities have formed their own networks and connected them together with wireless backbones, with uplinks to the wider internet established at several locations via secure VPN tunnels. A real-time map of one of these Freifunk community networks, connecting the municipalities of Mainz, Wiesbaden, and Umgebung, is shown in Figure 10-9.

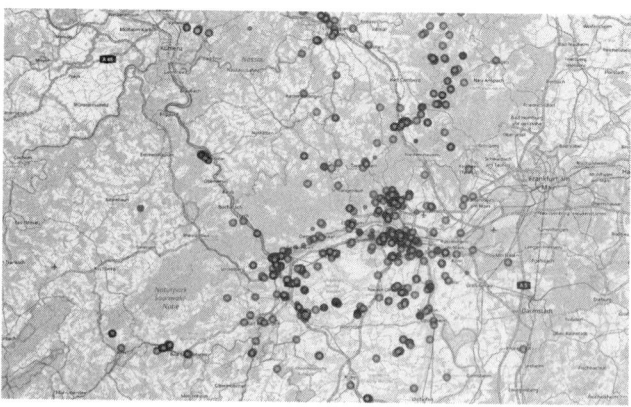

Figure 10-9: A real-time map of Freifunk community mesh nodes (OpenStreetMap, CC BY-SA 2.0)

As of this writing, more than a thousand mesh nodes are participating in this Freifunk region alone. Across Germany as a whole, this number exceeds many tens of thousands of nodes. All the devices in Freifunk operate as 802.11s mesh nodes using the same `batman-adv` protocol you've implemented here. Connecting to the network is done simply by flashing a supported router or access point with the Freifunk mesh firmware and powering it up. The device will then automatically mesh with other Freifunk router nodes that are within range.

Beyond free Wi-Fi, the Freifunk network provides many services to its participants, including chat via IRC and Mumble, radio and podcasts, collaborative writing, community calendars, and more. Perhaps most interestingly, the Freifunk Community API provides a mechanism for each community to make its resources known in a structured way. Powered by this API, a map of active Freifunk communities across Germany is available at *https://api-viewer.freifunk.net*.

The Freifunk initiative is an exceptional success story highlighting the potential of community-owned mesh networks. While a Raspberry Pi–based mesh network operating at this scale is theoretically possible, dedicated router hardware is generally better suited for this purpose. That said, I certainly encourage you to expand the `pi-mesh` network you've implemented here. To make it easier for others to join your `pi-mesh`, consider creating a baseline configuration based on the example in this chapter, then cloning the OS to create your own custom image. You can then distribute this image to other users so that they can more easily participate in the network.

If you're intrigued by the visual LED status indicators but find them lacking, the recipe from Chapter 3 can be modified to output any number of metrics associated with your mesh nodes. For example, you could parse the output of `batctl` to obtain a list of neighbors, originators, and gateway nodes within range of your node and output this to the TFT display. By querying these values at regular intervals, you can experimentally observe the process of hopping as nodes transit through the mesh.

Wrapping Up

In marked contrast to most of the other Wi-Fi networks covered in this book, this chapter has focused on implementing wireless mesh nodes that rely on an ad hoc routing protocol. The approach you followed uses low-cost, readily available components to create a mesh network that's both resistant to disruption and capable of scaling up as more nodes are added.

To achieve this, you interacted with network interfaces and the mesh protocol directly via the shell, and you used bash scripts from the companion GitHub repository to automate joining nodes to the mesh at system startup. Throughout this process, you saw how the mesh protocol operates entirely at Layer 2 of the OSI model, effectively emulating a virtual network switch to route traffic between nodes. You also learned about the vital role gateways play in providing an internet uplink to your network, as well as serving as an entry point for managing nodes in the mesh. To facilitate this, you used the mesh protocol and DHCP to designate a gateway node.

You examined the protocol itself to learn how messages are propagated between nodes, and you saw how nodes use this information to discover neighbors and route traffic efficiently. With this understanding of how mesh routing tables are created, you explored techniques for fine-tuning your mesh network. Finally, you looked at various methods for monitoring your mesh network, both via the terminal and by using hardware LED activity indicators.

11

WIRELESS DISPLAYS IN TWO WAYS

In the previous recipes, you've extended your Raspberry Pis with add-on components like mini TFT displays, LEDs, and status panels. These are great for indicating the status of a service or process, but otherwise they're pretty limited as output devices. All Raspberry Pi models support HDMI output, and many are capable of decoding 4K video at 60 frames per second (FPS). It's easy enough to connect your device to an external 4K-capable monitor via HDMI, but what if it could instead act as a receiver, streaming content wirelessly from mobile devices, laptops, and more?

In this recipe, you'll implement two popular wireless display technologies that enable you to stream content from a wide range of sources: Lazycast and RPiPlay. I'll also introduce *Wi-Fi Direct (WFD)*, a peer-to-peer protocol that's ideal for making this functionality possible.

Use Cases

There was a dark time when streaming media content required a tangle of cables and adapters. Today, thanks to wireless display technologies, we can effortlessly stream photos, video, web content, and more from a compatible computer or mobile device to a non-smart monitor, TV, or projection screen. The technology can roughly be described as "HDMI over Wi-Fi."

A wireless display receiver enables what is popularly known as *screen mirroring*. This has applications in home entertainment, work environments, and education, allowing you to mirror video, presentations, games, apps, photos—in short, anything you can display on a small screen—onto a larger one.

The main advantage of this technology is that it eliminates the need to track down the correct cable or adapter by removing the requirement for a physical connection to the primary display.

Hardware Required

Minimal hardware is required for this recipe. In addition to a Raspberry Pi, you'll need an inexpensive HDMI cable, which you might have on hand already. Optionally, depending on how you plan to deploy this project, a Video Electronics Standards Association (VESA)–compatible case is a nice finishing touch.

Compatible Raspberry Pi Models

A more recent device, such as a Pi 5 or 4 Model B, shown in Figure 11-1, is recommended if you anticipate streaming 4K video at 60 FPS. For less GPU-intensive activities, like sharing photos and apps, a Pi 3 Model B+ or even a Pi Zero 2 W will work fine.

Figure 11-1: The Raspberry Pi 4 Model B

The Pi 4 Model B is available from various online retailers for around $35. Table 11-1 lists this model's relevant video specifications. As you'll see, it's a very capable board for this recipe.

Table 11-1: The Raspberry Pi 4 Model B's Video Specs

Specification	Value
SoC	Broadcom BCM2711
CPU	4 × Cortex-A72, 1.5 GHz
GPU	Broadcom VideoCore VI
VPU decoding	4K @ 60 FPS video using H.265, 1080p @ 60 FPS video using H.264
VPU encoding	1080p @ 30 FPS video using H.264
Max screen resolution (16:9)	3840×2160 @ 60 Hz (2160p60)
OpenGL ES	1.1, 2.0, 3.0, 3.2 partially
RAM	1GB, 2GB, 4GB, 8GB (LPDDR4)

This Raspberry Pi model can decode up to 4K (3,840×2,160-pixel) video at 60 FPS, encoded in H.265. H.264 decoding is supported for up to 1080p (1,920×1,080 pixels) at 60 FPS. Both codecs are supported out of the box, so no extra licenses are required.

Of course, to see those extra pixels, you'll need a 4K screen. The Pi 4 Model B supports 4K resolutions at several refresh rates, up to 60 Hz. If wireless streaming of 4K video is a requirement, this is the board for you.

HDMI Cable

In addition to an official 15 W USB-C power supply, you'll need a single cable to connect the Pi to your desired display—usually, a 19-pin Micro HDMI to 19-pin HDMI cable like the one shown in Figure 11-2, as HDMI is the most common display input. (Yes, you will need a cable, but you'll need to connect it only once; thereafter, all content will be streamed wirelessly from your desired source devices to the receiver.) If you plan on affixing the Pi to your display, as discussed in the next section, consider buying a short cable. These are widely available from online retailers for about $4.

Figure 11-2: A Micro HDMI to HDMI cable

It's worth mentioning here that wireless HDMI transceivers are available, but they tend to be prohibitively expensive and are beyond the scope of this budget-friendly project.

VESA-Compatible Project Case (Optional)

If you're aiming for a more professional setup, choose a suitable case for your Pi and consider mounting it to the back of your display. Specialized cases with VESA-compatible mounting plates are inexpensive and make for a clean installation. The aluminum case shown in Figure 11-3 is available from the Pi Hut for around $14; it gives this project a nice finishing touch.

Figure 11-3: A VESA-compatible project case (from the Pi Hut)

There's no need to go overboard here; self-adhesive Velcro also works in a pinch (I've used it more than once). If you're using a digital signage solution, many of these units allow you to discreetly hide cables and small devices inside a protective housing.

Software Used

In this chapter, you'll implement two different wireless display solutions to support the broadest possible range of devices. (You can also choose to implement just one of these options, depending on your needs.) You'll be using open source software packages that provide an entry point to two competing standards: Miracast from the Wi-Fi Alliance and Apple's AirPlay. The reasons for these choices will become clear in the next section. For now, let's take a quick look at the software packages you'll be working with.

Windows and Android Support

For Windows and Android support with Miracast, you'll be using the *lazycast* GitHub project. Lazycast bills itself as a "simple Wi-Fi display receiver" originally targeted at the Raspberry Pi as the receiver and Windows 8.1/10 as source devices. However, it's been found to work equally well with a variety of Android-based sources.

This package is unique in that it includes Windows 10 support through *Miracast over Infrastructure (MICE)*, a feature that allows transmission of screen data over both Ethernet and secure wireless networks. Lazycast offers many runtime options, including support for multiple video players, and is highly customizable.

Apple Device Support

For iOS and macOS device support, you'll use the *RPiPlay* project, also available on GitHub. RPiPlay is an open source AirPlay mirroring server that was ported specifically for the Raspberry Pi. The code is based on an open source AirPlay project for Android, written in C. Thanks to the use of OpenSSL for AES decryption and the Pi's hardware acceleration, video packet decryption is reasonably fast on all currently available Raspberry Pi devices. The stated goal of RPiPlay is to "make it run smoothly even on a Raspberry Pi Zero," although you can expect better performance from a Raspberry Pi 5, 4, or 3B+.

Before delving into the implementation, let's briefly explore the relevant wireless display standards and the Wi-Fi technologies that underpin them.

Casting Call

When it comes to mirroring a device's screen wirelessly to another display, a variety of competing standards have fought it out for market share. Today, the dominant wireless display technologies are Apple's AirPlay, Miracast from the Wi-Fi Alliance, and Google's Chromecast. In 2010, Intel released its own technology, known as *Wireless Display (WiDi)*, to compete with Air-Play (known then as *AirTunes*), but it never gained broad adoption. Just a few years later, Intel sunsetted WiDi in favor of Miracast when Microsoft selected it for native wireless display support in Windows 10 and 8.1.

These standards all have similar features that make them good choices for wireless streaming, but they differ significantly under the hood, as you'll see in the following sections.

AirPlay

AirPlay is Apple's wireless display standard, introduced in 2010 as AirTunes to support audio and video streaming to the Apple TV. In 2011, Steve Jobs, then CEO of Apple Inc., demonstrated AirPlay Mirroring as a new feature in iOS 5, allowing a user to stream the screen from an iPad 2 to an HDTV wirelessly and securely. At the time, AirPlay was unique for enabling compatible TVs, speakers, and other devices to receive media from Apple devices (typically iPhones) when they were all connected to the same wireless network.

Unlike pure screen-mirroring solutions, AirPlay lets users multitask while streaming media content from a source device. Simply put, this means you can use your iPhone, iPad, or Mac for other tasks, and the playback controls won't appear on your Apple TV screen. AirPlay is clever enough to stream only the content you want to see.

While AirPlay works very well, it does have a few big limitations. First and foremost, it's compatible only with Apple devices, so you can't use it to mirror screens from or to Windows or Android devices. Second, AirPlay restricts the playback of Digital Rights Management (DRM)−protected content to authorized devices. If you try to stream DRM-protected movies or TV shows from services such as iTunes or Apple TV+, AirPlay is likely to enforce High-bandwidth Digital Content Protection (HDCP) to prevent unauthorized recording. Finally, AirPlay is currently compatible with only second- and third-generation Apple TVs, so you're out of luck if you have an older first-generation model. As is the case with other commercial standards, AirPlay also uses its own proprietary technology.

Despite its closed, or "walled garden," ecosystem approach, Apple's AirPlay set the bar for the competing wireless display technologies that followed it.

Miracast

Miracast is an industry-wide standard that was developed in large part as a response to AirPlay. Its specifications are defined by the Wi-Fi Alliance, with significant contributions from Microsoft. The protocol enables discovery, pairing, and rendering of multimedia content from a source device to a *sink*, or receiver. Miracast support is built into Android 4.2+ and Windows 8.1+, allowing Android smartphones, Windows tablets and laptops, and other devices to stream wirelessly to Miracast-compliant receivers. A wide range of consumer devices, from companies such as Samsung, LG, Amazon, and Roku, have native Miracast support.

The Miracast specification defines both Wi-Fi Direct and MICE protocols for device discovery and content streaming. We'll look at each of these methods more closely when you build your lazycast receiver. The Wi-Fi Direct protocol enables users to connect a source device, such as a laptop or phone, to a secondary display receiver (like a TV, projector, or monitor) using a secure peer-to-peer (P2P) link. One big advantage of this protocol is that DRM-protected content from providers such as Netflix, Apple TV+, and Blu-ray cannot be blocked. Miracast is agnostic in terms of the media streamed between source devices and receivers.

Of course, Miracast also has its limitations. For one, it's based on the connectionless UDP protocol, which, unlike TCP, doesn't guarantee data packet delivery. UDP is generally well suited for streaming because it provides low-latency communication, but the trade-off is that Miracast connections are more sensitive to network instability (for more on this, see "Expected Performance Levels" on page 370). In environments with unreliable Wi-Fi connectivity, performance may be less than optimal. By contrast, AirPlay and Chromecast use a combination of UDP and TCP for different aspects of their functionality (although this doesn't completely protect them from the effects of network latency).

Another drawback of Miracast is that it supports only display mirroring. You won't be able to stream video from your source device to a TV without the playback controls appearing on the screen.

Finally, while not a technical issue, Miracast doesn't mandate that devices be labeled with the Miracast brand name. As a result, manufacturers have developed their own names for the technology. For example, LG markets it as "SmartShare," Samsung as "AllShare Cast," and Sony as "screen mirroring." As a consumer, you might buy a new Samsung TV, see the

AllShare Cast logo, and not be aware that it's actually a Miracast-compatible display.

Chromecast

Google debuted its flagship Nexus 4 handheld in 2012 with much fanfare about its robust Miracast support, claiming that cheap Miracast-compatible receivers that you could plug into your TV's HDMI port would soon make ubiquitous wireless display a reality. The challenge of mirroring screens from Android and Windows devices would finally be a thing of the past (notably absent was any mention of Apple, of course).

However, those inexpensive, cross-compatible receivers never materialized. Instead, a year later, Google launched Chromecast, a device that plugged into a TV's HDMI port with power supplied by a USB cable. Sending video or audio to your non-smart TV was as simple as tapping a *cast* icon. Chromecast, as you might guess, was based on yet another proprietary protocol, *Google Cast*.

Google introduced Chromecast with a $35 price tag and a promotion for three months of free access to Netflix. The company deliberately chose not to position Chromecast as its version of Apple TV, but rather as a low-cost way to access online services on an HDTV. The product also debuted with a solid developer SDK.

Millions of Chromecasts were sold by 2014, and by mid-2015, consumers had made 1.5 billion casts (according to an announcement at the annual Google I/O conference). One might reasonably ask how Google knew how many casts its users had made. The answer lies in the privacy policies end users had to accept and the permissions granted during Chromecast's setup process.

While Chromecast played a major role in popularizing wireless casting, this chapter does not explore it further, for a few key reasons. Notably, unlike Miracast and AirPlay, Chromecast is tightly coupled with proprietary Google services and currently lacks a reliable, fully open source implementation suitable for self-hosted or offline use.

Casting Devices Compared

As is often the case, compatibility issues exist between these standards. To date, Apple's operating systems (macOS and iOS) do not support Miracast. Likewise, Microsoft's Miracast-based 4K Wireless Display Adapter excludes Apple device support. Only the Google Cast protocol is largely device-agnostic, although it still requires source devices to use software within the Google ecosystem, such as the Chrome browser or the YouTube app.

A summary of the most widely available commercial casting devices, their supported platforms, and their specifications is provided in Table 11-2.

Table 11-2: A Comparison of Popular Commercial Casting Devices

	Chromecast Ultra 4K	Apple TV 4K	Microsoft 4K
Power supply	AC adapter	AC adapter or PoE	USB
MSRP	$69.99	$129–$149	$69.99
Device support			
Windows	Google Cast	X	Miracast
macOS	Google Cast	AirPlay	X
iOS	Google Cast	AirPlay	X
Android	Google Cast	X	Miracast
Sharing			
Resolution	Up to 4K at 60 FPS	Up to 4K at 60 FPS	Up to 4K at 30 FPS
HDR	✓	✓	✓
Presenter mode	X	macOS	X

Now that you have a broad understanding of these wireless display standards and how they interoperate with popular consumer devices, let's turn our attention to one of the principal wireless technologies that makes them possible.

A Closer Look at Wi-Fi Direct

Not all Wi-Fi networks are created equal. As you learned in Chapter 1, wireless networks most often operate in either infrastructure or ad hoc mode. In infrastructure mode, Wi-Fi routers create the network, whereas ad hoc networks are usually spontaneous connections created by a laptop or other device. The latter are most useful when wireless infrastructure isn't available, such as when no access points or routers are within range. Instead of relying on a router, in an ad hoc network individual wireless endpoints (say, a laptop and another Wi-Fi–capable device, such as a smartphone) connect temporarily and forward packets between themselves for purposes such as file exchange or sharing a cellular internet link.

Ad hoc mode is also commonly referred to as *peer-to-peer* mode. The Wi-Fi Direct standard builds on this concept, allowing devices to communicate directly over wireless signals. We'll examine this more closely in the next section.

Operating Principle

Wi-Fi Direct allows a Wi-Fi–capable device to quickly find and interact with nearby devices, at a range beyond the capabilities of Bluetooth. These P2P wireless connections are among the simplest types of networks available in telecommunications. Wi-Fi Direct uses the same Wi-Fi technology that devices use to connect to wireless routers. In fact, a Wi-Fi Direct device essentially functions as an access point, enabling other devices to connect to it directly.

Although this is already possible with ad hoc networking, Wi-Fi Direct extends the concept with a streamlined setup process and a protocol known as *Device and Service Discovery (DSD)*. This protocol allows a Wi-Fi Direct device to quickly find a peer and determine if a session can be established with it. Refer to Figure 11-4 as I walk through this process step-by-step.

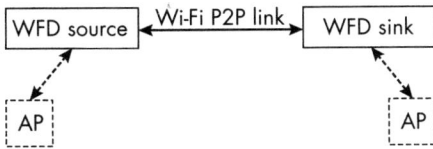

Figure 11-4: A Wi-Fi Direct connection between a source (left) and sink (right)

The first step in this exchange can be thought of as *initialization and group formation*. One device (we'll call it the WFD sink) initiates the Wi-Fi Direct session and acts as the P2P group owner (GO), while the other device (the WFD source) joins the session as a client. The GO broadcasts a beacon frame advertising its intent to create a Wi-Fi Direct group. This frame contains information about its capabilities and the group's intended purpose. The client scans for available Wi-Fi Direct groups, detects the beacon frame from the GO, and decides to join the group.

Once the initial connection is established, device discovery takes place. In this topology, one GO can have multiple clients connected, allowing several source devices to join the same group. The devices periodically broadcast probe request frames to announce their presence within the group. Each device in the group listens for these frames and extracts information about other devices in the group, such as their name, MAC address, capabilities, and supported services.

After discovering the presence of other devices in the group, service discovery is performed. Devices can use protocols like the Service Discovery Protocol (SDP) or Multicast DNS (mDNS) to find out about the services available on each device. The WFD sink may broadcast advertisements about the services it offers, typically in the form of service announcement frames. Upon receiving these announcements, a WFD source can request additional details about specific services by sending service query request frames.

Once a WFD source has discovered the services offered by the WFD sink, it can initiate connections to access those services. This might involve establishing TCP or UDP connections, depending on the nature of the service. During this phase, WPA2 encryption is used to secure the connection between the devices.

With a secure link established, data can be exchanged directly between the devices. This can include file sharing, media streaming, printing, or any other announced services the devices have agreed upon.

Interestingly, and relevant to this project, the service discovery phase can include details about the video capabilities of the Wi-Fi Direct devices, such as supported video codecs, display resolutions, and refresh rates. Other multimedia service information, such as stream formats and types of supported audio, might also be included.

Adapter Support

With an understanding of how Wi-Fi Direct works in practice, the next step is to verify that your wireless adapter hardware supports it. To check the supported interface modes of your wireless device(s), you can pipe the output of iw to grep as follows:

```
$ iw list | grep -A 7 'Supported interface modes'
    Supported interface modes:
         * IBSS
         * managed
         * AP
         * P2P-client
         * P2P-GO
         * P2P-device
    --snip--
```

In the output shown here, P2P-GO means that the adapter supports group owner mode, while P2P-client tells us it can also act as a device that connects to a group owner. The P2P-device interface mode is used during device and service discovery and for negotiating connections, to set up the group. These roles are explained in the comments for the nl80211_iftype enumerated type in the Linux kernel.

The good news is that all Wi-Fi–capable Raspberry Pis support these interface modes at the hardware adapter and driver levels. If you have an external wireless adapter attached to your Pi that doesn't support these P2P modes, it's best to disconnect it before proceeding with the lazycast installation. The reason for this will be made clear shortly.

Interface Combinations

Suppose you want to connect your device to an infrastructure Wi-Fi network, such as a wireless router, while also participating in a Wi-Fi Direct group. Alternatively, you might want to operate your device as an access point while joining a Wi-Fi Direct group. To find out whether your adapter is capable of these simultaneous configurations, run the following command:

```
$ iw list | grep -A 4 'valid interface combinations'
    valid interface combinations:
     * #{ managed } <= 1, #{ P2P-device } <= 1, #{ P2P-client, P2P-GO } <= 1,
        total <= 3, #channels <= 2
     * #{ managed } <= 1, #{ AP } <= 1, #{ P2P-client } <= 1, #{ P2P-device } <= 1,
        total <= 4, #channels <= 1
```

The output can be somewhat arcane, so let's take a moment to decipher it. Each line under valid interface combinations starting with an asterisk (*)

contains one possibility for a combination. If there are several lines, you can pick any one, as long as its restrictions are met. The adapter in this example has two lines, so we have two choices.

The notation #{ ... } can be interpreted as "number of interfaces of the following type." Consider the first line:

```
* #{ managed } <= 1, #{ P2P-device } <= 1, #{ P2P-client, P2P-GO } <= 1,
    total <= 3, #channels <= 2
```

In words, this reads: You can have a maximum of three simultaneous interfaces. Those interfaces can use at most two different channels (so at least two interfaces must share the same channel). You can have one managed interface (also called a station, STA, or client), one P2P-device interface, and either one P2P-client or one P2P-GO interface.

Now, let's interpret the second choice:

```
* #{ managed } <= 1, #{ AP } <= 1, #{ P2P-client } <= 1, #{ P2P-device } <= 1,
    total <= 4, #channels <= 1
```

This line tells you that you can have a maximum of four simultaneous interfaces. Those interfaces can use at most one channel (so every interface must share the same channel). You can have one managed interface, one access point (AP), one P2P-client interface, and one P2P-device interface.

While theoretically possible, in practice the Raspberry Pi's wireless physical (PHY) layer is not typically able to handle two concurrent client interfaces reliably. The takeaway here is that if your regular interface is configured as a client, the P2P interface should be a P2P-GO. Conversely, if your regular interface is operating in AP mode, the P2P interface must be a P2P-client.

This question of adapter support for various interface combinations with Wi-Fi Direct is entirely valid. As you now turn your focus to installing lazycast, it's recommended to leave your wireless interface idle or in standby mode. We'll revisit these configurations later in this chapter.

Installing Lazycast

Lazycast was chosen for its implementation of Miracast, which has good support for both Android and Windows and runs well on all currently available Raspberry Pi models. If your devices belong to these ecosystems, grab your chosen Pi and let's get started. If you're using only Apple devices, skip ahead to "Installing RPiPlay" on page 362.

You'll need to use the 32-bit version of Raspberry Pi OS Lite for this project, rather than the 64-bit version. This is because you'll be compiling the userland libraries, a set of GPU and multimedia libraries that were built and tested for the 32-bit ARM environment. The 64-bit user space is not officially supported; an --aarch64 option is provided, but in practice, it fails to compile all the libraries needed for this project. To simplify things, start with a clean install of the 32-bit version of the OS. This will ensure that you're able to compile the libraries you need and let you focus on more interesting tasks.

Disabling the Onscreen Prompt

If your Raspberry Pi is connected to a display via HDMI, you may be greeted with a "Please enter a new username" prompt. This wizard was added to the Bullseye release of Raspberry Pi OS to counter cyberattacks, which, regrettably, are an ever-present threat.

If you're running your Raspberry Pi headless and can't work through the wizard, you have a few options. The Raspberry Pi Imager tool allows you to preconfigure an image with a new user account. Alternatively, you can set up a user on first boot and bypass the wizard by creating a file called *userconf* or *userconf.txt* in the boot partition of the SD card (the part of the card you can access when it's mounted on a Windows or macOS computer). This file should contain a single line of text in the format *username:encrypted_password* (that is, your desired username, followed by a colon, followed by an encrypted representation of the password you want to use, with no spaces).

The easiest way to generate the encrypted password is to use OpenSSL on a Raspberry Pi that's already running. Open a terminal window and execute the following command:

```
$ echo 'mypassword' | openssl passwd -6 -stdin
```

This will produce what looks like a string of random characters, which is actually an encrypted version of the supplied password.

Finally, if you'd like to skip the wizard altogether (my preferred option), you can do so with the following shell commands:

```
$ sudo systemctl disable userconfig > /dev/null 2&>1
$ sudo systemctl enable getty@tty1
```

After a reboot, the `userconfig` wizard will be disabled for all subsequent terminal sessions.

Installing the Dependencies

Before building lazycast, ensure that your system is up to date, including the kernel and firmware. Again, be sure you're starting with the 32-bit version of Raspberry Pi OS Lite (Buster). Follow this with a reboot:

```
$ sudo apt update && sudo apt full-upgrade
$ sudo reboot
```

Next, ensure that you have the `cmake` and `git` packages installed:

```
$ sudo apt install cmake git
```

To compile lazycast, you'll first need to clone the official Raspberry Pi userland source code for ARM libraries. This is used to interface with the Raspberry Pi's GPU. Clone the repository into your Pi's home directory:

```
$ cd $HOME
$ git clone https://github.com/raspberrypi/userland.git
```

Then change to the project directory and execute the *buildme* script:

```
$ cd userland/
$ ./buildme
```

The build should proceed with output similar to the following:

```
~/userland/build/raspberry/release ~/userland
--snip--
Call Stack (most recent call first):
  CMakeLists.txt:24 (include)
-- Looking for execinfo.h
-- Looking for execinfo.h - found
-- The ASM compiler identification is GNU
-- Found assembler: /usr/bin/cc
-- Found PkgConfig: /usr/bin/pkg-config (found version "0.29.2")
-- Configuring done
-- Generating done
-- Build files have been written to: /home/pi/userland/build/raspberry/release
Scanning dependencies of target khrn_client
Scanning dependencies of target vcos
Scanning dependencies of target GLESv2_static
Scanning dependencies of target EGL_static
--snip--
-- Installing: /opt/vc/man/man1/dtmerge.1
-- Installing: /opt/vc/lib/libdtovl.so
~/userland
```

The build script may take several minutes to complete, depending on your hardware. At the end, you should see messages about the installation of various components.

Updating the Driver

To use GPU-based video players on the latest release of Raspberry Pi OS, you'll need to disable the DRM VC4 V3D driver. Otherwise, HDMI output may be turned off immediately after receiving a video stream. You can do this by editing */boot/config.txt*:

```
$ sudo nano /boot/config.txt
```

Locate the line

```
dtoverlay=vc4-kms-v3d
```

and comment it out or remove it. Next, add the following line below [pi4]:

```
dtoverlay=vc4-fkms-v3d
```

Save your changes to the file and exit your editor, then reboot your device for the changes to take effect.

Building the Lazycast Binaries

With the userland dependencies out of the way, you can proceed with building lazycast itself. Begin by installing the packages required for compiling the media players:

```
$ sudo apt install libx11-dev libasound2-dev libavformat-dev libavcodec-dev
```

There are quite a few packages to install here, so treat yourself to a break while apt does its job. When it's done, run the following commands to compile the *ilclient* and *hello_video* libraries:

```
$ cd /opt/vc/src/hello_pi/libs/ilclient/
$ sudo make
$ cd /opt/vc/src/hello_pi/hello_video
$ sudo make
```

Next, change to your home directory and clone the lazycast GitHub repository:

```
$ cd $HOME
$ git clone https://github.com/homeworkc/lazycast
```

Then compile lazycast:

```
$ cd lazycast
$ make
```

It's worth mentioning here that warnings are fairly common when compiling code using GNU make in Linux. Output like the following is generally harmless:

```
player.c: In function audioplay_get_latency:
player.c:729:16: warning: variable error set but not used
  [-Wunused-but-set-variable]
```

There's a good chance you'll see several of these warnings whiz by on the screen while the compiler is working.

Starting Lazycast

With the ARM libraries, media players, and lazycast itself successfully compiled, you're finally ready to launch the lazycast wireless display receiver. Ensure that you're in the */lazycast* directory, then execute the lazycast binary:

```
$ cd ~/lazycast
$ ./all.sh
```

After a moment, you should see output like the following:

```
Available interfaces:
p2p-wlan0-0
p2p-dev-wlan0
wlan0
OK
0    DIRECT-F5    ba:27:eb:01:d7:6a    [DISABLED][P2P-PERSISTENT]
Selected interface 'p2p-wlan0-0'
The display is ready
Your device is called: raspberrypi
PIN:
31415926
```

This indicates that the wireless display receiver has identified the P2P-compatible wlan0 interface and created the virtual p2p-wlan0-0 interface to handle Wi-Fi Direct. Take note of the default 31415926 PIN number (you'll change this later). You can now connect a Wi-Fi Direct–capable client device to your wireless display.

Connecting a Source

Miracast supports a broad range of Windows 8.1/10 and Android devices. I'll demonstrate connecting an Android handset here. Vendor implementations of Android will differ somewhat; on my device, I selected Connection & Sharing ▶ Cast and turned on the Cast Screen Contents to an External Monitor toggle to initiate a scan for available Wi-Fi Direct groups. The exact names on your device may differ, but you should be able to locate the correct option without too much difficulty.

After a few moments, the lazycast Wi-Fi Direct sink should appear. This will be identified by the device_name specified by your Wi-Fi Direct network, the default being raspberrypi. Tap the device name to connect, then enter the PIN when prompted, as illustrated in Figure 11-5.

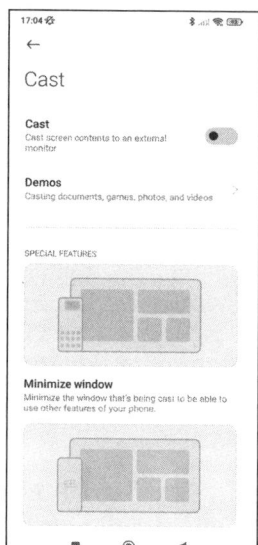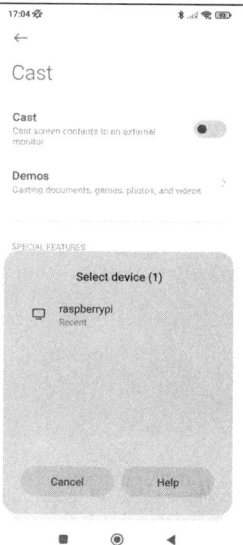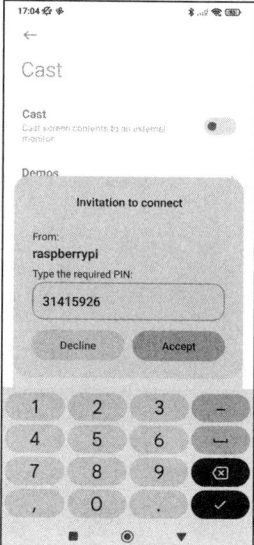

Figure 11-5: A series of dialogs illustrating connecting to a Wi-Fi Direct group

You can monitor the terminal output on your Raspberry Pi while doing this. You should see output like the following:

```
RTSP/1.0 200 OK
CSeq: 5
Date: Mon, Sep 15 2025 18:00:52 GMT
Session: 0000000a
Transport: RTP/AVP/UDP;unicast;client_port=1028;server_port=19022
--snip--
alsa init success
-------->
RTSP/1.0 200 OK
CSeq: 6
---- Negotiation successful ----
```

At this stage, your Wi-Fi Direct source (an Android phone, in this example) and the sink (the Raspberry Pi) have successfully negotiated a connection. You'll see some details about the connection in the terminal output, such as the protocol used (UDP) and ports used by the server and client.

Assuming your display is active, you should now see the Android phone's screen mirrored wirelessly to it. In the following output, you can see details related to the video and audio streams used between the devices in the Wi-Fi Direct group:

```
Input #0, rtp, from 'rtp://127.0.0.1:57823':
  Duration: N/A, start: 0.260000, bitrate: N/A
  Program 256
    Stream #0:0: Video: h264 (High), yuv420p(progressive), 1920x1080, 50 fps
    Stream #0:1: Audio: aac (LC), 48000 Hz, stereo, fltp, 255 kb/s
```

```
Rate 50 scale 1 time base 1 90000
Codec name h264
Codec name aac
Setting audio render format
Setting video decoder format
FPS num 50 den 1
Set frame rate to 3276800
Video decoder format set up ok
Default framerate 3276800
--snip--
```

Notice that the default video codec being used is H.264, with a screen resolution of $1,920 \times 1,080$ pixels at 50 FPS (my Android phone's screen resolution is $2,400 \times 1,080$ pixels). The audio stream is AAC stereo at 255Kbps.

Peeking Under the Hood

To understand how lazycast's implementation of Miracast works, you can investigate its operation by using some common Linux networking tools. While lazycast is running, execute **ip a** and take note of the presence of a p2p-wlan0-x device:

```
$ ip a
--snip--
3: wlan0: <NO-CARRIER,BROADCAST,MULTICAST,UP> mtu 1500 qdisc pfifo_fast state DOWN
    link/ether b8:27:eb:01:d7:6a brd ff:ff:ff:ff:ff:ff
4: p2p-wlan0-0: <BROADCAST,MULTICAST,UP,LOWER_UP> mtu 1500 qdisc pfifo_fast state UP
    link/ether ba:27:eb:01:57:6a brd ff:ff:ff:ff:ff:ff
    inet 192.168.173.1/24 brd 192.168.173.255 scope global p2p-wlan0-0
--snip--
```

In this output, you'll also notice that the wlan0 and p2p-wlan0-0 interfaces have the same MAC address, ba:27:eb:01:57:6a. What's happening here? In Linux, Wi-Fi Direct works by a creating a virtual interface, in this case p2p-wlan0-0, which is associated with the familiar wlan0 wireless interface.

For more insight into how lazycast creates the Wi-Fi Direct network, you need only examine *wpa_supplicant.conf*:

```
$ sudo cat /etc/wpa_supplicant/wpa_supplicant.conf

ctrl_interface=DIR=/var/run/wpa_supplicant GROUP=netdev
update_config=1
device_name=raspberrypi
device_type=7-0050F204-1
p2p_go_ht40=1
country=US

network={
    ssid="DIRECT-F5"
```

```
    bssid=ba:27:eb:01:d7:6a
    psk="wdoAQoqS"
    proto=RSN
    key_mgmt=WPA-PSK
    pairwise=CCMP
    auth_alg=OPEN
    mode=3
    disabled=2
    p2p_client_list=96:cf:15:ca:48:9f
}
```

Here, you'll find the network's SSID value (assigned as DIRECT-F5, the BSSID's MAC address, encryption settings, and more.

You can observe client connection events over the p2p-wlan0-0 virtual interface with the aid of wpa_cli, a text-based frontend program for interacting with wpa_supplicant. This tool operates in two modes: interactively and via the command line. Interactive mode will give you insights into connection events on the active interface. Start the program interactively, like so:

```
$ sudo wpa_cli

wpa_cli v2.9
Copyright (c) 2004-2019, Jouni Malinen <j@w1.fi> and contributors

Selected interface 'p2p-wlan0-0'

Interactive mode
<3>CTRL-EVENT-SUBNET-STATUS-UPDATE status=0
<3>AP-STA-CONNECTED 96:cf:15:ca:48:9f p2p_dev_addr=96:cf:15:ca:48:9f
```

With lazycast active, the p2p-wlan0-0 interface should appear by default, as this is the first interface found with a control socket. If not, you can explicitly specify the interface by appending the optional -i parameter. In the output, note the connection event to the Wi-Fi Direct sink (the Raspberry Pi) from the source device (the Android phone), and the phone's MAC address. In *wpa_supplicant.conf*, you can see that this MAC address is added to the p2p_client_list. This allows previously authenticated clients to reconnect to the Wi-Fi Direct group without needing to reenter the PIN number. Exit the wpa_cli program by typing **quit** and pressing ENTER.

The lazycast shell script, *all.sh*, spawns a Python process with *d2.py*, which has several user-configurable settings:

```
#################### Settings ####################
player_select = 2
# 0: non-RPi systems. (using vlc or gstreamer)
# 1: player1 has lower latency.
# 2: player2 handles still images and sound better.
# 3: omxplayer # Using this option for video playback on Android
sound_output_select = 2
```

```
# 0: HDMI sound output
# 1: 3.5mm audio jack output
# 2: alsa
disable_1920_1080_60fps = 1
enable_mouse_keyboard = 0

display_power_management = 0
# 1: (For projectors) Put the display in sleep mode when not in use by
# lazycast
--snip--
```

The default values are generally optimal for the Raspberry Pi with video playback from Android and Windows devices. Because the `vlc`, `gstreamer`, and `omxplayer` video players are not installed in Raspberry Pi OS, you'll need to use a value of either 1 or 2 for the `player_select` option.

Note that *all.sh* uses `wpa_cli` in command mode to enumerate available interfaces, create the Wi-Fi Direct group owner, set the PIN number, report on the network's status, and more. To change the PIN number from the default value, run the following command, replacing *new_pin* with the new eight-digit value:

```
$ sudo wpa_cli -i$p2pinterface wps_pin any new_pin
```

The Python process will execute continuously until it's interrupted. You can stop execution at any time with CTRL-C.

A Brief Detour into VideoCore

The Debian Bullseye release removed the OpenMAX player (`omxplayer`) and OMX libraries, which RPiPlay requires for video and audio rendering. To understand why this was done, it's helpful to take a quick look at the Pi's accelerated video and audio hardware and the software that supports it. The Raspberry Pi uses a *VideoCore GPU*, which is part of Broadcom's SoC (shown in Figure 11-6), to handle video and multimedia tasks.

Figure 11-6: The BCM2711 chipset, housing the Raspberry Pi's VideoCore GPU. Courtesy of Jeff Geerling (https://www.jeffgerling.com).

The VideoCore GPU is a multimedia processor used in many low-power devices, including mobile phones and all Raspberry Pi models. At its core is a *VPU*, a generalized video processing unit that manages media pipelines and runs proprietary firmware with its own OS and a set of multimedia-related APIs. Before Bullseye, the VideoCore APIs used OpenMAX (OMX), a standard set of C-language interfaces optimized for low-power and embedded audio and video processing. But over time, several factors led to OpenMAX becoming less suitable for the evolving Raspberry Pi ecosystem, chief among them a desire for greater compatibility and the performance improvements offered by more modern and widely adopted alternatives. For this reason, the decision was made to deprecate OMX support in favor of the *Video for Linux API version 2 (V4L2)* API.

However, many developers had come to rely on the performance and reliability of omxplayer and the OMX libraries, with the developers of RPi-Play being no exception. Fortunately, a relatively simple workaround is available, although it does require updating your system to the latest "bleeding edge" firmware and kernel. For the purposes of this recipe, you'll update the VideoCore firmware without going through the normal upgrade process by using a bash script called *rpi-update*.

In the past, *rpi-update* was, perhaps unfairly, disparaged by Raspberry Pi engineers as an inferior alternative to the normal apt firmware update process. More recently, it has been adopted by the Raspberry Pi Foundation and included in official OS images. You can obtain OpenMAX from this firmware package, allowing you to compile RPiPlay successfully.

The script downloads the latest prerelease version of the Linux kernel, its matching modules and device tree files, and the latest VideoCore firmware. It then installs these files to the appropriate locations on the SD card, overwriting any previous versions. For this reason, it's strongly recommended that you perform this step on a clean install of the OS. Fair warning: This procedure may introduce compatibility issues with other installed software packages.

Installing RPiPlay

In this section, you'll build an AirPlay-compatible wireless receiver that can stream media from your Apple devices. The project you'll use here, RPiPlay, differs from lazycast in a few important ways. First, while lazycast is based on Miracast (and, by extension, Wi-Fi Direct), RPiPlay uses Apple's AirPlay protocol, which operates over a standard Wi-Fi network with both devices connected to the same access point. Also, unlike with the lazycast installation, both the 32- and 64-bit versions of Raspberry Pi OS Lite are compatible. It's important to use the latest Bookworm release of the OS, as the steps you'll follow are specific to this distribution.

Installing the Prerequisites

As with lazycast, you'll be compiling many binaries and libraries from source. Begin by updating the package list on your system, including the kernel and firmware:

```
$ sudo apt update && sudo apt full-upgrade
```

Then run the *rpi-update* script introduced in the previous section, and reboot:

```
$ sudo rpi-update
$ sudo reboot
```

If for some reason your system doesn't have this utility, you can install it with:

```
$ sudo apt install rpi-update
```

During the update process, you should see the message "Updating Video-Core libraries," along with information about the firmware and kernel modules. After running *rpi-update*, you can confirm your GPU firmware version by running:

```
$ sudo vcgencmd version
Apr 17 2024 17:29:03
Copyright (c) 2012 Broadcom
version 86ccc427f35fdc604edc511881cdf579df945fb4 (clean) (release) (start)
```

Next, install the GStreamer dependency. This is a low-latency multimedia framework that supports linking various media processes:

```
$ sudo apt install libgstreamer1.0-dev libgstreamer-plugins-base1.0-dev
```

Then install the cmake and git packages, followed by several additional libraries required by RPiPlay:

```
$ sudo apt install cmake git
$ sudo apt install libavahi-compat-libdnssd-dev libplist-dev libssl-dev
```

Finally, install and create two symbolic links for the shared *libbrcmGLESv2* libraries:

```
$ sudo apt install libgles-dev libegl-dev
$ sudo ln -s /usr/lib/arm-linux-gnueabihf/libGLESv2.so \
    /usr/lib/libbrcmGLESv2.so
$ sudo ln -s /usr/lib/arm-linux-gnueabihf/libEGL.so /usr/lib/libbrcmEGL.so
```

Building the RPiPlay Binaries

With the prerequisites out of the way, change to your home directory and clone the RPiPlay repository:

```
$ cd $HOME
$ git clone https://github.com/FD-/RPiPlay.git
```

Change into this directory and create a new *build* subdirectory:

```
$ cd RPiPlay
$ mkdir build
```

You'll use this location for compiling the RPiPlay binaries.

At this stage, you're ready to start the build process. Change into the *build* directory and execute cmake with two build flags while referencing the parent directory:

```
$ cd build
$ cmake --DCMAKE_CXX_FLAGS="-O3" --DCMAKE_C_FLAGS="-O3" ..
```

You should see output like the following:

```
-- Found OpenMAX libraries for Raspberry Pi
-- Checking for modules 'gstreamer-1.0>=1.4;gstreamer-sdp-1.0>=1.4;
   gstreamer-video-1.0>=1.4;gstreamer-app-1.0>=1.4'
--    Found gstreamer-1.0, version 1.18.4
--    Found gstreamer-sdp-1.0, version 1.18.4
--    Found gstreamer-video-1.0, version 1.18.4
--    Found gstreamer-app-1.0, version 1.18.4
-- Configuring done
-- Generating done
-- Build files have been written to: /home/pi/RPiPlay/build
--snip--
```

Finally, execute make with the -j switch, which instructs it to run without limiting the number of simultaneous jobs. For the Raspberry Pi Zero or models with 1GB of RAM or less, use the -j1 switch instead of -j. Sample output from this command is shown here:

```
$ make -j
--snip--
Scanning dependencies of target playfair
Scanning dependencies of target h264-bitstream
Scanning dependencies of target llhttp
Scanning dependencies of target ilclient
```

```
[  1%] Building C object lib/playfair/CMakeFiles/playfair.dir/hand_garble.c.o
[  1%] Building C object lib/playfair/CMakeFiles/playfair.dir/modified_md5.c.o
[  2%] Building C object lib/llhttp/CMakeFiles/llhttp.dir/api.c.o
Scanning dependencies of target fdk-aac
[  2%] Building C object lib/llhttp/CMakeFiles/llhttp.dir/http.c.o
--snip--
```

GNU make will proceed through the project *Makefile*, compiling source files into the executables and libraries needed for RPiPlay. This process can take a while, and the compiler may use a substantial amount of your system's resources. You can monitor memory and CPU usage with htop in a separate SSH session, if you wish. If you receive the error "virtual memory exhausted" or experience an SSH session timeout, refer to "Troubleshooting" on page 369.

To verify your installation and get information about available command line options, use:

```
$ ~/RPiPlay/build/rpiplay -v
RPiPlay 1.2: An open-source AirPlay mirroring server for Raspberry Pi
Usage: rpiplay [-n name] [-b (on|auto|off)] [-r (90|180|270)]
   [-l] [-a (hdmi|analog|off)] [-vr renderer] [-ar renderer]
```

At this stage, you're ready to start the mirroring server and begin streaming content from your Apple devices.

Starting RPiPlay

When you start the *rpiplay* executable, an AirPlay mirroring target will appear on your network. For a good baseline setup, try the following options:

```
$ ~/RPiPlay/build/rpiplay -n "AirPlay" -vr rpi -ar rpi -a hdmi
```

This specifies AirPlay as the network name of the AirPlay server; you may change this value if you wish. The video renderer and audio output options are configured for optimal compatibility with the Raspberry Pi.

RPiPlay also supports several other command line options; the full list is given in Table 11-3.

Table 11-3: RPiPlay Command Line Options

Option	Description
`-n name`	Specify the network name of the AirPlay server.
`-b on|auto|off`	Show a black background always, only during active connection, or never.
`-r 90|180|270`	Specify image rotation in multiples of 90 degrees.
`-f horiz|vert|both`	Specify image flipping.
`-l`	Enable low-latency mode; renders audio/video frames as soon as they are received.
`-a hdmi|analog|off`	Set the audio output device.
`-vr rpi|gstreamer|dummy`	Select a video renderer to use.
`-ar rpi|gstreamer|dummy`	Select an audio renderer to use.
`-d`	Enable debug logging; will lead to choppy playback due to heavy console output.
`-v`	Display version information.
`-h`	Display help/usage details.

You can now connect an AirPlay-compatible iOS source device to your server.

Connecting the Source

RPiPlay supports screen mirroring and audio for devices running iOS 9 and later. Recent macOS versions have good compatibility as well, via the system Screen Mirroring feature. I'll begin with an iOS demonstration. Ensure that your AirPlay server is running, then select an item from your media gallery and tap the **Share** icon in the iOS toolbar. A menu similar to the one on the left in Figure 11-7 will appear. Tapping the **AirPlay** icon will reveal a list of available AirPlay servers, as shown on the right in Figure 11-7.

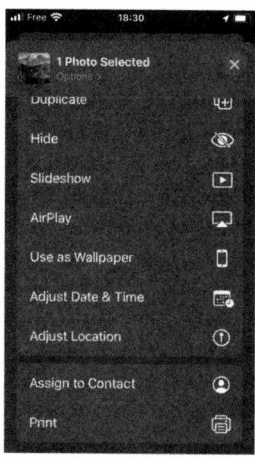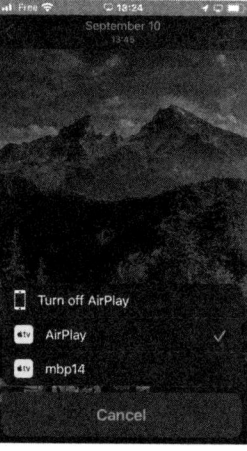

Figure 11-7: Connecting to the RPiPlay server with iOS

Tap **AirPlay** to connect to your AirPlay server. After a moment, your iOS device's top status bar should change color to indicate an active AirPlay connection, and the display will be mirrored to your remote wireless AirPlay monitor. You can observe this connection taking place in the Raspberry Pi's terminal. You should see output like the following:

```
Accepted IPv4 client on socket 15
Local: 192.168.1.49
Remote: 192.168.1.40
raop_rtp_mirror starting mirroring
```

Similarly, you can mirror the desktop in macOS by using the Control Center's Screen Mirroring function. Click or tap the Control Center icon in the top toolbar, then select the AirPlay server in the **Mirror or Extend To** list to connect to RPiPlay, as shown in Figure 11-8.

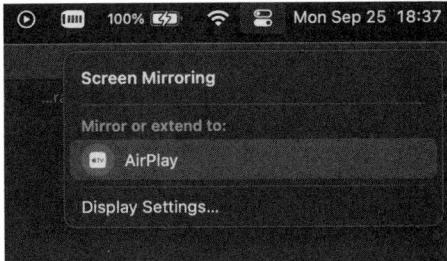

Figure 11-8: Using macOS's built-in Screen Mirroring function to connect to an AirPlay server

The Raspberry Pi's GPU is used for decoding the H.264 video stream. The Pi has no hardware acceleration for audio (AirPlay mirroring uses AAC), so the FDK-AAC decoder is used for this purpose.

Looking Under the Hood

As a strictly proprietary protocol, virtually all that is known about Apple's AirPlay has been gleaned through clever reverse engineering efforts. In early 2011, a talented hacker extracted the AirPlay private key from an AirPort Express device. This enabled third-party developers to finally start building open source AirPlay receiver (server) programs. By the following year, most of AirPlay's protocols had been reverse engineered and documented. If you're curious, you can view the unofficial AirPlay specification in its entirety at *https://openairplay.github.io/airplay-spec/*.

Fundamentally, AirPlay is a standard Apple Bonjour service that advertises itself and accepts playback requests via simple URLs. RPiPlay uses the Apple Bonjour compatibility layer of Avahi, a system that facilitates service discovery on a local network via the multicast DNS (mDNS) protocol. This component enables you to connect your laptop or phone to a network and instantly discover other devices and the services they advertise.

Bonjour effectively performs the same automatic discovery function as Wi-Fi Direct, described earlier in this chapter. AirPlay builds on this by using a reverse-HTTP protocol that allows a client to connect to a host and then reverses the way the connection (known as a *socket*) typically works. In practical terms, this means your AirPlay-compatible device searches for playback systems like an Apple TV or, in this case, an RPiPlay server. After finding a system, the device opens a connection to that system, then flips the normal client/server interaction style. Rather than the client requesting data from the AirPlay server, the server takes control and starts requesting information (such as what file to play) from the iOS or macOS client.

The reverse HTTP connection between the server and client looks like this:

```
HTTP/1.1 101 Switching Protocols
Upgrade: PTTH/1.0
Connection: Upgrade
```

This allows a client to receive asynchronous events, such as playback status changes, from the server. You can observe subsequent HTTP interactions by adding the -d (debug) logging option when executing *rpiplay*. Example output is shown here:

```
Local: 192.168.1.49
Remote: 192.168.1.40
httpd receiving on socket 15
conn_request
Handling request GET with URL /info
INFO len = 1915721940
httpd receiving on socket 15
conn_request
Handling request GET_PARAMETER with URL rtsp://192.168.1.49/18408912485133929897
httpd receiving on socket 15
conn_request
Handling request RECORD with URL rtsp://192.168.1.49/18408912485133929897
raop_handler_record
httpd receiving on socket 15
conn_request
Handling request SET_PARAMETER with URL rtsp://192.168.1.49/18408912485133929897
httpd receiving on socket 15
conn_request
Handling request SETUP with URL rtsp://192.168.1.49/18408912485133929897
httpd receiving on socket 15
conn_request
Handling request POST with URL /feedback
raop_handler_feedback
raop_rtp_mirror video ntp = 1695801474395659, now = 1695801474287773
--snip--
```

Notice that the connection request on the receiving socket is followed by an HTTP GET request to the RPiPlay server's */info* address. After this, service discovery is performed, and the iOS source device (an iPhone, in this case) sends an HTTP POST request to the server's */feedback* URL. At this point, the handler opens a video mirror stream to the client.

Troubleshooting

Supporting a broad range of Android, Windows, and Apple devices as media sources is no small task. Multiple operating system versions and media types raise the potential for errant behavior. Fortunately, the lazycast and RPiPlay projects provide runtime options that allow you to fine-tune settings and capture debug output when things don't work as expected.

The GitHub issues pages for the two projects are likely to cover the vast majority of reported problems, often with workable solutions proposed by the developers or other users. These pages will be your first and best line of support when troubleshooting problems.

For this chapter, a Raspberry Pi 3 Model B+ with 1GB of RAM was used as the wireless display server. This was chosen as a baseline to capture and resolve common issues associated with limited system resources. Code compilers are typically memory-hungry processes; in this section, I'll discuss ways to mitigate the problems you might encounter as a result, as well as some peculiarities of Linux networking. Finally, I'll cover expected performance levels and present methods to ensure smooth streaming from your wireless display servers.

Code Compilation Errors

While compiling code using make with either lazycast or RPiPlay, you may receive an error message like the following:

```
cc1plus: out of memory allocating 65536 bytes after a total of 741376 bytes
virtual memory exhausted: Cannot allocate memory
```

This indicates that the GNU C++ compiler has exhausted the available virtual memory on your system, which can happen if you're using a Raspberry Pi model with limited RAM (typically 1GB or less). In this event, use the optional -j switch to specify the number of jobs, or simultaneous commands, for make to run. Recommended values are make -j1 on a Raspberry Pi Zero or make -j2 on other models, to reduce parallelism while the compiler works.

With lazycast, you might encounter a compile error like this:

```
make[1]: [Makefile.include:19: h264.bin] Error 1
rm h264.o audio.o
make[1]: Leaving directory '/home/pi/lazycast/h264'
make: [Makefile:5: h264/.] Error 2
```

This indicates a problem compiling the H.264 video codec. In this example, it happened because the 64-bit version of Raspberry Pi OS Lite was used with the unofficially supported --aarch64 option while compiling the userland libraries, resulting in a nonfunctional video player. If you see this error, the best solution is to start over, making sure you're using the Buster release version of Raspberry Pi OS Lite (32-bit).

Linux Networking

As you've seen, AirPlay is built on Apple's Bonjour service coupled with an HTTP server, while lazycast relies on Wi-Fi Direct's peer-to-peer networking. The latter is facilitated by wpa_supplicant, an implementation of WPA-PSK security for wireless connections. In this context, a supplicant is simply a client process that must be authenticated to join a network.

With lazycast, you might see an error like this when launching the *all.sh* script:

```
Selected interface 'p2p-wlan0-0'
Available interfaces:
p2p-wlan0-0
p2p-dev-wlan0
wlan0
Failed to connect to non-global ctrl_ifname: p2p-wlan0-0 error:
  No such file or directory
```

This typically arises when the p2p-wlan0-x interface is unexpectedly terminated. This occurs at the level of the wireless adapter firmware, brcmfmac, usually when a lingering wpa_supplicant process is still present. The solution is to kill the old process and restart it, like so:

```
$ sudo pkill wpa_supplicant
$ sudo systemctl restart wpa_supplicant
```

If this fails, rebooting your device is an effective last resort.

Occasionally, even after a reboot, you may find that the lazycast server appears on your wireless network, but client devices are unable to connect to it. In this case, perform a full shutdown with:

```
$ sudo shutdown -h now
```

Then disconnect and reconnect the Raspberry Pi's power to reset its state completely.

Expected Performance Levels

I touched on wireless signal strength in Chapter 1. Expectations for reliable streaming media, in particular 4K video, are closely correlated with the performance of your existing wireless network. Table 11-4 lists expected streaming media performance based on measured signal strength.

Table 11-4: Wireless Signal Strengths and Their Impact on Streaming Media Quality

Signal strength	Expected quality
–30 dBm	Excellent; maximum achievable signal strength
–50 dBm	Very good; suitable for streaming 4K video @ 60 FPS and HD audio
–65 dBm	Good; sufficient for streaming non-HD video and audio
–70 dBm	Marginal; acceptable only for photo sharing, with streaming media unreliable
–80 dBm	Poor; packet delivery will be very unreliable
–90 dBm	Very poor; mostly noise, not usable

You can expect problems to arise when a wireless display receiver and its source device are too far apart, including packet loss of 10 percent or more and latency measured in seconds. This significantly degrades the quality of streamed media. As a rule of thumb, packet loss of less than 1 percent and latency within the 100 to 150 ms range are desirable targets. If in doubt about the performance of your wireless network, refer to "Evaluating Performance" on page 20.

Various free and commercial graphical tools exist for wireless network assessment, scanning, and analysis. These can be extremely useful when troubleshooting latency and quality issues. For example, with your lazycast Wi-Fi Direct network active, you can launch the tool of your choice and look for a network name with a *DIRECT-* prefix. This is shown in Figure 11-9 with NetSpot, a popular tool available for macOS.

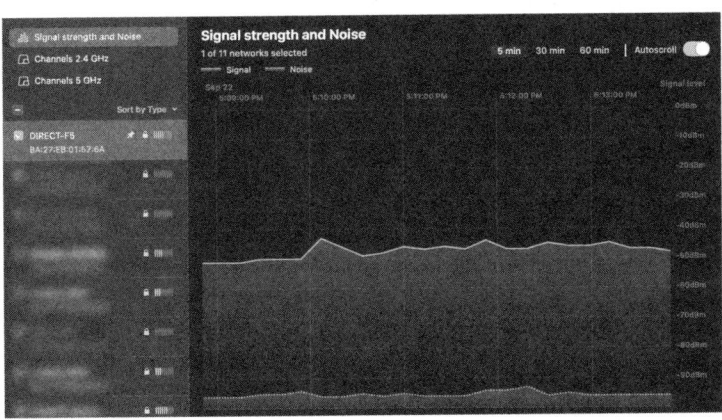

Figure 11-9: Lazycast's Wi-Fi Direct P2P sink seen in NetSpot

In Figure 11-9, notice that lazycast's Wi-Fi Direct network has a signal strength of between –40 and –50 dBm. At this level, you can expect generally very good performance, with video streaming capabilities up to 4K. If you observe a degraded signal or a higher noise threshold, verify that the devices in your Wi-Fi Direct group are within an acceptable range of one another.

Because of the overcrowded nature of the Wi-Fi spectrum (as discussed in Chapter 1), interference from other devices may cause video glitching, audio stuttering, or disconnections. You can mitigate this by performing a survey of your Wi-Fi neighborhood, using a tool like NetSpot to identify the least congested channel and making any necessary adjustments.

Going Further

Unlike in the other "Going Further" sections in this book, which mainly introduce related technologies or clever ways to extend the project at hand, my aim here is to empower you to take back control of your privacy by, in effect, taking ownership of the technology itself.

It may be tempting to simply purchase an off-the-shelf casting device, like those mentioned in "Casting Devices Compared" on page 349. Likewise, many of today's so-called smart TVs have some form of built-in streaming support, designed to spare you from needing such a device. However, as is often the case with smart technology, this convenience comes with a hidden cost.

In this case, the currency is your personal data, and the risks don't come from hackers or other malicious third parties, but from the TV manufacturers themselves. The truth is that nearly all modern smart TVs surveil your viewing habits and store this data remotely on private servers. Monetizing consumer data is a big part of the manufacturers' business models. The high prices fetched by this data, coupled with weak industry transparency, have led to massive volumes of viewer data being collected. During the initial setup, nearly all new TVs require you to accept lengthy user agreements that effectively waive your privacy rights.

Many smart TVs also have embedded microphones and cameras, ostensibly to enable features such as video calling, gesture control, and voice commands. Your TV listening to you or watching your gestures shouldn't be a problem—when you want it to, that is. The trouble is that manufacturers rarely guarantee any form of data security. Some, such as Samsung, even include disclaimers in their privacy policies explicitly absolving themselves of responsibility for third-party providers' privacy and security practices, while acknowledging that your personal information is recorded and shared with third parties.

Smart TV Spying

One concerning smart TV feature to watch out for is *automatic content recognition (ACR)*. Enabled by default on most TVs, ACR analyzes the video and audio streams from your TV and matches them against a remote database to identify what's being played. If it's unsettling to think about your TV watching you, consider that the vast majority of consumers are unaware that ACR exists, let alone that it monitors everything played on your TV, including DVDs and all forms of streaming content.

Known by a variety of other innocuous-sounding names (including Smart TV Experience, Live Plus, and Smart Interactivity), ACR is baked into TV firmware and marketed as a technology to recommend shows you might want to watch. However, the data is used not only for targeted ads but also to track viewers across other apps and services on the internet. If you stream a video to your TV from a phone or laptop, don't be surprised if YouTube starts showing you related content.

Streaming boxes and casting devices are no better, unfortunately. The most popular offerings are regularly evaluated for their consumer privacy protections. The results of a report by Common Sense Media are summarized in Table 11-5.

Table 11-5: The Top Five Streaming Devices Evaluated for Consumer Privacy Risks

Product	Rating	Default privacy	Explanation
Apple TV	79% (Pass)	Yes	Scored lower because Apple doesn't disclose how privacy is protected for K–12 students when the device is used in schools.
Google TV	81% (Warning)	No	Highest numerical score due to disclosures, but some of the worst privacy practices.
Amazon Fire TV	57% (Warning)	No	Data is used to track and target advertisements on other third-party websites or services.
Roku Stick	51% (Warning)	No	Sells users' data to third parties and tracks users on other apps across the internet.
Nvidia Shield TV	43% (Warning)	No	Targets users with advertisements and tracks users on other apps across the internet.

Among the top five devices, Apple TV is arguably the "least bad" offering. However, it barely receives a passing score. The bottom line: Whenever a streaming box or casting device is connected to your TV (and the internet), your personal data will almost certainly be collected, analyzed, and sold to third parties. If you opt to buy into this ecosystem, there's little you can do to prevent this from happening. Fortunately, this chapter has given you two viable open source alternatives.

An Alternative to Surveillance

You don't need to be a tinfoil hat–wearing type to be concerned about your privacy with these devices. There are some basic countermeasures you can take to protect yourself from smart TV spying, such as disabling ACR, opting out of personalization, and covering or disabling built-in cameras and microphones. Some users advocate for keeping their TVs disconnected from the internet and relying on a less intrusive streaming box. Depending on the manufacturer, many TVs also allow you to update their firmware offline using a USB drive.

As an alternative to the smart TV and casting device experience, other users opt for a non-smart monitor and a wireless receiver. Personally, I own a smart TV with a connected Google Chromecast device, although I rarely use it. Lately, my preferred devices are a 4K monitor with an attached Raspberry Pi configured as a wireless receiver. This setup performs double duty for work, including software development and writing, as well as entertainment. In my experience, there's almost no practical downside to using an open source, Linux-based wireless receiver under my control. In fact, I'd argue that there are only upsides to choosing this alternative.

Wrapping Up

In this chapter, you implemented two popular open source projects that enable wireless display receivers. To provide support for the broadest range of devices, you worked with both the Miracast and AirPlay industry standards and compared how they are used in commercially available casting hardware. You also explored how Wi-Fi Direct, the technology that underpins many consumer devices, operates in peer-to-peer mode to enable device discovery. By examining the roles played by Wi-Fi Direct sinks and sources, you gained insight into how this technology operates at the wireless hardware adapter and driver levels.

In building your display receiver, you installed dependencies and compiled the lazycast and RPiPlay projects from their source repositories. You observed how a Wi-Fi Direct sink works in practice when launching the lazycast binary, negotiating connections with a source device and ultimately streaming video and/or audio to an attached display. Then, with RPiPlay, you explored the inner workings of Apple's strictly proprietary (and subsequently reverse engineered) AirPlay protocol, including its unique use of reverse-HTTP interactions between the server and client to facilitate screen mirroring.

Finally, rather than focusing on technological enhancements, this chapter shed light on (and perhaps validated your suspicions about) the realities of digital surveillance, endemic in today's smart TVs and mainstream streaming devices. The open source alternatives presented in this chapter offer a concrete way to regain control of your media experience and your privacy.

APPENDIX

THE ENGINEER'S MINDSET

To illustrate the engineering thought process, I'll draw from a story that, in less of a roundabout way than you might think, connects stellar objects to coffee particles.

Jonathan Gagné is an astrophysics researcher and professor at the University of Montreal in Quebec, Canada. His PhD work focused on the search for brown dwarfs and low-mass stars. A prolific writer and speaker, Gagné's publications and talks cover topics ranging from imaging exoplanets to stellar kinematics and the study of planetary-mass objects. Among other programming projects, he's co-authored a Python package that estimates the age of white dwarf stars based on their observed temperature and surface gravity. Outside of astrophysics circles, though, he's best known for his contributions to coffee science.

Of Astrophysics and Coffee

Gagné admits to being a passionate coffee geek. When he developed an interest in brewing specialty coffee, one of the first annoyances he encountered was coffee enthusiasts' apparent inability to recommend precise grind sizes for different brewing methods, or to compare the quality of different grinders in an objective way. As a scientist accustomed to working with empirical data, he found brewing instructions like "use a grind size that's between salt and sand" to be very frustrating. The idea of measuring particle size distributions was neither new nor revolutionary; the coffee industry had been doing it for a long time. The problem was, the only methods available relied on laboratories with rare and prohibitively expensive laser diffraction equipment. The average coffee geek was left out in the cold.

Drawing on his academic research imaging distant objects in the universe, Gagné hit upon a solution. His idea was simple: Take a photo of coffee grounds spread out over a white background and use software to identify each discrete particle in the resulting image. If you invert the monochromatic scale of the photo on the left in Figure A-1, it's not a stretch to imagine a field of stars against the blackness of interstellar space.

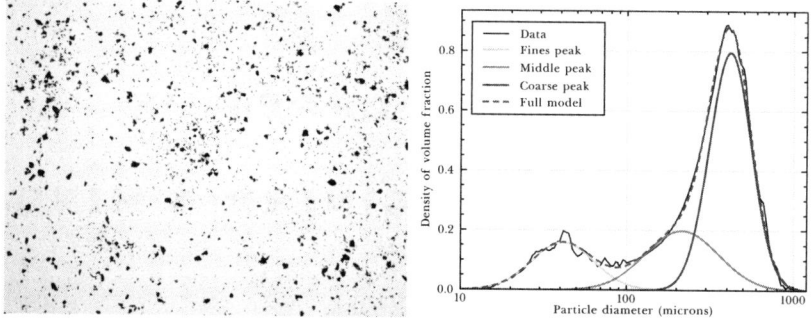

Figure A-1: An example image and particle size analysis returned by Jonathan's Coffee Grind Size software

By counting the number of pixels in each particle, it was then possible to calculate the grain distribution over various sizes. The resulting particle size analysis would permit someone to say, "With this recipe, I use a grind size that generates particles with average surfaces of 0.2 mm^2." Gone were the fuzzy, subjective measures, replaced by precise values that finally allowed coffee aficionados to calibrate their grinders accurately and share their exact brew recipes with one another. A graph of a coffee grind particle size distribution is shown on the right in Figure A-1.

The Coffee Grind Size software, written in Python, was the result. "It turns out writing Python software for coffee is a great way to relax after a day of writing Python software for astrophysics," said Jonathan. Released as an open source GitHub project, his application enabled coffee geeks everywhere to perform this sophisticated analysis—once the exclusive domain of industry labs—at home, using basic tools they had on hand. In turn, it helped users understand the effects of particle size distributions on the taste of their coffee. Moreover, as Jonathan remarked, "I don't think the industry really kept us in the loop with all the laser diffraction experiments, so hopefully we can help ourselves as a community."

You can find the Coffee Grind Size software at *https://github.com/ jgagneastro/coffeegrindsize*. If you'd like to follow Jonathan's coffee science experiments, you'll find his blog, *Coffee Ad Astra*, at *https://coffeeadastra.com*.

Developing an Engineer's Mindset

What does Jonathan's Coffee Grind Size software have to do with wireless projects in Linux? Quite a lot, actually. To make the link between astrophysics, coffee science, and this book, I'll first indulge in a brief exploration of how successful engineers view their world, approach design challenges, and develop solutions to the problems they encounter. Taken as a whole, this can be called the *engineer's mindset*. Next, I'll examine different types of constraints and how they can be harnessed to shape desirable outcomes. I'll then explain how a procedural, recipe-style format, like the one used in this book, can help readers develop fluency in creating wireless projects not just in Linux but in any software domain. Finally, I'll discuss a systems-level thinking approach and the vital role this plays in engineering.

Three Key Traits of an Engineer

In his popular book *Applied Minds: How Engineers Think* (W.W. Norton, 2015), author Guru Madhavan identifies the following three essential properties of the engineering mindset:

- The ability to "see" *structure* where none exists
- Adeptness at designing under *constraints*
- The ability to make *trade-offs*, or considered judgments about solutions and alternatives

Gagné was annoyed by subjective measures of coffee grind sizes. Applying these essential traits to his solution, he identified analogs between the structure of coffee particles viewed against a uniform background and the stellar objects he observed as an astrophysicist. At the same time, he faced a major constraint: a lack of access to the expensive laser diffraction equipment traditionally used to address the problem. So, he made a trade-off between this costly, high-precision lab equipment and more accessible alternative tools (a camera and a laptop) to arrive at an elegant solution. That it placed the analysis within reach of coffee geeks like himself was icing on the cake.

Madhavan elaborates on these qualities, saying, "Engineering is at the center of producing utility under constraints. Structure, constraints, and trade-offs are the one-two-three punch of the engineering mindset. They are to an engineer as time, tempo, and rhythm are to a musician."

Two Kinds of Constraints

Working within constraints is a central feature of software engineering. Limits imposed by CPU capabilities, memory, storage, and design requirements are inevitable in software projects of all kinds. However, these constraints can be expressed in different ways: either *imperatively*, with explicit steps and rules, or *declaratively*, by specifying desired outcomes and leaving the implementation details open.

This distinction is not unlike the contrast between a classical music composition and a jazz performance. In the imperative mode, the constraints define a strict sequence of actions, much like a written score. In the declarative mode, constraints guide the shape of the solution while leaving room for improvisation and interpretation. One is not inherently superior to the other; they're merely different approaches to arranging musical notes.

The recipes you've followed in this book, like those in any cookbook, are algorithmic and imperative in nature: Each step is clearly laid out, and the constraints are closed and explicit. You begin by collecting the ingredients, and the algorithm then guides you, step-by-step, through assembling the pieces: in this case, hardware and software components, prerequisites, configurations, code routines, and other elements needed to complete a project.

This is a useful way to get started in programming, and it mirrors my personal journey, retyping code snippets from *COMPUTE!* and *Scientific American* magazine. Years before I formally studied computer science, I had already acquired the building blocks of programming through imperative constraints and an algorithmic approach. As I gained experience, however, I found myself working more declaratively, defining what a system should accomplish, rather than how to do it, and letting tools, libraries, or my own abstractions fill in the gaps.

In a similar way, the building blocks you have acquired here can help you transition from a scripted, algorithmic methodology to a more open and declarative one. Throughout the recipes in this book, I've included cross-references to related concepts in other chapters and suggested open-ended ways to extend completed projects in the "Going Further" sections. You might opt to repurpose a portion of one project, refactor code from the companion source repositories, or create something entirely new. In short order, you'll be building original projects of your own while exploring wireless in Linux and beyond.

Systems-Level Thinking

A unique way of looking at complexity lies at the core of the engineer's mindset. Known as *systems-level thinking*, this involves logically breaking down a system into its component parts, without losing sight of the bigger picture. When confronted with an engineering challenge, it can be tempting to focus exclusively on the piece of the system that isn't behaving as you expect it to. But this narrow view can obscure other factors at play in related parts of a complex system. Instead of concentrating on an isolated component, a systems-level thinker sees it as part of an interconnected whole.

This is often easier said than done. Rather than a specific talent, systems-level thinking is mix of principles and techniques that can be cultivated over time. Curiosity, open-mindedness, and a willingness to explore root causes are part and parcel of this. To facilitate this way of thinking, engineers may use mapping techniques, various forms of process modeling, or simulations. On a personal level, I can't begin to count the number of times I've resolved an onerous software problem by stepping away from it, doing something else for a while, and later experiencing an "aha!" moment. In these instances, allowing myself time to reorient my perspective on the larger picture ultimately led to a solution. Ask enough engineers, and you're likely to hear many similar accounts.

The systems-level thinking process is a form of *decomposition*: breaking down a system into its basic modules, mapping their interdependencies, and observing how changes in one module affect the others. The focus here is on understanding how these pieces work, don't work, or could potentially work, and using this insight to achieve a desired result. The corollary is *recomposition*, reassembling the component parts into a functional whole.

Now that we've established a conceptual framework for the engineer's mindset, including the role of constraints and a systems-level view of complexity, let's turn our attention to how to apply this framework to create a methodology for analyzing systems, diagnosing faults, and finding solutions.

A Problem-Solving Methodology

We've established that the recipes in this book are a form of algorithmic programming with imperative constraints. While each was carefully selected, tested, and vetted, the reality is that in systems of any level of complexity, errant behavior may still occur. Where applicable, I've highlighted the most common issues you're likely to encounter and provided solutions in the "Troubleshooting" sections of these chapters. However, this guidance comes with the proviso that it's impractical to try to cover all the possible faults that may arise while implementing any of these projects, now or at some future date.

GNU/Linux is constantly evolving, as are distributions such as Raspberry Pi OS (itself a variant of Debian). Part of being an effective engineer is applying a systems-level view to these changes and equipping ourselves with a reasoned approach to understand faults when they happen. To that end, I'll describe here a methodology that you can apply to solve technical problems of nearly any kind. Think of it as a toolkit that, when coupled with the engineer's mindset, will give you the ability to diagnose these problems with confidence. I'll follow this with a real-world example of how this methodology can be applied in practice.

A big advantage of problem-solving in a Linux environment is its fundamentally open nature. Unlike proprietary, closed sourced systems, Linux is eminently knowable and therefore lends itself to the application of logic and reason. The steps you'll apply here are themselves a kind of algorithm, which ideally will produce a fix as its final output. This methodology is illustrated in Figure A-2.

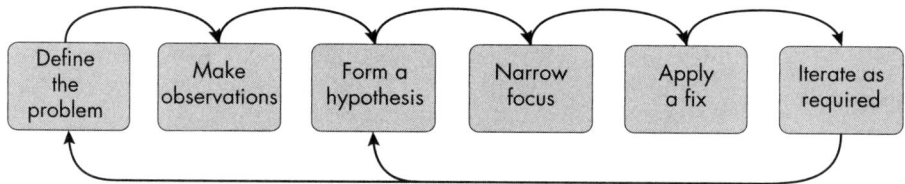

Figure A-2: The problem-solving methodology

If this looks familiar, you're already a step ahead. This approach is closely related to the scientific method, wherein empirical observations are used to formulate a hypothesis, conduct tests, and draw conclusions. I'll break down each of these steps in the next sections.

Defining the Problem

Before a problem can be solved, it must be defined unambiguously. A clearly articulated problem statement provides a solid starting point for the steps that follow. Put yourself in an investigator's shoes and consider how you'd characterize the fault you've encountered. The problem statement should be succinct but contain enough detail to inform the next phase of analysis. For example, rather than saying, "The API server isn't working," you could provide an additional layer of information: "I'm unable to establish a connection to the API server, which is running version x of the software." That sets the stage for a more targeted investigation.

Making Observations

Armed with a clearly defined problem statement, the next step is to collect observations. Linux systems generate a *lot* of logs, which are an invaluable source of information during this phase. Generally, the most important sources of log data are the kernel log, system logs, and logs generated by applications. Each may contain entries with different message levels, such as errors, warnings, or informational output.

Using the System Journal

As you might expect, these logs reside in various locations throughout the Linux filesystem. In Debian Linux, as well as in many other Linux distributions, the traditional */var/log* directory has largely been supplemented or replaced by the *system journal* for system and application log events. This journal, managed by systemd-journald, stores log data in a structured, binary format. It collects log data from several sources, including the kernel, service logs, and various user-space programs. You can view the journal entries via the journalctl command. When run without any options, it displays an unfiltered list, paginated for easier browsing, with the oldest entries at the top.

This can be a lot to digest, however, so a better option is usually to specify the -u or --unit option to filter the logs by the system unit you're interested in. This can be combined with the --since option to display only logs going back for a specified period. For example, to see log entries generated by the ssh.service since the previous day, run:

```
$ journalctl -u ssh.service --since yesterday
```

If you've logged into your device within the last day, this will display the system's record of your SSH session activity.

Another rich source of troubleshooting data is dmesg, which displays messages produced by the kernel. Combined with the system journal and application logs, this will provide a strong basis for your investigations in the observation phase. An ability to query these log sources effectively is critical, so I'll return to this topic in "Top Tips and Strategies" on page 387.

Viewing Debug Messages

Yet more observational data can be gathered at the application level. Many Linux executables include a --debug or -d option, some with different levels of verbosity, to enable debug messages. For example, running hostapd, the user-space daemon for wireless access points, with no arguments reveals two levels of debug output:

```
$ hostapd
--snip--
   -d   show more debug messages (-dd for even more)
```

When an application crashes or behaves unexpectedly, you can view its interactions with the system to gather clues as to what happened during its execution. One way to do this is with strace, a powerful utility that captures system calls made by a running process and the signals it receives. If a process is currently running, you can start a trace by specifying its *process ID (PID)*. For example, to trace the wpa_supplicant process, run **ps -efwH** to list all processes with extra width, in hierarchical format, and pipe the output to grep, like so:

```
$ ps -efwH | grep wpa_supplicant
root   10457   wpa_supplicant -c/etc/wpa_supplicant/wpa_supplicant.conf -iwlan0
```

This output indicates that the wpa_supplicant process with ID 10457, owned by *root*, is using the specified configuration file and is attached to the wlan0 interface with the -i option. Once you know the PID, you can trace its system calls with:

```
$ sudo strace -p 10457
strace: Process 10457 attached
getsockopt(13, SOL_SOCKET, SO_SNDBUF, [212992], [4]) = 0
ioctl(13, TIOCOUTQ, [0])
--snip--
```

The trace will display the name of each system call along with its arguments enclosed in parentheses. Signals received from the system are also captured. Depending on the process, strace can generate a considerable amount of output. However, it can also reveal granular details not otherwise reported by journalctl. In my experience, on several occasions strace has provided the key clue that led to an actionable hypothesis.

Using Command Line Tools

GNU/Linux provides a plethora of command line utilities that are invaluable in the observation phase. You've already seen many of these demonstrated throughout this book. Table A-1 provides a summary of the tools I used most often while implementing these projects.

Table A-1: Command Line Tools for Troubleshooting

Command	Description
dmesg	Prints kernel ring buffer messages
fuser	Identifies processes using files, directories, or sockets
gpioinfo	Displays information about available GPIO lines and their current state
htop	Runs an interactive process viewer for Unix systems
iostat	Reports CPU and I/O statistics for devices and partitions
iotop	Displays I/O usage by processes or threads
ip	Configures network interfaces and manages routing, devices, and tunnels
iptables	Administers packet filtering and NAT rules
journalctl	Queries and displays messages from the system journal
netstat	Displays network connections, routing tables, interface statistics, and so on
pdb	Runs the Python debugger, used for debugging Python programs
ping	Tests the reachability of a host on an IP network
ps	Reports a snapshot of current processes
ss	Investigates sockets
strace	Traces system calls and signals
systemctl	Controls the systemd system and service manager
tcpdump	Captures and analyzes network traffic
traceroute	Prints the route packets take to the network host
vmstat	Reports virtual memory statistics

Specific usage examples for several of these are provided in "Top Tips and Strategies" on page 387. Most of these tools are preinstalled in Debian Linux. Several additional ones can be installed with the sysstat package:

```
$ sudo apt install -y sysstat
```

It pays to invest some time in educating yourself on the effective use of these tools. When in doubt, use the man command to familiarize yourself with their associated manual pages, or consult online resources.

Whichever sources you use for this phase, collecting the right amount of observational data is key. Gather enough data to support your analysis, without drowning in a sea of log entries and debug output. I've developed the habit of copying specific sequences of observational data to a plain text file, annotated with any helpful supporting details.

Bear in mind that this isn't the time to fix the problem; your goal is to merely observe and record. You'll use these observations to first develop and then apply a hypothesis.

Forming a Hypothesis

With a set of well-documented clues, the next step is to form a hypothesis, or a preliminary explanation for your problem statement. This is where the art of problem-solving comes into play. Deducing the root cause of the issue from your observations involves a mix of intuition, past experience, and insights derived by recognizing patterns. It's perfectly fine to brainstorm at this stage by creating a list of hypotheses. This needn't be too formal; making notes in a plain text file, on paper, or on a whiteboard are all equally good methods. It's advantageous to be creative at this stage rather than restrictive; you'll be narrowing your search domain later, and it's better to have an abundance of hypotheses than to be economical and overlook a potential cause.

In some cases, you may arrive at a workable hypothesis quickly. For example, an error code in your logs might be referenced in an application, service, or software module's documentation. Other times, arriving at a workable hypothesis may require more extensive sleuthing. If you're unfamiliar with the symptoms you've observed, or the problem isn't resolved by using any of the methods known to you, let logic and reason be your guide. Take a step back and try to see the bigger picture. I find it helpful to remind myself that the observed symptoms are not the problem, but rather indications of the root cause.

Narrowing Focus

Now that you have a list of hypotheses to work from, it's time to narrow your focus. Although you've identified several things that *could* be the problem, you don't necessarily want to research every item on the list. Instead, try to pinpoint the most likely causes; these will be the candidates you pursue first. As you prioritize, pay attention to factors like kernel updates or recent changes to software components in your system. The reason for this will become clear in "Putting It into Practice" on page 385.

Working from your prioritized list, try to prove or disprove each hypothesis in turn. For example, if you suspect that you can't establish a connection with an API server because another process is using the network address, examine the list of local addresses and the programs listening on them. As you eliminate each potential root cause, you narrow your search domain further. Eventually, you'll arrive at a hypothesis that can't be disproved, and you can act on it.

On the other hand, if you exhaust your list of hypotheses without finding a root cause, you may have to return to the observation phase and gather a new set of clues. As you're testing your hypotheses, it's important to avoid introducing multiple changes to the system at once. Modify one component at a time, observe the results, and confirm whether the change resolved the problem.

Applying a Fix

Once you've validated your hypothesis, you can proceed with applying a fix. Usually, this phase is comparatively easy, as you've already completed the difficult part by deciding how to act. With the cause of the problem known, you can determine the correct repair action. The specific steps you take will depend on the root cause (or causes) you've identified. Often, this involves making configuration changes, updating or rolling back installed software versions, adjusting permissions, and so on.

Develop a habit of taking notes and keeping copies of configuration files as you apply your fix. This can help you avoid the pitfall of completing a series of tests only to find that the problem isn't resolved, or worse, that you've introduced a new set of issues and can't easily revert your changes.

Remember, the goal is to fix the underlying root cause, not just mask the symptoms. While engineers are sometimes forced to use workarounds or temporary fixes, these are expedient measures that will eventually need to be revisited.

Once you've implemented your fix, you'll need to test and validate it. In most cases, this means repeating the steps that produced the fault in the first place. If your repair is validated and the system behaves as expected, be sure to document your solution. This could be as simple as a comment in source code or a systemd unit file, or a note saved with your observations for later reference. It can be immensely satisfying to witness the moment a problem is resolved. Record it, learn from it, and add it to your arsenal of troubleshooting tools.

Iterating as Required

If your repair action fails the test, don't be discouraged. The truth is, troubleshooting problems in Linux seldom follows a linear path. In this event, iterate: Reprioritize your hypotheses, narrow your focus, and test again. If you've completely exhausted your list of hypotheses or discovered new information, you may even want to start over and redefine the problem.

This problem-solving methodology, coupled with the engineer's mindset, encourages continuous learning and improvement. With time, your experience and intuition will grow, and you'll feel increasingly confident navigating the intricate maze of Linux anomalies.

Bear in mind that even the most seasoned Linux guru can form an erroneous hypothesis or encounter a novel problem that surprises them. This process isn't merely about solving the immediate issue at hand; rather, it's about developing the skills and resilience to handle future challenges as they arise.

Putting It into Practice

Having a problem-solving methodology is all well and good, but how is it applied in practice? In this section, I'll walk you through a real-world example involving captive portal software and encryption. This ultimately led to a fruitful collaboration with an open source project maintainer. Each of the steps in the troubleshooting algorithm is demonstrated here, from crafting a clear problem statement and collecting detailed observations, to formulating a hypothesis and finally arriving at a fix.

Background

While developing the recipe in Chapter 4, I encountered some anomalous behavior with the implementation of an openNDS dynamic captive portal. Specifically, the issue involved the forward authentication service (FAS), which forwards a hashed client token together with several other parameters in a query string to a remote authentication server. Because this communication can occur over the internet, a strong AES-256 cipher is used to encrypt the query string. A pre-shared key (known as a faskey) is used to perform encryption and decryption on both the openNDS server and the FAS server.

For the process to succeed, the faskey values on the two servers must match. But despite me closely following the project documentation, every authentication request I sent was being rejected by the remote FAS server. It wasn't obvious where, or how, the fault was occurring; all I knew was that my dynamic captive portal was refusing to authenticate clients.

Problem Statement and Observations

Rather than immediately defining the problem as "the FAS server doesn't work," I first needed to study the issue more closely. With some investigative work, I was able to determine that the default faskey value I'd defined in my configuration was being changed. Thus, a better problem statement was: "A key mismatch occurs when using the default faskey value." At this stage, I didn't consider changing the default value. I was (perhaps obstinately) intent on using the project's recommended baseline settings from the outset.

With the problem statement in mind, I began collecting observational data, starting with the faskey values in my configuration and on the remote FAS server. The default faskey value in */etc/config/opennds* is shown here:

```
config opennds
    option debuglevel '3'
    option gatewayinterface 'wlan0'
    option fasport '2080'
    option faspath '/fas/fas-aes.php'
    option faskey '1234567890'
    option fas_secure_enabled '2'
    option list users_to_router 'allow tcp port 2080'
```

The corresponding key value is defined in */etc/opennds/fas-aes.php*:

```
// The pre-shared key "faskey" (this must be the same as in the openNDS
// config):
$key="1234567890";
```

Next, I needed to gather debugging data from the openNDS service. In the configuration, I enabled the most verbose setting, debuglevel '3', which writes a large volume of entries to the log. This is essential for troubleshooting. I then stopped and started the openNDS service while monitoring the system journal output:

```
$ sudo systemctl stop opennds.service
$ sudo systemctl start opennds.service; journalctl -f
```

On startup, the openNDS service indicated that the default faskey option value was set from the configuration file:

```
rpi3 systemd[1]: Started opennds.service - openNDS Captive Portal.
rpi3 opennds[70666]: option enabled is [ 1 ]
rpi3 opennds[70666]: openNDS Version 10.2.0 is in startup
rpi3 opennds[70666]: option gatewayname is [ openNDS ]
rpi3 opennds[70666]: The name of this gateway is openNDS
rpi3 opennds[70666]: option gatewayfqdn is [ status.client ]
rpi3 opennds[70666]: option statuspath is [ /usr/lib/opennds/client_params.sh ]
rpi3 opennds[70666]: option gatewayinterface is [ wlan0 ]
rpi3 opennds[70666]: option gateway_iprange is [ 0.0.0.0/0 ]
rpi3 opennds[70666]: option faskey is [ 1234567890 ]
```

However, several seconds later, the application generated a new faskey value:

```
rpi3 opennds[70666]: Executing command: /usr/lib/opennds/libopennds.sh "set_key"
rpi3 opennds[70666]: Reading command output
rpi3 opennds[70666]: faskey generated
```

The new key value was then written to the openNDS configuration and used to encrypt the query string passed to the authentication service. Because the FAS server still expected the original key, the key mismatch caused decryption to fail, and the authentication request was invalidated.

Hypothesis and Fix

Armed with these observational clues, I began to trace the root cause of the problem. My intuition told me that a change might have occurred recently in the openNDS project, and the documentation might not yet have been updated to reflect it. (This is common in development, and I'm often guilty of it myself.)

This is a great example of where open source software really shines. I cloned the openNDS repository and followed the logic in the C source code that dealt with the handling of the faskey. By following a clue in the debug output, which mentioned the *libopennds.sh* file, I discovered the following in *openNDS/src/conf.c*:

```
// Generate a unique faskey if not set in config
   if (strcmp(config.fas_key, DEFAULT_FASKEY) == 0) {
       setupcmd = safe_calloc(STATUS_BUF);
       safe_snprintf(setupcmd, STATUS_BUF, "/usr/lib/opennds/libopennds.sh
           \"generate_key\"");
   --snip--
```

This indicates that if the string value in the configuration is equal to DEFAULT_FASKEY, a new faskey is generated. Eureka! In this case, that debug clue quickly led to a workable hypothesis. I tested and validated it, and concluded that I'd found the root cause.

The repair was quite straightforward and didn't require any changes to the application code: Simply defining a unique hashed key string for the faskey value (rather than the default) in my configuration resolved the issue permanently.

Proximate vs. Ultimate Causes

My hypothesis confirmed that the default pre-shared key value was being modified by the system. What it didn't tell me was *why* it was being modified. As it happened, what I'd identified was the *proximate* cause of my problem. That is, it was immediately responsible for the behavior I'd observed but suggested that a higher-level *ultimate* cause (the "real" reason) had yet to be determined.

Examining the openNDS source code history, I soon found that a *Common Vulnerabilities and Exposures (CVE)* issue had been raised that concerned the use of faskey. The CVE system standardizes reporting and naming of publicly known cybersecurity vulnerabilities in software and firmware. It provides a reference for discussions about these issues and their ultimate resolutions. This particular CVE described how routers configured with the default faskey value allowed users to bypass the usual captive portal splash page sequence and authenticate directly with a Wi-Fi network. Given that openNDS is the de facto portal solution for OpenWrt routers, this vulnerability potentially affected many thousands of users.

The fix I'd found in the source, which had created my problem, resolved the CVE and closed the security hole. It could also be identified as the ultimate cause of the issue I had experienced. If, rather than following the documentation, I had used a strong pre-shared key in my implementation from the outset, the problem would have never occurred. In the end, the maintainer of openNDS and I collaborated on an issue that led to an improvement in the project.

Top Tips and Strategies

In "Making Observations" on page 380, I discussed how to gather observational data by using the system journal, debugging methods, and command line tools. In this section, I'll cover some techniques that I've found indispensable over decades of working with Linux systems. I'll begin by focusing on effective strategies for querying your richest source of observational data: the system logs. Then I'll elaborate on a method using command line tools to diagnose and resolve common Linux socket conflicts.

These are broad topics, so I've prioritized tips that will help you address the issues you're most likely to encounter while implementing the projects in this book.

Querying System Logs

As you saw earlier, the ability to gather clues effectively can make or break your hypothesis. With the volume of log data generated by a typical Linux system, it's easy to feel overwhelmed when trying to isolate the source of a problem. To help you get oriented, this section expands on two key sources of troubleshooting data and provides shortcuts you can add to your diagnostic toolkit.

Using journalctl

I briefly touched on `journalctl` in "Using the System Journal" on page 380. Here, I'll demonstrate using this tool to query, format, and analyze the log messages produced by journald, systemd's logging service. The journal includes kernel messages, syslog entries, and output from various services.

During boot, at service startup, or while a systemd service is running, each subsystem logs messages to the journal with varying levels of detail. In the past, each subsystem wrote to separate logfiles, usually located in */var/log/*. This required a Linux administrator to sift through messages from multiple files. The journal solves this problem by recording OS and application log entries in a single location.

Journald also indexes logs by boot sessions. If your system has crashed or became unresponsive, requiring a reboot, you can view messages from a previous boot by passing an offset value relative to the current one. To list available boots and their offsets, run:

```
$ journalctl --list-boots
IDX BOOT ID            FIRST ENTRY                 LAST ENTRY
--snip--
 -2 d85026a54ca24... Tue 2025-06-03 07:19:38 CEST Sat 2025-06-14 10:22:24 CEST
 -1 d7e1099adae54... Sat 2025-06-14 10:22:23 CEST Sat 2025-06-21 07:34:27 CEST
  0 793682f87a1c4... Sat 2025-06-21 07:34:26 CEST Thu 2025-06-26 08:18:07 CEST
```

In the example output shown here, we're interested in the previous boot with an index of -1. You can view its logs using:

```
$ journalctl -b -1
```

To show only messages from the latest boot, use the -b option with no arguments:

```
$ journalctl -b
```

There are various ways to further refine your search of the system journal. Often you may be interested in diagnosing a specific systemd unit. For example, to show all messages logged by the Bluetooth service, use the -u or --unit option with its unit name:

```
$ journalctl --unit bluetooth.service
```

You can specify multiple units. This is particularly useful if you want to examine the interactions between related services:

```
$ journalctl -u bluetooth.service -u pulseaudio.service
```

A typical Linux system usually has hundreds of unit files, each of which may be in an enabled, disabled, or masked state. If you're unsure of a unit name, you can get a list of all available units with:

```
$ systemctl list-unit-files --all
```

In "Problem Statement and Observations" on page 385, I demonstrated a method for outputting messages to the console as they're generated. This proved to be crucial in finding the clue that led to my hypothesis. To enable this behavior, add the -f or --follow switch. For example, to capture all system log messages after the hostapd.service is restarted, run:

```
$ sudo systemctl restart hostapd.service; journalctl --follow
```

If journalctl's default output isn't to your liking, or you want to analyze the logs with another tool, you can use the -o or --output switch. For instance, to display log messages from the hostapd.service unit to the console in an easy-to-read JSON format while simultaneously saving them to a logfile in your home directory, you could run:

```
$ journalctl -f -u hostapd.service -o json-pretty | tee $HOME/hostapd.log
```

In some scenarios, when examining messages from more than one source, error messages may appear to occur simultaneously. In such cases, it's useful to specify the short-monotonic output option, which includes high-precision timestamps:

```
$ journalctl -o short-monotonic
```

You can also restrict journal entries to a specific time window by using the --since option with a time descriptor. Combine this with the -o output switch, like so:

```
$ journalctl --since "1 minute ago" -o short-monotonic
```

Likewise, you can expand the time window and filter messages by piping them through grep to search for a specific pattern:

```
$ journalctl --since "10 minutes ago" | grep faskey
```

Manipulating the system journal by specifying unit files, following output, formatting messages, and defining time windows gives you a great deal of control and flexibility. Used in concert with tools like grep, this adds a powerful set of options to your diagnostic toolkit.

Using dmesg

The dmesg command is often overlooked, but it should be one of the first tools you reach for when troubleshooting. At the core of the Linux OS, the kernel is responsible for communicating with the hardware and managing system resources. Derived from *display message*, dmesg is primarily used to output messages from the kernel's ring buffer. These include messages related to system boot processes, hardware detection, module loading and unloading, drivers, and kernel-related events. This makes it your go-to utility for diagnosing hardware and driver-related problems.

You won't find user-space logs in the dmesg output, as its scope is limited strictly to the kernel. Additionally, the kernel ring buffer is *volatile*, meaning it's cleared on each reboot. Hence, dmesg shows only messages from the current boot session.

Running dmesg with no options will produce a firehose of all messages currently stored in the ring buffer. To make this output more digestible, you can pipe it through less:

```
$ dmesg | less
```

Alternatively, you can use the -H or --human option to enable more human-readable output, automatically piped to less:

```
$ dmesg --human
[Jun22 07:34] Booting Linux on physical CPU 0x0000000000 [0x410fd034]
[ +0.000000] Linux version 6.6.28+rpt-rpi-v8 (debian-kernel@lists...
[ +0.000000] KASLR enabled
[ +0.000000] random: crng init done
[ +0.000000] Machine model: Raspberry Pi 3 Model B Rev 1.2
[ +0.000000] Reserved memory: created CMA memory pool at 0x0.., size 256 MiB
--snip--
```

In the leftmost column, a high-precision timestamp (expressed as elapsed time since boot in seconds and nanoseconds) is associated with each kernel message. To exit the output viewer, press Q.

You can further restrict the message output by specifying the -l or --level option to filter messages by log severity level. For example:

```
$ dmesg --level err
$ dmesg --level=warn,notice
```

Of the available log levels, I most often use err, warn, notice, info, and debug (ranging from the highest to lowest severity). You can narrow the output even more by piping it to grep to search for a specific pattern, as shown here:

```
$ dmesg --level info | grep brcmfmac
```

This example produces an ordered list of timestamped messages relating to the brcmfmac kernel module, which provides support for the Broadcom WLAN chipset.

Likewise, dmesg supports a -f or --facility option that can be used to restrict output to a specific list of facilities or message categories. For example, to output messages from system daemons only, run:

```
$ dmesg --facility=daemon
```

Other useful facilities include kern, user, auth, and syslog; these should be self-explanatory. As with log levels, you can combine facilities. In this example, the -H or --human option is used together with two facilities, and the output is limited to info messages:

```
$ dmesg -H --facility=kern,syslog --level info
```

To restrict these informational messages to a specific subsystem, you can pipe the output through grep. In this example, messages related to the USB subsystem are displayed. The -i (case-insensitive) option is used with grep to capture all occurrences of the pattern:

```
$ dmesg -H --facility=kern,syslog --level info | grep -i usb
```

In some circumstances, you may want to inspect only the most recent kernel messages. You can do this by piping the output through tail with a numeric argument. For example, to display the most recent 10 messages, use:

```
$ dmesg | tail -10
```

Lastly, as with journalctl, you can monitor kernel logs in real time with the --follow option:

```
$ dmesg --follow
```

Tracing Socket Conflicts

Given enough time, most Linux programmers will encounter an error message like "Bind failed. Error: Address already in use." What's happening here? Linux provides several mechanisms for *inter-process communication (IPC)*, or ways for processes to share data and coordinate their activities. Signals, pipes, and message queues are common mechanisms, but here I'll focus on *sockets*, which provide a versatile interface for exchanging data over a network or within a single host.

A server uses the `bind()` system call to associate a socket with a specific IP address and port. Together, these form a local address that a client can use to connect to the server. Once bound, the server uses the `listen()` system call to wait for incoming client connections. After a connection is established, `send()` and `recv()` system calls are used to exchange data between server and client.

Process communication via sockets typically works exceptionally well—until two or more servers attempt to bind to the same local address, that is. Fortunately, there's a simple way to diagnose and resolve these conflicts. Begin by executing `netstat` on your system, as shown here:

```
$ sudo netstat -tulpn
Active Internet connections (only servers)
Proto Recv-Q Send-Q Local Address    Foreign Address   State    PID/Program name
tcp      0      0 0.0.0.0:22       0.0.0.0:          LISTEN   582/sshd
tcp      0      0 0.0.0.0:8421     0.0.0.0:          LISTEN   448/pisugar-server
tcp      0      0 0.0.0.1:8666     0.0.0.0:          LISTEN   453/pwngrid
tcp6     0      0 :::22            :::               LISTEN   582/sshd
tcp6     0      0 :::80            :::               LISTEN   631/bettercap
tcp6     0      0 :::8080          :::               LISTEN   476/python3
--snip--
```

The `-t` and `-u` options tell `netstat` to display TCP and UDP connections, respectively. The `-l` option limits the output to listening sockets, while `-p` is used to show the PID and the name of the program associated with each socket Finally, the `-n` option displays addresses and port numbers in numerical form.

In the example output shown here, `netstat` reveals the PIDs and names of several programs running on a Pwnagotchi unit, along with their corresponding listening addresses. The local address 0.0.0.0:8421 indicates two things worth noting. First, 0.0.0.0 is a special address that essentially means "all IPv4 addresses on the local machine." A service listening on this address will accept connections on all available network interfaces (`wlan0`, `eth0`, and so on). The number 8421 is the specific port on which the service is listening. In this case, you could say that the `pisugar-server` is bound to port 8421.

Now suppose another process attempts to use the same local address. Running that program would likely yield a "bind failed" or similar error message. A possible quick fix would be to execute `kill` with SIGKILL (signal number 9) and the process ID to forcefully terminate the first process:

```
$ sudo kill -9 pid
```

While expedient, this is often a temporary fix that may have unintended side effects. A more durable solution is to reconfigure one of the services to communicate via an unused socket. Locate its configuration file, assign a new port value, and restart the process.

Final Thoughts

In this chapter, I've endeavored to distill what it means to be an engineer: to think like one and to view the world through an engineer's lens. Within a systems-level framework, I've shared a problem-solving methodology that has served me well over decades of programming and working with Linux. Is it the final word on troubleshooting? Certainly not, and I hope you'll iterate on this process, find what works for you, adjust it accordingly, and consider passing it on to others. My own path to effectively diagnosing issues in code I've written and solving problems in Linux has been anything but linear.

I was drawn to the recipe format used in this book because it mirrors my introduction to computing. Whether you're a newcomer to Linux, a seasoned Linux developer, or somewhere in between, I sincerely hope you've found this format useful and made some new discoveries as you've worked through these chapters. This book has been a labor of love for me, and I'm deeply grateful that you've chosen to read it. I've learned a lot myself in developing these chapters, and it has reminded me that learning is a continuous and joyous process.

INDEX

The fonts used in *The Wireless Cookbook* are New Baskerville, Futura, The Sans Mono Condensed, and Dogma. The book was typeset with LaTeX 2_ε package nostarch by Boris Veytsman with many additions by Alex Freed, Miles Bond, and other members of the No Starch Press team *(2023/07/19 v2.4 Typesetting books for No Starch Press).*

RESOURCES

Visit *https://nostarch.com/wireless-cookbook* for errata and more information.

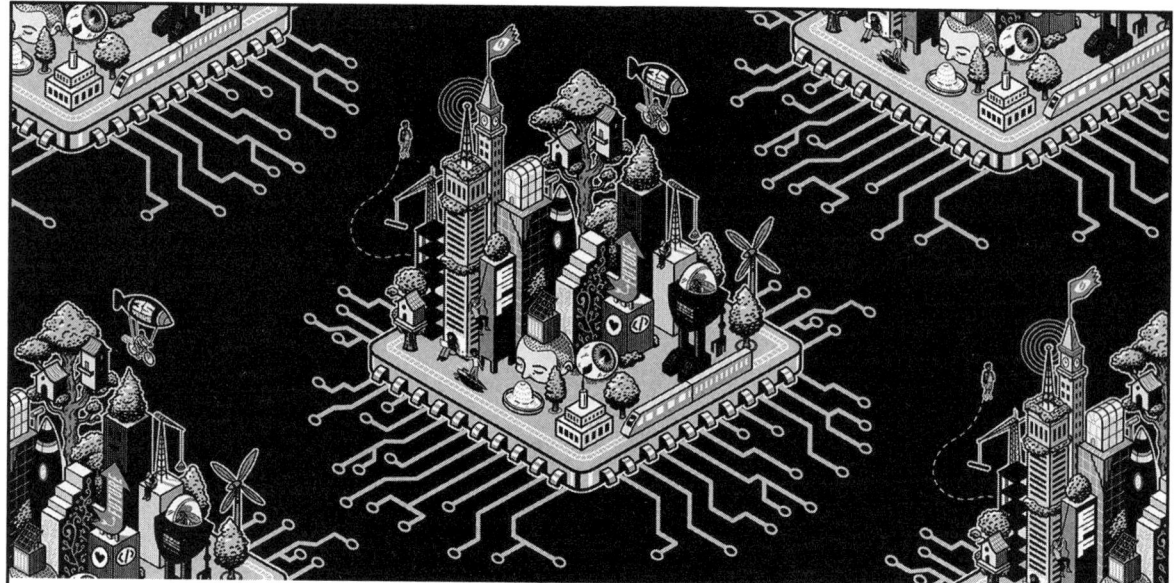

Never before has the world relied so heavily on the internet to stay connected and informed. That makes the Electronic Frontier Foundation's mission—to ensure that technology supports freedom, justice, and innovation for all people—more urgent than ever.

For over 35 years, EFF has fought for your rights through activism, in the courts, and by developing software because we believe in a better future—one where your device is truly yours, you can speak without being surveilled, and technology helps you connect with the people you care about. With your help, we can realize that vision for a brighter world together.

2 04